Created and Directed by Hans Höfer

INSIGHT GUIDES

SOUTHEAST ASIA

Edited by Joseph R. Yogerst
Featuring photographers of the APA Photo Agency

Editorial Director: Geoffrey Eu

APA PUBLICATIONS

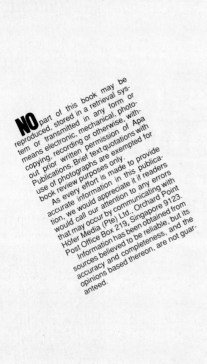
SOUTH EAST ASIA

First Edition
© **1992 APA PUBLICATIONS (HK) LTD**
All Rights Reserved
Printed in Singapore by Höfer Press Pte. Ltd

ABOUT THIS BOOK

Southeast asia is where it all began for APA Publications' *Insight Guides*. Going back over familiar territory while producing *Insight Guide: Southeast Asia* was both a sentimental journey and an eye-opener: writing about the eternal time-tested destinations invoked memories of previous *Insight Guides*, while newer but equally stunning locations and attractions revealed how much Southeast Asia has changed in the past decade.

Yet *Insight Guide: Southeast Asia* is also special for another reason. All destinations featured are part of ASEAN: the Association of Southeast Asian Nations, an international body formed in 1967 to foster economic and cultural ties among member states. This book is being published to coincide with a major tourism promotion, "Visit ASEAN Year 1992."

APA Publications boss **Hans Höfer** has a special attachment to Asia, having arrived in Indonesia in 1969, where he developed the *Guide to Bali*. This was the first of the popular *Insight Guide* series. He later founded a publishing company and, under his creative direction, the *Insight Guides* series has won worldwide acclaim.

The Right Staff

The concept of *Insight Guide: Southeast Asia* came about in early 1991 when APA editorial director **Geoffrey Eu** approached project editor **Joseph R. Yogerst** with a proposal to transform the existing *Insight Guide: East Asia*, winner of a PATA Gold Award for best travel book, into a new guide book based on the ASEAN countries.

Yogerst edited magazines in San Francisco and London before coming to Asia as the managing editor of *Discovery* magazine in Hong Kong. Since moving to Singapore in early 1990, Yogerst has been a contributing editor to *Conde Nast Traveler* magazine in New York, a special correspondent for the *International Herald Tribune* and editor of *Sojourn* magazine. Yogerst is also an accomplished travel writer, having won a Lowell Thomas Award from the Society of American Travel Writers and a PATA Gold Award for best magazine travel article in 1991.

Yogerst, who wrote the chapter on Brunei, was also responsible for expanding and revising the different sections on each country. He now spends much of his time traveling around ASEAN and the rest of the world.

Eu's first contacts with the travel business came from his undergraduate days in the School of Travel Industry Management at the University of Hawaii. He went on to complete his Master's at Northwestern University's Medhill School of Journalism before returning to his native Singapore. Eu, who journeys 'up-country' frequently, contributed the section on Malaysia.

Eric Oey's ties with APA go back a long way, having been a former marketing manager and editor of *Insight Guide: Indonesia*. He holds a Master's degree in Indonesian philosophy and linguistics and recently completed doctoral work in linguistics and Malay philology at the University of California, Berkeley. These impeccable qualifications made him the perfect choice for writing the Indonesia section.

Manila-born **Alfred A. Yuson**, a major contributor to *Insight Guide: Philippines*, is a modern Renaissance man of the Philippines. At various times in his career as a

Yogerst

Eu

Oey

"media mercenary" Yuson has been a novelist, poet, sportswriter, film and television scriptwriter, government speechwriter, documentary filmmaker, book designer and literary editor. Among the numerous awards received for his fiction and poetry are first prizes in the annual Philippines Free Press, Cultural Center of the Philippines and Palanca Memorial Awards. Yuson was also awarded an International Writing Program fellowship to the University of Iowa and a similar grant to attend the East-West Center Poetry Conference in Hawaii.

N. Balakrishnan, who wrote the chapter on Singapore, represents some of the new blood in Southeast Asia journalism. Armed with a Master's degree from Columbia University's Graduate School of Journalism, he traveled widely in Asia, Europe and the US. After a stint with a local daily in Singapore, Balakrishnan has since spent the past few years honing his journalistic skills in Hong Kong.

Steve van Beek is a transplanted American who has been living in Thailand since 1969. After graduating with a history degree from the University of Oregon, he served with the Peace Corps in Nepal before finding his way to Bangkok. Van Beek edited three local magazines, then turned freelance in 1977. He was written *The Arts of Thailand*, *Bangkok Only Yesterday*, the *Guide to Pattaya* and *Southeastern Thailand*, among others. Van Beek has made major contributions to APA's new *Pocket Guides* series, aimed at visitors with a limited amount of time in a place. He has penned Pocket Guides to Bangkok, Phuket, Chiang Mai and Tibet. The multi-facetted van Beek has recently turned his attention to river journeys. He navigated Thailand's longest river system (the Ping and Chao Phya) in a canoe in 1988 and recently completed a kayak journey through the Grand Canyon in Arizona. As a result of his river wanderings, van Beek was elected to the prestigious New York Explorers' Club in 1989.

Picture Perfect

An *Insight Guide* has been described as being a slide show between covers, a colorful souvenir of places you've been, or dreamed of going to. Indeed, the outstanding photography featured in the guides sets the series apart from other travel books. Whether the subject is a bevy of beautiful native women, an animal in the wild, a pristine landscape or a city skyscraper, the art of photography is on display an almost every page of an *Insight Guide* APA's evocative visual style offers a powerful incentive for a visit to any given destination. With access to many of the best travel photographers in the world, the pictorial coverage in an *Insight Guide* is second to none.

Insight Guide: Southeast Asia showcases the superb work of many different photographers, emphasizing the international nature of this book. Most are long-time contributors to the APA Photo Agency, a Singapore-and Hong Kong-based company that is prime photographic source for the *Insight Guides*.

—APA Publications

Yuson   *Balakrishnan*   *van Beek*

CONTENTS

Malaysia

—by Geoffrey Eu

Philippines

—by Alfred Yuson

Singapore

—by N. Balakrishnan

Thailand

—by Steve van Beek

Maps

TRAVEL TIPS

Dalanguer mons   CARDANDAN.   Sindinfu

Naugracot mons.   Vssonte   Qyianfu

mons   MANGI

PER   SIAE

siue So: phorum Im:

perij li: mites ad In:

dum flu: uium vsque

pertin: gunt

ORMVTII

REGNVM   MIEN.

TIPVRA

ARABIAE-

FELICIS   ARA   CAM.

PARS.   INDOS

BENGALA   TAN.   CACHV CHINA

CAMBAIA   MANDAO

DELLI   ORIXA

DE CAN.   VERMA

NARZINGA   AVA   BREMA

PEGV

BISINA-   SIAN.

GAR   MARTABAN   CAM.

PA.

Golfo di Bengala.   CAMB.   OIA.

Pulocampaa

Pulofirfir

Pulocondor

Zeilan Inf:Tenarism   MALA

incolis dicta   y.de Calantan

Natu.

na.

Andramania id

est aurea   Ariobo

insula.   Suma

IAVA MAIOR

INDIAE

ORIENTALIS,   BE:

INSVLARVMQVE   continentis

ADIACIENTI:

VM TY:

PVS.

Mare Cin

Satyrorum inſ.

AMERICAE, Siue Indiæ Occidentalis pars.

Quiuira

Cicuie

Tiguex

Inſ. de Miaco

Torza

Saendeber

Chela

Boxiaci academia

Bandu

Dinlai Hſani

IAPAN.

Amaguco

Hanc inſulam M.Paul.
Venet Zipangri vocat.

Menlai

Malao

Hormar

Negru Praſon

Cangoxima

Zanqua ins. Pilbo.

Baruquis

Scabana

OCEANVS

Liampo opp. et promſ.

Chequean

Mazacar

Lequio maior

y° Fermoſa

Reix magos

Bergatera inſula.

Lequio minor

Los dos hermanos

Los Bolcanes.

Tropicus Cancri

Malabrigo

La farſana

ORIENTALIS

Humunu vel y°
di buoni ſegni

Zamal

Reſtinga de
ladrones.

Cailan

Canhan

Aguada

Culuan

Poſſe de S. Clara

Cenalo.

Hibuſſon
Abarien

Huinangan

y° de mata-
lotes

*ARCHIPELA:
GO DIS.*

Inſ. de los
corales.

Los iardines.

Cataram

Paulogon

Eſpana inſula

Calagan

y° de arreciſes

Cimbubon

Chippit

Mindanao

Buran

y° de cocos

*ZABA
RO.*

Talon

Ziphar

Candinan

Cabuo

Talao, alijs Tarrao inſulæ

Doy

Inſulæ Moluccæ celebres ob maxima
aromatum copiam, quam per
totum terrarū orbem trans
ferunt, s. ſunt, iuxta Gilolo
nempe: Tarenate, Tidore,
Motir, Machiā et Bachian

Bibalon

Babatao

Zolo

Sanguin

Morotay

Calamba

Mamoro

Giloli

Circulus æquinoctialis.

y° de creſpos

y° de los
martires

Celebres

Guebe

Cainam

Celermoſo

S. Angeltna

Macaz

Pulola

NOVA GVINEA
quam Andreas Corſalus Ter-
ram Piccinaculi appellare vi-
detur. An inſula ſit, an pars
continentis Auſtralis incer-
tum eſt.

Bandan

Galiam

Neo Mamor.

zelot

Euae

Malha

Timor, Tidore inſ.

Cuto

Tidor

Arru

Japagna

Cimpegua

Sunbedit

Alifao

Subio

ſap

Cum Priuilegio.

A SOUTHEAST ASIAN PORTRAIT

At a distance, it's sometimes easy to view Southeast Asia as a single geographical entity. From a spatial point of view, it includes a massive archipelago (the world's largest collection of islands) and the adjoining mainland. One could also generalize by saying that the countries in this region are all tropical, with a common climate, vegetation, wildlife and terrain.

From a political standpoint, six of the countries in the region – Brunei, Indonesia, Malaysia, the Philippines, Singapore and Thailand – can be regarded as a collection of closely allied states, banded together as the Association of Southeast Asian Nations (ASEAN), formed in 1967, to foster cooperation in defense, culture, science and economics. But this is where the similarities end. For when it comes to calculating the human factors, these nations are as diverse a collection as you will find anywhere on the globe.

The reason is history. To be more precise, a 5,000-year-old heritage of cultural conquest and fusion. Hundreds of religions, languages, kingdoms and political doctrines set down on top of one another until the whole of the region becomes a giant melting pot of humanity. Take religion as the strongest example. Malaysia and the vast majority of Indonesia are staunchly Muslim. The Philippines is the only predominantly Christian nation in Asia. Thailand adheres to Theravadan Buddhism. The Chinese of Singapore are largely Confucianistic in outlook. Bali remains a relic of the time when Hinduism was the strongest religion among the islands, while the tribes of New Guinea and Borneo remain largely animistic.

The pace of modern development has also forged distinctions, not just among nations but also within the countries themselves. Brunei is the quintessential small oil state, Singapore the world's most dazzling example of what free trade (and an ambitious people) can accomplish almost overnight, while Malaysia marches forward into the industrial future. Bustling Bangkok and Jakarta are two of the fastest growing cities in Asia, yet rural Thailand and Indonesia remain bastions of bucolic serenity. Tropical beaches and highrise banks, ancient temples and modern resorts, traditional dances and high-tech discos – the variety of the region is simply astounding.

Perhaps the greatest advantage from the visitor's viewpoint, is that the myriad faces of Southeast Asia are close enough to be experienced within the framework of a single journey.

Preceding pages: the face of Malaysian youth; early map of Southeast Asia by Abraham Ortelius, published in 1570; a beauty from the street opera, Singapore; Muslim girls in Brunei; a Balinese poised in classical *Baris* dance; festive spirit at the *Ati-Atihan* festival, Philippines; young monk near the Thai-Burma border. **Left**, Asian warmth and friendliness welcomes the visitor.

BRUNEI: LAST OF A BREED

Of the hundreds of kingdoms, sultanates and vassal states that once constituted the Malay archipelago, the only one to survive as a sovereign entity in modern times is the Sultanate of Brunei, or Negara Brunei Darussalam as it is officially known.

In many respects, today's Brunei is a bit of an anachronism. It's one of the few nations in the world ruled by an absolute monarch, in this case His Majesty, Sultan Haji Hassanal Bolkiah Mui'zzaddin Waddaulah, the 29th ruler in a long-surviving dynasty, as well as the country's prime minister and defense minister.

Oil money has allowed the sultan and his advisors to transform once sleepy Brunei into a thriving modern nation. The population of 270,000 enjoys a per capita income of more than US$20,000 a year, one of the world's highest. The gross domestic product exceeds US$3.5 billion per annum. The government has no foreign debt; treasury reserves are said to be more than US$15 billion. Brunei was the first nation in Southeast Asia to have color TV, and there are almost as many cars as there are households.

Oil wealth has also percolated into social services. Education and health care are free. Many tropical diseases have been completely eliminated. Life expectancy is high; infant mortality is low.

The population is about 65 percent Malay, 20 percent Chinese and the remainder comprise various indigenous Dayak people and Europeans. Islam is the official religion and the creed of at least two-thirds of the people, but there are also sizeable communities of Buddhists and Christians.

Geographically, Brunei is one of the world's smallest nations, with just 2,226 square miles (5,765 square km) of land – about twice the size of Luxembourg or the American state of Rhode Island. It is bounded on the north by the South China Sea and on three sides by the Malaysian state of Sarawak, which actually divides Brunei into two parts. More than 80 percent of the total land area is still covered by forest, much of it primary jungle that has never been logged.

Brunei is a mixture of modern and ancient influences, and at the same time a paradigm of careful and well-thought-out development that is a model to the rest of the world. As it has for over 500 years, Brunei continues to show the world that it can look after itself.

Preceding pages: an illuminated Omar Ali Saifuddin Mosque. **Left**, Bruneian kids on the block.

Little is known about the early history of Brunei, but recent archaeological finds have determined that residents engaged in trade with China and other parts of mainland Asia as early as the 6th and 7th centuries A.D.

During the 10th century, the area that is now Brunei was a Buddhist kingdom, part of the Srivijaya Empire based in Sumatra. Later it became part of the Hindu Majapahit Empire of Java. By the 14th century, Brunei was a powerful seafaring state with a sultan based on Kota Batu on the Brunei River. Sharif Ali, a descendant of the Prophet Mohammed, came to Brunei at the start of the 15th century. Soon the sultan and most of his subjects converted to Islam, the foundation of a strong religious and cultural tradition that has endured to this day.

Despite being one of the world's smallest nations today, Brunei's rule during the 16th century extended over a vast area including most of the northwest coast of Borneo and many of the islands of the southern Philippines. The most prominent rulers at that time were Sultan Hassan and Sultan Bolkiah, who fashioned the lavish royal court that was the envy of the South China Sea. Bolkiah, known as the "Singing Admiral" because of his fondness for music, is credited with subduing the Sultanate of Sulu in the Philippines.

The remnants of Ferdinand Magellan's fleet – the first people to circumnavigate the globe – weighed anchor in Brunei in 1521 as the first Europeans to visit the sultanate. Italian Antonio Pigafetta, the historian of that voyage, described the sultanate as being rich, hospitable and powerful, with a strong Muslim monarchy and considerable influence in regional affairs. In the century that followed, other Spanish and Portuguese mariners explored the coast of Borneo. The Spanish made a vain attempt to conquer the sultanate, but instead had to settle upon hegemony over the Philippines including lands once ruled by Brunei.

Brunei's first permanent contacts with Europe came at the end of the 16th century, when a trading relationship was established with the Dutch East India Company. Somehow, against the odds, Brunei remained independent while the rest of the Indonesian archipelago was absorbed into the Dutch colonial empire. The sultanate remained a power to be reckoned with until the arrival of the British in the mid-19th century.

Although James Brooke became Rajah of Sarawak as a result of helping the Sultan of Brunei, Brooke spent much of his energy chipping away at the power of the sultanate. Brooke's political maneuvering and superior firepower forced the sultan into ceding large tracts of Brunei. In order to preserve his nation from being completely swallowed up

by Sarawak, the sultan asked for and received protection from Britain in 1888. The first British resident arrived in 1906 in order to advise the sultan on all matters except those pertaining to customs and religion.

Bruneians like to point out the fact that their country was never a "colony" of Britain as such. It never experienced a complete loss of sovereignty and there was continuity in the royal family, although some British influence was inevitable.

The history of Brunei took a sudden and dramatic turn for the better in 1929 with the discovery of oil at Seria. Thirty years later, the nation achieved full internal self-rule, although Britain continued to administer its foreign affairs and defense. The first off-shore oil deposits were found in 1963.

Despite intense pressure, Brunei refused to become part of the Federation of Malaysia. Sultan Sir Omar Ali Saifuddin – the father of the present ruler – chose to keep Brunei under direct British protection. As a result, the sultanate was drawn into a violent separatist revolt in late 1962. Inflamed by the Brunei People's Party, the revolt aimed to establish an independent nation in northwest Borneo comprising Sarawak, Sabah and Brunei, but it was quickly smashed with the aid of British Gurkha troops.

The late Sultan Omar abdicated in 1967 in million to B\$9.7 billion.

In 1979, the sultan signed a treaty of cooperation and friendship with Britain that set forth a five-year timetable for full independence. Then on January 1st, 1984, the sultanate became the sovereign and independent nation of Brunei Darussalam. That same year it became the 159th member of the United Nations, as well as a member of the British Commonwealth of Nations, the Association of South East Asian Nations (ASEAN) and the Organization of the Islamic Conference.

Sultan Haji Hassanal Bolkiah Mui'zzaddin Waddaulah is often lauded by financial publications as the world's richest man, al-

favor of his 21-year-old eldest son, the Sandhurst-educated Prince Muda Hassanal Bolkiah, who became the 29th Sultan of Brunei.

The 1970s propelled Brunei into the league of the world's richest nations. Increased production from new oil and gas fields combined with higher prices after the Arab oil boycott of 1973 to fill Brunei's coffers to overflowing. In just 10 years, from 1970 to 1980, Brunei's oil and gas revenues skyrocketed from B\$277

Left, Sultan Hassanal Bolkiah declared independence for his oil sultanate in 1984; above, youth and vigor at an Independence Day parade.

though the sultan makes a point of distancing his personal fortune from that of the state. A recent report estimated his wealth at US\$28 billion, based on his personal assets and government financial assets under his direct control. However, it should be pointed out that the average Bruneian has also benefited substantially from the oil boom. Brunei has a per capita income in excess of US\$20,000, making it the world's second richest nation in that category after Kuwait. Nearly a quarter of the goverment budget is spent on education and social services, and Brunei enjoys more than 95 percent literacy among its young people.

Bandar Seri Begawan

With no more than 60,000 people, **Bandar Seri Begawan** has more the feel of a small town than a national capital. It takes no more than 15 minutes to walk from one side of the central city to the other. But make no mistake, the good citizens of Bandar prefer their cars to walking. Oil money has transformed B.S.B. (as it is commonly known) into a strikingly modern city of skyscrapers, shopping malls and filling stations.

The **Omar Ali Saifuddin Mosque** not only dominates the skyline of the capital, but it has also become a shining symbol of Brunei, as much as the *Eiffel Tower* is for France or the *Statue of Liberty* for America. Built in 1958, it is a fantasyland of Arabian Nights architecture, with numerous arches, towers, columns, onion domes and a single slender minaret. The great golden dome rises to a height of 170 feet (52 meters) and can be seen from just about anywhere in the city. After the flamboyant exterior, the modern simplicity of the interior is a bit of a letdown. In the surrounding lagoon is a full-scale cement model of a 16th-century royal barge. The mosque is closed to non-Muslims on Thursdays and Fridays.

To the northwest of the mosque, obscured by modern apartment buildings, is the old **Istana Darussalam**. This green wooden structure, a classic example of *kampung* architecture, was the royal palace of Brunei until the 1960s. The present sultan was born here and his father insisted on dying here rather than in the new palace. The Istana is still guarded by Gurkhas, but unfortnely it's not yet open to the public.

The Christian community of B.S.B. centres around Jalan Kumbang Pasang, where the only structure of interest is **St Andrew's Anglican Church**. This old clapboard chapel looks like something out of the South Pacific, with palm trees in front, ceiling fans and simple wooden pews inside.

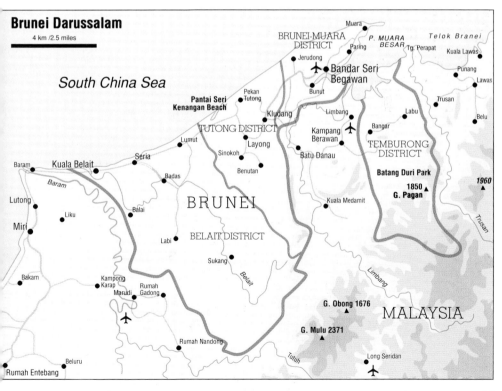

Brunei Darussalam

4 km /2.5 miles

South China Sea

BRUNEI-MUARA DISTRICT

Muara
Paring
P. MUARA BESAR
Telok Branei
Tg. Perapat
Kuala Lawas

Jerudong
Bandar Seri Begawan
Punang
Lawas

Pekan
Tutong
Bunut
Limbang
Labu
Trusan
Belu

Pantai Seri Kenangan Beach
Kludang

TUTONG DISTRICT
Lumut
Layong
Sinokoh
Kampang Berawan
Bangar
TEMBURONG DISTRICT

Seria
Benutan
Batu Danau

Baram
Kuala Belait
Badas
Batang Duri Park
1960

Baram
BRUNEI
1850 ▲
G. Pagan

Lutong
Liku
Balai
Kuala Medamit
Trusan

Miri
Labi
BELAIT DISTRICT

Sukang

Bakam
Kampong Karap
Rumah Gadong
Marudi
Belait

G. Obong 1676 ▲
MALAYSIA

Rumah Nandong
G. Mulu 2371 ▲

Tutuh
Long Seridan

Beluru

Rumah Entebang

At the junction of Jalan Stoney and Jalan Sultan is a complex that includes the bizarre **Churchill Memorial and Museum** bizarre in the sense that you don't expect to find anything dedicated to a sworn colonialist in this part of the world. Yet owing to the British protection afforded to Brunei over the years, the previous sultan had a fondness for things English, not the least of which was Sir Winston Churchill. There isn't much of real historical value in the collection-save for some old clothing and an artist's palette with colors and brushes as Churchill left them before his death-but the museum does remind us of what an extraordinary man Churchill was. He was not just statesman but soldier, writer, orator, horseman, pilot, painter and much more.

Sharing the complex are a number of other attractions. The **Hassanal Bolkiah Aquarium** showcases the marine life of the nearby South China Sea. The **Constitutional History Gallery** is a testimony to the inner workings of the nation's sovereignty while the **Dato Ibrahim Library** has been set aside as a research facility for those interested in Southeast Asian or ASEAN studies. Next door is the **Brunei Historical Center**.

Across Jalan Sultan from the cultural complex is B.S.B.'s other golden landmark, the crenelated roof of the **Lapau** (Royal Ceremonial Hall) which is used for important state occasions. Inside is the sultan's golden throne. Through the garden is the **Dewan Majlis** (Parliament House). Farther downtown, at the intersection of Jalan Sungai Kianggeh and Jalan Elizabeth II, is a small **Chinese temple** in the Taoist style. The thousands of Bruneians of Chinese origin come here to worship. Most of the deities are now behind glass, but there are some fine dragon columns and tiles on either side that reflect Chinese mythological themes. Opposite is **Pasar Malam**, one of the capital's two open-air markets, where you can watch boats offloading coconuts, bananas, pineapples and other tropical produce, or wander among the hundred or so stalls.

The center o activity for Brunei's Chinese community.

Downtown B.S.B. centers along a two-block stretch of **Jalan Sultan** that runs up from the waterfront. This is the place to find banks, embassies, airline offices, travel agents and luxury good shops. Climb to the roof of the multi-story car park on Jalan Cator for a fine (and free) view over the city, the Brunei River and the vast water-village. **Jalan McArthur** runs along the waterfront. Opposite is the **Teck Guan Plaza**, a kiosk which sells tickets for high-speed ferries to Labuan, Lawas and Limbang in nearby East Malaysia. Another open-air market can be found in the vacant lot fronting the **municipal pier**, which is the best jumping-off point for exploring the river.

Kampong Ayer is a massive community built on stilts above the **Brunei River**. As many as 30,000 people – half the population of Bandar Seri Begawan – are said to live in the village. It was proposed at one time that everyone be moved to modern housing on the mainland. But the residents steadfastly refused; the sultan agreed and so Kampong Ayer became a living anachronism of bygone life in Borneo.

Yet don't think that life in Kampong Ayer isn't modern simply because it's built over the water. Everything the residents could possibly need is also built on the water: mosques and schools, cafes and small neighborhood stores, police posts and fire stations, and even garages and gas stations that cater to boats. The residents get about in the ubiquitous water-taxis as easily as if they were on land.

The portion of Kampong Ayer around the golden mosque and across Kedayan Creek can easily be explored on foot along rickety elevated walkways and bridges. But to explore the full extent of the water-village you'll need to charter a boat from the municipal pier. There are plenty of eager pilots.

Beyond Edinburgh Bridge is **Seri district**, the thoroughly modern face of B.S.B. and a neighborhood of shopping malls, departmental stores, banks, gas stations and fast-food restaurants that wouldn't look that much out of place in

stana Nurul
man is His
Majesty's
official
esidence.

suburban America. The modern **Supreme Court** building sits next to the water as you cross the bridge, while on your right is a hill with an ancient **Muslim cemetery** and the very modern **RIPAS Hospital**, said to be the best in Borneo.

Continuing onto Jalan Tutong, you come to the impressive royal precinct, crowned by the golden domes and sway-back roof of the **Istana Nurul Iman**, the residence of his majesty, the sultan. With 1,788 rooms, this is said to be the world's largest palace. It was opened in 1984 in time for Brunei's independence celebrations, the product of an eclectic effort involving a Filipino architect, British interior designers, Japanese landscape gardeners as well as American engineers.

The palace is off limits to the public-except during *Hari Raya Festival* at the end of *Ramadan* when the gates are thrown open for three days. You too can shake the band of the sultan if you're wiling to line up with the thousands of Bruneians. However, you're free to drive

CHURCHILL

1874 – 1965

around the royal precinct any day of the year. See the royal polo grounds (the sultan's favorite sport), the royal heliport (the sultan flies himself), the former royal palace (used during the 1960s and '70s) and the various opulent homes bulit by the royal siblings.

Jalan Residency leads in the opposite direction from downtown, flowing east along the Brunei River in the direction of the South China Sea. The first building you come to is the **Brunei Arts and Handicrafts Training Center** where you can watch young artisans at work or choose from the selection of silver, brass, baskets and brocade. Two specialties are elaborate toy cannons and *kris* knives. Overlooking the center is the modern oriental outline of the **Ministry of Foreign Affairs**.

Three miles (5 km) east of B.S.B is the superb **Brunei Museum**. Older wings are devoted to the natural history, native customs and dress, and the oil industry in Brunei. But the most fascinating items can be found in the new Islamic Gallery with its collection of illuminated *Korans*, pottery, weapons, carpets, brass and glass from around the Islamic world.

Many of the items are from the sultan's private collection. Among the curiosities are a 19th-century Ottoman boot with a compass set in the toe, a scale model of the *Dome of the Rock* in Jerusalem in mother-of-pearl, a diamond-studded flywhisp handle and a complete set of chain mail armor from Mogul India, and 10th-century *kashgul* alms bowls from Iraq and Syria.

Down the hill is the **Malay Technology Museum** which is packed with traditional buildings that one rarely finds in Brunei these days. The three galleries are dedicated to the traditional crafts and technology of the land-dwelling Malays, the water-village people and the Dayak tribes of the interior. The adjacent **Archeology Park** displays the remains of Kota Batu, the medieval capital of Brunei, and the 16th-century **Tomb of Sultan Bolkiah**, the "Singing Admiral" who extended his realm into southern Philippines during Brunei's golden age.

The Churchill Memorial.

Beyond B.S.B.: Although no resort hotels have been built along the coast, Brunei has fine unspoiled beaches along the north coast. **Muara Beach** is 17 miles (27 km) northeast of the capital, near the main port of Brunei where freighters and passengers ships dock. **Pantai Seri Kenangan Beach**, 31 miles (50 km) west of the city near Tutong, has the open ocean on one side and a lagoon on the other.

The Brunei government is taking great pains to develop its wealth of natural resources into eco-tourism. One of the easiest means to explore the hinterland is to charter a boat from the municipal pier in B.S.B. The mangrove islands at the mouth of the **Brunei River** harbor typical Borneo wildlife including the rare proboscis monkey, crocodiles and a variety of birdlife.

Across Brunei Bay is the isolated **Temburong District** with a jungle river of the same name. The main town of this enclave is **Bangar**, which can be used as a jumping-off point for visiting the longhouses of the Iban and Murut tribes.

Water-taxis provide transport for the residents of Kampong Ayer.

Batang Duri Park in Temburong offers walks and swimming. Those with more adventurous spirit and energy might want to climb **Bukit Pagon**, Brunei's highest peak at 5,900 feet (1,800 meters).

West of the capital in the Muara District are the **Istana Nurul Izzah** (palace of the sultan's second wife), the royal polo field at **Jerudong Park**, and a collection of traditional buildings in an open-air museum at **Kampong Parit Park**. The oils fields are at **Seria**, 57 miles (92 km) from B.S.B., where the original Shell well was sunk in 1929. Tours of the oil complex can be arranged through travel agencies in the capital. Near Seria is **Sungei Liang Forest Park**, a small jungle reserve with nature trails.

From Seria, you can follow a primitive road inland to **Labi** where Dayak people live amid the rainforest. Farther west is **Kuala Belait**, on the Sarawak border. You can hire a small boat here and cruise the river demarcating the border. Several longhouses can be found upriver about an hour from the coast.

When embarking on a visit to the fabled "Spice Islands" of Indonesia, be sure to bring along a healthy sense of adventure – for found among these 13,677 tropical isles is the single most extraordinary collection of peoples, places, sights, sounds, smells, tastes and natural wonders on earth.

Known to naturalists and anthropologists as the fabulous Malay Archipelago, and remembered by many from the history books as the long-sought "East Indies" in a European "Age of Discovery," these islands still encompass an incomparable treasure trove of biological wonders and ethnological curiosities.

With over 190 million people, Indonesia also ranks now as the world's fifth most populous nation. Here, hundreds of distinct ethnic groups speak more than 350 mutually unintelligible languages, producing a cultural diversity of kaleidoscopic proportions.

Today's visitor to Indonesia follows in the footsteps of a long legacy of distinguished voyagers. One travelogue, penned by the Chinese monk Fa Hsien after being shipwrecked off the coast of Java, dates from the early 5th century A.D. Marco Polo sojourned along the eastern shores of Sumatra in 1292, and in the 17th century, Ferdinand Magellan plotted his historic round-the-world voyage in search of Indonesian cloves, nutmegs, pepper and mace.

In 1770, Captain Cook cruised into Batavia (Jakarta) bay for repairs after charting the coasts of Australia and New Guinea. And then, of course, Joseph Conrad plied these waters as a young sea captain in the late 19th century, and later used several of the islands as settings for his gripping tales of trial and survival in the East.

The modern visitor is faced with truly limitless opportunities for exploration in Indonesia, as literally hundreds of islands await your very own personal discovery. And the journey is relatively easy and comfortable – good accommodation and transportation facilities are now available throughout the archipelago.

Partly as a result, the number of visitors has been growing steadily. Tourist arrivals topped an estimated 2.1 million in 1990 – a fourfold increase in less than five years – and the Indonesian government has stepped up its efforts to promote tourism in order to boost foreign exchange revenues.

Seldom-visited corners of the archipelago welcome the truly adventurous traveler. More and more visitors are straying from the traditional Jakarta-Yogyakarta-Bali trail to explore some of Indonesia's remoter reaches – like Tanah Toraja in southern Sulawesi, Lombok and Kalimantan's Mahakam River.

So whether your particular interest is hiking through dramatic volcanic landscapes, diving amid colorful coral reefs, seeking out obscure antiquities or simply relaxing on the beach, remember that Indonesia is out there waiting to be "discovered."

Preceding pages: Light, color and composition come together effectively in the paddy fields of Lombok. Left, a *Legong* dancer.

The Indonesian archipelago is by far the world's largest – 13,677 islands strewn across 3,200 miles (5,160 km) of tropical seas. Superimposed on a map of Europe, it extends from Ireland to the Caspian Sea. On a map of North America, it stretches from Oregon all the way to Bermuda. Many of these islands are tiny, populated perhaps by a few seabirds, but a thousand of them are large enough to be inhabited. For instance, Java, Borneo and Sumatra are as large as England, France and California, while New Guinea ranks as the world's second largest island (after Greenland). With a total land area of 780,000 square miles (2 million square km), Indonesia is the world's 14th largest political unit.

Unique geologic and climatic conditions have created incredibly diverse environments. An amazing variety of flora and fauna are found here, including rare animal species, exquisite plumage birds and beautiful butterflies.

Born out of many millennia of violent tectonic activity, it is no surprise that many islands periodically experience the death and destruction of volcanic eruptions. In areas where the volcanic ash is basic rather than acidic, spectacularly fertile soils have been produced. Through the construction of elaborate irrigation networks, man has achieved rice yields among the highest in the world here.

Lying within the tropical zone, the islands enjoy consistent temperatures (with a mean of 78°F-82°F/25°C-28°C) and plentiful rainfall the year round. From November to May, rainfall and humidity increase markedly, while for much of the rest of the year, desiccating winds blow up from Australia bringing drier weather.

Vegetation is conditioned by rainfall, soils and altitude – and varies greatly. Lowland rainforests may contain up to 3,000 different tree species, hundreds of varieties of fruit-bearing palms, and many exotic orchids. At altitudes above 2,000 feet (600 meters), temperatures drop and species like chestnut, laurel and oak are found. Higher still, one encounters rhododendrons, edelweiss and alpine meadows more reminiscent of Switzerland than of the tropics.

Indonesian Melting Pot: The broad range of physical types found in the Indonesian archipelago has often been explained in terms of a "wave theory" of successive migrations. The original inhabitants of these islands were probably the so-called "Australoids" who today inhabit New Guinea and Melanesia. They have dark skin, kinky hair, pronounced brow ridges and broad, flat noses – much resembling the peoples of Africa, who evolved in a similar environment.

Later Malayo-Polynesian (or "Austro-

nesian") settlers are thought to have sailed to these islands via Taiwan and the Philippines about 6,000 years ago. Originally from southern China, and essentially "Mongolian" in appearance, with light skin and almond-shaped eyes, many groups later intermixed and acquired Australoid features, such as curly hair and brown skin – traits that are far more prevalent in the eastern islands.

Linguistic diversity also increases dramatically as one moves eastward in the archipelago. Over a hundred distinct languages are spoken in Irian Jaya alone by just over a million people! This indicates that the stability of these areas over many thousands of years, and indeed some New Guinean tribes have been headhunting and producing some tools well into this century.

Two major styles of agriculture are found here. *Ladang* or "slash-and-burn" cultivation is practiced mainly in outlying or marginal areas, and consists of burning a plot prior to the onset of rains to fertilize the soils. The *ladang* method does not support large populations and requires its practitioners to be semi-nomadic. Hence, it is generally associated with more "primitive" tribal groups.

Sawah or wet-rice cultivation, on the other hand, requires and supports large populations to work the soils and maintain the elaborate irrigation system. It also requires a high

religions practiced in the archipelago (Islam, Christianity, Hinduism and Buddhism), one generally finds a remarkable eclecticism.

Many ritual events here can be said to rank among the more extraordinary and dramatic spectacles in the traditional world. Central to most *adat* observances is the ritual sacrifice and communal feast, in which ceremonial foods are offered up to the spirits and then publicly consumed to ensure the well-being of the participants. The Javanese *selamatan* (literally "safe-guarding"), for example, is held on a wide variety of occasions: births, marriages, circumcisions, anniversaries, deaths and dedication of anything new. In Bali, an *odalan* or communal feast is held

The Temple of Boro Bodo in the district of Boro in Kedu.

degree of cooperation among members of the community, and often rewards them with an agricultural bounty.

Religious practices and beliefs in Indonesia are strongly tinged by local traditions – the body of public rites, private rituals, communal knowledge and customary laws that is passed from generation to generation and forms the distinctive fabric of each society. This is known throughout Indonesia as the *adat* (custom) of an ethnic group. And instead of strict adherence to any of the four major

Left, Indonesian native. Above, Borobudur, an ancient monument patterned on Indian models.

every 210 days to celebrate the anniversary of a village temple. Elaborate offerings, processions, symbolic ablutions (with specially-prepared holy water) and feasting characterize these ceremonies.

Such festivals are commonly thought to enhance the fertility and prosperity of the participants by strengthening their *semangat*, or life force. Considered by many groups to be concentrated in the head of humans, *semangat* was once "accumulated" by headhunting. Even today, locks of hair are exchanged in marriage rituals and human hair is applied to dance costumes in order to promote *semangat*. This life force is found elsewhere too. Pillars and weapons are often smeared with sacrificial blood to strengthen them. The cultivation of rice abounds with ritual observances designed to nurture the grain and guarantee a successful harvest. Souls of the deceased are treated with extreme care in elaborate funerary rites and shamanistic practices throughout Indonesia.

A Proud Heritage: Indonesia's earliest hominid inhabitant is popularly referred to today as "Java Man" – a member of the species *Homo erectus* who inhabited the Old World about 1.7 million years ago. A direct ancestor of *Homo sapiens*, "Java Man" was an omnivore and food-gatherer who lived in caves and open campsites, and was the first

kingdoms to enhance an already complex economic and social order.

At the end of the 7th century, a Buddhist kingdom based in eastern Sumatra took control of the strategic Malacca and Sunda straits. Srivijaya ruled these seas for 600 years, developing the largest ships on the seas, and sailing them regularly to India and China. Java, meanwhile, was the site of great inland empires, for here it was possible to support large populations with intensive wet-rice cultivation. A Hindu ruler, Sanjaya, was the first known great temple-builder. But the later Sailendra line of Buddhist kings replaced him, and erected the magnificent monuments of Borobodur, Mendut, Kalasan and Sewu.

creature to know the use of fire. He also produced an elaborate stone tool kit composed of choppers, axes and adzes.

During the neolithic period, the first agriculturalists must have grown taro before rice, and seafarers engaged in inter-island trade long before the dawn of written history. Megalithic stone monuments were erected on many islands to honor the ancestral spirits.

In the 2nd century A.D., highly sophisticated civilizations emerged whose cosmology, architecture and political organization were closely patterned on Indian models. Best known for the wondrous monuments they created, their rulers "Indianized" these

Rakai Pikatan, a descendant of Sanjaya, ousted the Sailendras in A.D. 856, and celebrated his victory by constructing the splendid Loro Jonggrang temple at Prambanan. Suddenly and mysteriously, however, the capital was shifted to East Java in about A.D. 930. Under King Airlangga's subsequent rule, Sanskrit classics were translated into Javanese, marking the flowering of an indigenous literature. A succession of East Javan rulers thereafter combined the benefits of a strong agricultural economy with income from the growing and lucrative overseas trade and, in the process, the Javanese became the master mariners of Southeast Asia.

The East Javanese empire of Majapahit was the first to embrace the entire Indonesian archipelago – numbering all ports around the Java Sea among its vassals. Majapahit reached the zenith of its power in the middle of the 14th century under King Hayam Wuruk and Patih Gajah Mada, after whose death the kingdom rapidly went into a decline. Control of the vital coastal areas passed to a number of new Muslim trading states, and when the central Javanese ricelands were subsequently conquered by Islamic forces, much of the Hindu-Javanese aristocracy fled to Bali.

Muslim traders from India and the Middle East had already visited Indonesia for centuries when the trading ports of northeastern

a growing force throughout the archipelago, with over 80 percent of Indonesians declaring themselves disciples of Mohammed.

Arrival of the Europeans: The Portuguese arrived in Indonesian waters in 1509, just 12 years after Vasco da Gama rounded the tip of Africa, but were refused access to the Islamic-controlled spice trade.

Though never able to dominate the region, the Portuguese left a lasting imprint. Mixed Portuguese-Indonesian communities are to be found today in many coastal areas, and numerous words of Portuguese origin have found their way into the Malay/Indonesian language. Even more significant, perhaps, was the conversion by Portuguese mission-

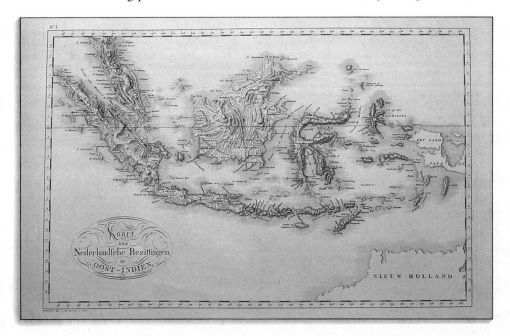

Sumatra began to convert to the new Islamic faith in the late 13th century. The dominant sect of these traders was Sufism – teachings of esoteric revelation, asceticism, dance, and poetry that were highly compatible with the earlier traditions of the Indianized courts.

The adoption of Islam seems not, therefore, to have disturbed the existing order. Moreover, conversion afforded many Indonesian rulers an economic advantage and protection from encroaching Thai and Javanese interests. Today, Islam continues to be

Left, slave trading in Timor. **Above**, 19th-century map of the Dutch East Indies.

aries of some 20,000 Indonesians to Catholicism during the 16th century. Though many later switched to Protestantism under Dutch rule, Christianity today retains a dominant presence in these areas of the archipelago.

The first Dutch expedition to Indonesia in 1596 met largely with disease and dissension, and returned to Holland after a year with only a third of its original crew and a meager cargo of spices. It nevertheless touched off a fever of speculation in Dutch commercial circles. In the following year, 22 more ships were dispatched to the Indies.

Zealous Dutch traders pooled their resources to form the United Dutch East India

Company, or VOC, in 1602, and it was soon empowered by the Dutch government to negotiate treaties, raise armies, build fortresses, and wage war on behalf of the Netherlands in Asia. The Dutch at this time dreamed of securing absolute control of the spice trade, and under the leadership of empire-builder Jan Pieterszoon Coen, they soon established a base at the pepper-port of Jayakarta (now Jakarta), and secured the tiny eastern Banda Islands which produced valuable nutmeg and mace.

During the 1640s and '50s, the Dutch tightened their grip on the eastern spice trade in a series of annual sweeps through the Moluccan islands, where clove trees grew in

led an invasion of Java and was made Lieutenant-Governor at the age of 31. He attempted to replace the old mercantile system with one deriving its income from taxes, but with Napoleon's defeat at Waterloo, Java was returned to the Dutch. Raffles' taxation plan was adopted and modified, however, and resulted in a century of windfall profits from the sale of Indonesian coffee, tea, sugar, quinine, rubber, palm oil, tin, petroleum and other vital commodities – profits that retrieved the Dutch from bankruptcy and financed new waterways, dikes, roads and a national railway system in Holland.

For Indonesians, however, the 19th-century "Cultivation System" (*Cultuurstelsel*) of

profusion. In other areas, they took military action to subdue rival European and Indonesian traders. So successful were these efforts that by the end of the 17th century, the Dutch had achieved effective control of the eastern archipelago and its lucrative spice trade.

On Java, however, official VOC corruption and a lengthy and costly series of wars bankrupted the company by the end of the 18th century. Iron-fisted Governor General Marshall Daendels, a follower of Napoleon, subsequently wrought numerous reforms and rebuilt Batavia (Jakarta).

Then in 1811, a brilliant Englishman named Sir Thomas Stamford Raffles planned and

land-use taxes and forced labor was oppressive, leaving them virtually slaves on their own land. Its injustices were exposed in novels such as *Max Havelaar*, written by a disillusioned colonial administrator, and liberal reforms were instituted. The Dutch also embarked on a series of bloody military campaigns that succeeded in imposing colonial rule throughout the archipelago by the end of the first decade of this century.

Nationalism and Independence: Ironically, Dutch efforts at educational and political reforms in Indonesia provided both an opportunity and an intellectual basis for Indonesian nationalism. Indonesians attending

Dutch schools began to form organizations dedicated to the betterment of their fellows, while Islamic labor unions formed to offer some hope of relief from the oppressive economic conditions.

Strikes often erupted into violence during the 1910s and '20s, and severe crackdowns ensued in which many union leaders were jailed or killed. The leadership of the anti-colonial movement thereafter reverted to the student elite. The first political party with independence as its goal was formed by a young engineer called Sukarno. His gifted oratory soon resulted in his imprisonment for "treasonous statements against the state" and by 1935, secular nationalism would seem

to have been effectively nipped in the bud.

Then came the 1942 invasion of Java by the Japanese, welcomed by many as liberators from Dutch rule. But it soon became apparent that the Japanese were there to exploit the Indies, not to free them. Still, they unwittingly contributed to a growing sense of Indonesian nationhood, while training and equipping a sizable Indonesian militia.

On August 9, 1945 – as the second atomic bomb was dropped – the Japanese Com-

Left, Dutch officials pay a visit to Bali in the 1930s. **Above**, Jakarta monument commemorating the "liberation" of Irian Jaya.

mander for Southeast Asia promised independence for all former Dutch possessions in Asia. Sukarno was appointed chairman of a preparatory committee, with Mohammed Hatta as vice-chairman. After Japan surrendered to the allies two days later, Sukarno and Hatta proclaimed independence. The Dutch attempted to regain their colony, but heroic sacrifices on the battlefield by thousands of Indonesian youths resulted in a military stalemate. Finally, in 1949, the United Nation's Security Council ordered the Dutch to sue for peace and a year later the new Republic was secured.

While independence brought in its wake a wave of euphoria, massive social and economic problems beset the new nation. Factories and plantations were shut, capital and skilled personnel were scarce, rice production was insufficient to meet demand, and the population was expanding rapidly.

With more than 30 rival parties vying for power, the political situation gradually deteriorated during the 1950s. Sukarno finally declared martial law in 1959 and proceeded to lay the blame for Indonesia's problems at the feet of foreign imperialism and the West. Meanwhile, foreign investments fled, deficits left the government bankrupt, and inflation skyrocketed.

Six leading generals were kidnapped and executed by a group of young radicals in 1965, causing General Suharto, then head of the elite Army Strategic Reserve, to move in and take command. Months of bloodletting ensued, as old scores were settled between rival Communist, army and Muslim elements. In 1967, Suharto consolidated his power and restored order.

One primary goal of the Suharto administration over the last 20 years is the integration of Indonesia into the world economy. The development strategy is two-pronged. On one hand, natural resources such as timber, copper, tin and oil have been harnessed to great effect. On the other hand, Indonesia has been able to attract substantial foreign investment in nascent manufacturing industries such as textiles and food processing. The resulting economic boom has transformed Jakarta and Surabaya into two of the fastest-growing cities in Asia. The government's strategy of promoting self-sufficiency and stimulating finished exports hopes to build a lasting prosperity for the nation.

JAKARTA

Capital to the world's fifth most populous nation and home to more than eight million Indonesians, **Jakarta** is a metropolis by any measure.

The city is still largely made up of small one- and two-story structures. Most of these have sprung up rather haphazardly over the past few decades: shops, offices and factories are found in residential districts; market gardens and makeshift *kampung* dwellings impart something of a village atmosphere to many backalleys, and the people live just about everywhere. But the Jakarta skyline is now changing rapidly with the advent of skyscrapers and glitzy shopping malls.

Though not particularly popular among tourists (due to its oppressive heat and snarled traffic), the city nevertheless boasts good museums and many interesting examples of colonial architecture, as well as an excellent array of shops, restaurants and performing arts venues. The people of Jakarta are her greatest asset, so give the city a chance.

Jakarta is located at the mouth of the **Ciliwung River**, on the site of a pepper-trading port that flourished here in the 16th century. In 1619, Dutch empire-builder J.P. Coen ordered construction of a new headquarters, a town that was subsequently dubbed "Batavia."

Under the Dutch East Indian Company (VOC) Batavia first prospered and then declined, as official corruption, decreasing market prices and frequent epidemics of malaria, cholera and typhoid took their toll.

Under Governor-General William Daendels (1808-1811), the old city was demolished to provide building materials for a new one to the south, around what is **Medan Merdeka** (Freedom Square) today. French Empire and neoclassical styles blended with tree-lined boulevards and extensive gardens to impart an atmosphere of grace and elegance, and by the turn of the 19th century, Batavia was once again prosperous.

Preceding pages: a breathtaking interior view of magnificent Istiqlal Mosque.

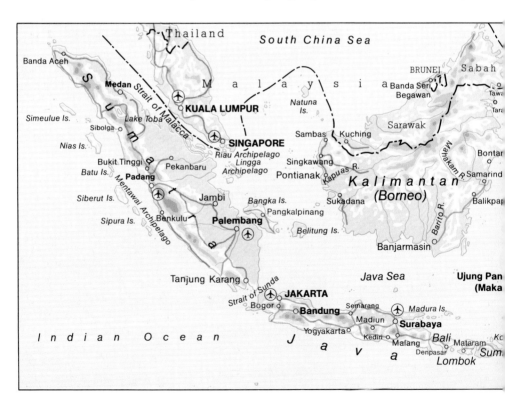

During the brief Japanese occupation (1942-45), Batavia was renamed Jakarta and quickly transformed from a Dutch colonial town of 200,000 to an Indonesian city of more than one million. Since then it has rapidly blossomed to become the unrivaled political, cultural and economic hub of the new nation.

City Tour: Much of **Old Batavia** (Kota) has been destroyed over the years, with the exception of the old town square, which has been restored and renamed **Taman Fatahillah**. On the north side of the square is **Si Jago**, an old canon regarded by many as a fertility symbol. Young couples sometimes approach the canon with offerings, the wife straddling the barrel in hopes of conceiving a child. Three of the surrounding colonial edifices are now museums.

The **Jakarta History Museum** on the south side of the square was formerly the city hall. It now houses 18th-century furnishings and portraits of the VOC governors, as well as many Hindu and Portuguese artifacts. The building was formerly the city hall (*Stadhuis*) of Batavia, a solid structure completed in 1710 and used by successive governors until the 1960s. Dungeons, visible from the rear of the building, were used as holding cells where prisoners were made to stand waist-deep in sewage for weeks awaiting their trials. Executions and public tortures, commonplace during much of the Dutch period, were carried out daily in the town square.

On the western side of the square is the **Wayang Museum**, which displays puppets and masks from all over Indonesia. There are buffalo-hide shadow puppets (*wayang kulit*), round-stick puppets (*wayang golek*), flat-stick puppets (*wayang klithik*), Chinese hand puppets (*potehi*), Thai shadow puppets (*wayang siam*), patriotic shadow puppets (*wayang suluh*), Biblical shadow puppets (*wayang wahyu*) and even a puppet of Batavia's founder, J.P. Coen. Interesting, too, are the simple puppets made of rice straw and bamboo. There is also a collection of *topeng* masks, and the tombstones of several early Dutch governors are on display.

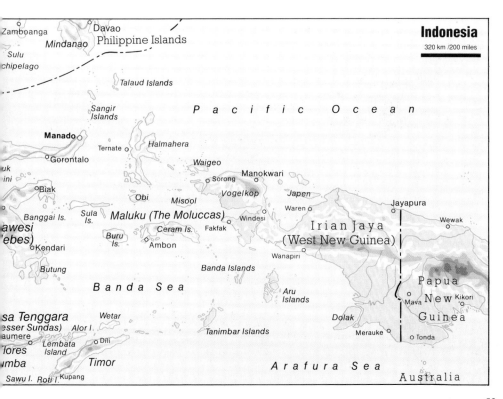

The **Fine Arts Museum** to the east is located in the former Court of Justice building (1879). It displays paintings and sculptures by modern Indonesian artists, as well as an exhibit of rare porcelains, including many Sung Dynasty celadons, Javanese waterjugs (*kendhi*) and terracottas dating from the 14th-century Majapahit period.

Behind the Wayang Museum are two **old Dutch houses** dating from the 18th century. Across the canal and to the left stands a solid red-brick townhouse built around 1730 by the then soon-to-be Governor-General Van Imhoff. The design, particularly the fine Chinese-style woodwork, are typical of old Batavian residences. Three doors to the left stands the only other house from the same period, now the offices of Chartered Bank. Several blocks to the north, an old wooden drawbridge spans a canal, recalling the days when Batavia was a Dutch town laced with waterways.

Glodok – Jakarta's Chinatown – is adjacent to the old European quarter. Give yourself at least an hour on foot to explore this district of narrow lanes and busy shopfronts. **Jin-de Yuan Temple** (1650) on Gang Petak Sembilan is the oldest of Jakarta's more than 70 Chinese temples. Numerous Buddhist, Taoist and popular dieties are enshrined within, including several deified Chinese notables of Old Batavia.

To the north lies the old harbor, **Sunda Kelapa**, with a mile-long wharf in use since 1817. This is where Jakarta began more than 1,500 years ago, as a Hindu spice-trading post. Moored there today are scores of Bugis *pinisi* – two-masted schooners that still ply the waters between Java, Kalimantan and Sulawesi. A morning or evening walk through this nautical hustle and bustle is one of Jakarta's unforgettable experiences.

Just opposite the port stands the **Uitkijk** lookout tower (1839), remains of the 17th-century Dutch fort that once guarded the harbor. Around the corner on Jalan Pasar Ikan are the remains of the old city wall and two Dutch East India Company warehouses dating from 1652, now the **Museum Bahari** (Mari-

Courtyard at the National Museum.

time Museum). Inside are traditional sailing craft from all corners of the archipelago and exhibits on the famous spice trade. Down the same street is the **Pasar Ikan** (Fish Market), beyond numerous stalls selling nautical gear. Be there at dawn for the fish auctions.

At the very center of Jakarta stands the **National Monument** (*Monas*), a 450-foot (137-meter) marble obelisk surmounted by an observation deck and a bronze flame sheathed in 73 pounds (33 kilograms) of gold. It was commissioned by Sukarno and completed in 1961 – a combination Olympic Flame/ Washington Monument with phallic overtones of an ancient Hindu-Javanese *lingam*. Catch the high-speed elevator to the top for a panoramic city view.

The **Presidential Palace** facing the northern side of Medan Merdeka is made up of two 19th-century, neoclassical mansions and adjoining executive office buildings. Whereas President Sukarno resided in the palace and often gave lavish banquets in the central courtyard, President Suharto prefers to stay in his modest home in the Menteng area. Farther east, the **Istiqlal Mosque** with massive dome and rakish minarets is said to be the largest in East Asia.

Lapangan Banteng (Wild-Ox Field) lies farther east, bounded on the north by the neo-Gothic **National Cathedral** (1901), on the east by the **Supreme Court** (1848) and the **Department of Finance** (1982), and on the south by the monstrous **Borobudur Hotel**. In the center of the square stands a muscle-bound giant bursting from his shackles. This is the **Irian Jaya Freedom Memorial** – placed here in 1963 by Sukarno to commemorate the annexation of western New Guinea.

On the western flank of Medan Merdeka lies the **National Museum**. Opened in 1868 by the Batavian Society for Arts and Sciences, it houses enormously valuable collections of antiquities, books and ethnographic artifacts acquired by the Dutch during the 19th and early 20th centuries. Upstairs is the exquisite **Treasure Room** – containing a plundered hoard of royal heirlooms –

Vessels anchored at the picturesque port of Sunda Kelapa.

open only on Sunday mornings.

Southwest of the square down Jalan Menteng Raya is **Taman Ismail Marzuki** (TIM), the massive Jakarta arts complex containing an exhibition hall, fine arts college, planetarium, dance studio, art gallery and five theaters. TIM presents a continuous bill of cultural events like Indonesian dance and drama.

To get quite a different view of Jakarta, hail a cab and brace yourself for the high-speed cruise down Jalan Thamrin to the **Blok M** shopping district in **Kebayoran**. Along the way, you'll pass the monuments to Indonesia's recent economic development – banks, shopping centers and gleaming office blocks. Dominating the district is a gleaming new U-shaped structure called the **Blok M Mall**. Visit the **Pasaraya Department Store** for a look at their extensive handicraft selection, then browse the shops around Blok M and have a meal in one of the chic restaurants – to get a feel for the standard of living to which many Jakartans have become accustomed.

If you have time, **Taman Mini** ("Indonesia in Miniature Park") should not be missed. Located about 6 miles (10 km) south of Jakarta and encompassing 247 acres (100 hectares), the park has 27 main pavilions, one for each of Indonesia's provinces, employing authentic materials and workmanship to exhibit a traditional style of architecture representative of that region. Inside are displays of handicrafts, costumes, musical instruments and other artifacts.

There are at least 30 other attractions here as well, including a **Tropical Bird Park**, an **Orchid Garden**, a **model of Borobodur** and the magnificent **Museum Indonesia** – a three-story Balinese palace filled with traditional textiles, houses, boats, puppets, jewelry and wedding costumes.

A modern theme park called **Ancol Dreamland** has been developed 6 miles (10 km) from downtown on the shores of Jakarta Bay. It features a Disney-like area called *Dunia Fantasi*, swimming complex with five pools, oceanarium, golf course and marina.

Thousand Islands: Lying just off the coast of Jakarta amid the turquoise waters of the Java Sea is a cluster of 600 offshore isles known collectively as the **Thousand Islands** (Pulau Seribu). Many of them are easy to reach by ferry or chartered boat from Tanjung Priok or Pasar Ikan on the Jakarta waterfront. Some of them are equipped with airstrips. Several of the closer islands, notably **Onrust**, were used by the Dutch East Indies Company as locations for warehouses and drydocks. The ruins of these colonial installations from the 17th and 18th centuries can still be seen.

Many other islands are privately-owned weekend hideaways for the rich and famous of Jakarta. Three of the islands – **Pulau Putri**, **Pulau Ayer** and **Pulau Bidadari** – have been developed as tourist resorts with air-conditioned bungalows. Only Pulau Ayer and Pulau Bidadari have supplies of fresh water, and Pulau Putri has access to an airstrip. The Thousand Islands is an excellent place for aquatic sports like snorkeling, scuba diving, water-skiing, windsurfing, fishing and sailing.

Left, West Sumatran wedding regalia on display at Jakarta's Taman Mini. **Right**, Jakarta skyline.

WEST JAVA

Little do most visitors suspect that within a few hours of Jakarta, the western third of Java offers beaches and landscapes as attractive as any in the more heavily toured parts of Indonesia. The Sundanese of West Java are known for their mellifluous language, hardy individualism and staunch adherence to Islam. The rugged highlands they inhabit (the so-called "Sunda Highlands") are famous for their cool climate, stunning vistas and excellent travel facilities.

This part of Java has been inhabited for many millennia, despite its relative impenetrability, and during the early 16th century, the coastal port of Banten was one of Asia's largest and most cosmopolitan trading emporiums. Having settled in Jakarta in the early 17th century, the Dutch were later ceded much of the so-called Priangan Highlands, and these tangled uplands were finally opened up when Governor-General Daendels ordered the construction of the great trans-Java post road linking Jakarta with other cities.

After 1830, the Dutch operated tea, quinine and rubber estates here, and modern industry has followed so that the area is now a cornerstone of the Indonesian economy. The highland towns of Bogor and Bandung were originally established as Dutch administrative centers and continue to attract new residents at a disproportionate rate, together with many textile, pharmaceutical and aircraft plants.

Escape from Jakarta: Besides the Thousand Islands (Pulau Seribu), another quick getaway from the capital is a journey to Java's sandy and secluded **West Coast Beaches** facing the Sunda Strait where you can enjoy a swim and snooze on the beach within three to five hours of leaving the city.

History buffs will want to stop along the way at the village of **Banten**, which was one of the most vibrant towns in Asia during the 16th century. Banten was razed by the Dutch in 1808. Today it's little more than a tiny fishing village straddling a tidal creek. But you can still see the ruins of two massive palaces and a Dutch fortress, plus an interesting old mosque with an adjacent museum and a famous Chinese temple.

From the small harbor at **Merak**, ferries depart for **Bakauhuni** on the southern tip of Sumatra. The nearby beach resorts of **Anyer** and **Carita** have comfortable accommodation bordering palm-fringed beaches. Marking the 14 miles (22 km) of coast that separate the towns are an old lighthouse and **Karang Bolong**, a huge rock forming a natural archway to the sea and a popular weekend swimming spot for Jakartans.

The infamous volcanic islands of **Krakatau** lie just 94 miles (152 km) to the southwest of Jakarta. From the port of Labuan, charter a boat for the smooth two-hour journey out to the volcanoes. Though dormant for centuries, Krakatau achieved instant infamy in 1883 when it erupted with cataclysmic force, ripping out a huge chunk of the earth's crust and forming a monstrous submarine caldera. The sea rushed in, causing tidal waves

Left, ubiquitous smiles of Javanese children. Right, misty montane forest on Mount Gede.

that claimed more than 35,000 lives. Undersea activity continued for decades thereafter, producing a newcomer with a gaping half-crater: **Anak Krakatau** ("Son of Krakatau").

Also available from Labuan are boats to **Ujung Kulon National Park** at the island's southwestern tip. The park is endowed with pristine tropical rainforest and many near-extinct Javan wildlife species like the *badak* or rhinoceros. If you wish to visit the park, make arrangements first through a travel agent or at the PPA (Conservation Department) offices in Labuan.

From Labuan, a scenic backroad winds east through the Parahyangan foothills to the highland home of the mysterious **Badui** people, sometimes called the "Amish of Java" because they refuse to live with modern objects.

Perhaps the most scenic of West Java's excursions is the ascent into the dramatic **Parahyangan Highlands** ("Abode of the Gods") to the south of Jakarta, The town of **Bogor** is only an hour's drive from the capital via the new Jagorawi Expressway. Here, the glorious **Botanical Gardens** (*Kebun Raya*) houses more than 15,000 species of tropical plants and trees, plus orchid nurseries, a zoological museum and a vast botanical library. The gardens were originally opened by the Dutch in 1817 and are now world-renowned. Next to the gardens stands the imposing **Presidential Summer Palace**, formerly official residence of the governor-general of the Dutch East Indies.

A good road leads over 4,863-foot (1,474-meter) **Puncak Pass** and down into the cool mountain resort of **Cipanas**, where many Jakartans maintain fashionable villas. This is a lovely place to spend a few days, hiking through the highland forest and tea estates. The nearby **Cibodas Botanical Gardens** – an extension of those in Bogor – has a famous collection of montane and temperate climate flora. From here, a six-hour climb takes you to the summit of either **Mount Gede** or **Mount Pangrango** – with their superb views, waterfalls and fascinating wildlife.

The Presidential Palace at Bogor.

The beautiful but dangerous southern coast of West Java is within easy reach of Bogor. The route winds south from Ciawi through an area lush with rubber trees, tea plantations and rice terraces. A scenic side road branches off at Cibadak and meanders down to the fishing village of **Pelabuhan Ratu**, where the ragged, wind-lashed Indian Ocean foams and crashes onto smooth black-sand beaches. A number of good swimming beaches line the coast for several miles past the village, but be warned that the surf and undertow here can be treacherous.

The highland city of **Bandung** offers another cool alternative to the oppressive heat of Jakarta. The population and cultural center of the Sunda Lands, Bandung sits in a basin at 2,300 feet (700 meters) above sea level and is surrounded by lofty peaks. Known as the "Paris of Java" before the war, it was then a small Dutch administrative and university town with broad boulevards and elegant homes. Still striking today, with a population of more than 1.5 million, Bandung offers several interesting sights. The **Geological Museum** on Jalan Diponegoro contains an array of rocks, maps and fossils, including replicas of the famous "Java Man" (*Homo erectus*) skulls found near the center of the island. The Publications Department upstairs sells topographic survey maps of most of Indonesia. Bandung's **Institute of Technology** (ITB) is the country's oldest and finest university. The campus library, built in the 1920s, is a honeycomb of massive wooden girders. Meanwhile, the old Dutch area around **Jalan Braga** contains many colonial Art Deco buildings.

The breathtaking peaks around Bandung are easy to visit. **Tangkuban Prahu** ("Upturned Boat") volcano lies only 20 miles (32 km) to the north of the city and has a road leading right to the crater rim. Here, cold mountain mists and sulfurous fumes swirl about jagged ridges. Visit the **Ciater hot springs** beyond the Tangkuban Prahu exit for a meal and a soothing soak in the piping-hot pools.

Tangkuban Prahu is surrounded by swirling mist.

YOGYAKARTA

The noble city of **Yogyakarta** (Yogya) sits astride a broad, green crescent of fertile ricelands on the southern flanks of towering **Mount Merapi**, where average population densities soar as high as 3,000 persons per square mile. Cultural attractions abound as well – for this was the site of Central Java's two great Mataram empires (one ancient and one modern). Yogyakarta is today a bastion of Javanese traditional life, as well as the jumping-off point for visits to the fabled monuments of Borobudur and Prambanan.

Ruled by a succession of Hindu-Buddhist kings from the 8th century to the early 10th century, the courts of Central Java suddenly and inexplicably shifted to the east after 928. The region then remained relatively deserted until the end of the 16th century when Muslim ruler Panembahan Senapati founded a New or Second Mataram Dynasty.

His grandson, Sultan Agung (1613-45), greatly expanded the empire, but their descendants became embroiled in an endless series of bitter and bloody disputes involving rival courts, the Dutch and the Madurese. In 1755, the Dutch finally imposed a treaty which divided the empire in half. Sultan Hameng-kubuwana I of Yogya then proceeded to build a new palace and an elaborate pleasure garden.

The subsequent history of the Yogyakarta sultanate is notably one of resistance to ever-increasing Dutch colonial influence in Central Java. Invaded by the Dutch and the British in 1810 and 1812, and swept up in the great Java War of 1825-30, Yogya later served as provisional capital for the new nation during the Revolution (1946-49).

"Navel" of the Universe: Despite all the changes of the past few decades, it is still Yogya's traditional attractions that most visitors come to see. The royal **Kraton**, a 200-year-old palace, exemplifies the Javanese belief that the ruler is the "navel" of the universe. The pal-

Two reflective Javanese men.

ace is thus both the center of the kingdom and the hub of the cosmos. It contains private chambers for the sultan, his family and the dynastic regalia, as well as a magnificent throne hall, meditational chambers, performance pavilions, a mosque, stables, barracks, an armaments foundry and two expansive parade grounds – all within a walled compound measuring a mile on each side.

The interior of the Kraton was remodeled in the 19th century along European lines, incorporating Italian marble, cast-iron columns, crystal chandeliers and rococo furnishings into an otherwise classically Javanese setting. The throne hall, an ancient *gamelan* set and two great *kala* head gateways all contribute to the visual effect.

The **Taman Sari** royal pleasure gardens lie just to the west and south of the Kraton. An opulent and architecturally ingenious complex consisting of an artificial lake, underground and underwater passages, meditational retreats, sunken bathing pools, and a two-story European-style mansion (known as the "Water Castle"), Taman Sari was constructed over a period of many years in the mid-18th century and then abruptly abandoned. It was once fortified, and was originally surrounded on all sides by a man-made lake. Today the complex borders on a crowded bird-market and a colony of young *batik* painters.

An underground passageway behind the Water Castle leads to a series of partially restored bathing pools. Designed for the use of queens, concubines and princesses, it is overlooked by a tower where the sultan "rested" during the day. The **Pesarean Pertapaan** to the south through an ornate archway is a small Chinese-style temple with galleries and a forecourt where the sultan and his sons are said to have meditated for seven days and nights at a time.

North of the bathing pools is **Sumur Gumuling** ("circular well"), a fascinating underground gallery often referred to by locals as a mosque. It was likely intended as a trysting place for the sultan and Nyai Loro Kidul, the powerful Goddess of the South Seas to whom

Puppet theater incorporates tales from Indian and old Javanese epics.

all Mataram rulers were promised in marriage by the dynasty's founder (and from whom they are said to derive their mystical powers).

A stroll down Yogya's main street, **Jalan Malioboro**, begins in front of the royal audience pavilion on **Alun-alun Utata**, the central town square north of the Kraton, and ends one mile away at a phallic *linggam* dedicated to the local guardian spirit, Kyai Jaga. Once a processional boulevard, this thoroughfare today bustles with cars, *becaks,* motorbikes and people. Both sides of the streets are lined with shops selling *batik* textiles, leather goods, baskets, tortoiseshell jewelry and endless knick-knacks.

The **Sana Budaya Museum** on the northwestern side of the square was established in 1935 by the Java Institute, a cultural foundation composed of wealthy Javanese and Dutch art patrons. Today it houses prehistoric artifacts, Hindu-Buddhist bronzes, *wayang* puppets, dance costumes and traditional Javanese weapons.

Yogya is known for its sophisticated performing arts. The *wayang kulit* shadow play undoubtedly lies closest to the heart of the Javanese. The *dalang* or puppeteer is the key to the performance, breathing new life into each retelling of familiar tales from the Indian *Mahabharata* and *Ramayana* epics. Performances for *selamatan* feasts, weddings, or circumcisions occur regularly, beginning around 9 p.m. and continuing until dawn. A full eight-hour presentation is held on the second Saturday of every month at the **Sasana Inggil** south of the Kraton, and mini-performances are held daily at 3 p.m. for the benefit of tourists at the **Agastya Art Institute** *dalang* school on Jalan Gedongkiwo.

Classical Javanese Dance is another highlight of Yogya's cultural scene. The weekly rehearsal on Sunday mornings at 10.30 a.m. in the Bangsal Srimangati within the Kraton should not be missed.

Yogya is also justly famous for its *batik* . Visit the **Batik Research Center** (*Balai Penelitian Batik*) at No. 2, Jalan Kusumanegara for an introduction to the wax-resist dyeing process, and to

Dusty Yogya street scene.

JAVANESE BATIK

Batik textiles are such an integral part of Javanese culture that it's difficult to imagine a time when they did not exist. Yet the *batik* process we know may not be old. Scholars debate whether the wax-resist dyeing method was brought to Java from India where it was known for centuries or whether it developed autonomously in Java.

An antecedent for *batik* might be the *kain simbut* of West Java, produced by smearing rice paste on cloth as a dye-resistant medium. Others say that Javanese *kain kembangan*, a method of tie-dying, led ultimately to the use of wax and resin resists.

Names for various *batik* motifs have been traced to 12th-century Javanese literary works. But the fact remains that the term "*batik*" (as applied to textile design) does not appear in the Javanese court records until the Islamic period, when Indian traders were already active in the archipelago. The name derives from "*ntik*," a Javanese word that means "creating with dots," which is basically what is done with the molten wax.

No one disputes, however, that Javanese *batik* is the world's finest. The reason is a small copper tool called the *canting*, a "pen" used to apply molten wax to cloth and capable of executing very fine designs. This method is called *batik tulis*.

The evolution of a complex technology of wax and resin compounding, dye preparation and fixing, and a whole repertoire of elaborate motifs, were also necessary for Javanese *batik* to become what it is today. Fine, tightly woven cloth was another prerequisite to high quality *batik*, but this was not imported into Java until very recently.

Fine *batik* requires extraordinary patience to produce. Starting with a piece of white silk or cotton cloth, the first step is to sketch a design. Areas which are not to be colored in the first dyeing must be covered with hot wax. This can take hundreds of hours of painstaking labor. The cloth is then immersed in a prepared dye solution and dried.

Next the cloth must be re-waxed in preparation for the second dyeing. Sometimes this is accomplished by boiling out the wax and starting over again; but at other times the task involves scraping certain areas and adding wax to others. The dyeing and re-waxing process can be repeated as many as 20 or 30 times in order to achieve the number of colors required.

An inferior method of production is called *batik cap*, in which the wax is applied with a copper stamp. This revolutionized the *batik* industry when it was introduced in the 1890s by allowing for mass production. It's often difficult for the uninitiated to tell the difference, but one sure test is to flip the *batik* onto its backside. *Batik tulis* should have identical color on both side because the wax is applied to both surfaces; *batik cap* is faded on the rear because the wax is applied to only one surface. A much newer form of production is "*batik* painting" on canvas – using a brush to apply acrylic or oil paints. ∎

the staggering variety of patterns and colors to be found throughout Java. **Jalan Tirtodipuran** in the south of Yogya also has over 25 factories and showrooms where you can see the cloth being drawn and dyed. **Toko Terang Bulan** shop on Jalan Malioboro sells finished *sarung*, *kain*, tablecloths, shirts and dresses at fixed prices. *Batik* paintings designed for framing and hanging are produced by a number of well-known artists.

Monumental Java: A visit to one of the hundred-odd *candis* or ancient stone monuments that lie scattered about the dramatic volcanic landscapes of Central Java is an unforgettable experience. Since 1900, a great deal of effort has been expended to excavate and restore them, but we still know little about their function within ancient Javanese society. There is no denying, though, that these awe-inspiring structures are among the most technically accomplished edifices of ancient times.

The legendary *stupa* of **Borobudur**, located 26 miles (42 km) to the north-west of Yogya, is the world's largest Buddhist monument. Built between 778 and 856, but then inexplicably deserted within a century of its completion, Borobudur has undergone a long process of "rediscovery" and restoration.

In 1814, English Lieutenant-Governor Thomas Stamford Raffles dispatched his military engineer to investigate what was rumored to be a "mountain of Buddhist sculpture." Sadly the uncovering of the monument led to years of plunder and abuse by local villagers and Dutch officials. A cry of outrage from within the colonial government in 1900 resulted in a massive campaign to reconstruct and preserve the monument. But the restorers soon realized that internal erosion was slowing eating away at Borobudur's foundation and would eventually destroy it.

Two world wars, the Depression and several earthquakes left Borobudur in a sorry state by the time UNESCO finally sponsored a fund-raising drive and feasibility study. In 1973, the massive project finally got underway.

Borobudur is the world's largest Buddhist monument, built 300 years before Angkor Wat.

It is estimated that it originally took 30,000 stonecutters, 15,000 carriers and thousands of masons 50 to 75 years to build Borobudur.

Seen from the air, Borobudur forms a *mandala* or geometric meditational aid. From a distance, it is a *stupa* or reliquary – a model of the cosmos in three vertical parts. The base has reliefs depicting *khamadhatu*, the lower sphere of bodily human desires. The middle terraces and galleries teach of *rupadhatu* or the sphere of "form," and contain reliefs depicting the life of Prince Siddharta on his way to becoming Gautama the Buddha. Statues of the meditating Buddha at the monument's highest levels symbolize *arupadhatu* – realm of formlessness and total abstraction represented by the central *dagoba*.

Borobudur was thus erected for the glorification of the Ultimate Reality – the serene realm of the Lord Buddha – and as a tangible lesson for priests and pilgrims. It was also a massive mausoleum, and may have once housed the relics of a Buddhist ruler or saint.

Two smaller temples lie just to the east of Borobudur. **Pawon** (the "kitchen" or "crematorium") is decorated with heavenly money trees and celestial musicians. **Candi Mendut**, now missing its crown, depicts scenes from moralistic fables and folktales. The main body of Mendut contains superbly carved panels depicting *bodhisattvas* and Buddhist sculptures reputed to be the finest found anywhere – a seated Sakyamuni Buddha flanked by the *Bodhisattvas* Vajrapani and Avalokitesvara.

Ten miles (16 km) to the east of Yogyakarta, in the center of a plain that is literally littered with ancient ruins (known by natives as the "Valley of the Kings"), lies the temple complex of **Prambanan**. Completed in A.D. 856 to commemorate the victory of Hindu Rakai Pikatan over the last Buddhist Sailendran king of Central Java, Prambanan is thought by many to be Indonesia's most elegant monument.

The complex consists of eight structures. The three main temples are arrayed north to south, with the large **Loro Jonggrang** ("Slender Maiden") Shiva shrine in the middle, flanked on either side by slightly smaller shrines dedicated to Vishnu and Brahma.

Legend has it that Loro Jonggrang was a princess wooed by an unwanted suitor. She commanded him to build a temple in one night, and then frustrated his efforts by prematurely announcing the dawn. Enraged, he turned her into stone. She now resides in the northern chamber of the temple – as a statue of Shiva's consort, Durga.

Loro Jonggrang is graced with a glorious symmetry and a wealth of sculptural detail. Celestial beings, animals, illustrations of the classical Indian dance manual or *Natyasastra*, and vivid depictions of the *Ramayana* are all carved in bas-relief on the temple's balustrades. The movement within these carvings is free-flowing and filled with fascinating detail. Not to be missed is the **Ramayana Ballet**, held under a full moon over four consecutive nights during the dry season (May – October) in front of Loro Jonggrang.

The Prambanan Temple complex.

CENTRAL AND EASTERN JAVA

Though most visitors make a beeline for Bali, the island of Java has much to offer to the intrepid traveler. All that's needed is a bit of time and a desire to stray from the beaten track.

The quiet, old court city of **Surakarta** (also known as **Solo**) lies just an hour east of Yogya by car. The main attraction, a still-functioning 18th-century palace called the **Kraton Kasusuhunan**, was constructed between 1743 and 1746 on the banks of the mighty **Bengawan Solo River**. Like the Yogyakarta palace, its outer walls enclose a labyrinthine network of narrow lanes and smaller compounds, two large squares, a mosque and an inner palace complex. Unfortunately, the elegant throne hall burned to the ground in 1985 and is yet to be rebuilt. Still, the area around the palace is well worth visiting.

The **Palace Museum** was established in 1963 and contains ancient Hindu-Javanese bronzes, traditional weapons and coaches dating back to the 1740s. Also be sure to visit **Sasana Mulya**, a music and dance pavilion belonging to ASKI, the Indonesian Performing Arts Academy, just to the west of the main palace gate. Here you may witness *gamelan* rehearsals, dance performances and *wayang kulit* shows.

Another branch of the royal family has constructed their own *kraton* about half a mile northwest of the main palace. Completed in 1866, the **Pura Mangkunegaran** boasts the largest *pendopo*, or audience pavilion, in Java. Built of solid teakwood, jointed and fitted in traditional manner without nails, it features a brightly-painted ceiling bordered by Javanese zodiacal symbols. Register at the east gate and ask for a tour of the inner sanctum, containing the exquisite private collection of Mangkunegara IV – dance costumes, *topeng* masks, jewelry and *kris* blades.

Solo is also an excellent place for the unhurried shopper who likes to explore out-of-the-way places in the hopes of finding hidden treasures. **Pasar Triwindu**, a sizeable antique market, lies just to the south of the Mangkunegaran Palace. *Batik* shops line the main streets; you should also visit **Pasar Klewar**, a huge textile market near the **Grand Mosque** and the town square.

Central Highlands: The handsome **Dieng Plateau** is often billed as a day trip from Yogya. But this sprawling tableland north of **Wonosobo** really deserves more than a passing look. The scenery itself makes a sojourn advisable. Dieng is all that remains of the caldera of a prehistoric volcano that exploded violently thousands of years ago, showering the surrounding region with ash and lava. The plateau is littered with volcanic remnants: sulfur springs, crater lakes, fissures, caves and petrified lava flows. The most famous lava cavern is **Gua Semar**, a well-known place of meditation and where the god Semar is said to live.

Dieng means "Abode of the Gods," a name that derives from its many temples. This was an active place of Hindu

Temples on the Dieng Platean.

worship during the 9th-century Saliendra Dynasty, but only eight of what is thought to have been several hundred *candis* remain. From an architectural point of view, they resemble much smaller versions of Prambanan. The largest temple cluster is situated in a swamp near **Dieng Village**.

North Coast: The north coast, once the site of Java's busiest and richest trading ports, is now one of the finest areas for handicrafts and the scene of eccentric palaces, holy graves, ancient mosques, bustling markets and colorful Chinese temples.

Cirebon is famous both for its seafood and its colorful past. At one time the seat of a powerful sultanate, it has two major palaces. The **Kraton Kasepuhan** displays a fascinating blend of Javanese, Chinese, Islamic and European influences. The **Masjid Agung** (Grand Mosque) next door was erected around 1500, making it one of the oldest Islamic landmarks on Java. The **Kraton Kanoman** behind the market has European furnishings and walls studded with Delft tiles and Chinese porcelains.

What the north coast may lack in scenic beauty it makes up for in *batik*. About 138 miles (220 km) east of Cirebon is a town called **Pekalongan** that announces itself on roadside pillars as "Kota Batik" – Batik City. Apart from the many factories and retail stores lining the streets, Pekalongan justifies this sobriquet by producing some of the finest and most highly prized *batik* on Java. The local style is unique – a blend of Muslim, Javanese, Chinese and European motifs executed in pastel tones. The town's hallmark is the floral bouquet with hovering hummingbirds and butterflies, a design derived from 18th-century Dutch porcelains.

Farther to the east is the bustling city of **Semarang**, a commercial hub and provincial capital. Visit the old **Dutch Church** with its copper-clad dome on Jalan Suprapto, and the **Chinatown District**, with ancient temples such as the **Thay Kak Sie** and very distinctive Nanyang-style townhouses.

The road south from Semarang climbs

Old Dutch warehouses overlooking the Kalimas Canal.

up into the foothills of **Mount Ungaran**. If you have time, make a detour to the cool mountain resort of **Bandungan** to visit the **Gedung Songo** temples – several of the oldest and most spectacularly situated antiquities on Java.

East Java: East Java is a paradise for rugged individualists who relish the search for ancient temples or the breathtaking views from the rims of desolate volcanoes. For five centuries after A.D. 930, the **Brantas River** valley of East Java was the locus of power and civilization on the island. The kingdoms of this period have left a rich heritage of temple art, literature, music and drama. Morever, the volcanic peaks of the eastern salient contain many secluded nature reserves and an unparalleled scenic beauty.

The metropolis of East Java is **Surabaya**, the largest seaport in the archipelago before the turn of the century and today a sprawling city of over four million. The old Arab, Chinese and Dutch quarters lie to the north of the city center. At the **Hong Tim Hian Temple** on Jalan Dukuh II/2, daily Chinese hand-puppet shows can be seen. From here, cross over the **"Red Bridge"** to see the old Dutch commercial district.

Just north of Surabaya in the Java Sea is the island of **Madura**, famous for its annual *kerapan sapi* or bull races. According to the locals, this sport began many centuries ago when plow teams raced one another across the rice fields. Today's racing bulls are specially bred and are a considerable source of island pride. Races take place in August and September with the grand finale in **Pamekasan**, the island's capital.

Tretes, 34 miles (55 km) south of Surabaya, is a delightful mountain resort where you can walk or ride horseback to one of three lovely waterfalls in the vicinity. A hike up **Mount Arjuna**, 11,000 feet (3,340 meters) through lush casuarina forests or across the **Lalijiwa Plateau** to neighboring **Mount Welirang** will appeal to hardier souls. Ancient temples are scattered throughout the area. **Candi Jawi** is on the main road, 4 miles (7 km) below Tretes – a

Bull races at Madura.

slender shrine dedicated to King Kertanegara. It overlooks **Mount Penanggungan**, site of 81 sanctuaries, grottoes and sacred pools.

Many more *candis* are found around **Malang**. At an altitude of over 1,460 feet (450 meters), this old Dutch colonial town is a welcome relief from the heat and humidity of the nearby lowlands. Just east of town are two interesting temples. **Candi Jago** is a 13th-century terraced shrine with reliefs depicting scenes from the *Mahabharata* and a frightening procession of demons in the underworld. Just 3 miles (5 km) to the southwest is **Candi Kidal**, a tall and slender temple from the same period.

East Java's only sizeable temple complex is **Candi Penataran**, 50 miles (80 km) west of Malang, just north of the city of Blitar. This was apparently the "state temple" of the Majapahit Empire, assembled over a period of 250 years between 1197 and 1454. It has no soaring pinnacle or massive *stupa*, rather a series of shrines and pavilions arranged before a broad platform. The pavilions are thought to have been originally roofed with wood and thatch, as was the body of the main temple, now partially reconstructed at ground level alongside the massive three-tiered base.

Nature lovers will revel in the moonscapes of **Mount Bromo**, the **Yang Plateau** and the **Ijen Crater.** The trek up Bromo for sunrise is a must on a backpacking trip across Java. Those who don't want to walk can hire ponies at **Cemoro Lawang** village. Either way, the ascent starts before daybreak with most of the climbing done in the dark.

At the far eastern tip of Java is **Baluran National Park**, a massive nature reserve which comprises volcanoes, seashore, grasslands, swamps and tropical forests. The wildlife inventory here includes wild buffalo, deer and leopards. On the southern coast near Sukamade is the **Meru Betiri Reserve**, where giant sea turtles lay their eggs on black-sand beaches at midnight. Heavy rain in this area has created dense rainforest which is the last refuge of the nearly extinct Javan tiger.

Bromo landscape is stark and spectacular.

BALI: PARADISE ON EARTH

In so many ways, Bali is the crown jewel in the treasure chest of marvels that comprise the Indonesian archipelago. Formed by an east-west volcanic range, drenched by tropical showers and bathed with radiant sunshine, the island is first and foremost a verdant masterpiece of nature. The people of Bali have done much to turn such natural blessings to their advantage, achieving great agricultural success through a fruitful cooperation with the land, gods and each other, in a culture that is both materially efficient and spiritually satisfying. For this reason, Bali has long been referred to as a "paradise on earth."

The tourist invasion of Bali since the 1960s has left many people wondering whether the island's fabled culture can take the strain. The government, in an attempt not to kill the proverbial goose that laid the golden egg, limits new hotels to no more than four storeys and has channeled resort growth into the southern tip of the island.

History has shown that the Balinese are incredibly adept at integrating foreign elements into their own flexible traditions. The polyglot nature of Balinese art is a striking example of the Balinese ability to digest and absorb while rejecting those elements not compatible with their sophisticated, conservative way of life.

Each person on Bali finds himself born into a complex web of social bonds. Children are privileged, for it's believed their souls are closer to heaven. Babies are carried everywhere, never permitted to touch the impure earth and always comforted by warm hands and soothing voices. Ceremonies are held at prescribed intervals, notably on the child's first birthday, when offerings are made by a priest. Thus begins the complex cycle of rites of passage which ushers the Balinese from cradle to grave.

On a larger scale, too, the society is elaborately defined in terms of groups bound together through ritual observances. Communal activities revolve around the three village temples, each with a separate calendar of local events, as well as participating in a schedule of regional and island-wide festivities. Within each *desa*, or village, are smaller cooperative units (*banjar*) whose members assist each other in marriages, festivals and funeral cremations. The *banjar* controls community property and has a kitchen for preparing banquets, a signal drum tower (*kulkul*), an open meeting pavilion (*bale*) and a communal temple.

Every Balinese is at once a member of his family, his *banjar*, his *desa* and the island-wide culture. This strong sense of community fosters an equally strong sense of personal identity, allowing each generation to be as fresh and dynamic as the one before it. The same can be said of each visit to beautiful Bali.

Preceding pages: The *Eka Dasa Rudra* rite is held once every hundred years at Bali's Pura Besakih temple. **Left**, dance is an all-important element of cultural life. This *Legong* dancer is from Bali.

SOUTH BALI

As the focus of Bali's tourism, commerce and government, the south is by far the busiest region. Bali's three famous beach resorts are all here, along with the international airport and the capital city of **Denpasar**. The entire area has experienced unprecedented economic and population growth during the last decades as a result of the tourist boom.

Yet beyond the hotels, shops and blaring discotheques, a traditional village culture manages to thrive on much as it did before. The south's temple festivals are legendary for the intensity of their trance dances and the earthiness of their rituals. Many village troupes now put on highly professional dance performances nightly.

Tiny **Sanur**, 6 miles (10 km) to the southeast of Denpasar, used to be a quiet fishing village. During the 1930s, its peaceful shores attracted Western intellectuals and artists, such as anthropologist Margaret Mead and painter Walter Spies. Mass tourism followed in the early 1960s, when several hotels were built along the edge of the lagoon.

Today, these hotels host thousands of visitors from Australia, Europe, Japan and the U.S., while still managing to preserve a sense of charm and quiet dignity. There are now three large hotels in Sanur and a number of smaller bungalow establishments. The beach and the main road are lined with souvenir shops, restaurants and money changers – but a quick, half-hour's walk inland will lead one down village lanes and through verdant ricefields.

Sanur's main attraction is leisure – a facet of life not unknown to those who live here. Strolls up and down the beach can easily occupy your day, capped by a fine meal and an evening dance performance.

With Sanur's beachfront all but used up, a new tourist development has been created with help from the World Bank at **Nusa Dua**, on the secluded **Bukit Peninsula** south of the airport. Nearly a dozen luxury hotels have been licensed,

the first of which opened in late 1982. All have magnificent beachfronts and extensive sports facilities, and are set in a vast expanse of manicured lawns owned and maintained by the Bali Tourist Development Corporation. As a result, Nusa Dua is blissfully free of souvenir sellers and garish billboards – offering all the advantages (and disadvantages) of a "total" hotel environment.

Nearby **Pura Uluwatu**, precariously perched on a cliff 330 feet (100 meters) over the ocean, is a sublime place to watch the sunset.

Kuta Beach on South Bali's western shore is a bargain basement beach party. Discovered by surfers in the early 1970s, Kuta's chief natural attractions are a broad, sloping beach, a pounding surf and technicolor sunsets. Informal accommodations line the beach and byways, along with a staggering array of restaurants, cafes, pubs, boutiques, discos, bike rentals, artshops and tour agencies. Thankfully, serene paddy fields and long stretches of sandy beach

Left, a prahu cruises Sanur Beach, looking for customers. **Right**, waters around Bali provide plenty of good fishing.

are never more than a few minutes away. Kuta is, incidentally, one of the best places to stop and eat in Bali – found here are some fine antique and clothing boutiques, as well as a wide variety of restaurants serving both Asian and Western fare.

To the north lies **Legian**, an extension of Kuta and now a tourist resort in its own right, though considerably quieter. Farther on is **Seminak**, and then empty space. The important estuary temple of **Peti Tenget** at the northern end of the beach is said to be where the first Hindu-Javanese priest and the first Dutchman both set foot on Bali.

Kerobokan lies even farther north along the main road, an outpost of rural charm and as instant a trip into the "real" Bali as one could hope to find. The main road is lined by a series of shrines and leads to a richly-carved palace. The "art nouveau" temple in nearby **Kaji** is also worth a visit, on the road back to **Sempidi** – itself a haven of mossy gulleys, streams, dams and waterfalls.

Denpasar has grown tenfold since 1945, to a bustling mini-metropolis of 200,000 today. But with the suburban sprawl are to be found a number of attractions. The main square was the scene of a *puputan* suicide in 1906, and successive governments have erected monuments in commemoration of this event. A 16-foot (5-meter) statue of Bhatara Guru, teacher and lord-protector of the realm, stands at the middle of an intersection, and in the square is a triple life-size bronze statue symbolizing the role of peasants in the nation's struggle for independence.

The **Bali Museum** on the eastern edge of the square houses a fine collection of archaeological artifacts and Balinese crafts. The architecture of the museum combines the two principal edifices in Bali: the temple and the palace. The split gate, the outer and inner courtyard, and the *kulkul* ("alarm drum") tower are characteristic of Balinese temples. Opposite the *kulkul* stands an elevated pavilion once used in palaces as a lookout platform for a prince viewing his lands. The main building with its wide pillared

Parasailing on Sanur beach.

veranda resembles the Karangasem palaces of East Bali; the windowless building on the right reflects the Tabanan-style palaces of West Bali; while the brick building on the left belongs to the northern palace style of Singaraja.

Every full moon, young people pay homage at **Pura Jagatnatha**, the recently built temple next to the museum, dedicated to Sanghyang Widi Wasa, the Supreme God (as opposed to a local deity or ancestral spirit). The tall *padmasana*, made from white coral, symbolizes universal order. The turtle and two *naga* serpents represent the foundation of the world.

Also near the center of town is the **Pasar Badung**, a four-story market building where one can find fruits and vegetables galore, clothing, spices, baskets, ritual paraphernalia, stainless and bamboo cooking utensils and more. The surrounding streets are filled with fabrics and goldsmiths, especially Jalan Sulawesi. Electronic shops and most of the major banks are on the main drag, **Jalan Gajah Mada**.

Just west of the canal is the **Kumbasari Shopping Center**, with movie theaters and handicraft stalls where you can snatch up some great buys. Nightlife in Denpasar revolves around Kumbasari and the other two night markets, located at the **Kereneng Bus Station** and the **Pasar Malam Pekambinan**, just off Jalan Diponegoro.

In the morning, visit **KOKAR/SMKI** on Jalan Ratna, the influential conservatory of dance, music and puppet theater – to see the island's graceful and handsome teenage stars rehearsing. The tertiary level of the school, ASTI, is located inside the new performing arts center, **Werdi Budaya**, at Abian Kapas.

Visitors are welcome to observe dance and music classes in progress. Evening performances are held regularly in the center's open-air stage. An Arts Festival is also held here annually in June and July, consisting of *gamelan* competitions, art contests, dance and theater revivals, and craft exhibitions. This has become a draw for thousands of art lovers and Baliphiles the world over.

Below, precipitous cliffs at Uluwatu. Right, the Bali Museum in Denpasar.

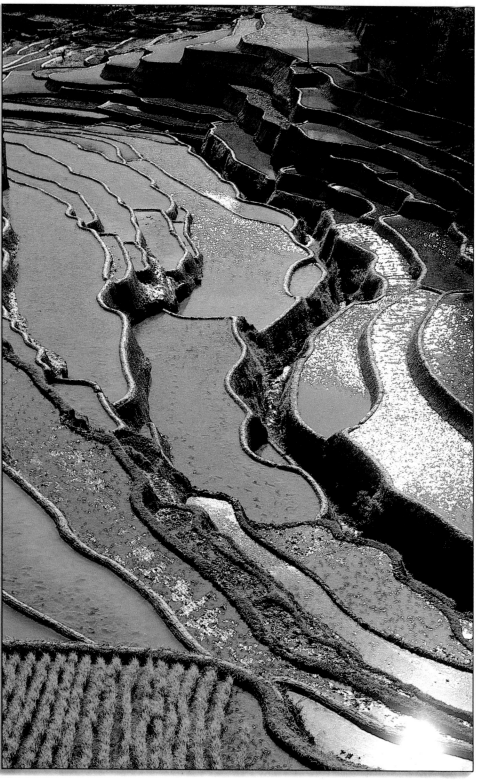

EXPLORING THE ISLAND

When embarking from the southern beach resorts on a tour of the island, the central district of **Gianyar** is your first stop. Easily the island's most exotic and artistic region, these villages have been patronized by Bali's rajas since the 17th century as a source for everything from carvings to jewelry to dancers.

Northeast of **Denpasar** is the village of **Batubulan**, where *barong* and *kecak* dancers entertain busloads of tourists daily. Also an area of beautiful temples, this is the source for the soft soapstone used to decorate most Balinese shrines with ornate carvings. Batubulan's **Pura Puseh** temple has a massive gate with the Hindu pantheon on one side and a meditating Buddha on the other.

Celuk is the center for gold and silver work. Here you will find fine filigree produced by craftsmen who learn the trade from a young age. The nearby village of **Sukawati**, once a center for Chinese traders, is now home to Bali's greatest puppet masters. **Batuan** residents are best known for their painting and dance. Under the patronage of German artist Walter Spies, the Batuan School of the 1930s was the first to produce secular paintings on Bali. The dancers of this village often win island-wide competitions and may be seen during the *odalan* anniversary rites for the village temples.

Mas is a village of master carvers. They originally produced only religious or court pieces, but today make decorative and expressionistic works for export. The famous Ida Bagus Nyana, whose visionary modernist sculptures of the 1940s are now on display in the gallery of his son, Ida Bagus Tilem, lived here. **Peliatan** is the home of an especially active dance troupe which presents excellent performances all year round.

Ubud has become a mecca for foreign and local artists who enjoy its quiet and creative village atmosphere. A local aristocrat, Cokorda Sukawati, joined forces with Walter Spies in the 1930s to form the Pita Maha art society. Many fine works from those years are exhibited in the **Puri Lukisan Museum** and **Neka Gallery**.

Among the Pita Maha artists, I Gusti Nyoman Lempad was probably the greatest. His ink drawings, cremation towers and temple stonecarvings are greatly admired – a few are on display in the gallery now operated by his children. Other well-known local artists include American Antonio Blanco, Dutchman Hans Snel and Javanese Abdul Aziz. Yet Ubud's greatest work of art is the surrounding countryside. Take some time to wander the backlanes – with a visit to the "**Monkey Forest**" temple about a mile to the south.

To the east of Ubud lies **Goa Gajah** (the "Elephant Cave"), whose carved opening was thought to portray the image of an elephant. Probably once a hermitage for Buddhist monks, the cave and its adjacent bathing pools were rediscovered and excavated in 1923. The nearby ruins of **Yeh Pulu** date back to the 14th century and feature a unique

Left, irrigation canals and rivers bring previous water to the rich farmlands of Central Bali. **Right**, a Balinese woodcarver.

frieze believed to have been etched by the thumbnail of a giant.

On the main road north of **Bedulu** is the **Archaeological Museum**, which houses a collection of neolithic axe heads, sarcophagi, weapons, bronze jewelry and Chinese ceramics. Several temples nearby contain objects of interest. Most famous of these is the **Pura Penataran Sasih**, containing the beautiful 2,000-year-old "Moon of Pejeng" bronze drum which is shaped like an hourglass and cast in one piece.

Two of Bali's holiest spots are found along the road to **Mount Batur**. Reached by descending a stairway through a stone arch into a watery canyon, **Gunung Kawi** is a spectacular ancient royal tomb. The **Pura Tirta Empul** spring at **Tampaksiring** was supposedly created when the god Indra pierced a stone to produce *amerta*, holy water with which to revive his poisoned army. The waters of Tampaksiring are still believed to have magical curative powers.

North Bali Round-Trip: Volcanic **Lake Batur**, viewed from the main road north of Tampaksiring, is Bali's most dramatic sight. The village of **Penelokan** perches on the lip of this 12-mile (20-km) wide caldera and you may hire motorized canoes at the lake's edge to visit the Bali Aga (pre-Hindu) community of **Trunyan** and the hot sulfur springs at **Toya Bungkah**.

The village of **Kintamani** crouches along the western rim of the caldera. Bali's highest temple is nearby, atop **Mount Penulisan**, and believed to have been the sanctuary of the ancient kings of Pejeng.

Roads leading over the mountains to the north of Bali were constructed by the Dutch only in the 1920s, so the cultures of north and south still differ. The language of the north is more rapid and less refined, the music more *allegro* and the temple ornamentation more fanciful. The carvings at **Pura Maduwe Karang** temple in **Kubutambahan**, for example, depict domestic scenes, ghouls, lovers and even a Dutch official riding a bicycle. The temple at **Jagaraga** is decorated with reliefs depicting Euro-

Entrance to Goa Gajah – a phantasmagoric cave.

THE SPLENDOR
OF BALINESE DANCE

The traditional Balinese polity has been described as a "theater state." While a culture as vital and as lively as Bali's has certainly not remained immutable, there are clear indications that dance and drama have played a central role in Balinese life since time immemorial.

A good deal of Indian influence is evident. In fact the Balinese dancers of today resemble those depicted in the classical Hindu-Javanese temple reliefs more than the court dancers of Java. Like his Javanese counterpart, the Balinese dancer adopts the basic "Indian" stance – knees bent, legs turned-out, body straight, head tilted and highly expressive hand and finger gestures.

In other respects, though, Balinese dance imparts a very different feeling. While the Javanese have developed slow, controlled, continuous movements performed with eyes downcast, and limbs held close to the body (in keeping with their aesthetic of refinement), the Balinese dancer is charged with energy – eyes agape, darting this way and that, high-stepping, arms up, moving with quick, cat-like bursts that would startle a Javanese.

All dances are connected in some way with rituals. Temple festivals always require a theatrical performance of some kind as entertainment for the gods (as well as for the participants). The Balinese, nevertheless, distinguish between those dances that are sacred (*wali*), ceremonial (*bebali*) and secular (*bali-balihan*).

The *Legong Kraton,* for example, has been the most popular dance in Bali since it was first performed in the villages in the 1920s. Now often seen at village temple festivals, it has become a big hit with tourists. Traditionally, the *Legong* is performed by two very young girls introduced by a court attendant, who first

sweeps the stage and presents the dancers with fans. Sheathed in glittering costumes, with headdresses crowned by frangipani blossoms, the two dancers then enact one of a dozen stories.

The best-known Balinese dance is undoubtedly the *Barong* – immortalized in the Margaret Mead film of the 1950s, *Trance and Dance in Bali.* It is a contest between the opposing forces of good and evil in the universe, embodied in the good beast Barong and the evil witch Rangda.

The powerful *Kecak* dance was adapted from

the *Sanghyang Dedari* trance dance in 1928, by isolating the chorus of the latter and treating it as Hanuman's monkey army in the *Ramayana* . Now performed by as many as a hundred chanting and swaying men dressed in loincloths, the *Kecak* is by far Bali's most popular tourist spectacle.

And in the 1930s, the legendary I Nyoman Mario introduced several new creations, such as the *Kebyar* and the *Oleg Tambulilingan.* The former is a solo virtuoso dance performed with the upper body only while in a sitting position. The latter depicts two bumblebees making love in a garden of flowers! ∎

Classic Bali mask – old man of the Topeng dance.

peans in a Model-T, a propeller plane diving into the sea and a steamship attacked by sea monsters.

The port of **Singaraja** was once a bustling center of commerce and government under the Dutch, but is today a quiet backwater. The **Gedung Kertya** on Jalan Veteran houses a vast collection of palm-leaf *lontar* manuscripts, and at the harbor you can see sailing vessels loading coffee, corn and rice.

Lovina Beach on Bali's northern shore is the ideal hideaway for travelers in search of quiet. Located 7 miles (11 km) to the west of Singaraja, it was once the site of a retreat built by the local ruler for his wife.

An alternate western road winds over the mountains, skirting the southern shores of peaceful **Lake Bratan**, where there is a government-run guesthouse and restaurant. On the edge of the lake is a graceful pagoda called **Uludanu Temple** where the water goddess Dewi Danu is venerated. Just below the lake is the village of **Bedugul** where orchids and tree ferns are sold at the market.

The road down from Bedugul passes through the village of **Mcngwi**, site of the magnificent **Pura Taman Ayun** with its moat, lotus pond and pagoda-like wooden shrines. Northeast of Mengwi is the famed **Monkey Forest** at **Sangeh**. Tall nutmeg trees, a moss-covered temple and a mischievous monkey tribe are to be found here.

The remarkable temple of **Tanah Lot**, founded by the Hindu saint, Naratha, perches on a large rock in the ocean at Bali's southwestern shore. At low tide, it is possible to cross over and ascend to the temple. And on the shore opposite, tables and chairs have been set up for visitors to witness the Indian Ocean sunset through the temple's twin towers.

Excursion to East Bali: Coming from the south, all roads pass through **Gianyar**, the center for Bali's weaving industry. Beautiful handwoven and hand-dyed textiles are still produced here; the use of machine-spun thread, quick chemical dyes and tinsel foil is now commonplace. Facing the town square, Gianyar's **palace** still houses the royal family,

Kecak dance in the shadow of Tanah Lot.

boasting intricately carved wooden pillars and stone-work exemplary of the opulence once enjoyed by Bali's rulers.

Nearby **Klungkung** was also once the site of a royal palace. In the middle of the village stand the 18th-century **Kerta Gosa** hall of justice and the **Bale Kambang** or "floating pavilion." On the ceiling of the former are depicted scenes from the *Bima Suarga,* Bali's answer to Dante's *Inferno.*

The mountain road north from Klungkung winds up through spectacular rice fields to **Pura Besakih**, Bali's "mother temple." Regarded as a holy site for centuries, this is the gathering place for all deities in the extensive Balinese pantheon. Each of the island's caste groups also has its own shrine here, with its own *odalan* celebrations. At every full moon, the *turun kabeh* ("all descend") ceremony is held to mark Besakih's consecration.

East of Klungkung on the coastal road is **Goa Lawah**, one of the nine great temples of Bali and the home of thousands of small black bats. The cave is also believed to be the terminus of an underground passageway up to Besakih

About 9 miles (15 km) past Goa Lawah is the picturesque harbor of **Padang Bai**, where the Lombok ferry departs and cruise ships anchor. Just east of this natural bay lies **Candi Dasa**, a newly-developed beach resort for the island's *cognoscenti.* Inland, in a hilly area of lush bamboo forests and banyan trees, is **Tenganan**, home to a pre-Hindu tribe which retains distinctive traditions of government, art and kinship. Sacred *geringsing* fabric – used in temple rituals and to ward off evil – is woven here.

The easternmost town in Bali is **Amlapura**, seat of the only Balinese raja allowed to retain his title and powers after the Dutch conquest. His palace, the **Puri Kanginan**, is an eclectic creation of European and Chinese design. Five miles (8 km) to the south lies **Ujung**, site of the ruins of an elaborate royal retreat. Just north of Amlapura are the **Tirtagangga** pools, used today for swimming. A number of inexpensive guesthouses have also sprung up here.

Besakih Temple, site of the *Eka Dasa Rudra* ceremony.

More than 60 percent of the two million visitors that come to Indonesia each year never travel beyond Java and Bali. While the latter islands undoubtedly comprise the heartland of Indonesian culture, there are more than 13,600 other islands in the archipelago. Most of them have their own unique cultures and customs, which makes Indonesia one of the globe's most diverse societies.

Sumatra is the world's sixth largest island, a huge horizontal belt of mountains, forest and swamp that runs parallel to the Malay Peninsula. In economic terms, Sumatra is the nation's most vital possession, earning tens of billions of dollars each year in receipts from oil and natural gas. The island also has large coal reserves and forest plantations. But Sumatra is also wealthy from a human point of view, with hundreds of interesting ethnic groups including the Batak and Minangkabau peoples.

The string of islands beyond Bali are known collectively as Nusa Tenggara. This is a fascinating transitional zone where Asia fades into the Pacific. The strength of Islam gradually gives way to Christianity and ancient animistic rites. Marsupials, giant reptiles and other Australian animal and plant species begin to appear. The music, clothes, housing and even the appearance of the people begin to take on a Pacific mien.

Indonesia controls two-thirds of Borneo, the world's third largest island. Known as Kalimantan, this is another area of rich natural resource: oil, gas, timber and hydroelectric potential. Yet away from the coast, Kalimantan remains a mysterious and primitive place, inhabited by hundreds of indigenous Dayak tribes, each with their own languages and customs.

Farther east is Sulawesi (Celebes), a massive odd-shaped island with four dangling arms. Though primarily known as the homeland of two flamboyant ethnic groups – the Torajans and the Bugis – Sulawesi boasts a large variety of exotic tribes, landscapes and natural wonders.

The hundreds of scattered islands of Maluku (the Moluccas) first brought Europeans to this distant shore. For these were the fabled Spice Islands, the domicile of nutmeg, cloves, mace and other spices that fetched their weight in gold in the markets of far-off Europe. Today, the once-opulent Maluku sultanates are but a shadow of their former self.

Farther still is Irian Jaya, the western half of New Guinea, the globe's second largest island. This is one of the last great frontiers of mankind, a largely impenetrable place that continues to defy attempts to drag it into the modern world. The terrain ranges from malaria-infested jungle to snow-capped mountains, while most of the hundred or so tribes live an existence barely removed from the Stone Age.

Preceding pages: light and shadow at work – to wondrous effect – in the rain forest of Indonesia. **Left,** the faraway feel of sparsely-inhabited islands to the east of Bali.

SUMATRA

The great island of Sumatra – third largest in the archipelago and sixth largest in the world – is Indonesia's most important territory. In just about every sense – strategically, economically and politically – Sumatra has always formed a pivotal "backbone" for the nation. It is second among the islands in population (30 million) yet first in exports, primarily of oil, natural gas, rubber, tin and palm oil. Sumatra stands at the crossroads of Asia, heir to an ancient and illustrious past and home to a broad spectrum of dynamic and fiercely independent peoples. Today the island is also the third most popular tourist destination in Indonesia after Bali and Java.

The southern half of Sumatra is the island's richest and most primitive region. Lampung province alone accounts for 40 percent of Indonesian government revenues through its oil and rubber resources, yet man-eating tigers still prowl the main highways. And while Javanese migrants have resettled and cultivated previously remote jungles, there are still animistic tribes like the Kubu and Sakai that roam the swamplands hunting for monkeys and birds.

Crossing the Sunda Strait from West Java, the Sumatran port of entry is **Bakauhuni**. The ferry passes within view of Krakatau, the famous volcanic island that erupted in 1883, killing 30,000 people and dramatically affecting the global climate for over a year. The southern terminus of the Sumatran railway is **Tanjungkarang**, but there is little of interest in either of these cities. Nearby, however, is the **Way Kambas Reserve** which is considered the best place on the island to see wild elephants and tigers.

Palembang is the boom town of south Sumatra, a city of 600,000 on the banks of the Musi River about 124 miles (200 km) from the coast. This is the center of a massive oil field that includes a major petrochemical complex at **Plaju** and a massive refinery at **Sungei Gerong**. As

Swamp forest of eastern Sumatra.

long ago as A.D. 800, Palembang was a thriving port and international bazaar, and also once a spiritual center where thousands of Mahayana Buddhist monks studied and translated texts. Today, there is little of interest to the visitor except for the **Rumah Bari Museum** with its art, crafts and weapons representing various eras in the region's history.

West of the oil fields are the **Pasemah Highlands**, a plateau dotted with carved megaliths, tombs, pillars and other stone ruins dating from about A.D. 100 and considered the best examples of prehistoric stone sculpture in Indonesia. Rocks have been fashioned into figures of armed warriors riding elephants, wrestling buffaloes or fighting snakes.

Farther west is the Indian Ocean port of **Bengkulu** (Bencoolen) founded by the British in 1685. One of the few remnants of British rule is **Fort Marlborough** (1762), with a gatehouse that contains old gravestones with English inscriptions. Sir Stamford Raffles was lieutenant-governor of Bencoolen from 1818 to 1823, when it

was handed over to the Dutch. Another worthwhile sight is the **Dendam Taksuda Botanical Gardens**.

Sumatra's largest nature park – the 600,000-acre (1.5 million-hectare) **Kerinci-Seblat Reserve** – straddles the frontier between Jambi and West Sumatra provinces. The focus of the park is **Sungai Penuh**, from where footpaths lead in all directions. The terrain here is amazingly diverse, from high-altitude marshlands around Danau Bentu, to the rainforests of Gunung Seblat, to Gunung Tujuh volcano and its crater lake. The wildlife inventory includes rare animals like elephants, rhinos, tigers, tapirs, clouded leopards and sun bears. Mythological creatures are also said to abound, including the *orang pendek* (half-man, half-ape) and the *cigau* (half-lion, half-tiger).

Padang dominates the coast of West Sumatra. Despite a population of over 250,000 and a bustling seaport at **Teluk Bayur**, the city's wide streets, traditional architecture and horse-drawn *dokars* give it the feel of a sleepy back-

water. Padang's culinary claim to fame is spicy *nasi padang* – a smorgasbord of 10 to 20 dishes eaten cold with rice. The local **museum** has fine exhibits of Minangkabau artifacts, but otherwise there are few sights.

The heartland of the gentle and sophisticated Minangkabau people lies north of Padang in the highlands. Their culture pervades this region and provides a striking contrast to the rougher Bataks of the hinterland. Anthropologists are fascinated by the Minangkabau who, despite their staunch Islamic devotion, comprise the largest matrilineal society on earth. According to legend, these people derive their name from victory (*menang*) in an ancient fight over land between water buffaloes (*kerbau*) from Sumatra and Java.

A few hours' drive north of Padang is **Batusangkar**, bygone home of the Minangkabau kings. There is a well-preserved *rumah adat* (clan house) in the town. Nearby is **Padang Panjang**, site of a conservatory of Minangkabau dance and music.

But the real fulcrum of the highlands is the delightful hill town of **Bukittinggi**, considered the "capital" of the Minangkabau people. Nestled amid mountain greenery at 3,000 feet (920 meters) above sea level, the town has a cool and sunny climate; people are relaxed and friendly. The central landmark is the old **Clock Tower** in the town square. Perched on a nearby hill is the **Rumah Adat Baandjuang Museum**, set within a 140-year-old clan house and featuring exhibits of Minangkabau culture such as wedding and dance costumes, headgear, musical instruments, weapons and crafts.

On another hilltop on the western side of town stands **Fort de Kock**. Built by the Dutch in 1825, it is a superb vantage point to look out over the surrounding farmland with smoldering Gunung Merapi volcano in the distance. You can also see **Ngarai Canyon**, the "Grand Canyon of Indonesia." A path leads through the gorge to the village of **Kota Gadang**, famous for its silver and gold filigree, and hand-embroidered shawls.

The Trans-Sumatran Highway winds north through the highlands, crossing the equator at **Bonjol**. A large globe and sign at the side of the road give ample notice. The next major town to the north is **Padang Sidempuan**, from where you can turn off to the east and drive two hours through the jungle to the 11th- and 12th-century Hindu ruins at **Padang-lawas**. The highway hits the coast again at **Sibolga**, terminus for boats to the isolated Nias islands.

A single feature dominates the geography of north-central Sumatra – the massive oval shape of **Lake Toba**. Situated on a high plateau, this blue-green body of water is the focus of the **Batak Highlands**.

More than three million members of the six major Batak tribes make their homes in the immediate region. Each tribe has its own dialect and customs. Despite being wedged between the fervently Muslim peoples of Aceh and Minangkabau, the Bataks remained animistic and cannibalistic until the middle of the 19th century, when German and Dutch missionaries converted

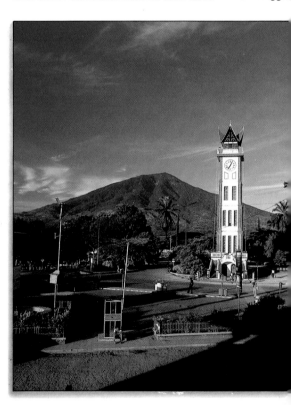

Clock Tower at Bukittinggi.

them to a mystical sort of Christianity.

Formed by a prehistoric volcanic eruption, Lake Toba is actually the largest lake in Southeast Asia (635 square miles/1,707 square km). It's also one of the highest (2,953 feet/900 metres) and deepest (1,476 feet/450 meters) lakes on earth. Enclosed by pine-covered mountain slopes and cliffs, the climate is cool but not bracing, sometimes rainy but never saturated.

Prapat is a large resort town on the lake's eastern shore, with hotels, golf course and a lively Saturday market. But the best place to experience Toba's spell is **Samosir Island** in the middle of the lake. Boats ply daily between Prapat and Samosir, and once on the island there is no shortage of *losmen* to choose from. **Tuk Tuk** is the main tourist village, with a community hall for Batak dances. A number of other villages are worth visiting, especially **Tomok** and **Simanindo**. But the most interesting place on the whole island is probably **Ambarita**, with three megalithic complexes. One of them includes a canni-

bal's breakfast table: the victim was beaten to death, decapitated, chopped on a flat stone, cooked with buffalo meat and served as the raja's breakfast, washed down with blood.

Thirty miles (48 km) east of the lake is **Pematang Siantar**, the rubber and palm oil center that is the second largest city in North Sumatra. Be sure to visit the **Simalungun Museum**, with an excellent display of Batak artifacts. From here, the highway leads to the coast of the Straits of Malacca and then northwest to Medan.

The sprawling, crowded city of **Medan** (population 1.5 million) is the largest city on Sumatra and the gateway to the north. It began its evolution into a thriving commercial city after the Dutch overran the Deli Sultanate in 1872. Medan has retained many architectural anachronisms from its colonial days when rococo, Art Deco and Art Nouveau styles were popular. The commercial hub is along Jalan Jendral A. Yani and around Merdeka Square. The bustling market district is adjacent to downtown.

Traditional Minangkabau-style house in West Sumatra.

Medan's two most imposing structures are the **Masjid Raya** (Grand Mosque) and the **Istana Maimun** (Sultan's Palace), built in the flamboyant Italian rococo style. The palace is still the residence of the sultan's descendants, but may be visited during the day. Across the Deli River is the **European town**, with wide avenues flanked by huge colonial villas and gardens. The Art Deco **Immanuel Protestant Church** (1921) is in this district, as is the **Bukit Kubu Museum** with its surveys of Sumatran tribal lifestyles and military history. Indonesia's largest Chinese temple is the **Vihara Gunung Timur**, on Jalan Hang Tua. Both Buddhists and Taoists worship here. It's said to be such a powerful place that photos taken within will remain unexposed. Still, cameras are prohibited.

Sumatra's northern and westernmost province is Aceh, the archipelago's first point of contact with external influences. Hinduism and Buddhism were introduced into Aceh in the 7th and 8th centuries by way of passing Indian traders; Islam gained a beachhead here in the 13th century through Arab and Indian Muslims. This was the first place the Portuguese landed in Indonesia in the 16th century, followed by the Dutch and English in the next century.

The quick way to reach Aceh is on the Trans-Sumatran Highway along the coast from Medan. But a much more spectacular route follows the **Alas Valley**. The first stop on this road is Brastagi, a hill resort and market town 42 miles (68 km) southwest of Medan. The Dutch built guesthouses, villas and an imposing hotel here. **Brastagi** has a mild climate, ideal for growing french beans, carrots, tomatoes, passion fruit, flowers and oranges. The Karo Batak tribe lives in this region and their massive wooden clan houses can be visited.

Kabanjahe stands at the crossroads of Aceh province and the Lake Toba region. This is a region of rich volcanic soils where rubber trees, oil palms, tea and tobacco flourish. Beyond **Kutacane** are the homelands of mountain tribes like the Gayo and Alas. The Sultan of

Lake Toba's blue-green waters sit in a caldera created by a prehistoric volcanic eruption.

Aceh didn't conquer this rugged plateau until the 17th century. He imposed Islam in the region, but many of the Gayos retain animistic beliefs.

A narrow road winds up the Alas River Valley through the **Mount Leuser Nature Reserve**, named after an 11,372-foot (3,466-meter) volcano of the same name. This reserve contains some of the island's most spectacular forests, which harbor wildlife like orangutans, rhinos, tigers and elephants. North of the park boundary is **Blangkeseren**, with numerous old Gayo and Alas clan houses.

By the time the inland highway intersects with the coast at Bireuen, you are firmly within the grasp of Acehnese culture. Villages in this region are surrounded by rice paddies or coconut groves, and the rectangular houses are built on stilts and covered with *nipa* palms. **Sigli** was known as Padri when it served as the chief port from which Acehnese *hajis* (pilgrims) departed for Mecca. The Dutch captured the town during the tragic Padri War of 1804, destroying it in the process. Remains of the **Padri Kraton** (fortress) can be seen on the outskirts of town.

Banda Aceh, the capital of the province, is built at the confluence of two rivers. Although the fortress and sultan's palace were destroyed when the Dutch invaded in 1874, vestiges of Aceh's glorious past can still be found. The **Gunungan palace** was built by Iskandar Muda or his son in the early 17th century. Sultanic tombs – including that of Iskandar Muda – surround the former aristocrat's house that is now the **Rumah Aceh Awe Gentah Museum**. Inside are *kris*, daggers, textiles and jewelry. The **Masjid Raya** (Great Mosque), though built of wood, was constructed without a single nail. This huge white structure with black domes is illuminated at night.

Beyond Banda Aceh are the wind- and wave-battered beaches of the northern tip of Sumatra. Indonesia's "Land's End" is the island of **Pulau Weh**, reached by plane or ferry. Besides the duty-free port of Sabang, it offers gin-clear water for scuba diving.

Banda Aceh's Grand Mosque.

NUSA TENGGARA: THE LESSER SUNDAS

The term Nusa Tenggara (meaning "southeastern islands" in Old Javanese) refers to the tightly packed necklace of sparsely inhabited islands lying east of Bali. In Dutch times, these islands were known as the Lesser or Eastern Sundas – a grouping which then included Bali. In 1951, Bali was made a separate province of the new Republic of Indonesia and the other islands were organized into two distinct provinces: West Nusa Tenggara (Lombok and Sumbawa) and East Nusa Tenggara (Sumba, Flores, Timor and other adjacent islands).

Whereas Java, Sumatra and Borneo (collectively known as the Greater Sundas) are bordered by the shallow Java Sea and have increased their land areas through the accumulation of vast alluvial deposits, the islands to the east of Bali rise from a deep seabed. The interstices between them have not been

"filled in" and this makes for a stepping-stone effect of small, adjacent islands with steep slopes, high mountains and very narrow coastal plains.

The depth of the seas and straits separating these islands is such that even at the height of the Ice Age, when world sea levels were about 450 feet (200 meters) lower than today, there were no land bridges between them. The great 19th-century naturalist, Sir Alfred Russell Wallace, spent several years studying these islands and noted a marked difference between the Eurasian species of monkeys, elephants, tigers, rhinos, deer, etc. of the Greater Sundas, and the Australian species of the eastern islands. He drew a line (now called the Wallace Line) separating Bali and Borneo from Lombok and Celebes, postulating this as a boundary between two distinct faunal groups.

More recent studies have shown that many Eurasian species persist throughout the Nusa Tenggara group and disappear only in New Guinea and Australia. Thus, these islands are a transitional zone (Wallacea) in which the wildlife of Eurasia and Australia coexist.

Nusa Tenggara is among the poorest and least fertile regions of Indonesia. Most of the 10 million inhabitants are subsistence farmers or fishermen. The government has invested heavily to improve communications, establish schools and provide health facilities in the islands. This has brought rapid change to some urban areas but, partly because the population is so scattered, many hinterland villages remain remote and relatively untouched by modern civilization.

Lombok: This is an island of startling contrasts and contradictions where Hindu rituals are incorporated into Muslim ceremonies, and lush rainforests back onto arid plains. Lombok has been spared, to a great extent, the more vulgar intrusions of Western culture. The island's polyglot populace – Sasak, Balinese, Chinese and Arab – continues its slow, traditional way.

Tourism is still in its infancy here, which means that a lack of amenities is more than offset by a relatively unspoiled

Spectacular landscape of Indonesia's southeastern islands.

culture rich in attractions, but with the "hard sell." Best of all is the fact that most of Lombok's sights and activities are concentrated on the western shore. The island's three main towns – Ampenan, Mataram and Cakranegara – bunch together along a 4-mile (6-km) stretch running east from the coast.

Ampenan, formerly the main port and once a vital link in the spice trade, is now little more than a broken-down wooden jetty with rows of deserted warehouses. At the main crossroads is the **Maritime Museum**, which attempts to recount the colorful history of Ampenan's overseas trade. Stop at the Regional Tourist Office (Diparda, 70 Jalan Langka) for information on island festivals.

From Ampenan, a small road leads north across river estuaries and through coconut groves to the **Batu Bolong Cliff Temple**. Situated on a high rock formation that juts out into the Lombok Strait, the temple is reached via a natural stone arch. Farther north along the coast is beautiful **Senggigi Beach**, quickly becoming the tourist hub of Lombok with its *losmen* guesthouses and resort hotels. The attraction is clear: several miles of unspoiled white-sand beach and a coral reef that is ideal for snorkeling.

Mataram is the modern provincial capital, yet other than providing banking, ticketing and other services, the town offers little for the visitor. Just south of Mataram are the white temples of **Mount Pengsong**, reached by climbing a long flight of stairs that rises from the road between ancient banyan trees. Monkeys cavort on the slopes.

Cakranegara, a short distance to the east, is the most interesting of the island's towns. It was the royal capital until the turn of the century and is still the major market town of Lombok. The crowded Arab quarter bustles with activity – this is the place to buy intricately patterned cotton *sarung*. The Balinese quarters, across the Ancar River, has many splendid courtyard homes in the unique Lombok-Balinese style. **Pura Meru**, the central temple of Lombok's

Aerial view of Lombok.

Hindu community, overlooks the main crossroads. Opposite is the **Puri Mayura** royal garden, with a pavilion that had once served both as a court of justice as well as a meeting hall for the island's lords. The **Royal Palace** behind the garden is surprisingly modest – a part-Dutch, part-Balinese style bungalow surrounded by a moat. It's now a museum filled with old photos and mementoes of Dutch times.

Dominating the interior of Lombok is towering **Mount Rinjani**, a 12,300-foot (3,800-meter) volcanic cone with a crater lake in the middle. The climb is strenuous and certainly not for everyone. It takes time and preparation, and should only be attempted during the dry season (April to October). Also in the interior is **Otakokok Falls**, a 55-foot (17-meter) cascade in a lush rainforest setting that is said to have medicinal properties.

Sumbawa: The island of Sumbawa is larger than Bali and Lombok combined. Its contorted form is the result of violent volcanic explosions, and indeed it appears on the map as two or three islands thrown hastily together. Sumbawa is now divided into three districts that roughly correspond to the island's former sultanates: Bima in the east, Sumbawa in the west and Dompu in the center. Most of the 800,000 inhabitants are farmers or fishermen, and the vast majority are devout Muslims. Bima district sends a higher percentage of pilgrims to Mecca than any other part of Indonesia.

The town of **Bima** (population 30,000) offers little of interest to visitors except for the **Sultan's Palace** which houses a fantastic collection of royal crowns and many *kris* with gem-studded gold and ivory hilts. To see them, you must contact the city government and negotiate a fee. There is another royal residence in **Sumbawa Besar** (population 40,000), the island's other metropolis. Built in 1885, the palace here is made entirely of wood, raised on stilts and crowned by two unusual carvings.

The hills east of Sumbawa Besar near the village of **Batu Tering** contain many large stone sarcophagi carved in low

Crater lake at Mount Rinjani, Lombok.

relief with human forms and crocodiles. It has been assumed that these megaliths are the royal tombs of a late neolithic culture which thrived here about 2,000 years ago.

Hikers and climbers might want to ascend to the crater of **Gunung Tambora**, site of the world's greatest volcanic explosion. In 1815, an estimated 130 million cubic yards (100 million cubic meters) of earth matter were ejected into the atmosphere with a force equivalent to that of several hydrogen bombs, in the process creating the famous "year without summer" of 1916. Today, the gaping 9,250-foot (2,820-meter) caldera offers a spectacular view of the island and sea. It's a day's walk to the rim from **Dempu**.

Komodo: In the center of the island-strewn strait between Sumbawa and Flores lies the island of **Komodo**, home of the world's largest reptile, the **Komodo Dragon** (*Varanus komodoensis*). This giant monitor lizard (called *ora* by the natives) is also one of the world's oldest animal species, and is a close relative of the dinosaurs who roamed the earth 100 million years ago.

Several hundred adult dragons live on Komodo. Adult males can reach 10 feet (3 meters) in length and weigh 330 pounds (150 kg). Females attain only two-thirds of that size and lay up to 30 eggs at a time. Though you may spot one by walking around the island, the safest and surest way to see a komodo dragon is to arrange a tour with the Indonesian Directorate of Nature Conservation (known by its Indonesian initials PPA). You will have an excellent opportunity to photograph a group of dragons devouring a goat. Be sure to bring a telephoto lens and keep well away from the lizards – their tails are lethal weapons and their saliva is extremely toxic.

Sumba: This island lies well to the south of the main Nusa Tenggara chain and has always been one of the major backwaters of the archipelago. Mostly flat, and normally barren throughout the long dry season, Sumba does offer visitors the opportunity to see the rem-

nants of an ancient pagan culture.

Villages with megalithic tombs are scattered around West Sumba. Among the best are those at **Tarung, Pasunga, Lai Tarung** and **Sodan**, but one can see tombs right in the district capital of **Waikabubak**. The island's most exciting ritual is *pasola*, in which scores of colorful horsemen on bareback battle with lances. The government has now declared that the spears must be blunt, but deaths still occur. *Pasola* takes place in February and March.

East Sumba is known for its warp *ikat* weavings, patterned by dyeing the warp threads before the weft is introduced. The process is long and tedious, taking several months to complete a single piece. You can see women dyeing and weaving in **Praliu** village just outside of **Waingapu**. Other major *ikat* centers are on the southeast coast, especially in the vicinity of **Ngallu** and **Baing**.

Flores: The name of this island derives from Portugese explorers who called it *Cabo das Flores* (Cape of Flowers) when they passed this way in 1512. Flores has long been susceptible to foreign influence. For centuries it formed a vital link in the inter-island trade and during the 14th century, it was drawn into the commercial and political sphere of the Hindu-Javanese empire of Majapahit. Some coastal communities began to convert to Islam in the 15th and 16th centuries after contacts with the Sultanate of Ternate. The Portugese arrived in the mid-16th century, establishing a mission at Larantuka and a fort on Solor Island to the east of Flores. Catholicism spread quickly and today claims roughly 90 percent of the island's one million people.

The westernmost of Flores' three main ports is **Labuhanbajo**, a beautiful harbor filled with native catamarans. From here, the trans-island highway winds up to **Ruteng**, a pleasant town in the western hills at an altitude of 3,600 feet (1,100 meters). There are good hotels in Ruteng and a market with embroidered *sarung.*

One of Flores' most inspiring traditions is the *Maha Kudus* mass, held once a year at **Bajawa**. The mass is preceded **The focus of visitor attention.**

100

by a ritual deer hunt in the nearby forest and followed by a lively procession of swordsmen and dancing villagers who follow a crucifix around the town.

Ende is the principal city of Flores. It has a distinctly Islamic flavor, the result of its role as an important Islamic trading post from the 17th to 19th centuries. However, today commerce is largely in Chinese hands. A few hours east of Ende is **Keli Mutu**, three adjacent volcanic lakes that are considered the island's chief tourist attraction. Two of the lakes are burgundy red, while the third is light turquoise. The residents of this area say that one red lake holds the souls of sorcerers, the other the souls of sinners, while the blue-green lake holds the souls of infants and virgins.

At the easternmost tip of Flores is **Larantuka**, a Portuguese colony for nearly 300 years. Local rituals still reflect a great deal of Iberian influence. A good time to be here would be Easter, when there is a procession of men in white hoods carrying the black coffin of the savior.

Adonara and Alor Islands: The old Portuguese fort (1566) on **Solor** island is in surprisingly good shape. Rusty cannons stand guard over the approaches from the sea. Nearby **Lembata** island is famous for its primitive whaling industry, while **Pantar** and **Alor** farther to the east are known for their bronze kettle drums. Hundreds and perhaps thousands of these *moko* drums are kept by natives as heirlooms or to pay the bride price.

Timor: The island of Timor has been known for centuries as a source of fragrant sandalwood. Chinese, Javanese and Islamic traders sailed to the island to obtain the wood. The Portuguese and Dutch later fought to control the trade, finally dividing the island into two halves: Dutch in the west and Portuguese in the east. East Timor remained a Portuguese possession until 1975 when it became independent. A year later, the Indonesian Army rolled across the border and annexed East Timor. Though technically possible, visits to **Kupang**, the capital of West Timor, are difficult to arrange.

Keli Mutu's coloured lakes.

KALIMANTAN (BORNEO)

Many exotic and often frightening images are traditionally associated with Kalimantan, the huge Indonesian portion of the island of Borneo. The name alone is enough to conjure thoughts of dense jungles and steamy swamps, primitive headhunters and savage animals. But Kalimantan today is not the godforsaken backwater that it once was.

The island's vast reserves of oil, natural gas, timber and diamonds (*Kalimantan* derives from the Malay term "diamond river") are now responsible for a hefty chunk of the country's exports, in addition to supplying raw materials for domestic consumption. As a result, there are now daily flights from Jakarta to major coastal cities, where fine tourist-class hotels and restaurants continue to proliferate. Yet the dedicated explorer will still have little trouble finding Dayak villages and wild orangutans in remote upriver jungles.

Borneo is one of the oldest islands in the archipelago. It has no volcanoes. Rather, the island's core is formed by a fold in the earth's crust, a weathered mountain chain that straddles the border between the Indonesian and Malaysian (Sabah and Sarawak) sectors. The highlands feed Kalimantan's major river systems, long and broad waterways with numerous interconnecting tributaries that form "roads" into the interior. These rivers are largely responsible for Borneo's immense size, for they carry enormous quantities of silt into the South China and Java seas, thereby pushing the coastline steadily outward.

As a consequence of thick mangrove swamps along the coast, most of the population of Kalimantan (about 5.5 million) lives inland. The large cities are generally located up to 30 miles (50 km) from the sea on the banks of major rivers. They are inhabited by a mixed bag of Chinese, Malays, Javanese and other ancestors of people who settled in Borneo centuries ago as miners, traders,

Banjarmasin, "Venice of Indonesia."

fishermen or pirates. In recent years, thousands of Javanese and Balinese families have been resettled in Kalimantan as part of the government's ambitious "transmigration" program. Farther upriver, in the remote and wild hinterlands, live a million or so members of more than 200 indigenous Bornean tribes, collectively known to outsiders as the Dayaks.

Pontianak, the rubber capital of West Kalimantan province, sits astride the equator on the Landak River. Most of the 250,000 inhabitants are Chinese. There isn't much of interest in Pontianak itself, but a good road runs north to **Singkawang**, noted for its Chinese temples and golden beaches. Farther north is **Sambas**, where handwoven *kain sambas* cloth can be purchased.

The largest city on the southern flank of the island is **Banjarmasin**, a good jumping off point for visits to the interior. The city is set on an island at the junction of the Barito and Martapura rivers, and the thousands of watercraft that flit about have earned the city the

This *gamelan* is from the Mulawarman Museum.

nickname "Venice of Indonesia." Most of the native Banjarese – pirates as recently as three decades ago – are devout Muslims. As the center of the Indonesian gemstone trade, Banjarmasin is the place to buy semi-precious stones such as amethysts, sapphires and agates.

Two hours by river to the west of Banjarmasin is **Mandomai**, gateway to Dayak villages near **Kandangan**. Prices for Dayak handicrafts are much lower here than in the city. The largest game reserve in the region is at **Cape Puting**, an animal-rich swampland that includes the **Camp Leakey Orangutan Rehabilitation Station**.

About 25 miles (40 km) east of Banjarmasin is a fascinating city called **Martapura**, the diamond capital of Kalimantan. Thousands of people work the diamond mines here, and hundreds more work in polishing factories. The best way to reach Martapura is by motorized canoe through the maze of inland waterways.

Balikpapan is the island's oil town and the metropolis of East Kalimantan province. Among its features are a massive oil refinery and modern harbor. Thousands of expatriate "oilies" (oil workers) and "chippies" (loggers) live in company compounds, shop in supermarkets and mini-malls, send their children to private schools and romp at "the club" on weekends. But most travelers don't stay long, using Balikpapan as a jumping-off point for trips up the Mahakam River into Dayak country.

Near the mouth of the Mahakam River is **Samarinda**, established as a trading post in 1730 and still the provincial capital. Dozens of big timber companies are based here, and the sound of sawmills competes with the cry of *muezzins* from the local mosques. Not far upriver is **Tenggarong**, founded two centuries ago as the court-town of the Sultan of Kutei. His residence is now the **Mulawarman Museum**, housing an amazing collection of ceramics from China, Vietnam and Japan, plus the Kutei royal heirlooms. The museum is surrounded by a garden full of Dayak woodcarvings.

Tenggarong is the principal starting

DAYAKS

The scattered and relatively primitive Dayak tribes of Borneo continue to live much as they have for centuries. The term "Dayak" is misleading as it's never used by the people themselves. In fact they find it rather insulting. Each of the 200 or so tribes has its own name, dialect, customs and lifestyles.

Dayaks are generally light-skinned - de-

scended from Mongolian immigrants who arrived in this region around 5,000 B.C. Since that time, their cultures evolved in isolation. With the arrival of Malays and Chinese in the coastal regions, the tribes moved farther inland. As the outer "civilized" world penetrated deeper into the Borneo hinterlands this century, the Dayaks have begun a slow but certain process of assimilation. Today, the governments of Indonesia and Malaysia encourage them to produce cash crops such as cloves and pepper, and many tribesmen have settled on the fringes of cities, towns, and timber or oil camps, hoping to find employment.

The most distinctive feature of the traditional Dayak village is the longhouse (*lamin*), a massive wooden building elevated on stilts housing as many as 50 families. Some longhouses are 600 feet (180 meters) long. Architectural styles vary greatly from tribe to tribe, but most longhouses have magnificently carved door frames, posts and railings with elaborate dragon, snake, bird and demon motifs. Each longhouse has a sacred herb garden and a collection of ancestral stone images. Most have large verandas where daily necessities such as paddles, nets, traps and blowpipes are stored. Kitchens are normally in a separate structure, connected to the main house by a wooden bridge.

Dayaks have a remarkably vibrant and graphic sense of design. Crafts are adorned with geometric patterns - mostly anthropomorphic and stylized animal images. Birds and reptiles are most commonly depicted. Spirals, hooks and meanders weave through every creation. A variety of barkcloth and *ikat* vegetable fibre clothes are produced.

Beadwork and basketry are also created by the Dayaks. Thousands of tiny glass beads are used to decorate purses, tobacco pouches, scabbards, baby carriers, basket lids, caps and headbands. Many types of shoulder bags and backpacks are made from rattan and bamboo strips, usually decorated with two-tone geometric patterns.

Not long ago, it was common to see human skulls hanging from the rafters or stored in woven baskets beneath the longhouses. In some remote villages, these can still be seen. Headhunting no longer exists, but formerly the capture of an enemy head was cause for village celebration. The powerful magic of a human skull - cured over a fire - was believed to strengthen the longhouse and protect the tribe from harm. The spirit of the dead person was "fed" from time to time with offerings of food and even cigarettes. Dayaks believed that as skulls became older, their magic power decreased and new skulls were needed. Tribes without skulls were considered weak and prone to pestilence. ∎

The intricacy of Dayak art is evident in this warrior's headdress and shield.

point for trips up the **Mahakam River**. Travelers can book passage aboard the regularly scheduled passenger boats which ply the river, allowing them to stop off at various places of interest. However, time is needed because most of the boats are slow, especially in the wet season when they must fight against stronger currents. Those who prefer organized tours can also arrange these in Tenggarong. Tours which last up to a week are available on riverboats reminiscent of the *African Queen*. Everything is provided, including food and sleeping gear.

Kutei National Park is farther north along the coast. This massive reserve embraces half a million acres (200,000 hectares) of lowland dipterocarp rainforest and is regarded as the largest park of its kind on the globe, richer than anything found in Africa or the Amazon. Wildlife here includes orangutans, monkeys, wild buffalo and more than 300 species of plumaged birds. However, tourist facilities are practically non-existent.

The oil-rich island of **Tarakan** is a waystation for those traveling on to Sabah or across the Makassar Strait to Sulawesi. The town has an interesting market, but not much else. Better to head for **Tanjung Selor**, 35 miles (57 km) to the south, where you can catch river launches into Dayak country along the Kayan River. The Kenyah tribe lives near the headwaters of the Kayan River. The *aso* dragon (a symbol of prosperity) and curling tendrils are the predominant patterns found on Kenyah homes, walls, pillars and shields. The Kenyah also practice tooth-filing.

From Tarakan it's often possible to arrange flights with some of the "missionary airlines" to remote settlements in the interior like **Longbawang** and **Longberini**. They lie close to the giant **Hulu Bahau-Sungai Malinau Reserve**, comprising 2.3 million acres (950,000 hectares) of rainforest and tropical savanna. Dayak tribesmen can be hired as guides for a full-scale expedition into the wilderness of this undeveloped park.

Hazardous Dayak country crossing.

SULAWESI

Although primarily known as the home of two flamboyant ethnic groups, the highland Toraja and the seafaring Bugis, the oddly shaped island of Sulawesi (Celebes) contains a great variety of exotic peoples, landscapes and natural wonders. Sulawesi's central position within the Indonesian archipelago has contributed greatly to her heterogeneity. Over the centuries, the island has received numerous influences from abroad, serving as a focus for inter-island migrations and trading operations.

Dramatic landscapes and remarkable peoples are the hallmarks of South Sulawesi, a province that is rapidly becoming one of the country's major tourist destinations. **Ujung Pandang**, the provincial capital, is a modern, bustling city of 700,000. Like all major Indonesian cities, it has undergone its share of growing pains in recent years, as the grandeur of the Dutch colonial town gives way to concrete boxes, roads and drainage canals that create a rather bland contemporary look.

Amsterdam Castle, the focus of the old town, is an outstanding examples of 17th-century Dutch fortress design. Within its walls is the **Ujung Pandang Provincial Museum**, with displays of old ceramics, coins, musical instruments and ethnic costumes. **Pantere Anchorage** at the north end of the city is a berth for many *pinisi* schooners.

The road around the south coast of Sulawesi goes through many ancient kingdoms. **Sungguminassa** was once the capital of the Sultanate of Tallo and many weapons and royal regalia of this period can be seen in the **Ballompoa Museum**. Also found here are the tombs of the 17th-century kings of Goa and the stone on which they were once crowned.

Cape Bira is the heart of the Bugis shipbuilding industry. Round-bellied *prahu* sailing craft are still fashioned here with ancient tools and without the use of metal or nails of any sort. Rituals are employed in all phases of construc-

Prahu in the Java Sea.

tion, from the selection of teak trees to the launching, to ensure the craft will be seaworthy. **Watampone** is the former capital of the Bugis Kingdom of Bone. This once-bustling port is quiet now, but notice the unusual architecture of the homes in the Bugis quarter. The **Museum Lapawawoi** houses the regalia of the kings of Bone.

Tucked away amid the rugged peaks and fertile plateaus of south-central Sulawesi are a cluster of isolated tribes called the Toraja or "highland peoples" who maintain many ancient crafts and customs. The Toraja traditionally live in small hamlets perched on hillsides and surrounded by stone walls.

The Toraja are perhaps best known for their elaborate, colorful funeral feasts, offered to make sure the souls of the dead pass into the afterworld in the appropriate manner. The funeral culminates in the ritual slaughter of up to 50 water buffaloes, each with a single stroke of the sword. Coffins are buried in *liang* (cave tombs) chiseled from bare stone on the sides of sheer cliffs.

Rantepao is the center of Torajaland tourist trade, with small hotels, restaurants and shops catering to foreign visitors. The nearby villages contain bustling markets and traditional houses, where Toraja practice their native crafts of weaving and wood carving and stage rituals and folks dances for themselves and the benefit of tourists. There are several cave tombs in the vicinity, with *tau-tau* effigies that stare out from the suspended balconies like guards.

North Sulawesi, though less developed than the south, is in many respects the most civilized and scenic area on the island, with dramatic volcanic landscapes, forested highland lakes and exotic wildlife. **Manado**, the provincial capital, is known for its cleanliness and mixed Indonesian-Chinese-European population. In the Minahasan hills is the **Tondano lake** district, with many interesting villages and megalithic monuments. Coconut plantations stretch for miles along the coast, and offshore coral gardens offer opportunities for snorkeling or diving.

Torajan burial procession.

MALUKU: THE SPICE ISLANDS

Every schoolchild has heard of the fabled Spice Islands, that source of exotic clove, nutmeg, pepper, cinnamon and mace which changed the course of history. The search for the passage to these isles touched off the expansive Age of Discovery, and the lucrative spice trade contributed greatly to the rise of the European mercantile and colonial empire that has shaped the modern world.

The name Moluccas (or *Maluku* from an Arabic term meaning "land of kings") applied originally to a chain of five small islands (Ternate, Tidore, Moti, Mare and Makian) lying just off the west coast of much larger Halmahera. Most inhabitants of this mini-archipelago engaged in tending and harvesting the world's supply of prime cloves. But now the province embraces a total of 999 far-flung islands including the Banda chain, Ambon, Buru and Ceram.

The center for government, commerce and communications is **Kota Ambon** on the island of the same name. Founded by the Portuguese in 1574, it is still predominantly Christian, although much of the colonial charm was wiped out by Allied bombing during World War II. **Fort Victoria** is the most visible reminder of the town's past, an old Dutch fort raised on earlier Portuguese foundations. Crowning a hill on the eastern edge of "K.A." is the **Museum Siwalima**, with an extensive collection of tribal artifacts such as carved canoe bowsprits, ancestor figures, magic and sacrificial objects, and talismanic skulls.

Southeast of Kota Ambon is **Mount Sirimahu**, famous for its outstanding views and prehistoric megaliths. An interesting old village called **Soya** rests on the side of the mountain, with a Dutch church (1817) and the residence of a former raja. Beyond Soya, the road forks into a number of other footpaths (known locally as the "Roads of Golgotha") that lead to the villages of **Ema**, **Kilang**, **Naku** and **Hatalai** on the southern slopes

View of Tidore from Ternate.

108

of the mountain. Each has its own ancient and sacred megalith. These villages remain little changed since St Francis Xavier converted them to Catholicism in the mid-16th century.

Ternate and **Tidore** islands are two perfectly shaped volcanic cones measuring less than 6 miles (10 km) in diameter, but each rising to about 5,600 feet (1,700 meters). For centuries, these were the most important parcels of real estate in all of Indonesia, for they owned a natural monopoly on the growing of cloves. The town of **Ternate** has grown up around the **Benteng Oranye**, a fortified trading post built by the Dutch in the early 17th century. The **Kedaton** (sultan's palace) is on a hill overlooking the town, now a museum with artifacts dating back some four centuries.

The 20-minute boat ride from Ternate to Tidore is spectacular and brings with it a change of atmosphere. **Soa-Siu**, the principal town, has the feel of a Mediterranean fishing village. Whitewashed houses with gabled Iberian archways climb the hill behind the port as a legacy of Spanish times. The sultan's palace and two Spanish forts are now in ruins.

Large and mountainous, the island of **Ceram** has peaks reaching to nearly 10,000 feet (3,000 meters). It's dotted with villages and old fortifications, but has few major towns and even fewer roads. Ceram is regarded as the homeland of the Hituese aristocracy.

Buru, similarly unknown, is surrounded by reefs and swamps, densely forested and inhabited by huge insects and tribesmen. Today logging is the primary industry. Special permission from the military authorities in Ambon is needed to visit the island.

The **Banda** chain – the "Nutmeg Islands" – simply oozes history. The capital **Banda Neira** rises dramatically from the sea, facing out across the narrow strait to another island. There are two old Dutch bastions – **Fort Belgica** and **Fort Nassau** – plus an old **Dutch Reform Church** in the center of town. Many of the large mansions of *perkeniers* or Dutch traders remain in a good state of preservation.

Below left, an Ambon girl in dance costume. Below right, nutmeg trees on Banda.

IRIAN JAYA

The western half of the huge island of New Guinea is called Irian Jaya. Formerly called Dutch New Guinea, it was ceded to Indonesia in 1963 following a brief but boisterous military campaign undertaken by President Sukarno.

Irian Jaya ranks as the most isolated and primitive region of the earth today. Impenetrable mangrove swamps seal much of the island's extensive coastline, while dense jungles and rugged peaks – some of them snowcapped and towering about 16,400 feet (5,000 meters) – dominate and subdivide the interior. Roads are almost non-existent; air and sea connections are few and far between; most villages in the interior can be reached only by walking up and down treacherous paths, sometimes for weeks.

Partly as a result of this extraordinary fragmentation, the province is home to a wildly diverse assortment of peoples and cultures. More than 100 mutually unintelligible languages are spoken in Irian Jaya by scores of distinct and colorful tribes, many of whom have barely emerged from the Stone Age.

A remarkable flora and fauna thrive on the island. Ferns, orchids and vines intertwine with the towering canopy of the lowland dipterocarp rainforest. About 700 species of birds have been identified, including the huge flightless cassowary and the fabled "Bird of Paradise" *(Paradisea apoda)*. Marsupials like the tree kangaroo, wallaby and flying phalanger inhabit the forests and grasslands. A variety of fierce reptiles, including the crocodile and "death" adder, are much feared by natives.

Oil was discovered at the western tip of New Guinea 50 years ago and the port of **Sorong** has boomed into a city of over 40,000 people, with attendant hotels, bars and expatriate workers. From here, the **Raja Empat Islands Nature Reserve** can be reached by boat. This is the best place to see the Bird of Paradise in its natural habitat.

Jayapura, the provincial capital and

Huts in the Baliem valley – the most accessible of the highland areas.

Irian Jaya's largest city (population 50,000) was founded by the Dutch to lay claim to New Guinea's north-central shore. During the last years of World War II, it was General Douglas Mac-Arthur's headquarters.

East of Jayapura is the **Yotefa Nature Reserve** on Yos Sudarso Bay, with many beautiful beaches and wreckage of several ships sunk during World War II. Farther east along this coast, one can find Sepik people, known for their primitive bark paintings and carved ancestor figures.

To the east of town is **Cendrawasih University** with its excellent **Anthropological Museum**. The main attraction is a collection of Asmat artifacts acquired through a grant from the John D. Rockefeller III Fund. Asmat figures and weapons are executed with a keen, dramatic sense of balance and beauty, prized by connoisseurs of "primitive art" around the world. Although the Asmat tribe lives on the south coast, a large selection of their carvings are available from the **Asmat Handicraft Project** warehouse in Jayapura.

The largest and most accessible of the highland areas is the **Grand Baliem Valley** in Central Irian Jaya, a 45-mile (72-km) corridor formed by the Baliem River. About 100,000 primitive Dani tribesmen inhabit the area, living in tiny settlements scattered across the broad valley floor. The only way in and out is by air – unless you plan to walk for a month – with regular scheduled flights from Jayapura to an airstrip near the village of **Wamena**. Villages throughout the valley are connected to Wamena by footpaths and an increasing number of crude vehicular tracks. Be sure to bring along warm clothes, sturdy shoes and a backpack. Porters and guides may be hired through hotels in Wamena, which can also arrange dance rituals.

Many visitors cross over the river and make the three-hour trek to **Akima**, where the chief's grandfather has been mummified and may be seen on payment of a small fee. It's several hours further to **Ywika**, where the Catholic mission offers comfortable lodgings.

The shields of these Asmat tribesmen are prized by connoisseurs of "primitive art."

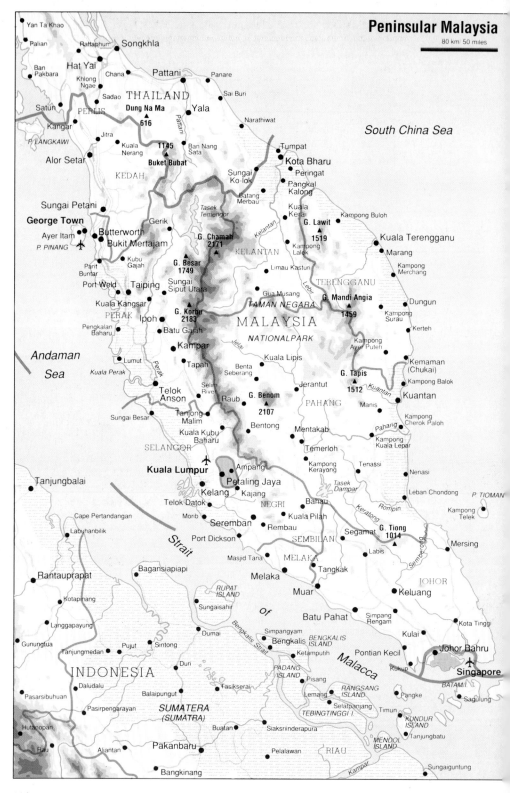

Yan Ta Khao

Palian

Ban
Pakbara

Rattaphum

Songkhla

Hat Yai

Chana

Pattani

Panare

Khlong
Ngae

Sadao

THAILAND

Sai Buri

Satun

PERLIS

Dung Na Ma
616

Yala

Narathiwat

Kangar

Jitra

Kuala
Nerang

1145

Ban Nang
Sata

Tumpat

P. LANGKAWI

Alor Setar

Buket Bubat

Sungai
Ko-lok

Kota Bharu

KEDAH

Batang
Merbau

Peringat

Pangkal
Kalong

Sungai Petani

Tasek
Temengor

Kuala
Kerai

Kampong Buloh

George Town

Gerik

G. Chamah
2171

KELANTAN

Kelantan

G. Lawit
1519

Kuala Terengganu

Ayer Itam

Butterworth

Marang

P. PINANG

Bukit Mertajam

Kubu
Gajah

G. Besar
1749

Limau Kasturi

Kampong
Lalok

Kampong
Merchang

Parit
Buntar

Port Weld

Taiping

Sungai
Siput Utara

Gua Musang

TERENGGANU

Kampong
Surau

Kuala Kangsar

TAMAN NEGARA

G. Mandi Angia
1459

Dungun

Pengkalan
Baharu

PERAK

Ipoh

G. Korbu
2183

Batu Gajah

MALAYSIA

Kerteh

Andaman
Sea

Lumut

Kampar

NATIONALPARK

Kuala Lipis

Kampong
Ayer Puteh

Kuala Perak

Tapah

Benta
Seberang

Jelai

G. Tapis
1512

Kemaman
(Chukai)

Perak

Selim
River

Jerantut

Kuantan

Kampong Balok

Telok
Anson

Raub

G. Benom
2107

PAHANG

Kuantan

Sungai Besar

Tanjong
Malim

Bentong

Mentakab

Manis

Pahang

Kampong
Cherok Paloh

Kuala Kubu
Baharu

Temerloh

Kampong
Kuala Lepar

SELANGOR

Ampang

Kuala Lumpur

Kampong
Kerayong

Tenassi

Nenasi

Tanjungbalai

Petaling Jaya

Tasek
Dampar

Leban Chondong

P. TIOMAN

Kelang

Kajang

Bahau

Rompin

Telok Datok

NEGRI

Kuala Pilah

Keratong

Kampong
Telek

Cape Pertandangan

Morib

Seremban

Rembau

Segamat

G. Tiong
1014

Labuhanbilik

Port Dickson

SEMBILAN

Semerong

Mersing

Masjid Tana

MELAKA

Labis

Bagansiapiapi

Melaka

Tangkak

JOHOR

Rantauprapat

RUPAT
ISLAND

Muar

Keluang

Kotapinang

Sungaisahir

Batu Pahat

Simpang
Rengam

Kota Tinggi

Langgapayung

Dumai

Simpangyam

Kulai

Gunungtua

Pujut

Sintong

Bengkalis

BENGKALIS
ISLAND

Pontian Kecil

Johor Bahru

Tanjungmedan

Duri

Ketamputih

Kukup

Singapore

INDONESIA

Daludalu

Tasikserai

PADANG
ISLAND

Pisang

Pangke

BATAM I.

Sagulung

Pasarsibuhuan

Balaipungut

Lemang

RANGSANG
ISLAND

Selatpanjang

Timun

KUNDUR
ISLAND

Tanjungbatu

Pasirpengarayan

SUMATERA
(SUMATRA)

Buatan

Siaksriinderapura

TEBINGTINGGI I.

MENDOL
ISLAND

Hutanopan

Rau

Pakanbaru

Pelalawan

RIAU

Kampar

Sungaiguntung

Aliantan

Bangkinang

South China Sea

Strait

of

Malacca

Kelantan

Lebir

Tembeling

114

MALAYSIA: A PERFECT TRAVEL CURE

The tourist brochures modestly claim that "only Malaysia . . . has it all." And so it does. Picturesque fishing villages, cozy hill resorts, unexplored tropical forests and miles of empty white-sand beaches. Mix into these scenes the cultural pastiche that is the Malaysian people, and the result is an irresistible combination of rural charm, intriguing lifestyles and a slight but ever-so-appealing hint of adventure that is guaranteed to send expectant visitors to travel heaven.

And that's just the tip of the coconut tree. Malaysia's multitudinous attractions also include traditional arts and crafts, colorful religious festivals and copious amounts of comestibles to pacify even the most epicurean tastes. In fact, sampling some mouth-watering Malaysian food comes close to being a religious experience in itself.

Situated smack in the middle of Southeast Asia, with a total land area of 132,000 square miles (342,000 square km), Malaysia is about the size of Japan, but with only a fraction of the population (about 17 million compared to Japan's 123 million). Peninsular Malaysia accounts for 40 percent of the land area, and 86 percent of the population. The East Malaysian states of Sabah and Sarawak are separated from the peninsula by 400 miles (640 km) of the South China Sea, but each of the 13 states has a charm and character of its own. Malay and indigenous tribes make up over half the population while Chinese, Indians and others also come under the broad spectrum that is covered by the term "Malaysian."

The country's economy was once based exclusively on agricultural commodities first cultivated during British colonial times, and Malaysia is still one of the world's major suppliers of tin, palm oil and rubber. But one of the major aspirations of the current government has been to shift the economy to a manufacturing and service base. The results have been nothing less than spectacular. Revenue from oil and natural gas reserves together with a substantial increase in foreign investment have helped diversified the economy into fields as diverse as car production and computer assembly. Almost overnight, Malaysia has become one of the great economic success stories of Asia.

Despite some physical changes – the inevitable outcome of living in an age of rapid development and high technology – Malaysia is still very much a land of *kampungs* (villages), jungles, beaches and rice fields, made that much more appealing by a friendly, deeply religious and uniquely diverse group of peoples. Malaysia really does have it all.

Preceding pages: top-spinning is a popular Malaysian sport.

Mula-mula. In the beginning. Traditional Malay tales of the country's origins always began with the words *"Mula-mula. . .,"* and if archaeological findings are to be believed, it all started back in 35,000 B.C. That's when the skull of possibly the first *Homo sapiens* in the East was found in Sarawak's Niah Caves. In the Malay peninsula, stone implements found in the limestone hills of Perak provided further evidence, although these date back only 10,000 years. Without doubt, though, Malaysia's strategic position, its abundant natural resources and ability to support human communities helped to make it an easy and logical place to settle.

Of present-day inhabitants, the earliest are the *Orang Asli* in the peninsula and similar tribes in Sabah and Sarawak, who still pursue a nomadic way of life. Their ancestors wandered down the peninsula from Yunnan in Southwest China, going through the mainland to the Indonesian archipelago and beyond. They were followed by the more sophisticated Proto-Malays, who probably established themselves around 2,000 B.C. The next wave of immigrants (Deutero-Malays) came equipped with knowledge of new agrarian skills, settling into the small, self-contained communities which have developed into the complex ethnic pattern of Malaysia and Indonesia today. The Malays of the peninsula had practically indivisible links with their counterparts in Sumatra, just across the Straits of Malacca.

Today, the peninsular Malays, along with the *Orang Asli* ("original people"), make up the indigenous peoples of Malaysia, and are collectivelly called *bumiputra* , or "sons of the soil." While differences do exist in the makeup of the various *bumi* groups, certain characteristics are shared, especially those rooted in the agricultural-seafaring economy and the village society that are even now so much a part of Malaysia.

Around the 1st century B.C., initial trading contacts were made between the peninsula and more established trading powers, particularly China and India. Over the next thousand years, Hindu and Buddhist elements of the Indian culture left their mark on the region, especially in the language and cus-

toms. These influences began to fade around the 14th century with the introduction of Islam into the area by Indian and Arab traders.

Islamic conversion in the peninsula centered around Malacca, a coastal village which had risen to prominence as a strategic trading post. Malacca was founded in 1403 by the Sumatran prince Parameswara, and his settlement blossomed into a prosperous and widely-respected port. Among its admirers was Admiral Cheng Ho, the famous "Three-Jewel Eunuch," envoy for the em-

peror of China. Parameswara paid a reciprocal visit to China, where the emperor extended him his protection and proclaimed him to be king of Malacca and beyond. Parameswara's successors later extended the kingdom to include the entire south of the peninsula. Malacca's status increased dramatically, while Parameswara and his heirs also ensured that Islam would be the religion of the realm. The Kingdom of Malacca dominated the Straits of Malacca for 100 years, a period which marks the classical age of Malay culture. Indeed, most of the peninsular states can trace their beginnings back to the Malacca sultanate.

In 1511, colonialism arrived in the form of a large Portuguese fleet led by Alfonso de Albuquerque, architect of Portugal's expansion plans in Asia. Malacca fell to a Portuguese assault, forcing the reigning sultan and his family to flee and establish themselves in other states. The Portuguese administrators lasted until 1641, when Dutch forces stormed the Portuguese-built *A Famosa* ("The Famous") fort and turned Malacca into an ordinary outpost of the Dutch empire. The Dutch government had already decided that Batavia (now Jakarta) was to be their capital. Malacca's halcyon days were over.

After the Dutch, it was Britain's turn to show the flag out East. This they succeeded

the Dutch gave up all their territory on the Malayan peninsula and the British gave up theirs in the East Indies, promising not to interfere in each other's domain.

In 1826, British domination of the peninsula became apparent when Penang joined Singapore and Malacca as part of the newly established Straits Settlements, a Crown Colony headed by a British governor. Six years later, the seat of British administration was transferred from Penang to Singapore which, by 1860, succeeded Penang and Malacca to become the area's premier port.

In 1874, the governor, Sir Andrew Clarke, arranged for the appointment of British Advisors to Perak, Selangor and Sungei Ujong,

in doing in 1786, when Captain Francis Light of the British East India Company secured trading rights on the island of Penang, off the peninsula's northwest coast. Meanwhile, Malacca was also transferred to the British in 1795, at the time of the Napoleonic Wars, part of a Dutch attempt to forestall the French from taking over.

The Dutch formally ceded Malacca to Britain under the Anglo-Dutch Treaty of 1824. According to the terms of the treaty,

Left, Alfonso de Albuquerque led the wave of colonizers. **Above**, Malacca was once a bustling trading port.

although it was not until 1891 before the system became acceptable. This led to the formation of the Federated Malay States of Selangor, Perak, Negri Sembilan and Pahang in 1896. The remaining four northern states of Kedah, Perlis, Kelantan and Trengganu, along with the southernmost state of Johore, became the Unfederated States of Malaya.

While affairs on the Malay peninsula were taking shape, the territories on the island of Borneo were themselves in a state of flux. Locals in Sarawak, a province of the Brunei sultanate, were voicing dissent against misrule by the governor there. Enter James Brooke, an English adventurer who happened to be sailing around the region. He first landed in Sarawak in 1839 and within two years, found himself installed as the Rajah of Sarawak, his reward for helping to put down a local rebellion. Brooke and his successors ruled Sarawak for over a hundred years, bringing it out of the dark ages by clamping down on the activities of headhunting natives and expanding trading ties.

In North Borneo, the British North Borneo Company had a rebellion of its own to deal with. Achieving local acceptance of white rule was not as easy, and recurring resistance was encountered until the Company finally gained full control with the death of local rebel chief Mat Salleh in 1900.

forces. For three and a half years, British, Malay and Chinese guerrillas fought World War II from their jungle bases. In September 1945, colonial authority was re-established by the British Military Administration. However, the Japanese experience had unleashed the potent and determined forces of nationalism. Faced with a totally new political environment, a change became inevitable.

The Straits Settlements were dissolved, with Penang and Malacca joining the Malay states of the peninsula to form a new Malayan Union, which was intended to have a central government and a governor. Sovereignty was to shift from the sultans to the Crown, in effect turning the whole country

The British spent the next 40 years consolidating their position in Malaya. One of their better experiments had been the planting of nine Brazilian rubber trees in 1878, an action which attracted little attention until John Dunlop invented the pneumatic tire and Henry Ford put the automobile on the assembly line. The man responsible for the crop that would take up three-quarters of all developed land in the nation was Henry Ridley, Director of the Botanic Gardens in Singapore. Tin mining, the province of the Chinese community, was already in full tilt.

Colonial supremacy suffered a rude awakening in 1941 with the invasion of Japanese

into a colony. The idea did not go down well with the Malays and, in March 1941, delegates from 41 Malay associations met in the capital, Kuala Lumpur, to oppose the Union. The United Malay National Organisation (UMNO) was born. As a result, the British abandoned the Union sheme and established instead the Federation of Malaya in 1948, which provided for the sovereignty of the sultans. The Federation consisted of all nine peninsular Malay states, plus Malacca and Penang, to be united under a federal government headed by a British High Commissioner. Singapore remained a colony and was later joined by North Borneo and

Sarawak, which did not have the resources to continue being run by the North Borneo Company and Brooke family, respectively.

By agreement, the Federation was the first step on the road to independence. Apart from nationalist pressure, the threat of communism also served to accelerate the independence process. Jungle-based guerrillas attacked colonial estates and harassed villages in a 12-year "war of nerves" against British security forces. Known as the Emergency, this period lasted until 1960, by which time most of the communists had been wiped out. In fact, the threat had diminished by 1955 so that the first federal elections could be held. UMNO and the Malayan Chinese Association

(MCA), the two principal communal parties, formed an alliance with the Malayan Indian Congress (MIC), winning 51 out of the 52 seats contested. The Alliance, led by Tunku Abdul Rahman, successfully pressed for independence and *Merdeka* ("freedom") was attained on August 31, 1957. The Tunku became the Federation of Malaya's first prime minister. Two days later, the *Yang di-Pertuan Agong*, "King and Ruler of the Federation of Malaya," performed a symbolic ceremony

Left, Tunku Abdul Rahman at the proclamation of independence, 1957. Above, modern-day religious architecture.

of acceptance of office by unsheathing his gold Kris of State and kissing its blade.

In 1961, Tunku mooted the idea of a new political entity called Malaysia, to include Malaya, Singapore, North Borneo, Sarawak and Brunei. Apart from Brunei, which opted out, the other territories voiced their enthusiasm for the plan. Considerable opposition, however, came from Indonesia, which denounced the scheme as a "neo-colonialist" plot and the Philippines, which staked a claim to North Borneo. In 1963, Indonesia embarked on a policy of "Confrontation," which included armed incursions across the borders of North Borneo (renamed Sabah) and Sarawak from Indonesian Kalimantan. A United Nations survey confirming the desire to join the Federation was rejected by both Indonesia and the Philippines. Nevertheless, the Federation of Malaysia was inaugurated on September 16, 1963. By 1966, a new Indonesian government had dropped its aggressive stance, as did the Philippines in 1977. Singapore, meanwhile, had left the Federation in 1965 to become a sovereign state in its own right.

In 1970, the widely-revered "Father of Malaysia," Tunku Abdul Rahman retired, handing over the reins to Tun Abdul Razak. He in turn was followed by Datuk Hussein Onn in 1976 and in 1981 by the current prime minister, Datuk Seri Dr. Mahathir Mohamad five years later. Mahathir's party was elected to another term of government in 1990.

Endowed with a clear-eyed determination to succeed, Malaysia's federal leaders have steered the country on a course of continued progress and economic development to the stage where its people now enjoy one of the highest standards of living in Southeast Asia. One of the cornerstones of government strategy has been the New Economic Policy (NEP), introduced to encourage a more equitable distribution of wealth among the various racial groups. Under NEP, rules were set down to ensure greater *bumiputra* involvement in all areas of the economy.

Emerging from the yoke of colonialism and the trauma of the Japanese occupation, it has taken several decades for Malaysia to cultivate a national identity and a firm democracy. Yet both of these goals have been achieved. The people can now look ahead to the 21st century with the realization that, as a nation, Malaysia has really come of age.

KUALA LUMPUR

"In the beginning, there was nothing but a lot of mud ..." Thus might begin an accurate but deceptively unappealing chronicle of **Kuala Lumpur**'s origins. Returning to its roots might seem redundant, as the Malaysian federal capital, situated in the heart of the peninsula, has never really left its past behind.

Despite the proliferation in recent years of highways, highrises and high society, "KL" is still very much a "down home" kind of town. Somehow, the seemingly incongruous blend of past and present, eastern mysticism and western technology, are able to gel into a unique entity.

On narrow city streets and six-lane super highways, expensive European cars and more modest Japanese makes rub hubcaps (often quite literally, given the Malaysian drivers' natural affinity for bumper-bashing) daily with a growing rash of Proton Sagas, Malaysia's national car since 1985 and the product of a joint M$230 million (US$88 million) project between the government and its Japanese partners.

Meanwhile, steel and glass skyscrapers of every conceivable design sprout almost indiscriminately amongst the older, more sedate buildings of the colonial past. And at night, as roadside hawkers enjoy a brisk business, royalty and jetsetters hobnob with mere mortals in chic meeting spots like the *Tin Mine* disco, its name a somewhat ironic reminder of the city's humble beginnings.

About 140 years ago, Kuala Lumpur was a precise representation of what its name means in Malay: "muddy river mouth." At that time, a group of tin prospectors, financed by the local Malay chief, journeyed upriver to the confluence of the less-than-crystal-clear waters of the **Klang** and **Gombak** rivers. Things eventually "panned" out, with the discovery of an abundance of tin slightly inland at **Ampang**.

Under Yap Ah Loy – a tough, astute administrator appointed by the local sultan to keep the peace among unruly Chinese miners – and later Frank Swettenham – the British Resident of Selangor – Kuala Lumpur blossomed into a Southeast Asian boomtown. Supported by a rapidly expanding infrastructure and growing lines of communication, then nourished by the tin and rubber bonanzas, KL quickly achieved capital city status.

In 1974, the 98 square miles (244 square km) encompassing the city and its population (currently 1.5 million) was formally declared the Federal Territory, separate from its mother state of Selangor. It continues to grow both upward and outward by leaps and bounds, as one of the most dynamic cities in all Asia.

Old City: Today's visitors to the still-muddied confluence of the Klang and Gombak rivers will find the magnificent **Masjid Jame** (Friday Mosque). Built in 1909 and nestled in a picturesque grove of coconut palms, the design is adapted from a Moghul mosque in northern India, although it was created by English architect A.B. Hubbock.

Preceding pages and left: Moorish minarets of Jame Masjid contrast with the city's skyscrapers. **Right**, the towering Dayabumi Complex offers a bird's eye view of KL and its surroundings.

Accessible from Jalan Tun Perak, the mosque features a walled courtyard (*sahn*) and a three-domed prayer hall flanked by two minarets rising above the height of the palms.

Behind the mosque, starting from the corner of Jalan Tunku Abdul Rahman and Jalan Raja, sits a line of former colonial-built public buildings, all designed in the distinctive Moorish style that British colonial administrators deemed appropriate for an Islamic possession. These are credited to A.C. Norman, one of Hubbock's colleagues in the Malaya Public Works Department. The **Information Department**, the old **City Hall**, the **High Court**, the former colonial **Secretariat** (now the Sultan Abdul Samad Building which includes the Supreme Court) and the former **General Post Office** were all completed around the turn of the century. They remain largely impervious to the changing times, functional and visually stunning monuments to an elegant past.

The **Supreme Court** is now the most photographed building in the city, with a 130-foot (40-meter) clock tower (the "Big Ben of Malaysia"), topped with a golden dome and flanked on either side by two dome-topped towers. During state occasions, colored lights twinkle in the arches of the Supreme Court, making it look like a setting for an Arabian night tale.

Opposite these buildings is another product of Norman's fertile mind, the **Royal Selangor Club**, a mock Tudor sports and social club that became the center of colonial society after its construction in 1890. Fronting the club is an expanse of green known as the **Padang**, on which some of the more notable social virtues – drinking tea and playing cricket – were practiced, and still are to this day. The Padang is also the venue for Independence Day celebrations which are held on August 31 each year. Beneath the green is a massive underground parking lot.

Festivities of a different kind are held each night at the Padang, as local transvestites and trans-sexuals make the rounds, like models on a catwalk, add-

The Padang's green expanse fronts the venerable Selangor Club.

ing some local color (literally!) to the neighborhood.

Across Jalan Raja from the old Post Office is another beautifully restored colonial building, this one housing **Infokraf**, an exhibition and information center for Malaysian arts, crafts and home furnishings. In stark contrast is the adjoining **Dayabumi Complex**, an interesting combination of Arabic and modern high-rise architecture that was labeled the most expensive building ever constructed in Malaysia when it was finished in 1985. This combination of government office and shopping center also features the new **Central Post Office**. For an elevated view of the city, take a ride to the building's 30th floor.

A pedestrian bridge across the Klang River links the complex with the Art Deco-style **Central Market** (1936), a former produce hall which has been spruced up in an effort to become KL's answer to London's Covent Garden and Boston's Quincy Market. The block-long structure now sports a pastel pink and baby blue facade, central air condi-

The Sultan Abdul Samad Building houses the Supreme Court.

tioning and a trendy wine bar. Although it contains the usual souvenir shops and fast-food outlets, Central Market is also a cultural showcase for Malaysian arts and crafts. The market is often the scene of concerts, *wayang* puppet theater and traditional dance performances.

The spiritual center of Kuala Lumpur, and indeed the symbol of Islam for the whole country, is the **Masjid Negara** (National Mosque). Built in 1965, it occupies a 13-acre (5.2-hectare) land-scaped site on Jalan Sultan Him-shamuddin. The complex is dominated by a jagged, star-shaped dome and a single minaret rising 240 feet (73 meters) from the center of a fountain. The 18 points of the dome represent Malaysia's 13 states and the five pillars of Islam. One of the largest in the region, the mosque blends traditional Muslim decorative art with modern day inter-pretations of Islamic design. The Grand Hall can accommodate 8,000 people and is busiest on Fridays, the Muslim holy day.

A.B. Hubbock also produced a

Moorish wonderland called the **Kuala Lumpur Railway Station**, which gives a brand new meaning to the word grandiose. Those arriving by train in Kuala Lumpur are confronted by a mass of turrets, spires, minarets and horseshoe arches that assault the eye from every direction. Despite a recent renovation, the old **Station Hotel** retains an air of faded grandeur.

Across Jalan Sultan Hishamuddin is another Moorish masterpiece, the **Malaya Railway Administration Building**. Down the road is the former Majestic Hotel, KL's contribution to grand colonial hostelries. Rescued from the wrecking ball in 1983, it has been converted into the **National Art Gallery**, housing a permanent collection of works by Malaysian artists in what used to be the hotel dining room and lobby.

Situated on a hillside overlooking Jalan Travers, about a 15-minute walk away, is the **Muzium Negara** (National Museum). It features a traditional Malay-style roof and two large murals of Italian mosaic flanking the main entrance.

Among the museum's varied collection of "Malaysiana" is a life-sized exhibit depicting a royal wedding and the circumcision ceremony of a prince.

Near the museum is the southern entrance to the **Lake Gardens**, a gently undulating, flower-carpeted and tree-filled oasis that provides a 173-acre (70-hectares) green "lung" in the middle of the city. The park owes its existence to a British official who managed to persuade Swettenham in 1888 that the young Kuala Lumpur needed a public park. Crowning the crest of a hill in the park is the gleaming white **Parliament House**, a mixture of modern design and traditional motifs opened in 1962. The building comprises an 18-story tower and transcepted chamber. On a smaller hill stands the **National Monument**, which commemorates those who died in the struggle against communist insurgency in the 1950s.

Just outside the park boundaries is **Carcosa**, the epitome of a colonial bungalow, built for the British governor of the Federated Malay States in 1897 and

Flower shop in downtown KL.

later became the residence of the British High Commissioner. Carcosa and the adjacent **Istana Tetamu** guesthouse were renovated into the exclusive **Carcosa Seri Negara hotel** in 1989, just in time to host Queen Elizabeth and Prince Philip on their visit to Malaysia for the Commonwealth Heads of Government meeting.

Chinatown is a concentrated area of frenetic activity that lies just east of the Central Market, bounded roughly by Jalan Bandar, Jalan Petaling and Jalan Sultan. Along these and adjoining side streets, a dazzling array of textiles, fruits, flowers, live animals, herbal medicines and other exotic delicacies are available around the clock, or so it seems. Organized chaos – more commonly called shopping – reaches a frenzied peak at dusk, when the middle section of **Jalan Petaling** is cordoned off and transformed into an open-air night market (*pasar malam*). The noble art of sidestepping pedestrian traffic while keeping an eye out for useful bargains can be honed to perfection here.

Lining the streets and sidewalks around Chinatown after dark are a variety of mobile kitchens, manned by hawkers who set up shop in narrow alleys along the walls of the commercial buildings. The quality of fare offered by these itinerant food vendors is almost uniformly excellent. The Malay equivalent of these sidewalk cafes can be found several blocks north at the **Munshi Abdullah** stalls on Jalan Dang Wangi and the **Campbell** stalls that appear at night in the nearby parking lot.

Fine examples of religious architecture can also be digested in this section of town. The elaborate, wildly decorative **Sri Mahamariamman Temple** on Jalan Bandar was built in 1873. Step inside to see Hindu worshipers offering prayers to the four-armed Lord Murugan, his two wives and a six-armed goddess.

Two prominent illustrations of Chinese shrines are the ornate **Chan See Shu Yuen Temple** at the southern end of Jalan Petaling, and the historic **Sze Ya Temple** opposite the Central Market off Jalan Hang Kasturi. The latter, a

Sikh fortune teller awaits a customer.

Taoist place of worship, was built by Yap Ah Loy in the 1880s.

Northeast of Chinatown is a district of tall office blocks, shopping centers and five-star hotels called the **Golden Triangle**, bounded by Jalan Ampang, Jalan Raja Chulan and Jalan Tun Razak. At the center of the triangle are the **Selangor Turf Club** and the old **Padang Lumba Kuda Race Track**, but all around the edge are the trappings of big-city life. There's enough nightlife in this area to satisfy even the most discriminating insomniacs.

Jalan Ampang once led to the rich tin mines at Ampang to the east of the city. Tin tycoons once built lavish mansions along this road, like the **Chan Chin Mooi** residence and the famous **Bok House**, now home to a wonderful old restaurant called **Le Coq d'Or** where some of the bygone ambience of KL persists. **Dewan Tunku Abdul Rahman**, another tin-boom mansion, was recently renovated into an art gallery and city tourist office. Farther up the road opposite Ming Court Hotel is

the **Khoon Yam Buddhist Temple**, the oldest Chinese place of worship in KL.

Tucked in one corner of the Golden Triangle is the **Karyaneka Handicraft Center** on Jalan Raja Chulan. Malaysia's 13 states each have their own *kampung* house with exhibits of their respective arts and crafts. Among the items on display are handwoven textiles, woodwork, *batik*, basketwork, silver and pewter goods, shellwork and pottery. You can see how many of these items are made, and some of the finished goods are for sale in the showroom.

The area north of the **Kelang River** has become increasingly popular with both locals and visitors. At the top end of Jalan Tunku Abdul Rahman is **Chow Kit**, the largest, loudest and most lively of KL's night markets. This is an area filled with cheap hotels catering to those with modest means, and many "ladies of easy virtue" ply their trade here. In the heart of all this activity stands the **Chow Kit Market**, reputedly the best and cheapest food market in town.

East of Chow Kit along Jalan Raja Alang is the **Sunday Market** (*Pasar Minggu*), which springs to life, not on Sunday as you might expect, but on Saturday night. The fun lasts into the early hours of Sunday morning. A variety of handicrafts are on sale at the various stalls including Malay caps (*songkok*), prayer books, hand-printed *batik sarongs*, Kelantan silverware and traditional earthenware pots (*labu*).

At the opposite end of Jalan Chow Kit is the massive **Putra World Trade Center**, with a conference hall, hotel and 40-story block housing the head office of the **Tourist Development Corporation** (TDC) of Malaysia. Many important international conferences and exhibitions take place here. Across the road is another impressive structure, **The Mall** shopping center. Arrayed around the atrium lobby are chic boutiques and luxury shops featuring Western designer goods. The sixth floor is modeled after a traditional Malay street market, with food stalls and souvenir shops, while the top floor is given over to an indoor fun park that includes a miniature rollercoaster and other rides.

Left, the wildly elaborate Sri Mahamariamman Temple. Right, The Mall is a popular KL hangout.

OUTSIDE KUALA LUMPUR

Petaling Jaya (PJ), the country's first satellite town, is just 6 miles (10 km) from KL on the southbound Federal Highway. This city of 250,000 is fully self-contained. While offering few tourist sights, PJ's laidback style – from open-air hawker stalls to smoke-filled jazz-and-gin joints – is a welcome and attractive entertainment alternative. Also located here is the **University of Malaya** and its **Asian Art Museum**.

After leaving PJ, the Federal Highway cleaves a path through the **Klang Valley**, passing the airport and the new Selangor state capital of **Shah Alam**. The Sultan of Selangor resides in the **Istana Bukit Kayangan**, but the city's most eye-catching structure is the **State Mosque**, with some of the world's largest domes and highest minarets.

At the end of the motorway is **Klang** on the banks of a river of the same name. **Gedong Raja Abdullah**, an old warehouse built in 1857, has been converted into a museum bringing the town's long, colorful and violent history to life. Five miles (8 km) west is **Port Klang**, the primary seaport for Kuala Lumpur. Most people come here for the fresh seafood in restaurants along the quayside.

About 8 miles (13 km) north of the capital off the Ipoh Highway are the **Batu Caves**. Formed within the framework of an imposing limestone outcrop, the caves were formed about 400 million years ago but not "discovered" until 1878 when American naturalist William Hornaday stumbled upon them quite by accident. This is the site of the Hindu *Thaipusam Festival*, held early each year in honor of the diety Lord Murugan. Chanting devotees carry a statue of the diety up the 272 steps leading to a shrine within **Cathedral Cave**. To seek penance, the entranced worshipers each carry a *kavadi*, an elaborately decorated wooden frame attached to their flesh with a variety of sharp skewers and hooks, to no apparent discomfort. Accompanied by the incessant beat of In-

dian drums and shouts of encouragement, the procession is testimony to the power of religious conviction.

If you have a desire for wide, open spaces, head for **Templar Park**, a 3,000-acre (1,200-hectare) jungle reserve located several miles farther north. Within its luxuriant green boundaries are numerous waterfalls, pools and jungle walks, designed to remove stress induced by city life. A similar distance from Batu Caves on the old Pahang Highway is a recreational park called **Mimaland**, with more lush gardens, a lake for fishing and boating, an enormous free-form pool and a mini-zoo to keep the children occupied. It's popular with locals, so avoid going on weekends.

On the northeast fringe of Kuala Lumpur is the **Selangor Pewter Factory** on Jalan Pahang, where Malaysia's famous pewter products are made and sold. Local pewter is made from an alloy of refined tin, antimony and copper. Farther out on the same road is the **National Zoo**, with a collection of more than 2,000 species.

Left, cavernous interior of the Batu Caves. Right, kavadi-carrying devotee offers penance to the gods.

MALACCA

Strategically situated on the famous **Straits of Malacca**, about 95 miles (150 km) south of Kuala Lumpur, **Malacca** (Melaka) is a place with a proud past. Prince Parameswara established the town in the early 15th century, naming it after a tree he was standing near. Malacca quickly developed into an important trading post. Admiral Cheng Ho (the Three-Jewel Eunich), an envoy of the Ming emperor, helped forge formal links between Malacca and the Middle Kingdom when he visited in 1409, the beginning of a long relationship between the town and China.

The descendants of Chinese settlers from this period came to be known as *Babas* (Straits-born Chinese), products of a unique fusion of their traditional Chinese origins and the Malay environment. These first Chinese immigrants were followed by a succession of European colonizers – the Portuguese in 1511, the Dutch in 1641 and the British in 1824. Architectural and cultural relics of their respective eras are apparent in Malacca even today. This is what makes the place a historical gold mine, despite the recent appearance of modern buildings and hotels on the periphery of the old town.

The richest vein of history is centered around **Dutch Square**, flanked by the salmon pink brick-and-laterite building of Dutch colonial times. The **Stadhuys** (Town Hall) was completed in the 1650s and is the oldest standing Dutch building in the Orient. It has been converted into the **Malacca Historical Museum**, whose exhibits trace the city's history from the time of the ancient Malay kingdoms through Portuguese and Dutch rule, and British occupation. Next door is **Christ Church** (1753), another unmistakably Dutch structure. It was started in 1741 to celebrate the centenary of Dutch occupation. Down Jalan Laksamana are the twin Gothic spires of **St Francis Xavier Church** (1849).

On the south end of the square is **St Paul's Hill**, with the ruins of **St Paul's Church** at the summit, constructed by the Portuguese around 1590 on the site of an even earlier chapel. St Francis Xavier first preached within its solid stone walls in 1545, and he was temporarily buried here in 1553. The ruins contain several large tombstones with epitaphs in Latin, Dutch and Portuguese. The hill itself was turned into a burial ground for Dutch notables in 1753.

At the base of the hill is the **Porta de Santiago** (Gateway of St James), the only remaining relic of **A Famosa**, a Portuguese fortress erected in the early 16th century. At one time, A Famosa encompassed the entire hill, its massive walls protecting the European settlement including a castle, two palaces and five churches. The Dutch later restored the fort, but the British demolished most of the fortifications in the early 19th century.

Opposite the gateway is a large open space called the **Padang Pahlawan**, where Tunku Abdul Rahman announced Malaya's independence on his return from negotiations in London. The

eft,
he distinctive
ed-brick
Christ Church
s a Dutch
egacy.
Right,
Peranakan
ulture in
Malacca.

Padang is now the venue for an evening sound and light spectacular, the first of its kind in Southeast Asia. Facing onto the Padang is the **Declaration of Independence Memorial Building**, which contains documents, photographs, films, videos and other materials connected to the campaign for sovereignty. How fitting that the building itself was once the exclusive Malacca Club (1911), where British colonial officials and planters gathered away from the prying eyes of the "natives."

Behind the Memorial Building is the **Melaka Sultanate Palace**, a recently completed replica of the 15th-century palace of Sultan Mansur Shah. Faithfully reconstructed from eyewitness accounts of the original palace, it fittingly serves as a cultural storehouse dedicated to the role of Malacca as the font of Malay culture and tradition.

Two miles (3 km) due south of Dutch Square, on another hill overlooking the town, are the ruins of **St John's Fort**. This is a Dutch construction of the 1770s, but its appearance has been undermined somewhat by the 20th-century water treatment plant and high-rise apartment block on either flank. To the east is **Bukit China** ("China Hill"), an ancient Chinese graveyard with tombs dating back to the Ming Dynasty. These are some of the oldest Chinese relics in Malaysia. With over 12,000 plots, this is said to be the largest Chinese cemetery in the world outside China.

The **Malacca River** – now clogged with silt, but once a thriving avenue of trade – divides the old European and Asian quarters, but it's easily crossed on a concrete bridge from the west side of Dutch Square. The area is known today as **Chinatown**, a fascinating neighborhood of temples, cafes and antique shops that is easily explored by foot.

Chinatown's most prominent landmark is the **Cheng Hoon Teng** (Green Cloud) temple on Jalan Tekong, the oldest Chinese place of worship in Malaysia. It was founded in 1645, with additions in later centuries. Figures from Chinese mythology made from broken porcelain and colored glass adorn the

The view of the Malacca River has changed little in recent years.

temple roof, ridges and eaves, images which blend Taoism, Confucianism and Buddhism.

Just up the road is the **Kampong Kling Mosque** (1868), with a typical Sumatran design that features a three-tiered roof and beautifully carved wooden ceiling. Next door is **Sri Poyyatha Vinayagar Moorthi Temple**, built by the Malaccan Hindu community in the 1780s.

One of the best known Malacca streets is **Jalan Tun Tan Cheng Lock**, named after a leading *Baba* who helped bring independence to Malaysia. The road is lined with the ancestral homes of the Straits Chinese. Sometimes called shophouses, these tightly packed, long and narrow structures offer an insight into local architectural styles of 200 years ago. Many of the buildings have intricately carved doors and elaborate interiors containing generations of family heirlooms and antiques. One of the old shophouses has been turned into the **Baba Nyonya Heritage Museum**.

Running parallel is **Jalan Hang Jebat** (Jonkers Street), famous throughout the Orient for its antique shops. Everything from Victorian brass beds to Chinese rosewood furniture to vintage photographs can be found here – but don't expect to find anything rare unless you are prepared to pay for it. The merchants here have well-honed sales pitches; the challenge is dickering them down to a mutually agreeable price. The street is also becoming known for its trendy eating places, especially the **Jonkers Melaka Cafe**, set within the cool and calm courtyard of an old shophouse.

About a mile from the town square, descendants of the early Portuguese live in a seaside community known as the **Eurasian Settlement**. Established in 1930, the district consists of a small number of *kampung*-style dwellings inhabited by residents who still speak *Christao*, an Iberian-influenced dialect from which many Malay words are derived. Each year the Eurasians celebrate the Feast of St Peter (*Festa de San Pedro*), in which fishermen decorate their boats for a ceremony in which they are blessed by the parish priest.

Colorful tiles characterize typical Malaccan designs.

PENANG

Take one tropical island, add a luxurious beach resort, augment with a significant amount of history, and toss in a liberal dose of superb local food. The result would be **Penang**, the "Pearl of the Orient." Pulau Pinang (Island of the Betel Nut Palm), as it is also called, lies just off the northwest coast of the peninsula and is indeed a gem, touted as a veritable heaven on earth. Visitors will be hard-pressed to deny it.

Originally a territory of the Sultan of Kedah, Penang was largely uninhabited until 1786 when the British East India Company decided to turn it into a commercial outpost as it was favorably located on the eastern end of the Indian Ocean. The island thus became the first British settlement in Malaysia, predating the other two "Straits Settlements" of Malacca and Singapore.

Since September 1985, the island's 114 square miles (285 square km) of

territory have been linked to the mainland by the 5-mile (13-km) long **Penang Bridge**. Previously, the only way to reach the island was by plane or the old but picturesque cross-channel ferries.

Apart from the bridge and glitzy resort hotels, one of the few visible signs of modern influence in Penang is the **Komtar** government complex, a cylindrical office block that dominates the skyline of **Georgetown** (Bandaraya Tanjung), the island's main city.

Reminders of the past are much more evident. **Fort Cornwallis**, on the northeastern tip of the island, was the site of the first British camp. Built by convict labor at the turn of the 19th century, only its outer walls remain. Next to the fort are the **Padang** and the **Esplanade**, which mark the heart of historic Georgetown. A prominent landmark here is the **Clock Tower**, presented to the city by a rich Chinese *towkay*, Cheah Chin Gok, to commemorate Queen Victoria's Diamond Jubilee. Old colonial buildings are much in evidence in this part of town. Take note of the **Supreme Court** and **St George's** (1818), the oldest Anglican church in Southeast Asia. Across Leboh Farquhar from the church is the **Penang Museum** and the **Penang Art Gallery**.

Farther west along the waterfront you stumble upon the stark white facade of the **Eastern and Oriental Hotel**, one of the grand dames of the East and once sister to Raffles Hotel in Singapore. The aura of somewhat faded glory is what gives the E&O its charm.

A short stroll around old Georgetown is an education in both cross-cultural fertilization and religious diversity. Near the museum on Leboh Pitt is the **Kuan Yin Temple**, one of the oldest and most revered sites in Penang. Built over 150 years ago, it's crowded year round, but especially during Chinese New Year when good luck is at a premium. In stark contrast is the Indian-influenced **Kapitan Kling Mosque**, built by the island's first Indian Muslim settlers around 1800. The eclectic nature of Penang's religious architecture is further enhanced by **Wat Chayamangkalaram** on Lorong Burma, which houses the world's third largest reclining Buddha, more than 100 feet (33 meters) long.

Yet perhaps the best known religious building in Georgetown is the **Khoo Kongsi**, at the junction of Leboh Pitt and Leboh Acheh. A *kongsi* is a clan house, which functions as a temple and assembly hall for Chinese of the same clan or surname. Built at the end of the 19th century and refurbished after fire destroyed the original roof, Khoo Kongsi features an elaborate blend of paintings, woodcarving and stonework.

Successful shopping in Georgetown requires a great deal of poking around in the narrow streets and alleys off **Penang Road**, where there are a multitude of handicraft and antique shops. Nearby on **Leboh Campbell**, it's possible to haggle with street vendors over the price of nylon shirts, fake crocodile-skin shoes and precious stones. The dusty streets of the area, with intriguing names like **Rope Walk** and **Love Lane**, are lined with a variety of shops flogging just about every imaginable type of paraphernalia, some of which might less charitably be de-scribed as junk. Still, the prospect of uncovering a memento or two is always there. A thirst for *mahjong* sets, Chinese name stamps, joss sticks and medicinal herbs is likely to be satisfied here.

A few miles west of Georgetown is the new **State Mosque**, an ultra-modern design topped by a shimmering gold onion dome. Near the center of the island, on a hill at **Air Itam**, is the towering pagoda of **Kek Lok Si Temple**. This is the largest Buddhist shrine in Malaysia and houses a great number of Buddha statues from different lands. Apart from the seven-story pagoda, the site also holds a three-tiered temple, turtle pond, souvenir shops and a huge statue of Kuan Yin, the Goddess of Mercy.

A short distance north of the temple grounds is the lower terminus of the vintage funicular railway that chugs up to the resort on the summit of **Penang Hill**. The half-hour ride (including a change of trains halfway up) will reward you with the cooler temperature and panoramic view of a 2,700-foot (830-meter) mountain. With pleasant

Komtar complex towers over Georgetown.

gardens and a small hotel, temple, mosque and police post, life at the top is redolent of a more romantic age. About 2 miles (3 km) northeast of Penang Hill are the **Botanical Gardens**, also called the Waterfall Gardens because they are arrayed around freshwater springs.

The dreamy-sounding **Temple of the Azure Cloud** might turn out to be more of a nightmare for those with an aversion to snakes. At one time, this temple about 8 miles (13 km) south of Georgetown was a must on the tourist agenda. It's not everyday that the green-and-yellow pit vipers can be found sliding up and down every altar, shrine and incense pot in a temple. Nowadays, the serpentine residents are so few that a sleepy snake or two is about the most excitement one can hope for. In one of the rooms, two decidedly non-aggressive looking vipers spend their time posing for pictures with out-of-towners.

Where the sightseeing ceases, the beach-bumming begins. Several luxury hotels are clustered at **Batu Ferringhi Beach** on the island's north shore. Ac-

tivities include sailing, horseback riding, hiking or just lying around on sun-baked stretches of white sand. The usual assortment of restaurants and art galleries offer some pleasing diversions. Nearby is **Telok Bahang**, a charming fishing village, while a mile farther on is the "world's largest" **Butterfly Farm**, a large caged enclosure with many species of butterflies and plants.

Finally, no visit to Penang would be complete without tucking in the taste-tempting, lip-smacking delights of local cuisine. It's no exaggeration to say that the people of Penang enjoy some of the finest fare in the region. Much of the best food is found at unfashionable roadside stalls and cramped coffee shops in the old parts of Georgetown. Anything from Indian curry to Malay *nasi* (rice) to Chinese *bah kut teh* (pork ribs in herbal soup) can be sampled at all hours of the day. The hawker stalls and centers of Georgetown, especially along **Gurney Drive** and **Jalan Burma**, are good spots for an initiation into some of the finer points of Penang gastronomy.

Bridges from different ages: the Penang Bridge is brand new, the wooden bridge has been around a while.

LANGKAWI

Tucked into the northwest corner of the peninsula and nestled in the warm waters of the Andaman Sea are the **Langkawi Islands**. Unlike the other islands off the west coast of Malaysia, the vast majority of the 30,000 people who live here are Malay. Of the 99 islands, just three are inhabited, and two of these very sparsely.

In recent years the government has been trying to promote Langkawi as a major tourist resort. To make the islands more appealing and accessible, an airport was built, regular ferry service was instituted from the mainland and Langkawi was granted duty-free status in 1987. Still, there hasn't been the rush that the government hoped for. Even during the high season, Langkawi retains the atmosphere of a quiet and relatively unspoiled tropical island.

Reaching Langkawi is quite easy. You can catch a ferry from **Penang**, or **Kuala Perlis**, on the mainland about an hour's drive north of Alor Star. The crossing takes about two hours. Or you can catch a flight from Penang, Kuala Lumpur, Alor Star or Singapore.

The main island is called **Pulau Langkawi** and its primary town is **Kuah** on the south shore. This small village has been transformed by the island's duty-free status and now nearly every shop is crowded with bottles of liquor, cartons of cigarettes and electronic items. There are also local craft shops with hand-painted fabrics, shellwork and stones with miniature paintings. Kuah has several small hotels and the government-run **Langkawi Island Resort**.

Until a few years ago, Kuah was the only part of the island where visitors could find accommodation. Now there are hotels, chalets and huts at a variety of locations. One of the most popular is **Pantai Cenang** in the southwest, where the big **Pelangi Beach Resort** and a number of beach chalets are situated. Another concentration of rooms can be found at **Pantai Rhu** on the north shore.

Away from the beach, there are a number of interesting places to see in the interior of Langkawi. **Telaga Tujuh** is a series of seven cool pools that tumble into one another down a mountainside. Legend has it that the mountain fairies came here to bathe and wash their long hair. As a contrast, visit **Telaga Air Panas** – the hot water pools near the center of the island. Not far away is **Durian Perangin Waterfall**, set amid thick jungle at the end of a rough track.

Boats can be hired for excursions to more inaccessible parts of the coast or to smaller islands in the Langkawi group. From Tanjong Rhu you can head around the northern cape to the gray limestone cliffs beyond. Here you will find **Gua Cerita** (Cave of Legends), inscribed with writings from the *Koran*. To reach the cave entrance, you must climb precariously up a bamboo ladder.

On **Dayang Bunting**, the second largest island, is the **Lake of the Pregnant Maiden**, separated from the sea by a narrow isthmus. The lake is a place of pilgrimage for barren women, who drink its waters in the hope of conceiving.

Left, sunrise over Pulau Langkawi. **Right**, resort facilities are readily available on Langkawi.

HILL STATIONS

The hill stations of Malaysia, as elsewhere in Asia, are essentially a colonial creation, developed by British bureaucrats as retreats from the heat and humidity of the lowlands. Since independence, they have taken on a variety of cloaks: some remain quaint anachronisms of the colonial past, while others have evolved into cosmopolitan resorts.

Genting Highlands: This modern hill resort is just 30 miles (50 km) from Kuala Lumpur. It boasts Malaysia's only casino, and claims to meet the needs of non-punters as well, but don't bet on it. True, the superb golf course, other man-made attractions and cool temperatures near the top of the 5,600-foot (1,700-meter) summit are inviting enough. But there's no doubt that roulette, blackjack, baccarat and other games of chances are the prime time events. Everything else is strictly loose change.

Fraser's Hill: Chances are that low-rollers in search of a mountain retreat will head another 30 miles north to Fraser's Hill – slightly lower than Genting at 5,000 feet (1,500 meters) – but sporting a more tranquil, relaxed atmosphere. Activity centers around the golf course, but the highlight of the day is likely to be a jungle walk or a swim at the base of **Jerlau Waterfall**.

The resort is named after Louis James Fraser, a 19th-century British adventurer who allegedly operated several questionable businesses from a shack in the hills. The shack is gone, but a series of colonial bungalows, complete with neat little rose gardens, have taken its place, rounding up the cool, clean, countryside charm of the place.

Maxwell Hill: This is Malaysia's oldest hill station, now renamed **Bukit Larut**, and situated on a 3,350-foot (1,020-meter) hill above Taiping in northern Perak state. Don't expect golf courses, fancy restaurants or swimming pools. The "attractions" here are a single badminton court and limitless jungle walks. Cool air and moist clouds hang low over the jungle below, and there is an ever-changing vista from Penang to Pangkor as the clouds wash off the Straits of Malacca. Comfortable bungalows with English names and fireplaces give Maxwell Hill the simplicity of a natural hideaway that sets one's heart and mind delightfully at ease.

The road to the top of Maxwell Hill is paved, but access is prohibited to private vehicles. Government-owned Land Rovers which operate from the far end of the Lake Gardens in **Taiping** serve as mountain taxis. They depart every hour between dawn and dusk, delivering you to the front step of your bungalow.

Cameron Highlands: The largest and most extensive of Malaysian hill stations, the Cameron Highlands is some 136 miles (220 km) north of Kuala Lumpur. They lie in Pahang state but can only be reached via roads through Perak. After turning off the Ipoh trunk road at **Tapah**, proceed another 29 miles (46 km) along a narrow, twisting road hewn from the raw mountainside. Along the way you are likely to encounter some *Orang Asli* (Original Men), aboriginal tribesmen

Left, picking tea leaves in the highlands. Right, towering trunks make an impressive sight.

TAMAN NEGARA: THE GREEN HEART

Malaysia's greatest jungle haunt is Taman Negara, a massive national park that sprawls across the mountainous interiors of three states - Pahang, Kelantan and Trengganu. Within this area, around the central mastif of Gunung Tahan, the highest peak on the peninsula, there are countless limestone hills cov-

ered in thick forest, fast-running streams and abundant wildlife.

The only way to reach Taman Negara is by boat, up the muddy Tembeling River from the dock at Kuala Tembeling. The journey takes three to four hours depending on the level of the river, and passengers might actually be asked to get out and walk along the shore at certain stretches of low water. The park headquarters is at Kuala Tahan, where there is a variety of accommodation ranging from rest houses and chalets to a youth hostel and campsites. Cooking facilities are available at the hostel, while nearby is a shop that sells basic food supplies. There are two restaurants at Kuala Tahan for those who don't want to rough it all the way.

Each night, the park service has a slide and film show to give information on Taman Negara and explain some of the wildlife you will see in the forest. Guides are also available from the reception if you wish for a conducted tour of plant and animal life. There are well-marked trails all around Kuala Tahan, and a few jungle hides where you can wait for animals to approach. Travel through the rest of the park is chiefly carried out by water. Boats are offered for hire through the park service.

Taman Negara is thought to be one of the earth's oldest forests, with a history that stretches back 130 million years. Many plants in this area have become highly specialized and are interlinked with other species in both parasitic and symbiotic ways.

The rainforest is not a quiet place. In some respects it's as noisy as any big city, with a cacophony of insect noises, bird calls and animal cries that goes on night and day. With more than 250 species recorded in the park, bird-watching is a delight. Look out for colorful hornbills in the tree tops, and kingfishers and fish eagles along the rivers. Long-tailed macaques and other monkeys are heard but rarely seen. But monitor lizards and otters are usually easy to spot. Larger wildlife is also present in the park, but they dwell deep in the jungle shadows, which makes them hard to spot. Deer and wild pigs are the most commonly seen animals close to park headquarters. Farther into the forest, you might be lucky enough to see a tapir, elephant, rhino or tiger.

Just downriver from Kuala Tahan and a 15-minute walk inland is the Gua Telinga (Ear Cave). After crawling along a narrow passageway through moss and guano, you finally emerge into a much larger underground room. With the help of a light, you can see thousands of fruit- and insect-eating bats suspended from the ceiling. Other cave dwellers include giant toads and a bat-eating snake. ∎

Visitors ca **hope to ca** **a glimpse** **a Malayan** **tapir.**

144

who have lived in Malaysia's jungles since prehistoric times. They sell fruit and carvings to passing motorists.

Ringlet is the outermost of the highland's three townships. The main town of **Tanah Rata** is 8 miles (13 km) farther on, and **Brinchang** lies another 2 miles (3 km) up the road.

Ranging in altitude between 5,000 and 6,000 feet (1,500 and 1,800 meters), the highlands were discovered in 1885 by a government surveyor named William Cameron, who mapped the area and found "a fine plateau with gentle slopes shut in by lofty mountains." He was followed by a steady stream of tea planters, vegetable farmers and wealthy colonials seeking relief from the lowland heat and humidity. The colonials successfully shaped the highlands into a tropical cousin of the English countryside, lining the main valley between Tanah Rata and Brinchang with mock Tudor homes overlooking a magnificent 18-hole golf course.

Much of the highlands are carpeted in a thick layer of tea. It's possible to arrange a visit to the **Blue Valley Tea Estate**, where visitors are shown the processes involved in making tea. Everywhere in the Camerons, the tea seems to taste fresher and its perfume sweeter than when drunk in the lowlands.

The whole of the Cameron Highlands is laced with jungle paths. Maps are usually available from hotels or from shops in Tanah Rata. They range from family strolls to very tough hikes. The ultimate goal is **Gunung Brinchang**, the highland's highest peak at 6,500 feet (2,000 meters). But be warned that the jungles here are deceptively dense. Tell someone where you're heading and stick to the paths for it's easy to get lost. Probably the most famous person to disappear here was Thai silk king Jim Thompson, the American entrepreneur who walked into the jungle in March of 1967 and never returned.

After your trek, head for **Ye Old Smokehouse**, the perfect copy of an English country inn, complete with roaring fire, pub grub and Guinness stout.

Malaysia's hill resorts are richly endowed by nature.

EAST COAST

From Butterworth, on the mainland opposite Penang, the East-West Highway runs a cross-country course of about 224 miles (373 km) along the Thai-Malaysian frontier, offering scenes of rural Malaysia at its best. The highway ends at **Gerik**, after which the quality of the road tends to decline. East of Gerik is the giant **Lake Temenggor**, with opportunities for fishing and hiking.

About 60 miles (100 km) farther on is **Kota Bahru**, capital of Kelantan and only a few miles from the Thai border. It's here that the charms of the East Coast become easily apparent. The big attraction here is the **Central Market**, a three-story complex where a mind-boggling array of fish, fruit, vegetables, meats and dried goods is available.

Slightly past the market is the **Padang Merdeka** and **Istana Balai Besar**, the original sultan's palace, built in 1844 and recently restored. To one side is the state mosque, **parliament** and **museum**. The museum is a converted palace and offers a variety of cultural riches. The display of local pottery, silverware, costumes, kites (*wau*), giant tops (*gasing*) and antique bird cages is ample proof of the claim that Kelantan has the country's most skilled craftsmen.

Kelantan is also the fulcrum of Malaysian *batik* and *sungkit* weaving. Young girls turn balls of cotton and silk into yards of material with hand-drawn, waxed-and-dyed designs. In addition to clothing, *batik* is used for many other aspects of the Malaysian lifestyle, from bedspreads to tablecloths to dishcovers.

Just outside Kota Bahru is perhaps the most famous stretch of sand on the East Coast – **Pantai Cinta Berahi** – the romantic-sounding "Beach of Passionate Love." In actual fact, the white sand is little different from the other miles of beach which line this coast.

Trengganu: South of Kota Bahru, the coast road runs beside a series of fishing villages and endless coconut palms before reaching **Kuala Trengganu**, capi-

East coast remedies: lots of beach and quiet.

tal of Trengganu state. Boats can be hired from the jetty at the end of Jalan Bandar to journey along the **Trengganu River**. The offshore islands of **Kapas** and **Redang** are also worthy sun spots; while the postcard-perfect **Marang** gives a good idea of coastal village life.

About 30 miles (50 km) farther south, the beach at **Rantau Abang** is the venue for the annual migration of huge leatherback turtles. They return to this particular stretch of shore between May and September to lay their eggs. The slow-moving *penyu* ("turtle"), one of the state's prime attractions, has been adopted as Malaysia's tourism symbol. The specter of one of these benign giants giving birth is an experience to treasure. After laboring up the beach, they dig a deep hole and deposit up to a hundred eggs, each about the size of a ping-pong ball. Then the mother crawls her way back to the sea.

Kuantan: Turtles can also be seen on the beaches of **Kuantan**, capital of Pahang state. Here too, craftsmen are noted for their woodcarving and weaving skills. Off the coast lie several tropical isles, each a mecca for the many swimming and diving enthusiasts who come between March and October each year (November to February being the rainy monsoon season). But the vast majority of beachcombers flock to **Cherating**, a cluster of seaside villages just north of Kuantan, where there is a broad range of accommodation ranging from beach chalets to a large Club Med.

An excellent sidetrip from Kuantan is an unusual and mildly adventurous journey to **Lake Chini**, which can be reached via an hour-long boat ride up two rivers. The lake itself is actually a series of 12 connecting bodies of water, covered between June and September by a carpet of lotus blossoms.

Mersing: About 120 miles (190 km) south of Kuantan is a busy fishing port called **Mersing**. Each May the festival *Kayu Papan* is held, during which a trance dance called the *Kuda Kepang* is performed. Mersing is also the jumping off point for a group of 64 idyllic volcanic islands in the South China Sea.

A *penyu* caught in the act.

The most famous of these is **Pulau Tioman**, which seems to be on everyone's list of the world's best islands. It was first mentioned 2,000 years ago when Arab traders made note of its good anchorage and freshwater spring. Ming pottery found in caves reveals that early Chinese traders also called on Tioman.

Nowadays the island is a tropical dream come true. When Hollywood was looking for a place to film *South Pacific*, they chose Tioman to portray the legendary Bali Hai. It's not hard to see why. Lovely beaches with lucid aquamarine water hug the western shore. The rugged interior of the island is dominated by jungle-shrouded twin peaks called the "Ass's Ears" and a rough trail leads to **Kampong Juara** and its lonely beach on the eastern shore.

The **Tioman Island Resort** with golf course, tennis courts and other amenities is the only modern accommodation on the island. Otherwise, visitors must choose from chalets and "longhouse" rooms along the beach at **Kampong Tekek** and **Salang** on the west coast.

A number of smaller islands are accessible from Mersing. All of the islands offer excellent opportunities for scuba diving, snorkeling and fishing. **Pulau Rawa**, only an hour away by boat, sports a "safari" resort with beach chalets. **Pulau Sibu Besar** – the "island of perilous passage" – is two hours by boat, noted for its lush tropical vegetation and golden beaches, but accommodation here is also quite basic. The deep blue waters around **Pulau Babi Besar** are said to teem with game fish like barracuda and grouper. **Pulau Hujong** features private bungalows that must be booked before leaving Mersing. **Pulau Tinggi** is the newest of these offshore isles to be developed for tourism, with a recently opened modern resort hotel built in the style of a Malay *kampung*.

Desaru: The southeast corner of Johor state was once deserted jungle country, but it is quickly being developed into an international "mega-resort" called Desaru. Already there is a big resort hotel, youth hostel, beach chalets and campsite, in addition to a country club

Tioman is on everyone's "world's best islands" list.

and scuba center. The current M$2-billion development plan calls for nine more hotels, 4,000 condos, theme park, marina, tennis center and four championship golf courses by 1994.

Johor Bahru: This thriving metropolis, at the tip of the Malay Peninsula opposite Singapore, is quickly developing into Malaysia's second most important city after the capital. Its population has exploded in recent years to more than one million, and the local economy is flush with new factories and foreign investment. Johor has also been drawn into a revolutionary "growth triangle" scheme with Singapore and the Riau islands of Indonesia that aims to pool joint talent and resources in developing an economic powerhouse that spans the Straits of Malacca.

The focus of "JB" is the famous **Causeway** that connects it to Singapore, completed in 1924 and partially demolished by the British Army in 1942 in a vain attempt to keep away the Japanese Imperial Army. The bustling downtown district overlooks this link.

Istana Besar (Grand Palace) was built by Sultan Abu Baker – the "Father of Modern Johor" – in the 1860s as his official residence. It no longer serves that function, but is still the venue for glittering state functions. The palace is stuffed full with antiques and Victoriana.

The present sultan lives in a much more modern palace, **Istana Bukit Serene**, crowned by an impressive 105-foot (32-meter) tower that is illuminated each night. Surrounding the palace are the **Istana Gardens**, with a replica of a Japanese tea house and the sultan's vintage car collection. Adjacent is the **Johor Zoo**, once the sultan's private animal sanctuary, but open to the public since 1962.

Commanding a conspicuous position above the straits is the elegant **Abu Bakar Mosque**, a mixture of traditional Islamic and classical Italian design. Completed in 1900, it can accommodate 2,000 worshipers. Another JB landmark is the **State Secretariat Building**, a massive Art Deco building finished in 1940 that functions as the state capital.

Nightlife in Johor Bahru is surprisingly lively.

SABAH

They call **Sabah** the "Land Below the Wind" because it lies below the deadly typhoon zone, an appropriately romantic phrase for a very exotic place. Not many tourists venture to her shores, but those who do come away with the impression that they have visited a most unusual place.

Sabah and Sarawak together make up East Malaysia, taking up about one third of the island of Borneo. Although their population accounts for only 14 percent of the country's 17 million people, their land area is larger than all the other 11 states combined. Both states are resource rich – providing vast amounts of timber, oil and natural gas to the Malaysian economy – which gives them economic muscle and political clout far greater than is usually possible with such tiny populations. Although Sabah and Sarawak share a common destiny, they were born of very different backgrounds.

Until the late 19th century, the coast of Sabah was under the control of local Malay sultans, Chinese traders and pirates. The inland areas were the realm of tribes such as the agrarian Kadazan and the primitive Murut. In 1881, the territory came under the control of the British North Borneo Company, which was interested in exploiting Sabah's natural resources. It remained a private domain of the company until after World War II, when Sabah became a crown colony. Sabah and Sarawak both became part of independent Malaysia in 1963.

Kota Kinabalu: The capital of Sabah is a sprawling, relaxed town on the west coast, which affords a splendid view of sunset over the offshore islands. Within the last decade, Kota Kinabalu has mushroomed in size and now has some of the most striking buildings in all of Malaysia, as befits the capital of one of the fastest growing states. Among the most impressive of these is the great tower of the **Sabah Foundation**, a 72-sided polygon that rises 30 stories. Inside are the offices of an institution created from state timber royalties.

Nearby is the monumental **State Mosque**, a fine display of modern Islamic architecture, and the splendid **State Museum**, built in the longhouse style of the Rungus and Murut tribes. The museum has a wealth of historical and tribal treasures, and a section on Sabah's fascinating flora and fauna. The complex also includes a **Science Center** with a large exhibition on the petroleum industry, and an **Art Gallery**.

The city center is a mixed bag of modern offices and Chinese shophouses with a water-village called **Kampong Ayer** along the seafront.

Just south of the airport is a 3-mile (5-km) stretch of beach called **Tanjung Aru**. The sea here is clear, the beach clean and seafood can be purchased at little stalls set up in the sand or in nearby restaurants. Offshore is the **Tunku Abdul Rahman National Park**, a group of tiny forested islands surrounded by azure-blue sea. The park headquarters is on **Pulau Gaya**, the largest island and only 15 minutes from the downtown jetty by boat. There are over 12 miles

Preceding pages: "The Pinnacles" in Sarawak's Mulu National Park. **Left**, Mount Kinabalu, Southeast Asia's highest peak. **Right**, ceremonial costumes evoke elegance and grace.

(20 km) of nature trails and a bungalow at Police Beach that can be rented for the night by prior arrangement. Wildlife inhabitants include monkeys, pangolin anteaters and the strange bearded pig. The offshore waters teem with coral, which makes the park ideal for scuba diving or snorkeling.

Mount Kinabalu: Everyone in Malaysia knows about this mysterious mountain. The closer one journeys towards its jagged profile, the better one understands the meaning it has for the local Kadazan people who named it *Aki Nabalu* or "Revered Place of the Dead." The spirits of the tribe's ancestors were said to roam these slopes and no one dared climb to the top to disturb them.

In spite of the taboos and myths surrounding the mountain, a young British officer named Hugh Low was still keen to reach the top. In the company of a Kadazan chief and his guides, Low reached the summit in 1851, leaving a small bottle with a note to mark his triumph. Little did Low know at the time, but he was standing on Southeast Asia's highest spot, in fact the highest ground between New Guinea and the Himalayas. Today this 13,450-foot (4,101-meter) summit is called **Low's Peak** in his honor, as is a deep gorge called **Low's Gully** that plunges a terrifying 5,900 feet (1,800 meters).

Accommodation is available at the headquarters of **Kinabalu National Park**, which features a hotel, chalets and dormitory-style sleeping, plus a shop selling basic food supplies to climbers. There are also mountain huts at 11,000 feet (3,300 meters) beneath the summit. Be sure to book all accommodation before departing from Kota Kinabalu. Park rules state that all climbers must obtain a permit (M$10) and hire a registered mountain guide for the ascent. Both are available at park headquarters or can be pre-arranged at the Sabah Parks office in Kota Kinabalu.

Besides the mountain, Kinabalu National Park contains a treasure chest of other natural features. The rainforest around the peak is unique in the world of flora in that it contains plants from al-

Mist-shrouded trees on Kinabalu's slopes.

most every part of the globe, including 1,500 species of orchids and the famous *Rafflesia*, the world's largest flower. There are 518 bird species, plus numerous reptiles and small mammals. Around the east side of the mountain is **Poring Hot Springs**, ideal to soothe those aching muscles after the climb.

Sandakan: On Sabah's northeast coast, about 240 miles (386 km) from Kota Kinabalu, is a thriving port called Sandakan which serves as a loading point for important commodities like timber, rubber and rattan. Besides the bustling waterfront, there isn't much of interest in the town itself. But Sandakan is a superb jumping-off point for numerous nature reserves found in the immediate vicinity.

A 20-minute drive outside the town is **Sepilok Reserve**, an orangutan "rehabilitation" center and the best place in Southeast Asia to see these gentle giants outside a zoo. The reserve takes in young orangutans that have been orphaned in the forest or outgrown their stay in human homes (although it's illegal to keep

them as pets, many people still flaunt the law). Wardens basically teach them how to be self-sufficient in the forest: how to climb, build nests in trees and forage for food in the jungle. Gradually they return to the jungle, although many return for visits in subsequent years.

Across the harbor from Sandakan are the **Gomantong Caves**, some of the largest in Borneo and home to more than a million swifts. The birds' nests are collected by men on bamboo ladders and sold as a delicacy to Chinese restaurants all around the Far East.

An hour off the coast by speedboat is the **Turtle Islands National Park**, which comprises three small islands where green and hawksbill turtles come to lay their eggs each night. Accommodation is available in rustic chalets on **Pulau Selingan**, the largest of the islands, but you must book ahead and bring your own food. Excursions can also be made up the **Kinabatangas River** to a proposed reserve for proboscis monkeys, but you must either hire your own boat or join a tour in Sandakan.

Looking down at the world from John's Peak.

SARAWAK

Once upon a time, a visit to the riverine state of **Sarawak** was likely to be a heady experience. Literally, that is. The Ibans, the state's largest indigenous tribal group, were belligerent headhunters until just a few decades ago. Even now, many Iban longhouses display the skulls of enemies taken in bygone encounters.

Sarawak has a unique and fascinating history. For about a hundred years, until the Japanese arrived at the start of World War II, Sarawak was the private domain of the White Rajahs – three successive members of the Brooke family whose lives were something akin to a novel.

James Brooke was a dashing young English nabob who sailed for the South China Sea in the late 1830s in search of adventure. After helping a vassal of the Sultan of Brunei crush a rebellion, Brooke was named Rajah of Sarawak as a reward. An ailing James abdicated his title to nephew Charles Brooke in 1863.

A much better administrator than his uncle, Charles expanded trade, reduced headhunting and built Kuching into a thriving city. The last rajah, Vyner Brooke, ceded power to the British after World War II. In 1963, Sarawak became part of independent Malaysia.

Kuching: Center of White Rajah rule and the gateway to a vast tropical hinterland is **Kuching**, perched on the banks of the **Sarawak River**. Although development has accelerated in recent years, the town retains much of its steamy tropical charm, like something out of an *Indiana Jones* movie.

The **Istana** was built in 1870 for newly married Charles Brooke, although it has undergone several renovations. Now the official residence of the governor of Sarawak, it commands a grassy bluff on the north bank of the Sarawak River. Farther downstream is **Fort Margherita**, named after Charles' wife, the Ranee Margaret. By the time it was finished in 1879, Sarawak was basking in a period of peace and calm, so the fort never saw hostile fire.

Sarawak River – the traveler's highway.

156

On the southern bank of the river is a huge open-air market along **Main Bazaar Road** and the **Courthouse** (1874), a rather plain colonial structure from where the White Rajahs dispensed their personal brand of justice. The **Charles Brooke Memorial**, erected in 1924, faces the Courthouse.

Dominating the skyline of Kuching is the massive **Masjid Negara** (State Mosque) with its golden domes. It may look ancient, but the mosque actually dates from 1968. At the eastern end of Main Bazaar Road is **Tua Pek Kong**, the city's oldest Chinese temple (1876). Its construction marked the firm establishment of the Chinese community in Sarawak, from a small nucleus of immigrants that James Brooke brought with him in 1839.

Perhaps the most enthralling of all the buildings in Kuching is the marvelous **Sarawak Museum**, set in lush grounds off Jalan Tun Haji Openg. Naturalist Alfred Russell Wallace spent many years in Borneo and became a good friend of Charles Brooke. With Wallace's encouragement, Brooke built the museum to house a collection of native arts and crafts, as well as specimens from Wallace's extensive fauna collection.

Although Kuching seems like an inland river city, it's actually quite close to the coast. The **Damai Beach Resort** is situated just 20 miles (32 km) north of the city, on a broad cove in the shadow of **Santubong** mountain. Swimming, windsurfing and snorkeling are popular pastimes here, or you can take a stroll along one of the marked nature trails in the nearby jungle.

Just 23 miles (37 km) north of Kuching is **Bako National Park**, located on a peninsula at the mouth of the Sarawak River. It comprises only 10 square miles (27 square km) of land but packs a lot of variety into a small area, including primary rainforest, sandy bays as well as steep cliffs. The park is also rich in flora and fauna. The jungle here is home to insect-eating plants and animals like the long-tailed macaque, wild pig and sambar deer. Within the park is a good system of well-marked paths and a rest-

Sarawak Museum links the present with the past.

house with overnight accommodation.

Longhouse Country: Beyond Kuching, cosmopolitan city life fades away and the innumerable rivers that mark Sarawak's green interior become more important than highways in reaching the many small settlements of the interior. Sarawak's longest and most important waterway is the **Rejang River**, which you can use to travel deep into the heart of longhouse country, where the Iban and other tribes live.

The sleepy town of **Sibu**, which lies at the junction of the trans-Sarawak highway and the Rejang, is the most convenient place to start your upriver journey. From here, express boats depart regularly for **Kapit** and **Belaga** on the upper reaches of the Rejang.

Kapit lies at the center of Iban country. Sarawak's largest indigenous people, the Ibans were once headhunters who gave Borneo its romantic yet somewhat gruesome reputation. Severed human heads were brought home to imbue the longhouse with protective spirits. James Brooke outlawed

headhunting, but the practice continued clandestinely until the 1950s. The Ibans are still known for their spirited war dances – to the accompaniment of chanting and gongs – and their various handicrafts.

A visit to an Iban longhouse is considered the pinnacle of any trip to Sarawak. Several hundreds have opened their doors to visitors for overnight stays. You can either book a guided trip in Kuching, or strike out on your own. But remember that it's important to bring your own food and drink, and gifts for the longhouse elders, which is a means of recompense for the warm hospitality that will be offered you.

Two weeks is the minimum for a trip upriver to areas far from the commercial and touristic world. The **Tourist Information Center** in Kuching can provide some details, but probably your best sources of information will be people you meet along the river in towns like Kapit and Belaga.

Niah Caves: More than four million swiftlets live in these caves, building nests that have been collected for centuries and sold overseas as an expensive delicacy. Although the area is protected within the framework of **Niah National Park**, nest collecting is still allowed. In fact, the caves are divided into private plots. Naturally, the nest collectors guard their trade jealously, passing their inherited plots to their sons. They live in villages and longhouses in the park area and during the collecting seasons – August to December and January to March – bring their entire family along to help gather up the riches.

Gunung Mulu: One of the newest (1985) and largest nature reserves in Malaysia is the vast **Gunung Mulu National Park**, in the far north of Sarawak near the border with Brunei. With the park is one of the earth's largest limestone cave systems – although no one is quite sure how big because the full extents of all the chambers have yet to be explored. The huge **Sarawak Chamber** measures 1,950 feet (600 meters) long, 1,462 feet (450 meters) wide and 390 feet (120 meters) high – the largest natural chamber in the world.

Left, the proboscis monkey, adopting an almost humanlike position. **Right**, bats take flight in Mulu.

158

Philippine Archipelago

400 km / 250 miles

All heights in meters

Luzon Strait

Philippine

Sea

BABUYAN ISLANDS

Calayan I.
Dalupiri I.
Camiguin I.
Fuga I.
Mayraira Pt.
Babuyan Channel
Escarpada Pt.

Laoag
Aparri
Tuguegarao
Vigan
L U Z O N
Chico
Palanan
Bontoc
Mt. Pulog
2933
Baguio
Solano
Casiguran
Dagupan
Cagayan
Agno
Tarlac
Pampanga
Cabanatuan
Olongapo
Quezon City
POLILLO ISLANDS
Manila
Polillo I.
San Pablo
Calauag
CATANDUANES I.
Lucena
Naga
Virac
Batangas
Buenavista
Mayon Volcano
2462
Calapan
BURIAS I.
Legaspi
Mamburao
Sibuyan Sea
MINDORO
Masbate
Catarman
CALAMIAN GROUP
Mindoro Strait
San Jose
MASBATE I.
SAMAR
Oras
Nabas
Catbalogan
Libro Pt.
Roxas
Visayan Sea
Tacloban
Culasi
PANAY
Cadiz
Ormoc
LEYTE
Cuyo I.
Iloilo
CEBU
Baybay
PALAWAN
DUMARAN I.
PHILIPPINES
Camotes Sea
Hinundayan
Roxas
Cebu
Palawan Passage
Long Pt.
Puerto Princesa
Binalbagan
BOHOL
Surigao
NEGROS
Tagbilaran
Cawit Pt.
CAGAYAN IS.
Tanjay
Mindanao Sea
Butuan

South

China

Sea

Mt. Mantalingajan
2085
Brooke's Point
Lianga
C. Buliluyan
Mt. Malindang
2425
Cagayan de Oro
Aguan
Sulu Sea
Ozamiz
Marawi
MINDANAO
Balabac Strait
Pagadian
Ragang Volcano
2815
Tagum
Mt. Tagubud
2804
Cotabato
Davao
Zamboanga
Moro Gulf
Upi
Davao Gulf
Tugubun Pt.
Basilan
Lebak
General Santos
Kudat
PANGUTARAN GR.
JOLO GR.
BASILAN I.
Mt. Busa
2083
C. San Augustin
Mt. Kinabalu
4100
Senaja
Jolo
TAPUL GR.
Tinaca Pt.
MALAYSIA
Hog Pt.
Tawi Tawi I.
SULU ARCHIPELAGO
Celebes
Sarangani Strait
INDONESIA
BORNEO
TAWI TAWI GR.
Sapulut
Sea
Tawau

162

THE PHILIPPINES: ASIAN FIESTA

The Philippines has long intrigued watchers of the Asian scene. The archipelago of some 7,000 islands continues to mystify with its curious turns of history and happenstance. "Discovered" in 1521 by a Spanish circumnavigating expedition led by Portuguese adventurer Ferdinand Magellan, and subsequently colonized, the experience has left an indelible mark. The result, though, is still uniquely Filipino.

The long Spanish rule has left such an imprint on the Filipino that he is often called the Asian Latino. A sense of fiesta appears to be his hallmark of character, one that allows too for the imperative siesta – an indication of lassitude often traced to his legacy of tropical sun and lush nature setting.

It was said that the native could toss the remains of a meal out the window and expect to have a new crop beside him next season. Fertile land was his birthright, together with the seas' munificence and a year broken simply into the rainy and the dry months.

When the Spanish arrived with "Sword and Cross," they found a people unfamiliar with adversity, living gently off a collection of disunited islands ruled by small sultanates. Proud regional differences persist to this day, having survived the waning Spanish empire as well as the second colonizing power in the form of the United States.

Some aspects of the Philippines seem remarkably familiar to visitors from North America and Europe. For one thing, it's the only predominantly Catholic country in Southeast Asia, and 70 years of English as the primary language of instruction makes it easier for the English-speaking visitor to strike up a conversation with a rural Filipino than any other Asian villager.

Long considered the least oriental of all Orientals, he enjoys a cuisine that is a sedate mixture of ascetic atoll diet, Chinese imagination and Spanish conservatism – with only a few areas where chilies come into their own.

The Filipino is also Asia's music man, marked by flair and friendliness, a person who is both capricious and volatile, but with an inordinate supply of unfailing good humor.

There is much that is contrary, and even contradictory, in the *Pinoy* (as the Filipino calls himself colloquially). But his innate Malay warmth and generosity, coupled with Latin temperament, allows for sudden shifts from Utopian optimism to moody fatalism. His odd mixture of brashness and grace, indeed, often makes the Filipino's fanciful act a hard one to follow.

Preceding pages: flags flying high at the *Ati-Atihan* festival, Kalibo-Aklan province.

Lying between 21 degrees north latitude and 5 degrees north latitude on the westernmost rim of the Pacific Ocean, the Philippines is actually a series of half-drowned mountain ranges, part of a great cordillera extending from Indonesia to Japan. The country stretches 1,100 miles (1,770 km) from north to south, and spans 685 miles (1,102 km) at its widest point.

Of the total land area of 120,312 square miles (311,600 square km), 96 percent is taken up by 11 large islands, and less than one in 10 of the Philippines' 7,000-odd islands is inhabited. The two largest islands, Luzon and Mindanao, account for 65 percent of the total land area and contain 60 percent of the country's population of 56 million. The land mass of the archipelago, taken as a whole, is about the size of Italy, slightly smaller than Japan, and slightly larger than the British Isles. Yet with so many islands dotted across such a vast expanse of water, it is not surprising that the Philippines coastline is double that of the U.S.

The highest elevations in the Philippines are volcanic peaks. Twelve of these are active and many more are either dormant or extinct. They are evidence of early linkage with the "chain of fire" at the borders of the Pacific. The dramatic vulcanism of these island groups' first million years are recorded in the Philippines by present fracture lines running the length of the archipelago. Also along these fault lines is the Mindanao Trough (east of Mindanao island) whose recorded depth of 35,210 feet (10,705 meters) makes it the world's second deepest trench.

A full 60 species of Bornean plants are found in the southern islands of Mindoro, Palawan and Mindanao. Flora identified with Celebes and the Moluccas are widespread in the Philippines, mainly in the form of ferns, orchids, and the dipterocarp, which makes up the country's primary forests as it does in Thailand, Indochina and Indonesia.

In the wilds of Palawan and Calamianes, the same mouse deer, weasel, mongoose, porcupine, skunk, anteater and otter are found as in Borneo's interior. Species of Palawan shrews, as well as a rare bat found in Mindanao, have kin in Celebes.

Fish in the waters of eastern Sumatra and western Borneo are much like those in southwestern Philippines, as are the fish between eastern Mindanao and New Guinea. Many Malaysian and Bornean birds make their home in Palawan.

The oldest human remains discovered in the country are the 1962 Tabon Cave find. High up a cliff facing the China Sea in Northern Palawan, the fossilized skullcap of a Tabon Woman was found with other human bones, flake tools and the fossilized bones of bats and birds. Carbon-dated at

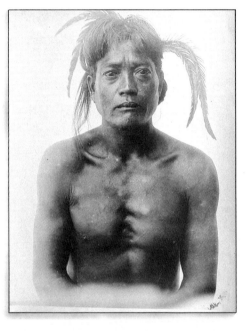

22,000 B.C., Tabon Woman and her fellow cave dwellers have been tentatively identified as Australoid.

Should this identification be corroborated, the growing speculation that early man in the Philippines was part of a huge and fascinating family tree comes closer to proof. It was a tree that included, at its roots, the prehistoric progenitors of the Chinese and all the Asian races. Scientists suggest that the Austronesian civilization could be older than either the Chinese or the Indian, and that it had Southeast Asia as its hearth.

The Philippines joined this scenario around the 3rd millennium B.C. when the

Austronesians came on outrigger canoes bearing pottery, woodcarvings, barkcloth and the art of tattooing with a highly developed geometric art style. Today many cultural minorities, still living on the fringe of the predominantly Christian civilization of the country, utilize this style in their mats, hats, jewelry, weaponry, pots and cloth.

Ethnohistory weaves its dazzling colors into the Philippine cultural fabric. There are over three dozen major ethnic groups scattered in relative isolation about the islands, each keyed to unique warps and wefts of time and custom.

Close to 10 percent of the total population are designated cultural minorities. These five called the Moslems or Moros, of old – constitute the largest cultural minority of the Philippines. They claim Mindanao and the Sulu Archipelago farther south as their own holy land. The Mindanao Autonomous Region has been established, granting autonomy to four provinces in Mindanao. The Muslims, fiercely independent and pugnacious among themselves, are divided into five major groups: Tausug, Maranao, Maguindanao, Samal and Badjao.

Contact with the outside world had been minimal until about A.D. 1,000, when Chinese, Indian, Arab and Indonesian traders brought in pottery, textiles, iron weapons, tools, jewelry and trinkets to barter for pearls,

million people, eking out a living outside the cultural mainstream of Filipino Christian lowlanders, comprise the most diverse and exotic population of the country. Sixty percent of this ethnic minority – Muslim Filipinos generally living in the southern islands of Mindanao and the Sulu Archipelago – color the most inaccessible mountain provinces of Northern and Central Luzon, and the highland plains, rainforests and isolated seashores of Mindanao and Palawan.

Considered as a whole, the Muslims – also

Left, Filipino native. **Above**, baptism scene from a painting of the Magellan Cross.

corals, gold and possibly rice, dried fish and handicrafts. They also introduced the first truly civilizing influences. By the 12th century, the Chinese were supplying prestige wares which acquired ceremonial significance – pottery and metal objects, for example – which are now being recovered from ancient graves.

Early in the 14th century, other traders introduced Islam which swept through the Sulu Archipelago and farther north. The new faith served to consolidate and to invigorate little sultanates that were later to vigorously resist the Spanish, the Americans and the Philippine national government.

The modern era in the Philippines dates from the arrival of Ferdinand Magellan on Samar Island (March 16, 1521). Magellan had set out on behalf of the King of Spain to find a route westward across the Pacific to tap the riches of the Indies. The "discovery" of the islands ended tragically when Magellan was killed shortly after, the result of an altercation with Lapulapu, petty chieftain of Mactan Island.

Four more Spanish expeditions failed to establish significant contact, and it was not until 1565 that Miguel Lopez de Legazpi, sailing from Mexico, gained a foothold in Cebu and claimed the islands of the archipelago in the name of King Philip II of Spain.

ducing sugar, tobacco, indigo and hemp as major cash crops, and ending the Manila Galleon monopoly on foreign commerce. But the reforms had been late in coming, and there was already an incipient nationalist movement led by the liberal clergy, professionals, and some students in Spain.

Nationalist and revolutionary movements developed rapidly in the last two decades of the 19th century. Jose Rizal, Andres Bonifacio and Emilio Aguinaldo emerged as the leaders, respectively, of the Propaganda Movement (demanding Filipino equality with the Spaniards), the Katipunan (a secret society advocating armed insurrection), and the first declaration of a Philippine Republic

Thus did the islands gain the name *Filipinas.*

Bands of conquistadores, newly-arrived from Mexico, spread out to conquer Luzon and Visayas. They encountered little opposition, and soon entrenched themselves as lords of great estates worked by native peons. The accompanying friars quickly converted the population. The various religious orders competed vigorously with one another and with the civil and military authorities for prestige, privilege, power and wealth.

In the late 18th and early 19th centuries the Spanish effected important political, economic and social reforms, allowing some native participation in government, intro-

(June 12, 1898).

In the meantime, Spain and America had gone to war on the question of Cuba. The answer came on May 1, 1898, when, Commodore George Dewey sailed into Manila Bay and defeated the Spanish fleet. The Spanish commander surrendered the city after token resistance. With the end of the Spanish-American conflict, Spain ceded the Philippines, Puerto Rico and Guam to the U.S.

Filipinos had sided with the Americans against the Spanish, but were now angered because the Americans offered not independence but a new colonialism. The Philippine-American War lasted from 1899 until 1902. The Americans, defining their role as one of trusteeship and tutelage, promoted rapid political, economic and social development. On November 15, 1935, the Philippines was constituted a Commonwealth nation with the promise of full independence in 1945. But World War II intervened.

On December 10, 1941, the Japanese landed an expeditionary force, which fought its way down the Bataan Peninsula (despite the heroic resistance of General Douglas MacArthur's American and Filipino troops), stormed the island fortress of Corregidor, occupied Manila, and overran the whole of the archipelago. As he made his escape from

Even after the granting of independence on July 4, 1946, Philippine-American relations have not been untroubled. The major conflicts have related to "parity" (special American business privileges), "bases" (American military installations), and what the Filipinos have perceived as unduue American influence in the nation's economy and political scene.

Successive Philippine administrations have encountered a string of recurrent problems. Ferdinand Marcos, elected President in 1965, declared Martial Law in 1972, and ruled with a firm hand until political events and long-standing social unrest ended his 20-year rule. In 1986, a four-day bloodless revolution

besieged Corregidor on May 6, 1941, General MacArthur pledged "I shall return" – and he did, on October 20, 1944, with a massive American invasion force.

With the aid of Filipino and American troops who had campaigned as guerrillas during the three-year Japanese occupation, the Americans fought their way back into Manila in February 1945. The Philippines' liberation cost the Filipinos enormous losses in lives and property, but it was greeted with jubilation.

**Left, mural of the country's national heroes.
Above, Cory Aquino amidst "people power."**

installed the hitherto unknown Corazon Aquino, widow of an assassinated opposition leader, as President.

Despite her popularity with the masses, Aquino's presidency has had to deal with a faltering economy, several attempted military coups and terrorist attacks by communist insurgents in Luzon and the Moro National Liberation Front in the south. Yet in the face of awesome obstacles, the Filipino people continue to push bravely and optimistically forward.

In mid-1992, the nation will see a change in leadership when it goes to the polls to elect a new president.

MANILA

The logical place to start on a tour of Manila would be **Fort Santiago**. It is easily reached by taxi from the **Ermita** district, the so-called "tourist belt" where most hotels are.

Manila is bisected by the **Pasig River**, so that most city areas are known to be either north or south of the Pasig. Fort Santiago is situated south, close to where the river empties itself into **Manila Bay**. On this site, four centuries ago, stood the bamboo fortress of Rajah Sulayman, a young warrior who ruled the palisaded city state of about 2,000 inhabitants.

The Spanish conquistador Miguel Lopez de Legazpi arrived in 1571. After a battle, he took over the ruins of Sulayman's fortress which, according to legend, the recalcitrant chieftain razed to the ground upon sensing his impending defeat.

Legazpi founded Spanish Manila that same year, beginning construction of a medieval fortified town that was to become Spain's most durable monument in the East. The city fortress, an expanded version of the original Fort Santiago, and defended by moats and turreted walls 33 feet (10 meters) thick with well-positioned batteries, was called **Intramuros**, or "within the walls."

Four gates connected the Walled City to the outlying boroughs, where lived the *indios* (as the Spaniards called the natives), the *mestizos*, Chinese, Indians and other foreigners, including a number of Spanish commoners. Trade and commerce flourished to such an extent in these suburbs that they soon outstripped the city proper in area and population.

A tour through Intramuros should start from within the inner gate of Fort Santiago, where parapets allow one to walk around the well-preserved walls. A stately building houses the memorabilia of Dr. Jose Rizal, national hero. On another end of the quadrangle is **Rizal's Cell**, where he wrote his farewell poem to his people on the eve of his execution by the Spanish in 1896.

The open-air courtyard beside it is now the **Rajah Sulayman Theater**, where a theater group carries on a season of plays in *Pilipino*.

Across Fort Santiago is the **Manila Cathedral**, an imposing romanesque structure which is constructed of Philippine adobe.

Intramuros' perimeter measured some 2.5 miles (4 km). Following Legazpi's blueprint for the capital, succeeding Spanish governors constructed 18 churches, several chapels, convents, schools, a hospital, a printing press, a university (as early as 1611), palaces for the governor-general and the archbishop, soldiers' barracks and houses for the "in" community. These were laid out over a pattern of streets intersecting at right angles to form 64 blocks within an uneven pentagon served by seven gates.

The single structure spared (miraculously, say some) by the American bombing holocaust of 1945 is the **San Agustin Church and Museum**. Walk down General Luna Street, past the western side of the Cathedral, and after four short blocks you come upon the intersection of General Luna and **Calle Real**, the main street of Intramuros' fabled time. Here, incongruous Chinese lions carved of granite guard the entrance to the church courtyard.

The original structure on this site, built of bamboo and *nipa* (a local palm), was the first church of Intramuros, constructed shortly after Legazpi defeated Sulayman in 1571. Another structure was started in 1599 and completed in 1606, and this is what remains to this day, surviving both natural and man-made calamities which have, at one time or another, leveled other old churches of Manila.

Adjoining the church is the monastery-museum containing a treasure trove of Philippine artifacts and religious art. Here on permanent display are the remains of the vast collection amassed by the Augustinians in their 400 years' work on the islands.

Across the church courtyard is the **Plaza San Luis** complex, a block of reconstructed houses featuring antique galleries, restaurants, a cafe and **Casa**

Preceding pages: Mayon Volcano's gentle symmetry. Left, Roxas Boulevard at night.

Manila, a museum replicating the aristocratic lifestyle at the turn of the century. Cultural presentations are performed in the courtyard and house proper, where costumed actors recreate a day in the life of old Intramuros.

From this area you have several options to continue your tour. You can turn eastward at Calle Real and prowl the remains of Intramuros till you reach **Muralla Street**. Here you can follow the walls or pass through one of the restored gates which will lead you back to the Pasig River or to a plaza called **Liwasang Bonifacio**. On this busy square is a statue of the revolutionary leader Andres Bonifacio. The plaza is bordered by the **Post Office Building** to the north, and to the east the newly-restored **Metropolitan Theater** with its original art deco appointments.

Between these two landmarks is a system of overpasses handling, at all hours, a great bulk of Manila traffic. The left lane leads to **Jones Bridge**, the center lane to **MacArthur Bridge**, and the right one to **Quezon Bridge**. These three bridges are the major passageways across the river, leading to the half of Manila known as "north of the Pasig."

If from San Agustin Church you turn left or westward at Calle Real, you wind up shortly at **Bonifacio Drive**, which leads southwards to Roxas Boulevard by the bay. It's a pleasant stroll along these parts, with the walls of Intramuros rising to your left, its ancient moats now converted into fine lawns and golfing grounds.

Bonifacio Drive ends where Roxas Boulevard begins, at the site of the vast **Rizal Park** formerly known as *Luneta* (or little moon, for its crescent shape), where Rizal was shot in 1896. Towards the right is the grand old **Manila Hotel.** At the central portion of the park is a monument to the hero, the object of much wreath-laying by visiting dignitaries the whole year round. It is under 24-hour guard, and the regular drill maneuvers of the sentries have become an attraction. This spot also has the distinction of being kilometer zero, or the point of reference in land travel

Filipinos partying in traditional dress – the women in *baro't saya* and the men in *barong tagalog*.

throughout the island of Luzon.

Behind the **Rizal Monument** is a series of plaques on which are inscribed Rizal's poem *"Mi Ultimo Adios"* (My Last Farewell) in the original Spanish and in various translations. A marble slab marks the spot where Rizal met his martyr's death by musketry.

The central section where the monument stands is bordered by Roxas Boulevard to the west, Kalaw Street to the south, Orosa Street to the east, and Padre Burgos Street to the north. Close to the Burgos side are the **Japanese Garden** and **Chinese Garden**, which charge token fees for entrance. Here too is the **City Planetarium**, where an audiovisual show is conducted twice daily.

On the Kalaw Street side of the park's central section is the **National Library**. The park's eastern section, across Orosa Street, is dominated by the **Department of Tourism Building**. Travelers may call upon the tourism staffers for guides, books, information and any such assistance. The eastern side is bounded by **Taft Avenue**, clearly the major artery cutting through the Manila "south of the river." Both Burgos and Kalaw streets end up at Taft Avenue. If you follow Burgos you reach the former **Legislative Building**, where the **National Museum** continues to be housed on a temporary basis. Proceeding northward through Taft Avenue, you will pass the **Maharnilad** or Manila City Hall and end up at Liwasang Bonifacio, from where the three bridges give you options for further browsing north of the Pasig.

From Taft, turn right at any of the perpendicular streets beginning with United Nations Avenue, where the Manila Hilton stands. This will lead you to Ermita.

Ermita is an unusual district in many respects; its "tourist belt" reputation is built on the strength of its proximity to Rizal Park and Manila Bay. There is an abundance of hotels and lodging houses in the area, and these in turn attract a conglomeration of eateries, nightspots, beer gardens, boutiques, antique shops, handicraft and curio stalls, and travel

Postcard shows a Manila street scene of old.

M-14 – Escolta, Main Street, Manila, Philippines.

agency offices. The two major streets, narrow enough to necessitate one-way traffic, are the southbound **M.H. del Pilar** and the northbound **A. Mabini**.

Scattered here and there within the area are reputable nightspots featuring Filipino folk singers and rock and jazz groups. Here, still another facet of the Ermita spirit may be glimpsed – the bohemian character of its younger residents. The boundary between the twin districts of Ermita and **Malate**, which is actually **Pedro Gil Street**, remains unobserved, so that the catch-all "Ermita" often stands for both. A number of good restaurants can be found in the area.

A worthwhile stop when in the Ermita area is **Solidaridad Bookstore** on **Padre Faura Street**. It is rich in Filipiniana as well as the latest imported titles and periodicals. It also doubles as an art gallery.

Running parallel to the major Ermita streets is Roxas Boulevard by the bay. Past the Philippine Navy Headquarters on the seaward side of Roxas Boulevard

rises the **Cultural Center of the Philippines,** otherwise known as the CCP Complex. The center, built on reclaimed land, houses two theaters, two art galleries, a museum and a library. Manila Proper ends on Buendia Avenue, past the CCP Complex.

Ninoy Aquino Avenue at boulevard's end leads to the **Manila International Airport** as well as the **Domestic Terminal**. A large Duty Free Emporium is available for arriving and departing passengers. Anyone shopping for lady luck, meanwhile, may visit various casinos located in and around the city. A popular casino is at the **Silahis Hotel** on Roxas Boulevard.

Close to the airport is another favorite tourist haunt, the *Nayong Pilipino* (**Philippine Village**), where the country's regions are represented in miniature in a landscaped village designed to allow visitors a glimpse into the archipelago's attractions and diverse cultures. The **Philippine Museum of Ethnology** is found within the grounds. It showcases the arts and crafts of the minority groups,

The main altar of San Agustin Church in Intramuros.

and is a good bet for buying souvenirs which otherwise may only be made by traveling the length and breadth of the country.

From Ninoy Aquino Avenue you can take a short bus or taxi ride to Makati via the **Epifanio de los Santos Highway** or EDSA. Makati's main street, **Ayala Avenue**, has been dubbed the Philippine Wall Street, being the financial hub of the metropolitan area. Off Ayala Avenue, on Makati Avenue is the **Ayala Museum**. The museum has an outstanding archive and a permanent exhibit of dioramas portraying significant episodes in Philippine history, along with detailed replicas of boats and ships which have plied Philippine waters. An aviary, formerly part of the museum, has now been converted into a park.

From Ayala Avenue's end at the EDSA, you can cross the highway to enter the plush residential village called **Forbes Park**, which continues to enjoy the highest status among the affluent burgher villages in the area. Forbes Park's McKinley Road leads to the **Manila Polo Club** and the **Manila American Memorial Cemetery**, where the remains of 17,000 Allied dead rest below row upon row of unmarked white crosses. The *Libingan ng Mga Bayani* (**Graveyard of Heroes**) is close by with its eternal flame burning by the **Tomb of the Unknown Soldier**.

The half of Manila north of the Pasig does not have as many attractions for the foreigners as the southern side, except for a few landmarks scattered around the residential districts.

Manila's **Chinatown** may be reached by crossing over Jones Bridge from Liwasang Bonifacio. If Quezon Bridge is used, you will wind up immediately at **Quiapo**, an area which has long been considered the heart (some say the armpit) of downtown Manila. Beside the **Quiapo Church** you'll find sidewalk stalls offering herbs and ointments of all persuasions, amulets, candles, religious calendars, local almanacs, flowers and lottery tickets.

Down **Quezon Boulevard** towards **Recto Avenue** is a mercantile strip of

The palm-fringed Roxas Boulevard is popular for its famous Manila Bay sunset.

A FILIPINO FOR ALL SEASONS

Traveling widely through the Philippines, one easily recognizes recurring landmarks. In town after town, the plaza has to include a basketball court, a small concrete stage for political and beauty contests, and a statue of a man revered as the national hero.

The man is Dr. Jose Rizal, born in 1861, whose execution by the Spanish 35 years later provoked the first war of independence launched by an Asian country against a foreign colonizer. In his short life, Jose Rizal earned himself such sobriquets as "The Great Malay" and "Pride of the Malay Race."

He was an artist, sculptor, poet, playwright, novelist, musician, naturalist, scientist, linguist, engineer, doctor, propagandist and above all, a social reformist.

His two novels written in Spanish, *Noli Me*

Tangere (*Touch Me Not*, 1887) and *El Filibusterismo* (*Filibusterism,* 1891) were produced while he nearly starved in Europe spearheading the Filipino propaganda movement. The novels established his reputation as the leading spokesman of the Philippine reform movement. The books, printed with the help of friends overseas, were declared seditious by the Spanish authorities. Satirizing abusive religious and political figures in Spanish officialdom, while also presenting an allegory of latent nationalism about to explode into revolution, the novels were cited as evidence in the mock trial that doomed Rizal.

There were truly many facets of the man, some of them in apparent contrariety. Rizal believed in peaceful reform and rejected the call of revolutionaries for an armed uprising. Against the advice of his parents and friends, he returned home in 1892. On exile in the lonely isle of Dapitan in the Southern Philippines, he turned down a plan to spirit him out. He was content with designing a waterworks system for the town, practicing as an eye doctor, and exploring the countryside for new species of lizards to send to Europe, one of which was named after him.

He was also quite keen on romance, having taken to heart and home Josephine Bracken, daughter of an Irish patient visiting from Hong Kong. Inspired by her, he composed sonatas celebrating their idyllic life in exile. When the Cuban War broke out, he volunteered his services for the medical corps. The authorities allowed him to leave, but in mid-journey he was recalled to face trial for subversion.

On the eve of his execution, he wrote a long poem of farewell to his beloved country (*Ultimo Adios*), then hid it in a gas lamp. He faced his death by musketry with calm and dignity. When the volley was ordered, his last supreme effort was to twist his body around for a last glimpse of his country's sunrise. Such was the intense patriotism of the man to whom generations of Filipinos owe a debt of genius, martyrdom, and inspiration. ∎

One of the many monuments to patriot Jose Rizal.

textile shops, army surplus stores, pawnshops, hole-in-the-wall palmists and astrologers, martial arts schools, bike shops, restaurants and moviehouses. You can turn right at Recto Avenue towards the "university belt," where several institutions disgorge thousands of students daily. Close to where Recto Avenue becomes Mendiola Street is the **San Sebastian Church**, reputedly the only pre-fabricated steel church in the world. Every single piece of its neo-Gothic structure was fabricated in Belgium and shipped here for assembly at the end of the 19th century.

Mendiola Street leads past several private colleges to the **Malacañang Palace**, office-residence of Philippine Presidents. Since the end of the Marcos era, Malacañang has become the top tourist attraction in Manila. Tickets for the hour-long tour are distributed by the Department of Tourism. The tour takes you through the luxurious halls of the Palace, and includes a peek at former President Marcos' study and bedroom, as well as the more lavish accouterments of the former First Lady. A high point of the tour, curiously enough, is the basement where Imelda Marcos kept much of her inordinate wardrobe, including the bulk of her now world-renowned collection of footwear.

Backtracking up Mendiola Street and Recto Avenue, turn at Nicanor Reyes Street and you will shortly find yourself on **España Street** where the large campus of the **University of Santo Tomas** is located. The university antedates Harvard by a good 25 years, having been founded by Dominicans in 1611. It is the oldest university in Asia. The U.S.T., as it is more commonly called, also boasts a library with a rare manuscript collection of 12,000 volumes and a first-rate museum, the nucleus of which is as old as the university itself.

España Street leads straight to the boundary between Manila Proper and **Quezon City**, the country's official capital before its integration into Metro Manila. Where España ends, Quezon City's **Welcome Rotunda** marks the beginning of the former capital's two major thoroughfares. Forking right is

Rodriquez Avenue which leads to **Cubao**, a commercial center whose endearing landmark is the **Araneta Coliseum**, billed in the early '60s as the world's largest domed coliseum.

The other major street, Quezon Avenue, leads straight to the **Capitol Site Rotunda** or **Elliptical Circle**, off which are found a number of government buildings including the **Quezon City Hall** and the **Philippine Heart Center for Asia**. On the last stretch of Quezon Avenue before the circle are **Fr. Aguilar's Zoo** and the **National Parks and Wildlife Grounds**. Within the large rotunda area is the **Quezon Memorial Hall** which contains the memorabilia of Philippine Commonwealth President Manuel Luis Quezon as well as the modest beginnings of a projected Quezon City Museum.

Beyond this circle is **University Avenue,** which leads to the sprawling main campus of the **University of the Philippines.** Here, the air is cooler and the atmosphere has a distinctly laid-back feel to it.

BEYOND MANILA

The usual coach tour itinerary for the short-term Philippine visitor covers day excursions from Manila to Tagaytay to view the Taal Lake and Volcano, Pagsanjan Falls in Laguna to "shoot the rapids," and Corregidor Island at the entrance to Manila Bay.

Tagaytay is a leisurely hour's drive south on a fine highway traversing the verdant countryside of Cavite province. There are three ways to get there from Manila. One is the new Cavite coastal road from the end of Roxas Boulevard, which bypasses the traffic-prone suburbs from Parañaque onwards. Another is to use Quirino Avenue from the airport area, and this is recommended for those wishing to make a stop at the **Las Piñas Church** to see the historic and unique **Bamboo Organ**. The third way is to take the South Superhighway until the turn-off to Carmona.

There are scenic views of **Taal Lake** and **Volcano** from any of several sheds lining **Tagaytay Ridge**, or from several resorts in the area, such as the **Taal Lodge** or **Villa Adelaida**.

At a junction before Tagaytay Ridge, a steep and rough road descends to **Talisay**, a small lakeside town where you can hire a boat to take you across to **Volcano Island**.

Farther south, in Batangas Province, are the popular and picturesque beaches of **Matabungkay** and **Nasugbu**, which offer moderately priced lodging. They are another hour's drive from Tagaytay. A number of specialized resorts catering to diving and other watersports enthusiasts can be found at **Anilao** off **Batangas City**.

The **Calatagan Peninsula** in southwestern Batangas is a wonderfully charming place, with an old Spanish town set in what used to be a single huge *hacienda* and forest preserve. The peninsula has relatively isolated white-sand beaches and an interesting resort called **Punta Baluarte**, hewn out of rocky cliff and reminiscent of Spain's Costa Brava.

On your way back to Manila, detour through the historic towns of Cavite, including **Kawit**, where the former residence of President Emilio Aguinaldo – who declared independence from Spain in 1896 at this site – has been turned into an interesting museum.

Fresh oysters and mussels sell cheaply on Cavite's roadsides. Beach resorts on a modest scale are plentiful in the area. But the top of the line is **Puerto Azul** in **Ternate** town, whose attractions include a spectacular golf course designed by Gary Player, deluxe hotel, charming beach cottages and a full range of watersports facilities.

Pagsanjan is a two-hour drive southeast from Manila, or halfway round the Laguna Bay Loop. The route takes you past the southern lakeside towns, the first of which you'll pass on the South Superhighway from Makati.

Hot spring resorts cluster in the towns of **Los Baños** and **Pansol** on the south shore of the lake. Private roman pools, cottages and picnic huts are the standard features of these resorts.

eft, rafting
y the falls of
agsanjan.
ight,
erapeutic
aters of
aminos'
idden Valley
prings.

Some 25 miles (40 km) before Pagsanjan is **San Pablo City** with its seven miniature lakes. In nearby **Alaminos** town is the popular **Hidden Valley** resort in a lush tropical setting with soda pools, waterfall and giant age-old trees. **Lake Caliraya**, a man-made lake fringed by plush resorts, is close enough to Pagsanjan for a side-trip.

Pagsanjan's name derives from *sanga*, or branch, the town being at the fork of two rivers. A number of resorts and hotels in Pagsanjan offer boatmen's services for upriver rides to the falls. For the more daring, a small cave behind the falls can be reached by a rope-guided raft. The sensation of going under a wall of cold water is sure to stir your spirit of adventure.

Afterwards, with well-timed shoves, the two boatmen skillfully navigate the *banca* (outrigger canoe) downriver past the rocky shallows. It's really no whitewater experience, but an appreciation of a *bangkero's* (boatman's) dexterous talent could make your day. On the way back to Manila is

Calamba, birthplace of Jose Rizal. The old Rizal house on the main street is now a national shrine landscaped with Philippine fruit trees. It's a pure treat to wander through this fragrant garden and then duck indoors to feast your eyes on the opulent appointments of 19th-century Laguna gentry.

Corregidor, a strategic tadpole-shaped island commanding the approach to Manila Bay, can be reached daily by hovercraft and ferry boats from a pier near the CCP Complex in Manila. The Rock, as Corregidor is fondly known, receives many nostalgic visits from World War II veterans and history buffs. A memorial to the Filipino and American war dead stands in a lovely park at the heart of the fortress island.

At a promontory called **Suicide Cliff**, where Japanese soldiers jumped to their deaths rather than accept the changing fortunes of war, a small Buddhist shrine has been set up by Japanese veterans.

A tour of Corregidor will take you through **Malinta Tunnel**, where Fil-American troops mapped out their tactics in the dark summer of 1942, **Battery Way** close to Suicide Cliff on the northwest coast, and the ruins of **Topside Barracks**, sited on a plateau overlooking the Bataan coast across the channel.

Elsewhere on the island are limestone caves where Japanese troops holed up in 1945 while the Allied forces mounted recapture operations to recapture the island .

Corregidor Inn, perched atop a hill in the island's middle, provides panoramic views from a breezy terrace. North across the channel, the rugged coast of Bataan is almost close enough to touch. Turning southward, you aim a curious squint at Cavite's shimmering white coves. Ships glide in and out of the timeless picture.

Bataan: Two hours to the northwest of Manila is **Bagac** in Bataan province, where a white-sand beach and complete watersports facilities are available. Bagac and nearby **Mariveles** were the starting points of the infamous Bataan Death March in 1942, which took a heavier toll among the Allied prisoners

The Bamboo Organ at Las Piñas Church

than the actual combat. The route is traced by several markers along Bataan's east coast.

On the approach to Bagac on the west coast is a **Friendship Tower**. It was erected by a Japanese Buddhist society, with a massive tree trunk serving as clapper to a great bronze bell.

Bataan, like Corregidor, is hallowed ground for the war veteran making a return to the scene of his earlier valor and wartime suffering.

Wreath-laying is a year-round affair. However, the most important speeches are usually reserved for April 9, the date of Bataan's fall. On that day, the president of the Philippines leads a throng of heroes up **Mount Samat**, which was once the site of fierce fighting in 1942 before the Fil-American forces finally capitulated.

Near the summit stands the *Dambana ng Kagitingan* (Shrine of Valor), a massive cross marking a memorial shrine to the war dead. An elevator takes visitors up the cross, from where there is a fine view of Manila Bay on one side and the South China Sea on the other.

North of Bataan is **Zambales** province, a rugged strip of mountains and picturesque coastline that forms a western border to the Central Luzon provinces. The huge American naval base at **Subic Bay** lies near **Olongapo City**. The bay between the two – and the fine coastal stretch from San Antonio to Iba – is lined with beach resorts catering to the ubiquitous American serviceman.

North of Zambales is **Pangasinan** province. The most famous of the province's tourist destinations is the **Hundred Islands** off **Alaminos** town. Ferries depart from the wharf at Barrio Lucap for a collection of isles strewn along the Lingayen Gulf. Only **Quezon Island** has drinking water and overnight lodging.

Pangasinan is also noted for its preponderance of faith healers. They are found mostly in the towns of **Villasis**, **Rosales**, **Asingan** and **Urdaneta** off the MacArthur Highway, which leads from Manila to Baguio City and the Ilocos region.

Ruins of the army barracks at Corregidor Island.

THE ILOCOS REGION

Hugging the northwest coast of Luzon is the fascinating and picturesque **Ilocos Region**. This fertile shore is framed by the dull blue outline of the Cordillera mountain range to the east and the South China Sea to the west, creating a classic situation in which the inhabitants have had to battle both these geographical extremes in order to survive. Under the stern conditions of their environment, the Ilocos people have learned to coax the soil with more skill; mine the open sea with more cunning. Ilocos is the sort of place that breeds tough temperaments and restless souls.

The region doesn't start until you're past the town of **Sison** in Pangasinan province, where the road forks right toward Baguio City, and left to **La Union**, the southernmost of the Ilocos provinces. The capital, **San Fernando**, can be reached in four hours from Manila. Before San Fernando is **Agoo** town at the entrance to La Union where the **Museo Iloko**, a repository of Ilocano artifacts, and the nearby **Agoo Minor Basilica** (Our Lady of Charity Shrine), are worth a stop. First built of *nipa* and bamboo in 1578 by the Franciscans, the shrine was destroyed by an earthquake in 1892 and only recently restored.

Bauang town is 14 miles (23 km) north of Agoo, and from there a 6-mile (10-km) coastal stretch to San Fernando is marked by a series of beach resorts frequented by Baguio visitors and American servicemen.

The former **Marcos Highway** connects Agoo to Baguio, while **Naguilian Highway** does the same for Bauang. Both are an hour's drive from the mountain resort city. Agoo features a park and golf course lorded over by the controversial Marcos Bust, a large cement likeness of the former president.

Once you reach San Fernando, treat yourself to some fresh seafood, including something called "jumping salad" – fresh shrimp cooked with a dash of *calamansi*, a local lime – and fish

Harvesting rice near San Fernando in Vigan.

kinilaw, chunks of raw fish steeped in vinegar spiced with shallots and chilis.

Past San Fernando, on the **Maharlika Highway** that hugs the Ilocos coastline, the old churches at San Juan and Balaoan are worthwhile stops. Fine woven blankets and handcrafted *bolos*, or machetes, the best in the region, are sold on the roadsides of **Bangar** town.

The next province, **Ilocos Sur**, is known for its charming old churches. The church at **Sta Maria** squats on a hill. The leaning belltower has become more noteworthy than the main edifice, having figured in important scenes of a classic Filipino movie from the early 1950s. Six miles (9 km) farther north is **Santa**, where a small church with a pure white facade and slight greenish tint stands close by the sea, ringed by low hills in the background. The neo-Gothic church at **Bantay** stands on a vast elevated plaza commanding a good view of the surrounding area.

Between Sta Maria and Santa, a smaller highway forks right and climbs the mountains toward **Bangued**, capital of Abra Province, the least developed part of the Ilocos region. At Bangued and the nearby valley towns you can pick up some fine handicrafts – small bags and baskets woven from local reeds – produced by a minority group called the Tingguians. The interior of Abra is seldom visited for lack of an extensive road system. **Mapasu Hot Springs**, **Lagayan Caves** and the **Ar-Arbis Waterfalls** are all accessible by car, although the terrain can be tough.

From Bantay, a road veers left off the national highway to enter **Vigan**, the provincial capital. Close to the imposing **Vigan Cathedral** is the birthplace of martyr-priest Father Jose Burgos. The **Burgos House**, a colonial two-story structure, has a good antique collection, iconographic archives and library. A series of paintings depicting scenes from the Basi Revolt of 1807 titillates with its curious imagery set in folk perspective. Fronting the plaza is **St Joseph's Antique Shop**, the most reliable of the capital's numerous dealers in bygone items. **Syquia Mansion**

Ilocos folk celebrate a town fiesta in front of the Bantay church.

in Vigan's *mestizo* quarter is a depository of President Elpido Quirino's memorabilia.

Follow the coastal highway north, passing the interesting baroque churches of **San Vicente**, **Magsingal**, and **Cabugao**. Also of note is the **Magsingal Museum**, a small yet eclectic affair that features items as diverse as Tingguian blowpipes and antique Spanish altar pieces. Two miles (1.5 km) past Cabugao, a side road turns left toward **Pug-os Beach**, an undeveloped large cove with warm placid waters. A few more miles northward and you cross the provincial boundary to **Ilocos Norte**.

The first town is **Badoc** where the **Luna House** calls for a stopover. Exhibited in the reconstructed ancestral house are reproductions of the 19th-century Filipino painter Juan Luna. **Badoc Church** is also worth a visit. But the prime example of the centuries-old churches in the region is to be found in **Paoay**, two towns north. Here the **Paoay Church** is a real stunner, a successful hybrid creation wedding the strong fea-

tures of "earthquake baroque" (such as massive lateral buttresses) with an exotic oriental quality reminiscent of Javanese temples. Built at the turn of the 18th century, restored and repaired in 1793, it is the most celebrated of all Ilocos churches.

Half a mile (about 1 km) from the town proper is **Paoay Lake**. Overlooking the shores is the **Malacañang Ti Amianan** (Malacañang of the North), Marcos' former resthouse which has now been converted into a highlight of the Ilocos' tour attractions. About 9 miles (14 km) farther up the coast is **San Nicolas**, home of the traditional Ilocos *burnay* jars. Primitive glazing adds to the homely charm of these squat, strong earthenware jars.

Farther north is **Laoag City**, the provincial capital. **Laoag Cathedral**, dating back to the 16th century, is another notable example of "earthquake baroque" architecture. A road leads east from Laoag to **Sarrat**, birthplace of Ferdinand Marcos, where the **Marcos Museum** houses family memorabilia, including the four-poster bed where the controversial Great Ilocano was born, the clock beside it set to the exact hour and minute of his birth. The **Sta Monica Church and Convent** in Sarrat, connected by a massive bridge-staircase, are well-preserved specimens of colonial architecture.

Continuing on the coastal highway you come to **Bacarra**, one of only two places in the Philippines where residents still carve and play the 17-stringed wooden harp for town fiestas. Bacarra is also known for its quake-damaged belltower, which stands a little way from a church whose facade has needlessly suffered from restorative zeal. Outside Baccara are the **La Paz Sand Dunes**.

Cape Bojeador Lighthouse off Burgos town stands over a dramatic coastal expanse of jagged rocks. Some miles past is **Bangui** town, then **Pagudpud** with its little-known but spectacular **Saud Beach**, a long curving stretch of white sand. Shortly beyond you'll have reached the northern coast of Luzon and the road now turns east toward Cagayan province.

Left, the Paoay church is a stunning blend of baroque and oriental architecture. **Right,** relic in wood.

BAGUIO AND THE NORTHERN SKYLAND

Baguio is the summer capital of the Philippines, a mountain resort perched amid pines at more than 5,000 feet (1,500 meters) above sea level. Tragically, much of the city and surrounding region was devastated by a huge earthquake in 1990, and Baguio has yet to recover fully from the destruction.

The first-timer in Baguio city may find a weekend all too brief for making the mandatory rounds of attractions. It is not so much the number of "tourist spots" that will induce you to prolong your stay, but the sense of leisure that comes inevitably with the first invigorating whiff of pine air. With an average temperature of 65°F (18°C), clean parks and lovely gardens, winding roads set against a backdrop of rugged mountain ranges, Baguio offers a fine respite from the lowland dust, heat and bustle. Not a few visitors have decried Baguio's commercialism, but most transients would agree that Baguio's charms easily offset such a gripe.

Long walks become the most popular form of recreation, the time-honored constitutional being up and down **Session Road** with its mainstreet gamut of commercial shops. At the lower, northern end of Session Road, you can cross over to the bountiful **Baguio Market** for highland fruits and vegetables, seafood from the coastal towns an hour away, fresh mushrooms, jams, handicrafts and army surplus goods. Alternatively, you may take the left fork towards **Burnham Park**, where you can relax on a bench under a weeping willow, or watch the lovers boating in the lagoon.

Driving around in Baguio without a proper map can become a frustrating experience, unless you're casually airing your driving skills or are naturally predisposed to winding mazes. Getting somewhere seems easier by cab or any of the drab-looking jeepneys clustered

Hilltops serve as playground for local kids.

186

on the side streets of Session Road. They follow regular routes, but are inclined to take you on a "short trip" to any part of the city for a set fee. Cabs can also take you to any point, even to the relatively far reaches of the city proper like **San Carlos Heights** off Naguilian Road for a spectacular view of the sunset over the Pangasinan coastline, or **Mount Santo Tomas** where a radar station competes with the view of the China Sea in the distance.

Between these two points, located west and southwest of the city center respectively, may be found the **Lourdes Grotto** perched above 225 steps where devotees test their zeal and heart condition, and farther on, a woodcarving village on the way to **Asin Hot Springs**.

North of the city center down **Bokawkan Road** is the **Easter Weaving Room** where native cloth and curio items sell for bargain prices. Weavers at work are an attraction for camera bugs. Farther north down **Magsaysay Avenue**, some 10 minutes' drive from the downtown area is **Bell Temple**, an edifice of gracious lines bedecked with dragons and Chinese ornamentalia. It is open to visitors during certain hours. Its priests, who practice a blend of Buddhism, Taoism, Confucianism and Christianity, are inclined to cast fortunes for the curious.

In the northeast part of the city, down **Leonard Wood Road**, you'll find the former Botanical Garden now named **Chion Park**. A replica of an *Igorot* village (*Igorot* being the blanket term for the diverse ethnic groupings in the mountain provinces) has been structured with prototypes of native architecture representing the different mountain tribes. These are ringed by handicraft and silver jewelry shops.

Farther up is **Mansion House**, summer residence of Philippine presidents. Fronting it is **Wright Park**, featuring the **Pool of the Pines**, the end of which overlooks a riding field with horses for hire. Up Gibraltar Road and into Torres Street you come upon another cluster of souvenir shops across **Mines View Park**, a familiar image for having be-

Vegetable seller at Baguio market.

come *the* classic Baguio postcard. It is really just a viewdeck overlooking Baguio's mineral bowl. Children in a nearby gully have made it a tradition to call out for coins, which you toss over and they scamper in the brush for.

South of Mansion House is the **Baguio Country Club**, and past it the former John Hay Air Base, now a government-run resort. A cute stop within the rolling manicured grounds is the **Cemetery of Negativism**, a series of mock tombstones depicting characteristic loser types, with witty epitaphs suggesting that the visitor bury his negative vibes here.

Accommodation is no problem in Baguio City except during Holy Week, the high point of the summer excursion time when the city's population of some 200,000 is nearly quadrupled. A listing of lodging places, a map of the city, and other pertinent information are available at the local Tourism office at **Governor Pack Road** connected to the southern end of Session Road.

Baguio also serves as the gateway to several points of interest in the Cordillera region. The most popular destinations are Bontoc which is six hours away, Banawe which is two hours further, and Sagada which is just off Bontoc. All points to the north are reached through the **Halsema Highway**, a rugged but pleasantly scenic road carved out of the mountainside. An expansion of the old mountain trail, it offers vistas of the Grand Cordillera chain at every turn, reaching elevations of more than 7,000 feet (2,120 meters) at certain points.

Buses leave early in the morning. Sixty-two miles (100 km) from Baguio, the road ascends to **Mount Data**, a lumber town often enshrouded by mist and an eerie quiet faintly hinting at Olympian settings.

Some two hours further are **Bontoc** and **Sagada**, the latter reached by forking off the highway at a junction before Bontoc. Much of the charm and coziness lacking in Bontoc, the provincial capital, can be found in Sagada which is popular with foreign backpackers for its cool climate, pretty scenery, interesting hiking trails, caves, ponds and falls.

Nestling on a low valley by the **Chico River**, Bontoc is much warmer in the daytime, and has a somewhat harsh-looking trading post exterior. The **Bontoc Museum** is an interesting stopover, however. From Bontoc, you can take the early morning bus to Banawe to view the famous **Banawe Rice Terraces**. From Banawe, you may travel directly back to Manila without passing the same route through Baguio.

Also worth a sojourn is **Kabay-an** about four hours' drive from Baguio. Nearby is **Mount Pulag**, the highest peak in Luzon and a sacred mountain to the Igorots. But Kabay-an is more famous for its burial caves where 500-year-old mummies are kept. Unlike their Egyptian counterparts, the cadavers are not wrapped in gauze but are naked with geometric tattoos still visible on the skin. Some of the mummies are displayed in the town hall, but most are found in man-made burial caves on the outskirts of town, like **Banagao Mummy Cave** and **Tenongchol Burial Rock**.

Left, Ifugao woman with tattoos on her hands, a symbol of womanhood, and headband of snake vertebrae. Right, Batad village tucked in the midst of rice terraces.

THE VISAYAS

Hanging like a necklace of odd-shaped beads strung together by various geographical threads, the **Visayan Islands** of Central Philippines lend themselves perfectly to the sort of languid exploration that is perhaps more identifiable with the South Pacific. People from Luzon, when asked about these islands, generally point to the slower pace, the seductive lilt of Visayan speech and the sensuous local women.

Travel through the Visayas is best done by sea. Only then can you share in the islanders' immemorial sense of the dubious qualities of speed. Jets will take you from Manila to Cebu and most other Visayan capitals in less than an hour. But the impression is simply of having been whisked from one Filipino city to another, not having savored the interim plentitude, the subtleties of transition that can only be achieved with the proper kowtows to distance.

Samar: This large island lies opposite the southern tip of Luzon and can easily be reached from Manila via the Maharlika Highway and a brief ferry. The first landfall on Samar is the town of **Allen** with its nearby hot springs. The main roads wind along the northern coast to **Catarman**, capital of Northern Samar province. Several interesting waterfalls are found in the interior of this part of the island, but reaching them requires considerable hiking through roadless terrain.

In the southwest corner of the island is the **San Juanico Bridge**, the longest in the Philippines, linking Samar to adjacent Leyte Island. Near the approach to the bridge is **Basey** town, known for the **Sohotan National Park** and several other natural wonders.

Leyte: The trading center of the Eastern Visayas is **Tacloban**, capital of Leyte Province. The **Capitol Building** features in bas-relief a scene of General Douglas MacArthur's historic landing in 1945, while the actual site is marked by the **Leyte Landing Marker** a few miles south of town on Red Beach. Not far away is the **Sto Nino Shrine and Heritage Museum**, a repository of art and antiquities assembled by native daughter Imelda Marcos.

Cebu: A major destination in the Philippines is **Cebu City** – the "Queen City of the South" – capital of Cebu province and second only to Manila in terms of trade and commerce. It's the hub of all activities in the Visayan region. Normally, one flies from Manila to Cebu's Mactan International Airport. The alternative is a 14-hour sea journey.

The small island of **Mactan**, connected by bridge to the Cebu mainland, is of historical importance. Ferdinand Magellan landed here in 1521 during the first circumnavigation of the globe, but the Spanish explorer was killed at the hands of Chief Lapulapu during the Battle of Mactan. The **Magellan Monument** erected in 1886 marks the spot where he died on the beach, while the **Lapulapu Monument** stands at the plaza fronting the **Lapulapu City Hall**.

Mactan's beach resorts cater to hordes of foreign visitors, especially during the

Left, lighting up at the *Ati-Atihan* festival, one more excuse to have a good time. **Right**, lazing around on Tambuli Beach in Cebu.

peak season of July and August. Among the better beaches are **Costabella** and **Tambuli**. A top divers' destination is **Olango Island**, on the far side of Mactan.

Magellan left a large wooden cross to commemorate the Philippine's first encounter with the West. **Magellan's Cross** is now Cebu's most important historical landmark, the remnants encased within a black cross of of *tindalo* wood and housed in a kiosk on Upper Magallanes Street in Cebu City.

Close by, on San Juan Street, is **San Agustin Church**, built in 1565 to house the country's oldest religious relic, the *Image of the Holy Child Jesus* presented by Magellan to Queen Juana of Cebu upon her conversion to Christianity. One of Legazpi's men found the image intact some 40 years later when Spain resumed its colonization. The church is now known as the *Basilica Minore of Santo Nino*, its conversion ordered by the Pope in 1965 in recognition of its importance and that of Cebu City as the cradle of Christianity in the Far East.

Near the waterfront is **Fort San Pedro**, started by Legazpi in 1565. Finally completed in 1738, the triangular bastion stood close to the sea to serve as a lookout against Muslim marauders from Mindanao. The Department of Tourism office is within the fort, a favorite promenade ground.

Close to the fort is **Colon Street**, the oldest street in the Philippines. This part of town is called the **Parian district**, the city's original Chinatown. The Chinese community is very much in evidence in Cebu and is largely responsible for its continued growth as an industrial and commercial center. Among the more interesting cultural attractions within the city are **Casa Gorordo** (which replicates turn-of-the-century aristocratic lifestyles), the **University of San Carlos Museum**, **Jumalon's Family Cultural Project** (which displays fascinating lepido-mosaic art utilizing butterfly wings as medium) and the **Medalle Collection of Old Cebu Photographs**.

Bohol: A 20-minute flight southeast of Mactan is **Bohol Island**, which for its relatively small size has much to offer in

A piece of Magellan's cross is encased in a larger one in Cebu City's history kiosk.

ATI-ATIHAN

Filipinos know how to throw a good party, which means the islands are endowed with more than their fair share of fiestas and festivals, holy days and holidays. But the third week in January is a red letter day in the country's crowded festival calendar. A ceremonial catharsis for more and more Filipinos who flock to Kalibo town in Aklan province on the island of Panay to celebrate the most spirited of all annual events: the *Ati-Atihan Festival*.

Ati-Atihan is three days of organized chaos, a soot-black orgy wherein disparate images from myth and media, box office and boob tube, childhood nightmares and the Catholic Church march through the streets of Kalibo in a laundry day of the Filipino subconscious.

By 10 a.m. in the morning on each festival day, the whole of the town has turned out on the streets, mingling with the plane- and boatloads of tourists. Everyone has blackened their faces with soot. The first layers of the drunken haze have already settled in. Drumbeats pound at the sea breeze like a vibrating sonar field. Frenzy rises thick in the noonday heat. Congolese warriors engage in mock battle with Spanish *caballeros*. Cowgirls wiggle a *salsa* with King Kong. A Japanese lion dancer corners a tipsy burlesque queen.

The festival traces its origins to two events in Kalibohon history. One was a 13th-century real estate deal that transpired after a dozen *datus* fled a tyrant in their native Borneo and bartered for land in Panay. After initial mistrust, the indigenous Ati aborigines exchanged their ancestral lowlands for gold. Overjoyed, the Borneans threw a humorous feast for their new neighbors, blackening their faces with soot to become a shade closer to the dark pygmy hue.

The other event transpired four or five centuries later. The now Christianized people of Panay lived in constant fear of looting and

slave-hunting pirates from Mindanao. In the chaos of one such raid, the Christ Child is said to have appeared and driven off the marauders. This miracle persuaded the Kalibohons to time their harvest festival on the feast of Santo Nino in late January.

Kalibo's *Ati-Atihan* has become so popular that similar festivals have cropped up through the Western Visayas. Antique province has launched its own "*Binirayan*" and "*Handugan*" festivals. Iloilo City has recently been staging a more lavish and choreographed edition called "*Dinagyang*," and Bacolod City is also starting

to mount its own. All the new versions have something or other to do with the landing of the Bornean *datus* on Panay and their subsequent barter with the aborigines. In fact, the *Ati-Atihan* fever has spread as far north as Manila, where bastardized versions are performed in Ermita's "tourist belt" and at a resort hotel on the city's outskirts.

Ibajay, northwest of Kalibo, claims a more pristine if modest interpretation - the townsfolk alleging that the original *Ati-Atihan* took place in their community when the small black Atis came down from the hills to celebrate with the descendants of the *datus*. ∎

Fire-breathing reveler at the Ati-Atihan Festival, Panay Island.

terms of historical and natural attractions. Legazpi anchored briefly off the island in 1563 and is recorded to have sealed a blood compact with a native chieftain named Sikatuna. The **Blood Compact Marker** commemorates the site a few miles from the capital, **Tagbilaran City**. A good road system traverses the entire island. Bohol's coastline is marked by a fascinating array of picturesque coves and clean white-sand beaches.

Four miles (7 km) from Tagbilaran is **Baclayon Church**, the oldest stone church in the country. Built in 1595, it has an interesting museum housing a rich collection of religious relics, vestments, icons and old librettos of church music printed in Latin on animal skins. Off the south coast of Bohol is **Balicasag Island**, a marine reserve and favorite scuba diving spot.

North of Tagbilaran is the old **Punta Cruz Watchtower** in **Maribojoc**, and farther up, **Calape Church** with its reputedly miraculous image of the Virgin. A visit to the inland town of **Antequera** on an early Sunday morning will allow you a pick of the cheap handicrafts woven of vine, reed and grass.

But Bohol's most famous attraction – with which in fact the island has become synonymous – is a unique panorama in the vicinity of **Carmen**, a town 34 miles (55 km) northeast of Tagbilaran. Here several hundred haycock hills formed by limestone, shale and sandstone rise some 100 feet (30 meters) above the flat terrain. These are the **Chocolate Hills** of Bohol, so-called for the confectionary spectacle that unfolds at the height of summer when their sparse grass cover turns dry and brown.

Negros: To the west of Cebu is a much larger island called Negros. You can either take a direct sea connection from Cebu City to Bacolod or Dumaguete in Negros, or a combination of bus and ferry across the Tanon Strait.

Dumaguete City, the capital of Negros Oriental province, is a small college town built around the prestigious Protestant-run **Silliman University**. Fine swimming and snorkeling beaches dot the coastline north and south of town. Offshore is **Siquijor Island**, long considered the center of sorcery in the Southern Philippines. There are some 50 *mananambals* or folk healers on the tiny island, classified as "white" or "black" sorcerers depending on the nature of their abilities.

Dominating the northwest shore is **Bacolod City**, capital of Negros Occidental province. It has its fair share of hotels, restaurants and shopping malls, but points of interest do not go beyond several fine antique collections, ceramic shops and weaving centers producing *hablon* fabric.

North of Bacolod is charming **Silay City** with quaint old houses recalling the Castilian past. The **Hofilena Art Collection** includes the works of Dr. Jose Rizal and turn-of-the-century Filipino masters Juan Luna and Felix Hidalgo, plus a few paintings by Picasso and Goya. Farther north is the **Chapel of the Angry Christ** within the Vicmico Compound, with its psychedelic mural and mosaic of pop bottles depicting an irate Jesus with the saints

Bohol's "Chocolate Hills" turn into a confectionery spectacle in the summer.

depicted by Filipinos in native dress.

Panay: From Bacolod, it's two hours by ferry to **Iloilo City** on Panay Island. At the mouth of the harbor is **Fort San Pedro**, built by the Spanish to defend against the Muslims, as well as the British and Dutch who made repeated incursions into the Visayas at the turn of the 17th century.

The **Museo ng Iloilo** (Iloilo Museum) on Bonifacio Drive showcases prehistoric artifacts dug from the many burial sites around Panay. Two miles (3 km) outside town is the village of **Molo** where the **Tiongco Antique Collection** is a must for pottery lovers. The churches in the towns around Iloilo City are all fascinating specimens of colonial architecture. The most celebrated is the **Miagao Fortress Church**. A squat, sturdy structure, it has a beautifully ornate facade featuring native flora in relief carving.

On the north coast of Panay is **Roxas City**. There isn't much of interest in the town, but the coast on either side is rich fishing ground. Close by is **Pa-nay** town, with coral reefs offshore and a village church with marble floors and 10-foot (3-meter) thick walls of white coral.

The interior is decorated with scupltured *retablos* (altar pieces) of silver and hardwood.

Boracay: No one outside the Philippines had ever heard of this tiny island until a couple of years ago. Now Boracay is a mecca for young overland travelers and strung-out Western executives from Hong Kong and Manila. Opposite the northwest tip of Panay, the island is a place of pristine beauty where beaches are great, the eats cheap and the electricity is on for only a few hours each day.

Romblon: Lying close to the northwest coast of Panay is a group of 20 islands that form **Romblon Province**, a name that has become synonymous with marble. Stalls full of marble items crowd the waterfront. Coffee tables made from solid marble are the most expensive, but there are also chess pieces, mortars, eggs, ashtrays, paperweights, candleholders and more. Many of the items are expertly designed and carved.

Miagao Fortress Church is a splendid example of colonial church architecture.

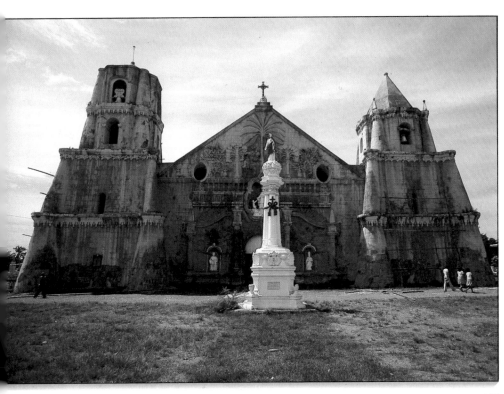

MINDANAO

South of the Visayas is **Mindanao**, the second largest island in the Philippines and the most southerly of the 11 large islands. Mindanao is big on superlatives: the rarest eagle in the world (the Philippines money-eating eagle); the largest city on the earth in terms of area (Davao); one of the planet's most expensive shells (*Gloria Maris*); the richest nickel deposits (Surigao del Norte); and one of the world's most obscure tribes (the Tasaday).

Of irregular shape, Mindanao comprises five major peninsulas and five major mountain systems, some of volcanic origin. The island has an extremely long coastline, and more than two-thirds of the terrain is covered by forest. Mindanao has an abundance of minerals including copper, silver, gold, coal, limestone and 72 percent of the Philippines' iron ore reserves. It is also rich in agriculture, producing more pineapples, corn, coffee and copra then any other island in the archipelago. And if that isn't enough, the waters around the island are also blessed with an abundance of colorful corals, spectacular shells and giant fish.

Perhaps more than anything else, Mindanao is known as the Muslim enclave of the largely Catholic Philippines. By the time Miguel de Legazpi and the Spanish arrived in 1565, the entire region was bowing toward Mecca. Indeed, only the arrival of the conquistadores halted the northern drive of Islam through the entire archipelago. The Spaniards called the Muslim people of the south "Moros" – after the Arabs whom they had recently driven from southern Spain – and that epithet still applies today.

As a result of a 1989 referendum, four provinces in Muslim Mindanao (Maguindanao, Tawi-Tawi, Sulu and Lanao Del Sur) formed the Mindanao Autonomous Region, an autonomous Muslim state under Filipino sovereignty.

Zamboanga City: Situated at the southern tip of the most western of

Mindanao's arms is **Zamboanga**, a charming city known for its rich Castilian heritage and lovely gardens. But more than anything, the *vinta* sailboats of the Badjao and Samal (Sea Gypsy) peoples are a symbol of this southern city. With their multi-colored sails, the boats are much in evidence in the bay, as the Badjao and Samal sell resplendent *pandanus* mats and shell and coral items directly from their watercraft.

Immediately behind the wharf lies **Plaza Pershing**, named after the general who was the first American governor of Moro country. The quasi-Baroque **City Hall**, completed in 1907, stands southeast of the plaza and houses the post office. A short way down Calderros Street is the **Lantaka Hotel** where the Department of Tourism offices are located. You might try *curacha* crab, a Zamboangan culinary specialty, on the seaside terrace at the Lantaka.

A 25-minute boat ride from the hotel takes you to **Santa Cruz Island** with its pinkish-white sands. On the island corals and shells are sold at markets and

eft,
Muslim boy
looking
casual in a
room filled
with brass
collectibles.
Right,
King Faisal
Mosque.

shops in town. The seafaring Samal people have a graveyard here. Strange that only in death do they go ashore.

Just past the hotel is **Fort Pilar**, its 3-foot (one-meter) thick coral walls overgrown with moss. A bronze plaque at the eastern gate tells not only its dramatic story, but much of the colorful history of Mindanao. Originally built in 1635, the fort has been a bastion through the centuries against Muslim, Dutch, British and Portuguese attacks. Built into the eastern wall is the open-air shrine of the patron saint of Zamboanga, the Lady of Del Pilar.

A few hundred yards to the east of the fort is a large Samal water village called **Rio Hondo** which – fortunately for residents, but sadly for tourists – is losing much of its ethnic charm. Urban renewal is making its mark. Gone are the tilted *nipa*-palm huts and the zigzag walkways with missing planks. **Taluksangay** is a quieter, more sedate village on stilts, 12 miles (19 km) east of the city center. Notice how the silver dome of the village mosque reflects in the adjacent lagoon.

Davao: The largest city in Mindanao and the third largest in the Philippines, Davao is situated at the head of the Davao Gulf in the southeast quadrant of the island. At the airport, a gaily painted statue in tribal attire holds a durian in one hand. Locals say the figure is a Manobo aborigine, but others claim it's none other than Pinocchio.

Midway between the airport and the city is the **Insular Hotel**, possibly the area's major attraction. Relax over a glass of fresh *tuba* (palm-wine) or stroll through the immaculately kept grounds which have been described as a smaller tropical version of Versailles.

Davao itself has little to offer. The city's 18 colleges and two universities are testimony to the fact that the Philippines has more people pursuing higher education than any other country except the United States. Davao has the largest Chinese population in Mindanao, and there is a beautiful **Buddhist temple** on **Leon Garcia Street**.

Pumpboats can be rented in the harbor

Below left, Fort Pilar is a shrine to Zamboanga's patroness, the Lady of Del Pilar. Below right, natives call Mount Apo "*Sendawa*" or Mountain of Sulfur.

198

for a pleasant one-hour journey across the gulf to the large island of **Samal.** A visit to San Jose village makes an interesting diversion.

Mount Apo: When the weather is right, majestic Mount Apo – the highest peak in the Philippines – can be seen to the south of Davao. Called the "grandfather of Philippine mountains," this dormant volcano stretches to a height of 10,000 feet (3,000 meters) and covers an area of 188,000 acres (76,000 hectares).

Although there is no recorded eruption, the jagged crater walls are mute testimony to ancient activity. Locals believe the mountain is the sacred abode of two gods, Apo and Mandargan, and that landslides are caused by the latter in order to satisfy his lust for human sacrifice. The best time to climb Apo is April and early May. Allot four days for the trek, which is tiring rather than trying, delightful rather than difficult.

North Coast: At about the middle of the island's north shore is **Cagayan de Oro**, a city of innumerable banks and government offices, as well as a superb harbor.

This large sprawling city is bisected by the Cagayan River, on the banks of which is **San Agustin Cathedral** and **Lourdes College**. Nearby is **Xavier University**, which boasts an excellent small museum with archaeological relics, Hispanic antiquities, tribal artifacts and a shell collection.

About halfway between Cagayan de Oro and Butuan City is the port of **Balingoan**, from where you can board a ferry for **Camiguin Island.** Beachcombers and lovers will find this place absolutely irresistible. Dominating the landscape is the volcanic peak of **Hibok-Hibok**.

Iligan City is an uninteresting but prosperous town that owes much of its wealth to hydroelectric power. Six miles (9 km) south of town are the **Maria Christina Falls**, the most beautiful and the tallest in the country at more than 170 feet (58 meters). More superlatives are in store at **Lake Lanao** – 23 miles (37 km) due south of Iligan City – which is the second largest and deepest lake in the Philippines.

THE MARGINAL ISLANDS

Popular destinations for the beach and underwater fancier include several out-of-the-way places in the marginal islands, especially Marinduque, Mindoro and Palawan.

Marinduque, an isolated volcanic mass surrounded by coral reefs, lies between Mindoro and the Bondoc Peninsula of Quezon province on Luzon. According to legend, the island rose from the sea as a consequence of a tragic love story that bears resemblance to *Romeo and Juliet*.

During Holy Week, the island comes alive with the famed *Moriones Festival*. Residents don masks and garb themselves as Roman soldiers to enact a vivid and uniquely Filipino rendition of the Passion of Christ. On Good Friday, a masked Jesus emerges from a fortress-like church in the village of **Boac** and leads a mournful procession up a hill to his crucifixion. Old women wander about in black veils with leafy wreaths on their heads, while flagellants whip themselves with great fervor. The festival reaches its climax on Easter Sunday as a one-eyed Roman centurion named Longinus leads a "rebellion" through Boac before he is "beheaded" before a milling crowd on a platform next to the river.

A favorite among budget travelers and beach freaks is **Puerto Galera** on **Mindoro Island**. The area is known for its coral beaches, tranquil seascapes, artifact collections and the famous **University of the Philippines Zoological Undersea Garden**. But word of mouth has made Puerto Galera such an "in" place in recent years that fears have risen that it may soon be spoiled. Mindoro's close proximity to Manila is both a boon and bane. Puerto Galera can be reached from the capital via a two-hour bus ride to Batangas City and then another two-hour ride by ferry across the Verde Island Passage.

Off the northeast tip of Mindoro is the **Lubang Island** group with an excep-

Mindoro's coral beaches.

tional array of beaches and coves. The waters here are a favorite for sports fishermen. Down on the southwest coast is the town of **San Jose**, from where it's a 30-minute pumpboat ride to three small islands that can turn the head of the most jaded beach fanatic. Six hours by pumpboat from San Jose is the fabulous **Apo Reef**, reputedly the best dive spot in the country.

Palawan's position, 420 miles (672 km) southwest of Manila, has made it the destination of choice for those wishing to take a break from the pace of urban life. There are daily flights from Manila to Puerto Princesa, or take the twice-weekly ferry which stops off at Coron in the Calamianes.

Situated near the middle of the eastern coast, **Puerto Princesa** is both the island's capital and the hub of travel to other parts of the Palawan group. Roads branch out from the town to other ports, from where further travel is done in coast-hugging boats.

It's about 38 miles (60 km) from Puerto Princesa to **Baheli** town, and then three hours by boat to the famous **St Paul's Subterranean National Park**. Marble cliffs tower over a dome-shaped, cathedral-like chamber that leads to the 5-mile (8-km) long Underground River. **Quezon** town is a five-hour drive to the southwest of Puerto Princesa. From here it's just a half hour by boat to the **Tabon Caves**, a huge complex of some 200 caverns of which only 29 have been explored by archaeologists since their discovery in 1962.

Close to the northern tip of the island is **El Nido Resort**, perhaps the poshest resort in all the Philippines. Charter flights from Manila can take you directly to this exquisite and exclusive playground. El Nido boasts secluded coves, emerald lagoons leading to secret caves, untouched coral reefs and exotic tropical fish that feed out of your hand.

Nearby, towering black marble cliffs provide the swiftlet with enough nooks and crannies on which to build its nest – much fancied by gourmets as the key ingredient to *nido* (bird's nest soup, a popular Asian tonic).

SINGAPORE: THE LION CITY

Visitors to Singapore wishing to sample some of the mystique associated with its founder Sir Stamford Raffles will find a choice awaiting them.

They can of course stay at the legendary and newly refurbished Raffles Hotel, home of the *Singapore Sling* and the epitome of colonial charm. Alternatively, they can walk next door to "Raffles City" where the 73-story Westin Stamford, the world's highest hotel, (746 feet/226 meters), stands in all its ultra high-tech aluminum splendor.

The contrast between the two hotels brings out in tangible form what has been said about this 238-square-mile (616-square-km) island with just over 3 million people so many times that it has become a cliché – that Singapore is an exciting amalgam of the East and West, old and new.

Though more than three-quarters of its population is Chinese, Singapore's official language is English and it is so widely understood that the visitor can use it to order snake soup in Chinatown or French cuisine at Maxim's.

Besides its Chinatown, Singapore also boasts a Little India, an Arab Street and Geylang, where Malay culture predominates.

Visitors from the West are pleasantly surprised to find superclean taxis driven by cabbies who don't expect a tip and a gastronomical paradise they can enjoy without ever having to worry about what may be in the water. The tree-lined roads are invariably the cleanest anywhere and the epithet "Garden City" is aptly named for Singapore, whose well-planned public housing system and island-wide parks are justifiably lauded by urban planners around the world.

A few blinkered people from the developed countries, fed on wartime tales about an exotic, sin-filled Singapore, are surprised to find that trishaws are no longer that common or that, far from being filled with opium dens, Singapore actually has one of the toughest drug control laws in the world. There are also some self-appointed *cognoscenti* of world travel who, on the basis of a few travel articles, have concluded that there is nothing to Singapore except sterile skyscrapers and shopping centers.

A more detailed look would reveal that the Singapore of today remains as interesting a place as it was in the past, if not more so. It is still very much an Asian society, one that represents the descendants of three great cultures from Asia.

Stone and concrete monuments have their appeal, as do mechanically-created theme parks that purport to show us the future. But nothing beats the lively and dynamic fusion of the past and the present in a living society. And nowhere is this global drama of old societies and values changing into the present and peeking into the future as easily or as comfortably viewed as from Singapore.

Preceding pages: the impressive and frequently-changing Singapore skyline. **Left,** Raffles immortalized at the site of his historic landing.

When Sir Stamford Raffles, one of the few British colonial pioneers with both vision and a scholarly mind, set foot on Singapore in 1819, he did so with the conviction that the island, located at the crossroads of the South China Sea, would one day become an important port.

But the history of Singapore does not begin with the arrival of Raffles. The Malay Annals record that Singapore derives its name from *Singa*, which means lion. Since the animal was not normally found in these parts, we can only conclude that the anecdote of a Malay prince naming the city after sighting the beast in the island belongs to that realm of history generously mixed with mythology.

The first written records of Singapore's history begin around the 13th century and chronicle the island passing through the hands of various regional empires. The Thai kings, the Javanese and even the Chola kings from far-away India seemed to have invaded and controlled Singapore for various periods.

The mighty Majapahit empire that was centered in what is modern-day Indonesia brought Singapore under its control in the early part of the 15th century. But they went on to develop Malacca, farther north in Malaya, into a big port and Singapore became an obscure fishing village until the landing of Raffles in January, 1819. Raffles himself spent only a year in Singapore but after his arrival, Singapore's population had grown to 5,000 and the first official census in 1824 showed an increase to 11,000.

Despite a lack of lions, there was no shortage of tigers. Records indicate that in the 1850s, when immigrants tried to clear the thick jungle covering the island to make way for commercial crops, as many as 300 people were killed by tigers. But under a combined onslaught by the multitudes of immigrants, the jungles were soon cleared and Singapore emerged as a thriving trading port, becoming one of the most important trading posts of the British empire before the end of the 19th century.

The main items of trade were tea and silk from China, timber from Malaya and spices from Indonesia. The colony also imported opium and fabrics from India as well as English-manufactured goods from Britain.

Singapore's free port status attracted many merchants and its development was accelerated to such a pace that it soon overtook much older British colonial ports in the region, such as Penang and Bencoolen in Sumatra. Its commerce and reputation grew by leaps and bounds with the arrival of thousands of Chinese and Indian immigrants in the later part of the 19th century.

World War I did not affect Singapore

directly and in fact it was a time of great prosperity for the island as it was enjoying the fruits of the Malayan rubber boom.

The war did cause the German community in Singapore to be ostracized by the colony's British administration. There was also a revolt by some of the Indian soldiers stationed in Singapore, incited by an underground Indian independence movement and the German secret service. But the British were able to suppress the revolt in a few days with the help of the Japanese, who were at that time allied with the British.

By 1911, the population of Singapore had grown to 250,000 and the census recorded 48 races speaking 54 languages in the island.

The Great Depression that gripped the West in the late 1920s had its reverberations in Singapore too as the prices of commodities such as rubber collapsed. But even in its relative poverty, Singapore was secure as the greatest naval base of the British empire, east of Suez.

That security was rudely shattered when the Japanese invaded Malaya in 1941. Rather than confront British naval might from the sea, the Japanese landed in North Malaya on December 8 of that year and advanced down the peninsula towards Singapore.

Despite an appeal by Winston Churchill to the local governor to fight to the "bitter end,"

Malaya and made it into a Crown Colony. The returning British also had to face problems from the Communist Party of Malaya in both Singapore and Malaya. With the assumption of emergency powers, however, the Communist challenge was contained.

But as older residents of Singapore, including many of its senior political leaders, have testified, the Japanese occupation taught Singaporeans the unreliability of depending on Britain or anyone else for their protection. That lesson eventually led to an independent Singapore which was not willing to depend on any external powers for its protection.

Sensing the post-occupation mood, the British in 1948 allowed a limited form of

the British administration in Singapore surrendered on February 8, 1942.

The Japanese renamed Singapore *Syonan*, "Light of the South." Under their occupation many civilians, particularly the Chinese, suffered unspeakable hardships.

The commerce of Singapore died down and the population had to cultivate tapioca in their backyards to survive. The Japanese three-and-a-half years' rule ended in August, 1945 with the landing of Allied troops.

The British then separated Singapore from

Left, Sir Thomas Stamford Raffles. **Above**, early 20th-century photograph of Raffles Place.

elections to the legislative council. But it was only in 1955 that full elections were held and self-government was granted to Singapore.

As befitting the polyglot nature of Singapore, a descendant of Iraqi Jews and a brilliant British-trained lawyer, David Marshall, became Singapore's first chief minister. Marshall remained in power for less than a year and the chief minister who followed him, Lim Yew Hock, negotiated for full self-government under a new constitution in 1959.

The dramatic changes that propelled Singapore from a sleepy colonial port into the metropolis it is today are due largely to the party that came to power in the elections of 1959, the People's Action Party (PAP) and the man who led it, Lee Kuan Yew, who was to become the country's prime minister.

First, the PAP had to fight tooth and nail to convince Chinese Singaporeans, many of whom were under Communist influence in those days, that their destiny lay with joining the proposed Federation of Malaysia that would be dominated by the Malays.

The Communists too thought that the destiny of Singapore lay with Malaya but they denounced as an imperialist plot, the British proposals to join not just Malaya and Singapore but also North Borneo and Sarawak into one federation to be known as Malaysia.

leadership to a young technocrat named Goh Chok Tong. Yet Lee will always be considered the man who steered Singapore through her toughest times.

Few thought that Singapore had a chance to survive for long, let alone prosper. The skeptics had facts on their side. Singapore had a population that was booming and few natural resources. The British troops and their dependants, who at one time numbered 100,000 and provided employment to thousands of Singaporeans, were scheduled to leave for good. But, in the face of adversity, Singapore succeeded even beyond the expectations of its well-wishers.

The only real resource Singapore has be-

The PAP was able to persuade Singaporeans to overcome their primordial loyalties and in an historic referendum, they voted to join Malaysia in September 1963. But differences between the leaders of Malaysia and Singapore became serious enough for a separation and Singapore became an independent nation on August 9, 1965.

Singapore has now weathered more than a quarter century of independence, during which time it has made a relatively smooth transition from third to first worlds. At the national helm for most of those years was Lee Kuan Yew, who resigned as prime minister in late 1990, passing the mantle of

sides its people is the deepwater port that lies in one of the busiest trading routes of the world, at the entrance to the Straits of Malacca. Oil from the Middle East to Japan, minerals from Australia to Europe, manufactured goods from Europe and the U.S. all find it convenient to pass through Singaporean waters.

But the leaders of Singapore felt that the port alone was not enough to employ a burgeoning labor force of about one million. They set out to scour the developed nations for industrial investment in the republic and cleared the formerly marshy land of Jurong in the island's west coast for ready-made factories that were leased to industrialists who arrived.

Labor laws were tightened, making strikes more difficult under the premise that it is better to employ people, even under low wages, than to drive away foreign investment with demands for high wages.

The government also set about building affordable highrise apartments in an ambitious public housing development program. A compulsory savings scheme was also introduced. About one-quarter of every wage earner's salary is automatically deducted and individually credited into the government-sponsored pension fund, the Central Provident Fund (CPF).

The government considers Western-style welfare benefits as anti-work ethic and an anathema. You can, however, use your CPF funds to buy an apartment or a house. The government finds this a good way to house the population as well as to give citizens of immigrant origin a real stake in the future of the country. National service was introduced for all males over 18 and this, more than anything else, has been responsible for the development of the "Singaporean identity."

Trying to point out how difficult it was to

Above, showing the flag during National Day celebrations.

have built a "Singaporean identity" at all, the present Prime Minister Goh Chok Tong said there are Singaporeans alive today who have undergone four changes in nationality. Before the Japanese occupation they were British "subjects." They then became Japanese subjects under occupation, only to be British subjects again after liberation. They became Malaysians in 1963 and Singaporeans again in 1965. The prime minister added that he hoped Singaporeans would not have to change nationalities again.

Despite its recent turbulent history, Singaporeans bear very few emotional scars of the past. They generally look to the future rather than live with the bitter memories of the past. The Japanese, British, and most other nationalities are equally welcome in the Singapore of today which, despite its free enterprise economy, maintains diplomatic relations with most Communist states and has a thriving trade with them.

The Singapore government does not believe there are things that cannot be planned for. With slogans such as "Make Courtesy Our Way of Life," "Speak Mandarin," "Keep Singapore Clean," and medical benefits that favor the less fecund, it has succeeded so well in controlling the population that this country, which once used to worry about how to provide employment to its people, now has to import foreign labor. A nation that had to build in a frenzy to put a roof over the multitudes is now saddled with excess capacity in everything from luxury condominiums to highrise office space.

The fear that Singaporeans of various races would drift apart has receded into distant memory. The nation now confronts the problem of how to preserve the traces of old ethnic cultures for tourists who are disappointed to find a Singaporean who is not "native" or "colorful" enough to meet their preconceived notions.

Singaporeans of the next generation will confront a different set of problems. They will have to deal not with problems of over-population, shortages and poverty, but declining birthrates, excess capacity and maintaining a strict work ethic that has been softened by a comfortable and secure lifestyle.

There is no doubt, however, that more than a few developing nations would like to swap Singapore's problems of affluence with their own problems of poverty.

A nation o

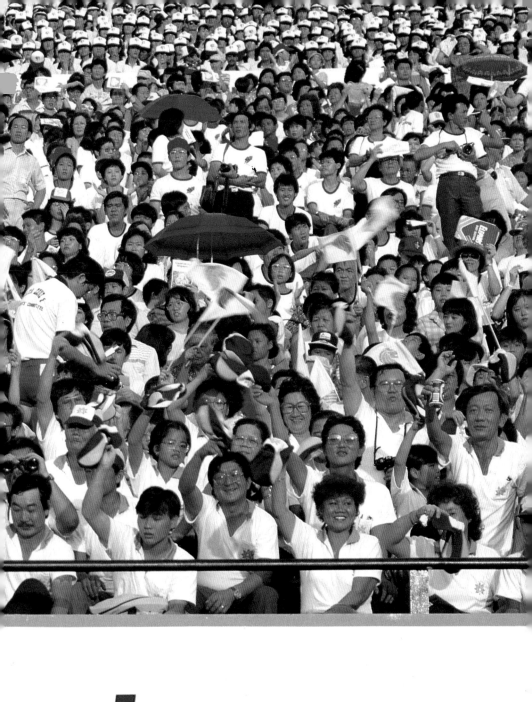

the move

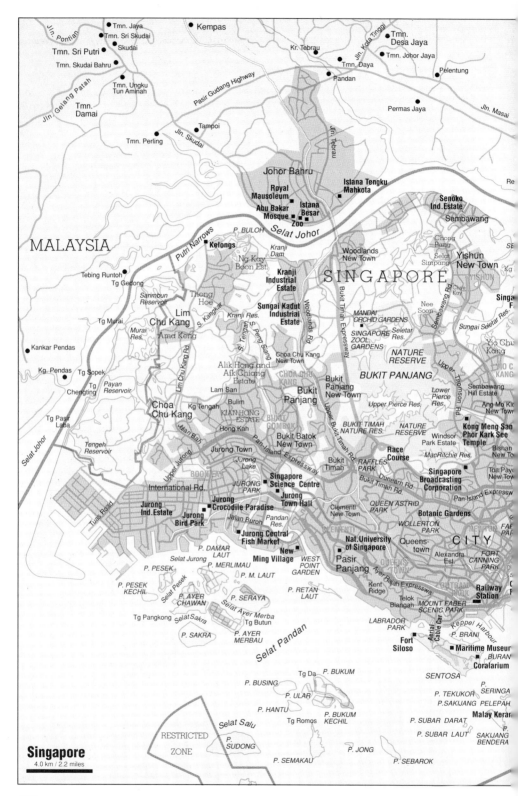

Singapore

4.0 km / 2.2 miles

212

Kong Kong

MALAYSIA

Kg. Tg. Langsat

sai

asai

Kg. Pasir
Gudang

Kg. Ayer
Biru   Pasir

Kg. Puteh

hor

Tg Tajam

Tg Punggol

Kelongs

Tg Balai

to PULAU TEKONG

P. SERANGOON

PULAU UBIN

Kg Melaya

S. Punggol

Punggol

P. KETAM   Tg Jelutong

Tg Chek Jawa

Kg Serangoon
Kechill

CHANGI BEACH
PARK

kang

Serangoon Harbo

Changi

S. Serang

Pasir Ris
New Town

Kelongs

ngoon

Kg Teban

Kg Loyang   **Ind. Estate**

Loyang

ougang
ew Town   Fish
Farming Est. Hun Yeang

PASIR RIS

Kg Tampines

**Changi
International
Airport**

Tampines Rd.

Yan
Kit

**Changi
Prison**

rocodile Farm

Tampines
New Town

Tampines
Expressway

Est.

Kg Batak   Bedok
Res.

Ho Tong Jen
Estate

Kg Bugis

Somapah
Changi

Pan-Island Expressway

Airport Boulevard

Changi Coast Road

eft

Kg Landang

Kg Reteh

Simpang
Bedok

S. Bedok

Kg Pachitan

Sims Avenue

Opera Est.

BEDOK

Bedok

Katong

**Nat. Inst.
of Commerce**

East Coast Parkway

Straits   of   Singapore

Sea View
Park

EAST COAST
PARK

HUDC Chalets

arium

MARINE PARADE
PARK

MALAYSIA

Selat Johor

Tg Renggam

P. UNUM

Tg Todak

Pulau
Tekong
Res.

Tg Balai

Kg Salabin

P. TEKONG
KECHIL

Kg Pahang

Kg Ayer
Samak Darat

Kg Pasir

Tg Chek Jawa   Tg Ladang

Kg Ladang

PULAU TEKONG

Kg Sanyongkong

CHANGI BEACH
PARK

Tg Batu Koyak

Kg Batu Koyok

Pulau Tekong

At its most elemental, Singapore is but a modest lump of rock and soil thrust up from tropical seas, an island of 238 square miles (616 square km) not much larger than the city of Chicago. But overlaid on this geological foundation is a more dynamic topology, of which glass-and-steel towers are only the most visible and schematic signs. Behind the scenes, government and private enterprise conduct an orchestra of automation that makes Singapore one of the world's most efficient societies. Buses roar, container cranes groan, mercury lamps hum, computer drives whirr and elevators whisper in a cacophony of high-tech wizardry.

But there is a third element that is even more complex, one which pervades this island, nation and city from its basalt heart to its chrome exterior – the people, their culture, their moods, their eccentricities and their charms. To wander around Singapore is to wander through a mosaic of cultures and histories and their respective artifacts. Sometimes a seemingly inconsequential decision – to turn down a Chinatown alley, for example – can quite dramatically plunge the visitor into another century or civilization.

It is these recurring apogees, this visual and visceral contrast, that makes Singapore such a treat. In this, the island epitomizes the modern Asia; despite the shade cast by 20th-century skyscrapers, Singapore's ancient and venerable culture refuses to fade away.

The Colonial Heart: Directly at the center of action in Singapore is a huge, flat green space called the **Padang**. The word means "plain" in Malay, which is exactly what this area was when the British first arrived. It was the only dry spot on what was then a swampy waterfront and it quickly became the fulcrum for European society.

Arranged around the Padang in the so-called "Historic District" are memories of the colonial era that so shaped this city-state. The steps leading up to the Greek columns of the neoclassical **City Hall** (1929) are where Lord Louis Mountbatten accepted the Japanese surrender in 1945. The magistrates still don powdered wigs for proceedings in the **Supreme Court** (1939) next door. On the green itself is the old but very active **Singapore Cricket Club**.

St Andrew's Cathedral (1862) on Coleman Street sits in the middle of its own large green. Raffles himself designated this site for the original church, later replaced by the early English Gothic structure still standing today. Inside the cathedral, sunlight pierces stained-glass windows, cascading hazy pastels over the dark wooden pews and hassocks. Church bells cast by the makers of Big Ben peal above a congregation of more than a thousand worshipers.

Just beyond are three other historic churches. The **Cathedral of the Good Shepherd** (1846) at the intersection of Queen Street and Bras Basah Road is the oldest place of Roman Catholic worship in Singapore. Older still is the **Armenian Church** (1835) on Hill Street, funded by the once-thriving Armenian community.

Two of those immigrants, the Sarkies brothers, built what is unquestionably Singapore's most famous colonial building – **Raffles Hotel** – at the junction of Bras Basah and Beach roads. Established in 1887, the hotel quickly blossomed into the flower of Victorian society. Over the years it has played host to kings and queens, presidents and prime ministers, and to literary giants like Somerset Maugham, Joseph Conrad and Rudyard Kipling.

Yet equally, the area around the Padang also reveal the glittering facade of modern Singapore. Dominating the district is massive **Raffles City**, which boasts the world's highest hotel in the 70-story Westin Stamford. To the south is the stark brown profile of **Marina Square**, the city's largest shopping center and hotel complex. And rising between the two is gargantuan **Suntec City**, which will embrace the Singapore Convention and Exhibition Center when completed in the late '90s.

Preceding pages: nationalistic fervor on display. Below left, the Westin Stamford Hotel towers over the Padang. Below right, the Supreme Court.

Between the Padang and the Singapore River is a trio of superb colonial buildings. **Parliament House** (1827) started life as the mansion of a wealthy merchant, and later served as a courthouse before it became the seat of Singapore's post-independence government in 1965. The adjacent **Victoria Theater** dates from the 1860s and is now the venue for drama, dance and music. Next to the river is **Empress Place**, a former government office building recently converted into a cultural complex with restaurants, shops, art gallery and an upstairs hall that is hosting an ongoing series of art and history exhibits from the best museums in mainland China.

On the quay behind Empress Place is a monument to **Sir Stamford Raffles**, on the spot where he first set foot in Singapore in 1819. The view across the river from this spot is remarkable for its summation of old and new Singapore in a single glimpse. Spanning the river is **Cavenagh Bridge**, now given over to pedestrians and bicycles. An elegant iron structure built in Scotland, it still has an old sign that forbids bullock carts from crossing.

On the western bank of the Singapore River is the bustling **Financial District**, Most of the colonial-era buildings here have been replaced by the glass-and-steel hulks of modern banks and corporate headquarters. The largest collection of skyscrapers are along **Shenton Way** and around **Raffles Place**. The triangular OUB Center is tallest at 918 feet (280 meters), the maximum allowable height of buildings in Singapore.

Still history survives in nooks and crannies. The **Telok Ayer Market** at Shenton Way and Cross Street is a Victorian wrought-iron masterpiece, originally built in Scotland in the 1890s, shipped halfway around the globe and re-assembled on the Singapore waterfront. Recent renovation has brought it back to life. Two Art Deco structures that have survived the building boom are the **Fullerton Building** and the **Bank of China Building** on Boat Quay.

Farther along, **Boat Quay** is lined with old shophouses and godowns, the ware-

Elgin Bridge spans the Singapore River.

houses that once stored goods offloaded from small and medium-sized trading vessels. The river itself was once choked with lumbering bumboats, but these were forced downstream into **Marina Bay** in the late 1970s as part of a comprehensive government drive to clean up the Singapore River. However, you can still catch a cruise from Boat Quay on the half dozen bumboats that have been converted into river tour boats. Upstream beyond Coleman Bridge is **Clarke Quay**, another huge area of godowns that has been earmarked for renovation.

At the confluence of the Singapore River and Marina Bay is the **Merlion** statue, a half-lion, half-fish that has become a symbol of modern Singapore. Nearby, **Clifford Pier** is a hive of activity. Here you can catch ferries to Batam and Bintan islands in the nearby Riau Archipelago of Indonesia (often visible from the Singapore waterfront) or negotiate with wizened old captains over the price of a bumboat trip to the outer islands. **Change Alley** behind is a depressing skeleton of its former self.

The large landfill area on the opposite side of the bay is **Marina South**, a multipurpose recreation area with bowling alleys, tennis and squash courts, driving range and yacht club, plus a bustling hawker center and a cluster of upmarket restaurants called **Marina Village**. But this entire area is earmarked for an expansion of the highrise profile of the central business district, once the land settles in about 20 years.

More reminders of the colonial past can be found in the **Tanjong Pagar Conservation Area**, a recently refurbished district of old buildings that lies in the triangle bounded by Neil, Craig and Tanjong Pagar roads. The several hundred historic shophouses in this area were completely gutted (except for their facades) and rebuilt from the ground up with modern fixtures. Since the first phase of renovation was completed in 1990, Tanjong Pagar has evolved into a district of trendy restaurants, bars and antique shops that is especially lively after dark.

The Port: Schooners and clipper ships

Old buildings given a new look in the Conservation Area.

used to pull right into Marina Bay. But that was in the days before mega-ships and steel containers. Nowadays the "big league" port activity is farther west along the waterfront at **Tanjong Pagar Terminal**. Most shipping activity goes on behind closed doors, so those interested in a firsthand look at the bustling harbor and the enormous stacks of colorful containers may want to take a harbor cruise from Clifford Pier.

Tanjong Pagar is the largest and most active of Singapore's port facilities. How appropriate that it should thrive on the site that Raffles handpicked for his new port when he claimed Singapore for the British Empire in 1819. It seemed the perfect place: quick access to the strategic Straits of Malacca, which connects the South China Sea to the Indian Ocean. Raffles decreed his port open to all maritime nations. More than 300 international shipping lines still take advantage of that decree.

At any one time, more than 400 ships weigh anchor in the harbor in a maritime panorama that stretches to the horizon. One arrives or departs roughly every 10 minutes. Four tons of cargo are hoisted onto or offloaded from a ship every second, every day of the year. Such is the frenzy of activity that Singapore surpassed Hong Kong and Rotterdam as the world's busiest container port in 1990. Singapore's lead will increase with the opening of the new Brani Island Container Terminal by the end of the '90s.

Besides its function as a container port, Singapore has also grown into the region's largest shipbuilding and repair center, a major feeder port and a financial and insurance center for shipping. The port is also a major staging post for oil exploration (in Sumatra and the South China Sea), the location of Southeast Asia's largest collection of oil refineries and the home base for a large international merchant fleet. Today, giant 300,000-ton supertankers and container ships dominate the scene, leaving the bumboats to bob in their wake as they plough through the shimmering waters of Singapore Harbor.

At sunset, the PSA container port is still a hive of activity.

ORCHARD ROAD

There's no other street in Asia quite like **Orchard Road**. This is the shopping and entertainment heart of Singapore, but, with a plethora of hotels, it's also a mecca of tourist activity. Orchard Road is at its luminous best during the Christmas period, when it becomes an "electric avenue" of flashing lights and decorations to usher in the festive season.

Numerous hotels, shopping centers, cinemas and department stores line Orchard Road, as well as **Scotts Road** and **Tanglin Road** which join it. In addition, the boulevard is served by three Mass Rapid Transit (MRT) stations: Dhoby Ghaut, Somerset and Orchard.

Nightclubs of the Chinese and Western variety are readily available in the Orchard Road area, so bar-hoppers will have no great distance to travel. They tend to alternate between DJs and live bands, and it should be pointed out that drinks aren't cheap. Almost everyone is well aware that the "sin" in Singapore has been largely eliminated since independence. It's no longer the raucous port city it was once. Therefore those looking for pleasures of the flesh would do better in Manila or Bangkok. But positive aspects of the cleanup include the absence of the sleaze and crime that normally accompanies the world's oldest profession. Still, if you're desperate for a thrill, check out the transvestites that prowl the sidewalks of Orchard Road in the early hours of the morning.

At the top end of the Orchard Road corridor is **Tanglin Shopping Centre**, a beehive of antique shops and souvenir stalls, silk salesmen and carpet dealers. It's a good place to compare prices for various items. The nightclubs on the top floor are some of Singapore's more highly-spirited after dark venues.

Around the corner on Orchard Road is the new **Forum The Shopping Mall**, with Singapore's biggest toy and electronics shops. Directly behind in Cuscaden Road is the rowdy **Hard Rock Cafe**, a bastion of loud music and hardy food in the best American tradition.

Orchard Tower is another place with lively nightlife scenes, ranging from the now legendary **Top Ten** disco to a smokey country-western bar called **Ginivy** where the Filipino band sounds straight out of Nashville.

Among the more important names in this area is **Tang's**, the big building with the green Chinese-style roof at the corner of Orchard and Scott roads. This one-time Chinese curio store has been transformed over the years into a huge department store selling everything from Western appliances and fashions, to Chinese silks and handicrafts.

Up Scotts Road are a number of large hotels and the eclectic **Scotts Shopping Centre**. **Brannigan's** pub in the basement of the Hyatt Regency is Singapore's closest thing to a traditional American "fern bar" with lots of singles to mix it up. Near the junction of Scotts and Stevens roads are two of the city's more exclusive venues, the ultra-modern **American Club** and the venerable **Tanglin Club**. A further 10-minute walk down Scotts Road will bring you to the

THE SPICE(S) OF LIFE

One can never overestimate the importance of eating to Asians. With such a diversity of ethnic backgrounds, it is not surprising that Singaporean taste buds have been honed to a highly refined and discriminating level.

It is possible to find much of what Singapore offers elsewhere, but nowhere else can one find in one place such a variety of food at such reasonable prices.

As visitors to China and India will tell you, you can get better Chinese and Indian food in Singapore than in the countries of origin themselves. After all, gourmet eating is a function of affluence and Singaporeans are certainly affluent by Asian standards.

complex on reclaimed land at the mouth of Marina Bay. The selection ranges through Chinese, Malay, Indonesian and even Thai food. The Newton Circus hawker stalls are popular at night, especially after midnight, while those along the Boat Quay are favorites with lunchtime office crowds.

Seafood prepared the Singapore way, grilled or barbecued with spices, is usually an instant hit with visitors. Chili crab – fresh crabs on the shell, stirfried with garlic, sugar, soy sauce, tomato sauce, chilies and eggs – has already garnered a place in the Singapore foodhall of fame. Do not be afraid to ask for the dishes to be modified to your tastes with less spices if that is the way

But it is the area of "informal" dining that Singapore really excels. Eating Singapore-style at "hawker stalls" is a must. The seats and cutlery may be basic but the food is clean and tasty. Among the more popular items are chicken rice (much more exciting than it sounds!), *satay* (local kebabs), *mee goreng* (fried noodles), *rojak* (local salad) and desserts like *ice kachang* (shaved ice with an assortment of fillings topped with syrup) and *goreng pisang* (banana fritters).

One of Singapore's largest hawker center is at Marina South, a sprawling

you prefer it. A wide selection of seafood can be found at the UDMC Seafood Center.

Those who value air-conditioned comfort and proper cutlery over the native charm of hawker stalls will find no shortage of upmarket restaurants serving Chinese food from the various regions, including Cantonese, Szechuan, Peking and Teochew cuisine.

One particular variation worthy of trying by those who prefer lighter meals is *dim sum* (literally "touching the heart"). Served at lunch and as a brunch during weekends, *dim sum* is a series of light snacks that is washed down with cups of Chinese tea.

Hawker food can be a fiery affair.

popular **Newton Circus** hawker center, where you can sample many of the culinary delights of the Orient.

About halfway down Orchard Road is a relic of old Singapore, a cluster of old buildings that have been renovated into modern shops and restaurants with more than their fair share of charm. The most prominent is **Peranakan Place**, which features a pleasant outdoor cafe and **Bibi's** a bar with an atmosphere redolent of turn-of-the-century Singapore. At the rear is a small but fascinating **museum** that showcases a unique segment of local history. The museum is set up like a typical Peranakan home of a hundred years ago. Peranakans are descendants of early Chinese immigrants who have absorbed indigenous Malay influence into their language, cuisine and customs.

Behind Peranakan Place is **Emerald Hill**, a little gem of a street that has its own special restaurants and shops. Farther up the hill, commercial gives way to residential, as many of the old shophouses have been refurbished for residential purposes. A bit farther down Orchard Road is **Cuppage Terrace**, another row of antique shophouses, with several sidewalk cafes and a popular jazz club called **The Saxophone**.

Some of the largest shopping malls in Singapore can be found along the lower section of Orchard Road. **Centrepoint** boasts a whole floor of bookshops and **Robinson's** department store, no longer a store appealing to the colonial British but to anyone looking for good buys. Robinson's sales are the stuff of legend along local housewives. Near the end of the road is the massive **Plaza Singapura** mall.

Well-concealed behind the highrise facade of Orchard Road is the **Istana**, the official residence of Singapore's president. Its extensive gardens were once part of a nutmeg plantation, while the mansion, built in 1869, served as the home of Singapore's British governor. The Istana is normally closed to visitors, except for a number of public holidays when the gardens are open to the general public.

Straits Chinese traditions live on at the Peranakan Place.

ETHNIC ENCLAVES

When Sir Stamford Raffles alighted in Singapore in 1819, he meant to leave nothing to chance in establishing the trading colony of his vision. Thus, the growth of the town was meticulously planned, and each of Singapore's major racial and cultural groups was alloted its own section of the new city. "European Town" is now the area around Raffles Hotel and the Padang. "Chinese Kampong" became Chinatown. "Arab Kampong is now the district around Arab Street, while the adjacent "Bugis Kampong" has recently seen new life as a historic conservation area.

Chinatown: Though it may at first seem odd to have one in a city where three-quarters of the population is of Chinese origin, the Chinatown in Singapore has a certain something the rest of the city is lacking. The main part of Chinatown fits into a neat little square bounded by New Bridge Road and South Bridge Road, but the district also spills over into Club Street and Telok Ayer Street closer to the Financial District.

In a way, Chinatown has always been the heart of Singapore. Although the Malays were the island's first inhabitants and the Tamils the first traders to stop here, it was the 19th-century explosion of Chinese immigration that set the foundation for turning Singapore into the metropolis it is today. Many of these first Chinese worked as coolies and lived in appallingly crowded conditions. One early 20th-century census counted more than 18,000 Chinese living in just the few blocks of Chinatown – an astounding one person for every 2-foot by 4-foot (1.2 meter) patch of land.

Things have thinned out considerably since then. The vast majority of the island's population is now housed in towering apartment complexes and new towns on the edge of the central city. Chinatown, in its key position between the center of government along the river and the center of finance and trade along the bay, has been steadily squeezed down and crowded out by skyscrapers.

Yet the Chinatown that lingers is a sight to behold. It still largely comprises two- and three-story Victorian shophouses, the ground floor flung open by day to expose an offering of tropical fruit and cold drinks, baskets of dried seafood, joss sticks and carved deities. Overhead, the day's laundry is draped over bamboo poles so that it dries in the sun. The buildings show their age – the tiled or corrugated tin roofs are patched in places with sheets of tar paper, and ferns sprout from the eaves and downspouts – but the district is being renovated block by block to insure that it's around for generations to come.

At 14B Trengganu Street in Chinatown is the **Chinaman Scholars Gallery**, a small museum dedicated to traditional Chinese life in Singapore. The gallery is a "living museum" of the 1920s and '30s with kitchen, living, dining and sleeping areas decorated and furnished as they would have been at that time. There are also collections of old photographs and Chinese musical instruments.

Left, pain is transcended as Hindu devotees fulfill their vows during Thaipusam. Right, tourists can have their names written on good-luck scrolls in Chinatown.

Chinatown is endowed with an amazing array of religious shrines. Perhaps the most stunning landmark in the district is the **Sri Mariamman Temple** on South Bridge Road, the oldest Hindu temple in Singapore. As soon as an industrious Indian laborer named Narayana Pillai stepped off Raffles' ship in 1819, he set about finding the best site for a temple. What he founded has since blossomed into an other-worldly shrine of Hindu deities peering down on devotees. The temple hosts an annual fire walking festival called *Thimithi* in which the participants run across a pit filled with burning embers.

Of the half dozen Buddhist temples in Chinatown, the most outstanding is the **Thian Hock Keng** (Temple of Heavenly Happiness) on Telok Ayer Street. This is Singapore's oldest place of Chinese worship, founded in the 1820s as a modest joss house on what was then the waterfront. Chinese sailors used the temple as a place to offer thanks for a safe journey. Once a refuge for fresh immigrants from Fukien province in China, the temple retains an old world charm that cannot be found in the larger and more modern Chinese temples.

Just down the street is **Nagore Durgha Shrine**, a light green building with twin minarets built in the late 1820s by Muslim immigrants from India. In the other direction up Telok Ayer Street is the **Al-Abrar Mosque**, opened in 1855 by the same Indian Muslims.

Across New Bridge Road from Chinatown is a modern yet slightly downtrodden building called the **People's Park Complex**. This warren of shops, stalls and sidewalk vendors is the closest thing Singapore has to Hong Kong's Stanley Market or the Weekend Market in Bangkok. Lots of cheap clothes and electronic goods.

Two of the more noteworthy Buddhist temples in Singapore are outside Chinatown. Among all deities touching the hearts of the Singapore Chinese is Kuan Yin – the Goddess of Mercy – and for that reason the **Kuan Yin Temple** on Waterloo Street is one of the island's most popular places of worship. Legend

Below left, the goddess Kali tramples in the Sri Veeramakaliamman Temple. **Below right,** Muslim ladies wear a head shawl when praying.

has it that Kuan Yin spurned entry to heaven upon hearing cries of anguish from the earth and returned to work for the alleviation of human suffering. The temple itself is quite modest. Decorations are scarce: instead of gilded wooden beams and antique lanterns, the ceiling is covered with coils of incense.

Siong Lim Temple is on Kim Keat Road in Toa Payoh, near the center of the island. The name means "Twin Grove of the Lotus Mountain Buddhist Temple." It was built in 1908 by two wealthy Hokkien businessmen as the most grandiose of Singapore's Buddhist shrines. The entrance is guarded by imposing statues of the bodyguards of the gates of Heaven. But the inner sanctum is a serene place where the Laughing Buddha and the merciful goddess Kuan Yin reign. The temple's sagging roofs, upturned eaves and twisting woodwork will appeal to students of traditional Chinese architecture.

Little India: Bounded by Serangoon Road, Jalan Besar, the Rochor Canal and Syed Alwi Road, Little India is a bustling neighborhood of peddlers, shopkeepers and the best curry cooks this side of Calcutta. Along the sidewalks here, you can buy *saris* of all colors, garlands made from jasmine or artificial flowers, posters of various deities and spices. Dozens of renovated and restored shophouses comprise a pleasant venue for the sale of Indian items and the enjoyment of Indian cuisine.

Along **Serangoon Road**, the smells are of tumeric, cardamon, coriander and cumin – the ingredients of curry. The raw spices are sold by the kilo from huge baskets lined with plastic. If cooking the dishes at home isn't your thing, you can walk over to **Race Course Road** to sample the spices in fishhead curry, the local specialty, or the many vegetarian dishes on offer.

Little India claims a number of interesting temples. The **Sri Srinivasa Perumal** Hindu temple on Serangoon Road is capped by a 65-foot (20-meter) *gopuram* gateway encrusted with elaborate carvings depicting the five manifestations of Vishnu.

The Temple of A Thousand Lights has the aura of a Siamese wat.

Just behind on Race Course Road is the **Sakya Muni Buddha Gaya**, the so-called "Temple of a Thousand Lights." For a small donation, the worshiper may illuminate the thousands of tiny electric bulbs that border a great nimbus enclosing a 50-foot (15-meter), 600-ton Buddha image. What distinguishes the temple is its personal touch. The shrine was built many years ago by a Thai monk named Vutthisasara. Later he added finer relics, including a mother-of-pearl replica of the Buddha's footprint and a piece of bark from the sacred Bodhi tree in India.

Another fascinating Hindu shrine is the **Chettiar Temple** on Tank Road. Built in the 1850s by Chettiar Indians, money-lenders by trade, the original temple was demolished in 1984 to make way for the present masterpiece of Indian craftsmanship. There is an awesome 75-foot (23-meter) high *gopuram* gateway and a spectacular ceiling decorated with lotus petals, chandeliers and glass panels. Chettiar Temple is the scene of the culmination of the mesmerizing

Thaipusam festival in January or February, and the joyful *Navarathi* (Nine Nights) festival in October when traditional Indian music fills the temple precinct each evening.

Kampong Glam: In Sir Stamford Raffles' original town plan for Singapore, this was the Muslim district. Although hemmed in by highrise, the *kampung* retains much of its bygone charm. The most famous thoroughfare in this district is **Arab Street**, once a center for Middle Eastern traders but now a quaint street where basket, rugs and cloth by the bolt are offered for sale. At the center of the district is a dilapidated palace called the **Istana Kampong Glam**.

The shimmering golden domes of **Sultan Mosque** on Muscat Street can be seen miles away. Raffles donated $3,000 to help the Sultan of Johor build the first mosque on this site, but the original building came tumbling down 100 years later to make way for the opulent domes and spires of the present shrine. This is still Singapore's largest mosque and the focus of *Hari Raya* celebrations after *Ramadan* each year.

Slightly to the west of Kampong Glam is Singapore's infamous **Bugis Street**, once known to sailors and soldiers the world over for some of the raunchiest and most raucous nightlife this side of Pearl Harbor. The lane was especially notorious for its transvestites and transsexuals. Bugis Street was bulldozed in the mid-1980s to make way for the MRT station that bears its name. After an outcry from old patrons around the globe, the government decided to rebuild Bugis in a somewhat more docile form at a nearby site. The new squeaky clean Bugis Street opened in late 1991, with many (but not all) of the old merchants returning.

A couple of miles to the northeast is a much larger Malay neighborhood called **Geylang Serai**, which thrives not on the tourist trade but on business from the Malays themselves. The shops and markets of Geylang are quite lively. Many of the old buildings have so far escaped the wrecking ball. Particularly nice are the old shophouses at the junction of Katong and Dunman roads.

Left, the aroma of spices fills the air in Little India. **Right**, time for quiet study. This Muslim has made a pilgrimge to Mecca and earned the right to wear his white *haji* cap.

PARKS AND GARDENS

One of the most remarkable things about the island of Singapore is that in addition to some of the highest buildings and slickiest highways in this part of the world, it also has some of the most lavish parks and gardens.

Singaporeans are determined to let concrete prevail. Parks, gardens and neatly trimmed hedges border the sidewalks of even the busiest streets. A battalion of gardeners employed by the Ministry of Environment ensure that even the smallest plant is well-manicured and scour the roads in search of fallen leaves.

In fact, nature is handled with such care that very few places remain relatively untouched by the hands of man. Only the water catchment area at the center of the island, the few nature reserves and a couple of the small outlying islands recall the primeval Singapore. In 1990, four of Singapore's more significant green spaces – the Botanic Gardens, Fort Canning Park, Bukit Timah Nature Reserve and the Catchment Area – were combined into a new National Parks system.

Overlooking the central business district is **Fort Canning Hill**, a historic site. The ancient Malays called this place Bukit Larangan or "Forbidden Hill" because it was said to be haunted by the ghosts of prehistoric tombs. Nevertheless, the early rulers of the island built palaces and a powerful fortress on this strategic site overlooking the port. Raffles chose the hill for his private bungalow – later to become Singapore's first Government House – and the British built a battery here in 1859. In the days of the Raj, a cannon was fired from Fort Canning to mark dawn, noon and dusk, while signal flags fluttered to announce ship movements in the harbor.

What the visitor finds today is a Christian cemetery with the graves of early European settlers dating back to the 1820s, and a sacred Malay tomb said to be that of Iskandar Shah, the last

Modern art fronts the entrance to the National Museum.

sultan of Singapura. Massive metal gates, a derelict guardhouse and earthworks are all that remains of the colonial fort.

At the base of Fort Canning Hill is the **National Museum** on Stamford Road. This sumptuous Victorian structure was first opened in 1887 to house an extensive collection of natural history and anthropological items that had been started more than 40 years before by Raffles himself. Today it embraces a number of Asian treasures including the fabulous Haw Par jade collection, ceramics, bronze and stone sculptures, and stone age artifacts. The History of Singapore Gallery has 20 dioramas tracing the history of the island from Raffles' landing to the present while the National Art Gallery showcases the works of prominent local artists.

The **Botanic Gardens** off Holland Road have been in bloom for over a century, although their lineage can be traced back to the 1820s when Sir Stamford Raffles planted an experimental spice garden near his bungalow.

More than half a million species of flowers and plants can be found within its 79 acres (32 hectares), a lush tropical collection that is second only to the Bogor gardens in Indonesia. The landscape ranges from beautifully designed parklands to primary jungle to an Orchid Enclosure with more than 2,500 plants of 250 different hybrids and species.

It was here in 1876 that botanist Dr. Henry Ridley – nicknamed "Mad Ridley" because he once stuffed rubber seedlings into his pockets and went round plantations like a door-to-door salesman begging them to venture a trail – introduced the first Brazilian rubber trees to Southeast Asia from samples brought from Kew Gardens in London. From this humble beginning sprang the Malayan rubber boom.

Jungle walks weave in all directions through **Bukit Timah Nature Reserve**, about 8 miles (12 km) from the city center. The thick tropical vegetation resembles the entire scenery of Singapore when Raffles first arrived. This 148-acre (60-hectare) park plays host to

the island's highest point and a rich collection of local fauna including long-tailed macaque monkeys, flying lemurs, tropical squirrels, civet cats and brilliant forest birds. The snake population includes pythons, tree snakes and poisonous cobras and kraits.

Many of these same creatures live in the vast **Catchment Area** in the middle of the island which includes MacRitchie, Seletar and Pierce reservoirs. Most of the parks comprise lush secondary rainforest, but some areas are landscaped with lawns and picnic areas. The Catchment Area is popular with joggers, walkers and young lovers. On the southern shore of Pierce Reservoir are the undulating fairways and smooth greens of the exclusive **Singapore Island Country Club**.

The **Singapore Zoological Gardens**, regarded as one of the best zoos in the world, has the finest wildlife collection in Southeast Asia. The place bills itself as an "open zoo" – few of the animals are in cages or behind bars. Instead, they wander in free-form enclosures sepa-rated by natural barriers like water and rockwalls. It's hard to imagine a more idyllic setting for the animals.

The zoo specializes in Southeast Asian animals. Among the rare or endangered species are the Komodo dragon (the world's largest lizard), Malay tapir, clouded leopard, Sumatran tiger, Bawean hog deer and the largest group of orangutans in captivity. The polar bear and crocodile exhibits are both state of the art, while the elephant, primate, snake and seal shows stress education as well as entertainment. In the mornings, the zoo offers a rare treat – breakfast with an orangutan. But be sure to book ahead.

Not far from the zoo are the **Mandai Orchid Gardens**. Situated on a gently sloping hillside bounded by secondary jungle, the gardens export three to four million sprays per year to flower shops around the globe. This is one of the world's largest displays of orchids, with exotic names such as *Arachnis*, *Renanthera*, *Aerides* and *Vanda*.

From flowers to fowl. True to Singa-

Below left, out on a limb at Jurong Bird Park. Below right, one of the star attractions at the zoo.

pore's flair for international personalities, the **Jurong Bird Park** is globally oriented. If you haven't seen an Australian emu lay its huge black-spotted eggs, or overheard the giggle of the Indian white-crested laughing thrush, this is the place to come.

The grounds house more than 3,500 birds of nearly 400 species from around the world, including an incomparable collection of Southeast Asian varieties. In the world's largest walk-in aviary, a waterfall cascades into a lush tropical valley where rainbow-colored birds fly free. Day turns to night in the nocturnal house, where you can view rarely seen species such as owls, night herons, frogmouth and New Zealand kiwi bird. While the stunning penguin exhibit transforms equatorial Singapore into the chilly South Pole, the best of the live performances is the "birds of prey" show which features eagles, vultures and other predators.

Sharing the same suburban site as the bird park is the **Jurong Crocodile Paradise**, home to more than 2,500 of the ferocious reptiles. See men – and women – wrestle, pet and even kiss the creatures, or head for the underwater gallery where you can gaze eyeball to eyeball with a fearsome croc. More crocodiles can be found at the **Singapore Crocodilarium** off the East Coast Parkway and at the **Crocodile Farm** on Upper Serangoon Road. But before you go and accuse Singapore of having a reptile fetish, realize that it's nothing more than "shoe" business.

Jurong Park is one of the island's biggest green spaces, a massive park that embraces two golf course, several islands, a river and a lake. Within the grounds is the **Chinese Garden**, based on the design of the Summer Palace gardens in Beijing and with waterside pavilions built in the Sung Dynasty style. You enter the gardens via a traditional tiled archway and gently curving bridge, leading to a nine-tiered pagoda, weeping willows, lotus blossoms and a courtyard with fountains.

Nearby is the equally delightful **Japanese Garden**, billed as one of the

Chinese mythology is relived at the Haw Par Villa.

largest of its sort outside Japan. In trying to communicate the Japanese love for beauty, order and tranquility, the garden is a serene collection of carp-filled ponds, stone lanterns, waterworn stones and exquisite compositions of green.

On the eastern flank of Jurong Park is the popular **Singapore Science Center**, which counts a planetarium, the largest aviation gallery in Asia, and a host of other exhibits that range from nuclear power to human birth. The emphasis here is on education, through computers that test your knowledge, easily understood displays and hands-on exhibits. The museum's **Omni Theater** has a giant IMAX screen with a double bill that includes a short documentary on Singapore history called *Homeland*.

The world of myth and legend is explored at **Haw Par Villa** on Pasir Panjang Road, about halfway between Jurong and the central city. Also known as **Tiger Balm Gardens**, the grounds have recently been transformed into the world's first high-tech, Chinese mythological theme park. Among the new attractions are the popular Wrath of the Gods flume ride, the Tales of China boat ride through the belly of a huge dragon, several multi-media shows featuring lasers and other special effects, and two live shows that include audience participation. But the best thing about the park are the old plaster statues: tableaux of Singapore life in the 1930s and '40s.

Just to the west of the central business district are two hills that have played their own peculiar roles in Singapore history. Crowning the crest of **Telok Blangah Hill** is the handsomely restored **Alkaff Mansion**. Until the 1940s, this was the stately home of a wealthy local family, but they fell on hard times and the mansion sat empty and derelict for nearly 40 years. In 1990, it was saved from its ill fate and transformed into Singapore's most romantic dinner/drinks venue. Not far away is **Mount Faber**, with a panoramic view of downtown and the port, a small crafts market, and cable cars over to Sentosa Island.

Sentosa is the largest of Singapore's smaller outlying islands and a good re-

Harmony with nature at the Chinese Garden.

treat if the city gets too hectic. Besides the cable car, you can reach the island via a short ferry ride from the **World Trade Center** on Telok Blangah Road. The name Sentosa means "Island of Tranquility" but it was formerly called Blakang Mati or "Back of the Dead" allegedly because pirates buried their victims here. No matter, nowadays Sentosa is a lively playground that offers many things to many people.

The splendid new ferry terminal is surrounded by a colonial garden with illuminated musical fountains that spray and spin to the sound of music each evening. Farther up the hill is the superb **Pioneers of Singapore** exhibit which traces the history of Singapore and the **Surrender Chamber** which details the island's place in the story of World War II. A real-life remnant of the war is **Fort Siloso** on the western tip of Sentosa, where the old British fortifications have been turned into an open-air museum.

Nature lovers can choose from among the **Butterfly Museum** with its aviary full of free-flying insects, the hands-on exhibits at the **Coralarium**, or the splendid new **Underwater World** with its walk-through aquarium. Other activities include two golf courses, roller-skating rink, cycle and hiking paths and a swimming lagoon where you can rent kayaks and paddle boats. Two resort hotels are currently under construction on the island.

The World Trade Center is home to the new **Guinness World of Records** museum and also the place to catch ferries to Singapore's other outlying islands. **Kusu Island** is best known for its hilltop *keramat* or Malay tomb, and the beautiful Tua Pekong Chinese Temple, dedicated to the turtle god. During the ninth lunar month, thousands of devotees flock to the island's religious shrines to pray for fertility and prosperity. Otherwise, Kusu is a quiet island that's perfect for swimming or sunbathing. Opposite is **St John's Island** with fine white-sand beaches, jungle walks and overnight bungalow. It can also be reached by ferry from the World Trade Center.

Sentosa's musical fountain provides a romantic backdrop for the open-air disco there.

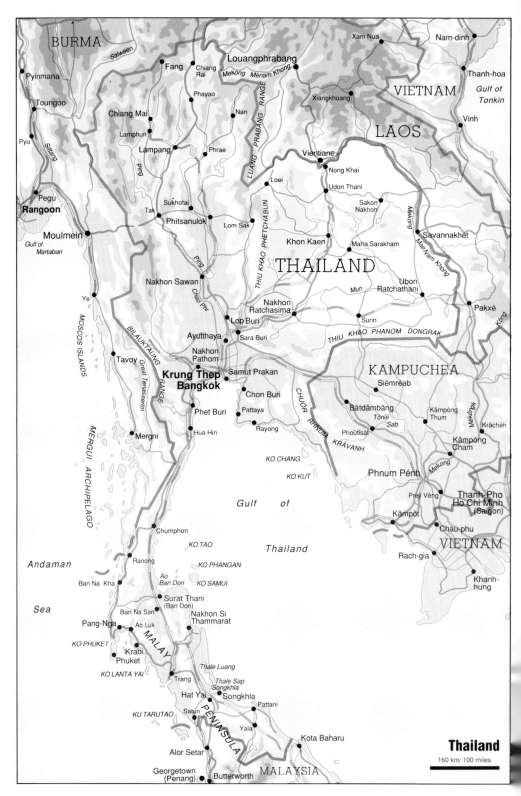

BURMA

Pyinmana

Toungoo

Pyu

Salween

Pegu

Rangoon

Moulmein

Gulf of Martaban

Ye

MOSCOS ISLANDS

Tavoy

Great Tenasserim

BILAUKTAUNG RANGE

Mergni

MERGUI ARCHIPELAGO

Fang

Chiang Rai

Phayao

Chiang Mai

Lamphun

Lampang

Phrae

Nan

Mekong

Mènam Khong

Louangphrabang

LUANG PRABANG RANGE

Ping

Sukhotai

Tak

Phitsanulok

Lom Sak

THIU KHAO PHETCHABUN

Nakhon Sawan

Ping

Chao Phr

Loei

Vientiane

Nong Khai

Udon Thani

Sakon Nakhon

Khon Kaen

Maha Sarakham

THAILAND

Xam Nua

Nam-dinh

VIETNAM

Gulf of Tonkin

Xiangkhoang

LAOS

Vinh

Thanh-hoa

Savannakhét

Mae Nam Khong

Mekong

Ubon Ratchathani

Pakxé

Kong

Lop Buri

Ayutthaya

Nakhon Pathom

Krung Thep Bangkok

Sara Buri

Nakhon Ratchasima

Mun

Surin

THIU KHAO PHANOM DONGRAK

KAMPUCHEA

Siĕmréab

Samut Prakan

Chon Buri

Phet Buri

Pattaya

Hua Hin

Rayong

CHUÔR PHNUM KRÂVANH

Bătdâmbâng

Tônlé Sab

Phoŭtîsât

Kâmpóng Thum

Krâchéh

Kâmpóng Cham

Mékông

KO CHANG

KO KUT

Phnum Pénh

Mekong

Prey Vêng

Kâmpôt

Thanh-Pho Ho Chi Minh (Saigon)

Chau-phu

VIETNAM

Gulf *of*

Thailand

Rach-gia

Khanh-hung

Chumphon

KO TAO

Ranong

Ban Na Kha

Ao Ban Don

KO PHANGAN

KO SAMUI

Andaman

Sea

Surat Thani (Ban Don)

Ban Na San

Pang-Nga

Ao Luk

Nakhon Si Thammarat

KO PHUKET

Krabi

Phuket

MALAY

KO LANTA YAI

Trang

Thale Luang

Thale Sap Songkhla

Hat Yai

Songkhla

KU TARUTAO

Satun

Pattani

PENINSULA

Yala

Kota Baharu

Alor Setar

Georgetown (Penang)

Butterworth

MALAYSIA

Thailand

160 km/ 100 miles

THAILAND: THE LAND OF SMILES

Imagine a land of infinite variety with high, tree-carpeted mountains; jungles rich with wildlife, orchids, and exotic plants; shining rivers tumbling to the plains on their way to a warm-water gulf rimmed by miles of golden sands. This is what the gods have given Thailand.

Picture orange temple roofs, golden spires glowing softly in the dusk light, silver canals criss-crossing the lowlands through a patchwork of fertile rice fields; fragile arts of breathtaking beauty. This is what Thais have created from their exquisite land. Together, god-made and man-made Thailand has for eons served as a magnet of endless appeal for travelers, many of whom journeyed for a look and stayed a lifetime.

Land of the Free. Land of Smiles. The former is a literal translation of the name "Thailand," the latter describes the cheerful demeanor of its people. Thais are proud of their ancestors' rejection of foreign domination, making their country the only one in Southeast Asia to escape the yoke of colonialism. This independent spirit is evident in everything they do. Beneath their graciousness is a strong sense of self, a humility without subservience, a willingness to suffer the consequences rather than to curry favor. It is this pride in themselves which underlies their sense of nationalism and their ability to smile at the vicissitudes of life.

But then, Thais have much to smile about: a sunny culture filled with color and brilliance, sparkling waterways that offer cooling comfort to the heat of the sun, food that is a match for any other cuisine in Asia, handsome men and beautiful women, a healthy economy, and a tolerance for religions and politicians. All these contribute to the Thais' natural warmth, hospitality, and genuine concern for the traveler.

Boasting a population of 55 million and a land area of 198,460 square miles (514,000 square km), Thailand is very nearly the size and shape of Central America. Its climate is tropical with three seasons: hot (March-June), monsoon (July-November) and cool (December-February). Its capital, Bangkok (population five million) lies on the same latitude as Madras, Khartoum, Guatemala City, Guam, and Manila.

The country is commonly divided into four regions; the Central Plains which includes Bangkok, the North, the Northeast and the South. Each region has its own culture and appeal and must be explored thoroughly to gain a proper appreciation of Thailand's vast richness. Bangkok is but one small patch in the cultural quilt. When a Thai says "I'm heading upcountry tomorrow," he could mean anywhere outside Bangkok's city limits: north, east, south or west. This is where the real Thailand begins. Upcountry.

Preceding pages: monks taking a leisurely stroll down a country road.

OF KINGS AND KINGDOMS

In 1966, in a small village on the Korat Plateau, a boy tripped over the root of a kapok tree and fell into the 36th century B.C. Surrounding him, exposed by erosion, were hard rings, rims of baked clay pots that would prove to be 5,600 years old. Beneath them were bronze tools, jewelry, and musical instruments. The boy walking through the village of Ban Chieng near the banks of the Mekong River that afternoon, had literally stumbled onto one of the great archaeological finds of the century – the vast remains of what may well have been the world's first Bronze Age culture and the first civilized settlement in Thailand.

At an unknown date, these people of the high plains disappeared, likely scattered by invaders sweeping down from the north. These new people would later forge the great empires of Cambodia and create the fabulous stone cities of Angkor Wat and Angkor Thom as well as myriad temples and monuments scattered throughout Thailand's northeast.

The next few millennia are blank pages in history books. There may have been well-developed communities living in the Chao Phya Valley as early as the 4th century B.C. By the 7th and 8th centuries A.D., the towns of Nakhon Pathom and Lopburi to the west and north respectively of Bangkok were centers of learning and religion with famed monks traveling from as far as India to preach Buddhism. In the south, there is evidence of Hindu settlement, merchants from southern India who established trading posts in the communities and minor chiefdoms which dominated the river mouths. Little is known about the rest of the country.

In the 11th century, the power of the Khmers, the dominant tribe in Cambodia, extended into Thailand nearly to the border with Burma. Master builders, they erected monuments hewn from laterite or stone at sites in the northeast and in Si Thep, Sukhothai, Lopburi and as far south as Petchburi. By the 13th century, however, the Khmer empire, beset by internal problems, began to wane and its former realms were taken over by a new race that would one day dominate the region.

For over a century, a new and more vigor-

ous race of people had been filtering south out of China, crossing the misty mountains that form the eastern end of the Himalayas to establish small fiefdoms in the fertile valleys of northern Thailand. These people called themselves *Thai*, or "free." Growing more powerful steadily, they soon found themselves strong enough to challenge the hegemony of the Khmers. In 1238, King Intradit of Sukhothai bonded neighboring principalities into a federation and Sukhothai, translated as "The Dawn of Happiness," be-

came Thailand's first capital. The date also marks the dawn of Thailand as a nation.

Sukhothai reigned as the capital of Thailand for only a century. Its greatest monarch, King Ramkamhaeng the Great (1279-1299) gave his people the Thai alphabet, codified laws, a peaceful kingdom and the respect of its neighbors. It was not to last. Later Sukhothai kings appear to have spent more time in religious devotion than in statecraft, leaving the mantle of power to pass to more aggressive Thais downriver at Ayutthaya.

Ayutthaya became the nation's capital in 1350. A succession of strong kings made it the most powerful kingdom in the region

238

with one of the richest and most cultured civilizations in Asia.

At the height of its power in the 17th century, Ayutthaya had a population of one million, more than contemporary London. In their journals, visitors marveled at its more than 2,000 gold spires and Buddha images, its wealth of architecture and the gorgeously decorated boats which plied its waters. Merchants came from far and wide to trade in its city. France, Britain, Portugal and Holland vied for favor, the Thais cleverly playing off each against the other to keep any one from becoming too influential. Foreign meddling in Thai politics led to the expulsion of all foreigners in 1688.

river from present-day Bangkok. For 15 years, Thonburi served principally as a staging area for continuous battles against the Burmese.

In 1780, a young general succeeded in driving the Burmese from the country and in 1782, he ascended the throne as King Rama I. The Chakri dynasty he founded has lasted to the present day, the reigning king Bhumibol Adulyadej being the ninth in the line.

King Rama I was a visionary who foresaw a great future for his new realm now that peace had been restored. One of his first acts was to move his capital across the river to Bangkok, a small village (*bang*) located in a plantation of plum olives (*kok*). He then built the beautiful *Wat Phra Kaew*, the "Temple

For centuries, the Burmese had cast covetous eyes on Thai wealth, sending expedition after expedition to attack Ayutthaya's ramparts. In 1767, they succeeded in storming the gates, and went on a rampage of looting and arson which razed the major buildings of the city. Remnants of the Thai army succeeded in ejecting a Burmese garrison force from Ayutthaya but one look at the ruins told them that the once glorious capital could never be rebuilt. They chose, instead, to relocate to a new, more easily defended site farther downriver at Thonburi, across the

Left, native Thais. Above, view of Bangkok.

of the Emerald Buddha," the glittering centerpiece holding the most revered Buddha image in the kingdom. With its transformation from a few motley merchant homes and plum olive trees to a glittering city, its name was also transformed from Bangkok to *Krung Thep*, "City of Angels."

Bangkok soon became a thriving metropolis. Early in the 19th century, foreign traders were welcomed back into the realm but under the strict authority of the palace; the Thais were not about to repeat earlier mistakes. But by mid-century, foreign merchants, travelers and even Christian missionaries were welcomed with open arms. The initiator of this new policy was one of the most remarkable monarchs in Asia of that or any other time.

King Mongkut (1851-1868) is, unfortunately, known to the West as the foolish despot portrayed in the film still banned in Thailand, *The King and I.* He ascended the throne armed with the wisdom gained from 27 years as a Buddhist monk. He also enlisted the aid of American missionaries to teach him English, using it to pursue an avid interest in science and technology. Once on the throne, he used his newfound knowledge and reforming zeal to modernize his nation.

Until his reign, transportation through Bangkok had been by elephant-back and

try's first rail lines snaking deep into the countryside, and sent his sons and nephews to study at universities in England, France, Germany and Russia thereby providing the country with skilled leadership. He made state visits to the capitals of Asia and Europe, his wife acting as regent in his absence, both acts diverging sharply from tradition. It was due to the innovativeness of these two monarchs and the execution of a very advanced foreign policy that, while neighboring countries were being colonized, Thais remained, as their name suggests, "free."

The 20th century saw Thailand emerge as one of the most developed, enlightened nations in Asia. Modernization did not come

canal boat. In 1863, Mongkut built Bangkok's first road, New Road, a macadamized street that wound through the heart of the city and along the river banks, thereby facilitating communication and heralding a new era in trade and commerce. In 1868, he scientifically predicted a solar eclipse and took unbelieving Europeans to the site. As the moon covered the sun, he was hailed for his grasp of science. Tragically, he contracted malaria and died on his return to Bangkok.

Mongkut's son, Chulalongkorn (1868-1910) was no less impressive. Continuing his father's work, he established universities, developed the economy, sent the coun-

without a price to the monarchy that had conceived it. Thai students caught up in the revolutionary fervor that swept Europe during the 1920s returned home to foment rebellion. In 1932, they staged a *coup d'etat* and in one night overturned 700 years of absolute monarchy. They replaced it with a constitutional monarchy, with the king as titular head of a government run by a prime minister, a two-house parliament and an independent judiciary, the system which prevails today.

Since 1932, Thailand has been ruled under a series of constitutions and by a series of governments, many of them installed by *coup d'etats* and functioning primarily as extensions of military power. Except for a brief period between 1973 and 1976 when the country experimented with true representative democracy, the military has been a pervasive force in the country, ruling either directly or from behind the scenes.

Throughout its history, Thailand has been characterized by its tolerance for alien religions and beliefs. Although 92 percent of its populace professes Theravada Buddhism, the country has always extended religious freedom to its 6 percent Muslim subjects, and its Hindu, Sikh and Christian minorities.

Though geographically closer to China, Thailand's principal cultural influences have come from the west. Buddhist missionaries

were sent to the Chao Phya Valley by the Indian Emperor Asoka in the 3rd century B.C.; 13th-century Theravada Buddhists from Sri Lanka arrived to give the religion more substantive form. The five-tone Thai language was enriched with polysyllabic Sanskrit and Pali words introduced by Brahmin priests captured when Thai armies overran Angkor Wat in 1431. The same priests also introduced and oversaw the ceremonies of statecraft and the rites of passage

The monarchy is revered in Thailand. **Left**, the king at the investiture of the crown prince. **Above**, the royal couple preside over a ceremony.

for Thai royalty that are still practiced today.

In the arts, it is the Indian classical tale, the *Ramayana* (*Ramakien* in Thai), which forms the principal theme for literature, *khon* masked drama, *lakhon* dance-drama, and puppet and shadow puppet theater, all of which were once considered palace arts. Variations, often quite bawdy, appeared outside the palace walls and regional arts, notably folk dances, arose in the north and northeast, *Manohra* drama in the south.

Architecture, sculpture and painting were, until the 20th century, devoted exclusively to religious themes. Architects created distinctive temples which held bronze, wooden, stone or stucco Buddha images. A walk through a temple is a visual trip through a religious work: scenes of the Buddha's life and past incarnations painted on the interior walls, each element rich with meaning.

A number of Thai festivals are directly associated with Buddhism. *Magha Puja*, *Visakha Puja* and *Asalaha Puja*, falling on the full moon nights of February, May, and July, celebrate the birth, death, first sermon and enlightenment of Buddha.

Two of the most charming holidays, *Songkran* and *Loy Krathong*, are purely secular festivals. Though the eve of *Songkran* is devoted to anointing the revered *Phra Buddha Sihing* image as it is paraded through Bangkok, the festival itself on April 13 is a riotous affair. *Songkran* is traditionally regarded as the start of the Thai New Year (though Thailand now follows the solar calendar), and is celebrated by sprinkling (and sometimes throwing) water on one's friends to bless them for the coming year. Though not an official holiday, *Loy Krathong* is celebrated on the full moon night of November and also centers on water. It is popular with lovers who launch tiny banana-leaf boats laden with candles, incense sticks, and flowers onto rivers, ponds and canals in the hope that their prayers will be answered.

Thailand was plunged once again into constitutional crisis when the elected government of prime minister Chaitichai Choonhaven was overthrown in early 1991 in a bloodless military coup. Other than political strife, Thailand must also contend with massive environmental destruction and pollution brought about by careless exploitation of natural resources and rapid economic development of some areas.

BANGKOK:
ANGEL IN DISGUISE

It is easy to forgive the first-time visitor for wondering if the angels of **Bangkok** have taken to their heels, driven away by the dust and din, heat and hullabaloo the city dishes out. How the angels could remain amid the chaotic traffic, noise, smoke-laden air and broken, heat-baked pavements is a mystery. There is no denying that Bangkok, or *Krung Thep* (City of Angels) as the Thais call it, is an assault on the senses, a city easy to dismiss and to wonder how one's friends, normally people of taste and discernment, could have made such a fuss about it.

What one soon discovers is that the angels are there. They can be found by doing what everyone must eventually do: delving beneath Bangkok's skin and searching for its hidden heart. The delights to be discovered are glittering temples, rich art, and cool canals; fragrant flowers and incense assailing the nostrils; tinkling chimes and monks' chants caressing the ears; succulently-prepared food tempting the palate. Most delightful of all are the warm and friendly people, the true angels of this vast city.

Bangkok began its life on the banks of the **Chao Phya River**, the "River of Kings," the "Mother of Waters." Though the city is some 400 years old, it became the nation's capital only in 1782 when the royal dynasty which now rules Thailand was established. The first king, Rama I (1782-1809) ordered a canal to be dug across the neck of an oxbow in the river, thereby creating an island which could be easily defended.

Bangkok's first major building was **Wat Phra Kaew**, the **Temple of the Emerald Buddha**, the holiest Buddha image in the realm. Wat Phra Kaew is a complex of sacred buildings erected over the course of Bangkok's first century in a seemingly random pattern and a delightful variety of styles. Walking through it, one's eyes are assaulted by twinkling pinpoints of sunlight reflected in hundreds of thousands of tiny colored mirrors that cover every jewel-like surface of the temple.

At the center of the complex is the *bot* or "ordination hall" that holds the Emerald Buddha. Gilded *garudas* (mythical birds) line its ramparts while *singhas* (mythical lions) protect the stairs and ferocious guardians carved on the doors see to it that evil spirits do not enter. The image they guard is rather small. Seated high on a pedestal, it is made of jasper and is clothed in the raiment of the season.

North of the *bot* are the pantheon holding the ashes of past kings and important royal personages; the library, repository for the Buddhist scriptures; and a tall golden mosaic-tiled spire with a summit clad in pure gold.

Surrounding the complex is a portico whose walls are covered, comic-strip fashion, with episodes from the Thai classic, the *Ramakien*, the story of the god-king Rama which is the principal work of Thai dance-drama, literature and puppet theater, and whose name the present dynasty's kings have assumed.

A major part of the murals' charm lies in the off-stage areas which show the life, dress and pastimes of the common man, subjects the artists took particular relish in depicting.

The **Grand Palace** also evolved piecemeal, beginning with the **Dusit Mahaprasad Audience Hall** which sits on the west of the great courtyard. In front of it is perhaps the most charming structure, the jewel box-like **Aphon Phimok** pavilion where kings once dismounted from their royal elephants.

The most impressive building, the **Chakri Mahaprasad**, was in fact the last to be built. It sits at the center of the complex, fronted by a garden of sculpted trees. Built as a royal residence and audience hall in 1890, it was designed by British architects on an Italian Renaissance plan.

The original blueprints called for a rather plain roofline but, sensitive to Thai aesthetic sensibilities, King Chulalongkorn ordered that three spires crown it. The addition prompted wags to dub it "the *farang* (foreigner) wearing the *chada*," the headdress of a Thai classical dancer. The building is open to the public only on special days.

A stroll south of the Grand Palace leads to **Wat Chetupon** or, as it is popularly known, **Wat Po.**

Few statues are more impressive than Wat Po's mammoth **Reclining Buddha** which occupies the entirety of a long building in the northwestern corner. Regarded less for its artistic merit than its awesome size, the soles of the enormous image's feet are covered in 108 intricate mother-of-pearl signs by which a living Buddha can be recognized. Wat Po is also a center of herbal medicine. Of special interest to visitors who have spent the day tramping through temples is the traditional massage hall where 120 baht acquires a soothing hour-long massage at the hands of expert practitioners.

Cross the street northeast of Wat Phra Kaew to **Lak Muang** which houses a tall *lingam* dedicated to Shiva and demarcates the official center of the city. Here, devotees come to make wishes or **The Royal Palace at Bangkok.**

246

to repay the spirits for wishes granted by hiring the resident *lakhon* dance-drama troupe to perform a small piece.

Wat Mahathat, the **Temple of the Great Relic**, although of little note architecturally, contains the **Buddhist University** where monks are trained. North of the *wat*, the **National Museum** houses some of the best sculptures the nation's artists have produced. It also contains the **Buddhaisawan Chapel** which holds the **Phra Buddha Sihing**, the kingdom's second most important Buddha image. Its murals are among the finest in Thailand.

Between Wat Mahathat and the riverbank is the **Amulet Market**. Thais are great believers in the power of clay amulets stamped with portraits of the Buddha to protect them from harm. Some amulets are said to be so powerful they will stop bullets or knives entering the wearer's body. Vendors are willing to help you test the theory or you may simply prefer to take their word for it.

Although amulets are theoretically a profanation of Buddhism, having its roots in animism, they are worn by nearly every Buddhist. It is here and at a second amulet market next to **Wat Rajnadda,** that they flock, connoisseurs of the occult in search of talismans which will improve their lot in life.

Thieves Flower Market, on the banks of **Klong Lawd**, is a plant lover's paradise. Orchids, shrubs, trees, line the sidewalks, a veritable jungle of exotic species. Walk a bit farther north to **Wat Indraviharn** with its colossal gilded **Standing Buddha.**

The core of nearby **Wat Rajabhopit** is a tall *chedi* or spire surrounded by a circular cloister. On the northern side is a beautiful jewel-box *bot* on whose doors are beautiful mother-of-pearl depictions of royal decorations.

Wat Suthat was completed in the reign of King Rama II (1809-1824) to house a 28-foot (8-meter) tall Buddha image brought downriver from Sukhothai on a raft and then laboriously hauled on a chariot through the city streets. The doors, carved to a depth of 2 inches, are the creation of King Rama II himself, a talented artist who is said to have thrown his specially designed tools into the river so no one could duplicate his feat. The interior murals depict fantastic sea creatures.

In front of Wat Suthat is one of the city's most famous landmarks, the **Giant Swing**. The tall structure was once the site for a ceremony, now discontinued, to honor the god Shiva. On a special day, a team of four athletic men would sit on a seat suspended from long ropes and attempt to swing high enough to snatch a bag of gold set atop a long pole.

On the boundary of the original city is **Wat Saket** whose fame stems from the artificial mountain which rises beside it. The **Phu Kaew Thong** or **Golden Mount**, once the city's tallest structure, provides a superb panorama of the city for those with stamina to climb its many stairs.

Wat Trimitr near the **Hualampong Railway Station** is famed for its Buddha image. When moving the huge plaster image in 1957, a sling broke, cracking the plaster and revealing a

A painstakingly crafted interior frames the Emerald Buddha.

second image hidden inside. When the plaster was stripped away, the inner image was found to be made of solid gold, 5.5 tons of it.

The heart of "Victorian" Bangkok is north of the Grand Palace, beyond Klong Phadung. This area became the fulcrum of Thailand's government at the turn of the 20th century. A pleasant tree-lined boulevard (Rajadamnern Avenue) leads straight into the square in front of the imposing **National Assembly**, a white marble monolith with a huge cupola in the neoclassical style that was built by King Chulalongkorn in 1907 as his throne room. Later it became the seat of Thailand's first Parliament.

Just behind is the **Vimanek Palace** ("Cloud Mansion"), billed as the world's largest teakwood building. It was built by Chulalongkorn as a rural residence for his family in, what was in 1900, the suburbs of Bangkok. The 100-room palace is filled with crystal, Faberge jewelry and other European objects. The spacious **Ampron Gardens**, still the venue for many royal social functions,

lie west of the National Assembly. Just across the street is the **Dusit Zoo**, one of the most popular places in Bangkok for family outings.

Also facing onto the square in front of the National Assembly is **Wat Benchamabhopit**, also called the Marble Temple. It was built in 1901 and was the last major temple constructed in Bangkok. The architecture bears a number of departures from the usual Thai style. The most obvious are the lavish use of Carrara marble from Italy in the main buildings and courtyard, and the yellow Chinese tiles of the roof. Try to be there in the early morning or the evening when the monks come to chant in the *bot*. The temple is also a superb site to watch the candlelight procession that circles the complex three times on the nights of three principal Buddhist holidays: *Visakha Puja, Magha Puja,* and *Asalaha Puja*.

Down Sri Ayutthaya Road from the temple stands **Chitralada Palace**, which is the residence of the current king. Unfortunately, it is not open to the pub-

Parliament Building, gloriously decked out with strings of lights, in honor of the King's birthday.

lic. The Royal Turf Club is opposite.

Even well into the 20th century, Bangkok's "streets" were really canals, overhung with palms and plied by tiny *sampans* paddling past houses built on rafts. Those days are largely gone, but a trip on the Chao Phya River still provides an educational glimpse of traditional life on the water. Water-buses called *rua duan* make regular stops at landings along the river. You can pick one up outside the Grand Palace and cruise all the way down to the Oriental Hotel, or vice versa. A few baht will take you an hour upriver to the provincial market town of **Nonthaburi**.

To discover the remnants of canal life, head into the narrow waterways on the **Thonburi** side of the river. The best way to get around is in a *rua hang yaow* ("long-tailed boat") with a low draft and tilted propeller shaft that allows it to negotiate the shallow canals. If you follow the canals far enough, you'll find yourself in the countryside amid coconut plantations, quaint rural temples and villages built on stilts.

After sundown, Bangkok shows a different face.

While you're on the Thonburi side, visit **Wat Arun**, the Temple of Dawn, which rises 284 feet (86 meters) above the river. The great *prang* (rounded spire) is covered with millions of pieces of broken Chinese porcelain embedded in cement. The builders actually ran out of porcelain during construction, prompting Rama III to solicit contributions of broken crockery from his subjects. You can climb about halfway up the tower for a fine view of the city's bizarre oriental skyline. Downriver is the old **Portuguese Quarter**, with several Iberian-inspired structures, including the **Santa Cruz Monastery**.

The spectacular **Royal Barges** are housed in a warehouse farther north along the Thonburi side. These splendidly carved boats were originally used by the king when he made his royal *kathin* (river procession) at the end of the rainy season, bringing robes and gifts from the Grand Palace to the monks at Wat Arun. Today they are put afloat only on the rare special occasion, but the warehouse is open to the public.

Back on the left bank, a short distance to the southeast of the Grand Palace area, is a large and rather ill-defined area called **Chinatown**. It basically spreads from Charoen Krung (New Road) down to the river, a boisterous maze of back alleys and tiny streets that reaches a noise level impressive even by Bangkok standards. The shops carry out brisk business in everything imaginable, from motorbikes and stereos to birds' nests and paper lanterns. One area of claustrophobic old streets is known as **Nakorm Kasem** or the **Thieves Market**. The name is something of a misnomer, since it happens to be an eminently respectable district on the whole. The lure here is about two dozen antique shops that spill their treasures onto the sidewalks. The bustling **Bangrak Market**, an emporium for fresh fruit and vegetables, is on the southern fringe of Chinatown near the river.

Farther downstream near the intersection of New Road and Silom Road is an area that could rightly be called the tourist heart of Bangkok. Many of the city's best known hotels hug the riverbanks of this area, while the nearby streets are choked with antique shops, tailors, restaurants, bars and sidewalk stalls catering to the tourist trade. The old and venerable **Oriental Hotel** is situated here. Be sure to check out the old wing, where many of the Western world's literary stars have stayed. The outdoor terrace of the Oriental is especially good for watching traffic flit up and down the Chao Phya. Nearby is a huge, modern shopping mall called **River City** with two entire floors given over to Thai antiques and handicrafts.

Bangkok's allure, indeed much of its ill-earned reputation, is based on nightlife. Travelers with a cultural bent will flock to restaurants that offer superb Thai cuisine and an evening of classical dance. But sooner or later, they find themselves gravitating toward one of Asia's most famous streets for what is usually a bit of harmless fun.

The infamous **Patpong** is known for its stripbars and wealth of feminine

Sampan chitchat on the Floating Market in Bangkok.

pulchritude. Bar patrons are welcome to watch the girls dance, have a quiet chat over a drink or simply watch the anomalies of human behavior as men and women negotiate the details of the world's oldest profession. Patpong also offers massage parlors, gay bars and music joints. In recent years, the street itself has become the venue of a lively night market selling cheap clothes, fake watches and pirate tapes. This may be the only street in the world where the blue-rinse set comes face to face with ruby lips.

Touts and taxi drivers offer to transport those with jaded tastes to more "lively" entertainment located in the backstreets of town. **Soi Cowboy** off Sukhumvit Road is a rowdier version of Patpong with a score of bars lining a single street. Here you will meet a much different sort of angel.

Not a five-minute walk from Patpong are the tranquil confines of **Lumpini Park**, where the "action" usually consists of early morning joggers and late-night couples. Not far from the park

Evening peace embraces Lumpini Park.

entrance is the **Pasteur Institute Snake Farm** where live cobras are milked each morning at 11 a.m. The extract is used to produce anti-venom serums.

North of the park is the **Royal Bangkok Sports Club** (horse-racing on Saturday afternoon during the dry season) and beyond that a thriving retail hub centered along Rajdamri Avenue, Rama I Road and Ploenchit Road. At the intersection of the three is the famous **Erawan Shrine** where, in a strange example of religious fusion, Thai Buddhists make offerings to Hindu god Brahma in order to improve their luck.

Rajdamri Avenue boasts chic new shopping centers like the **Peninsula Plaza** and **Galleries Lafayette**. Down Rama I Road is the Intercontinental Hotel, with its expansive gardens, and **Siam Center**, a huge air-conditioned shopping center that caters to tourists. Just across the street is **Siam Square**, a warren of shops, cafes and movie houses that caters mostly to Thais. There are also many antique shops and English-language book shops in this area. On either side of Ploenchit Road are the massive **Central Department Store** (the "Macy's of Bangkok") and **Amarin Plaza**, with enough American fast-food outlets to keep you fed for days.

In this same area are two much older sights. The wonderful **Jim Thompson House** and its lush gardens on Soi Kasemsan II offers a unique look at Thai lifestyle before they discovered concrete. The house actually comprises three old wooden structures, transported from Ayutthaya and reassembled on the banks of what was then a peaceful canal in suburban Bangkok. Thompson, the American who introduced Thai silk to the world, mysteriously disappeared in the Cameron Highlands of Malaysia in 1968. The house contains his priceless antique collection.

Suan Pakaad on Sri Ayutthaya Road is a private palace comprising old Thai houses and containing an excellent collection of lacquer and gold antique book cases, Ban Chieng pottery and jewelry. The **Lacquer Pavilion** is regarded by some as Asia's finest example of gold-and-lacquer decoration.

OUTSIDE BANGKOK

The hinterland of Bangkok is filled with a rich variety of sights and experiences that can be visited as a daytrip from the capital. Excellent highways now lead out of Bangkok in all directions, and what used to be a three- or four-hour trip can now be made in just over an hour, enabling the visitor to cover a lot of ground in a few days.

As night turns to dawn, tiny splashes can be heard along the **Damnern Saduak** canal in Ratchaburi province as women paddle tiny *sampan* laden with fruit and vegetables to the **Floating Market**. For early risers, a tour to the market is one of the most fascinating experiences in Asia. The market lasts until around 10 a.m. and is especially famous for its exotic fruit which comes from the surrounding orchards.

Not far away is the **Rose Garden**, located on the bucolic Tachin River. The brainchild of the former lord mayor of Bangkok, the landscaped grounds sprawl across a large area embracing not just roses, but also a modern hotel, several fine restaurants, a golf course, swimming pool and a model Thai village where there is a cultural show, work elephant demonstration and handicraft stalls.

Beyond the Rose Garden, just 34 miles (54 km) west of Bangkok, is **Nakhon Pathom**. As you drive toward the town, a colossal landmark seems to rise above the plains – this is the **Phra Pathom Chedi**, the tallest Buddhist monument in the world at 420 feet (127 meters). Set in a huge park, the massive *chedi* rests upon a circular terrace planted with trees connected with the Buddha's life. In November each year, a gay fair in the temple grounds attracts crowds from near and far. Also in the grounds is **Sanam Chand Palace** with a fine *sala* (meeting pavilion) now used for government offices and a mock Tudor building used for Shakespearean drama.

The name **River Kwai** conjures images of a wooden bridge and Allied

River Kwai tragedy re-enacted at the light and sound show.

POWs made to work under horrendous conditions by their Japanese captors. In fact, the movie depicting the World War II incident was shot in Sri Lanka rather than Thailand, and the real bridge is actually a mundane iron trestle affair. Guaranteed to evoke emotion, however, is the **Allied War Cemetery** with its rows of gravestones honoring the men who toiled to build the "Death Railway" between Thailand and Burma. Nearly half of the 16,000 Allied prisoners who worked on the line lost their lives from beatings, starvation, disease and exhaustion. Much of the infamous bridge was destroyed by British bombers shortly before the end of the war, but the Japanese government rebuilt the central span as part of their war reparations.

Kanchanaburi, 76 miles (122 km) northwest of Bangkok, is the jumping-off point for explorations of the River Kwai region. You can explore the river itself from the relative comfort of a floating bungalow – thatched houses built on bamboo rafts. The area is bountifully blessed with caves and water-falls. **Erawan Falls**, in particular, is worth a visit for its tranquil setting, considered by many as one of the most beautiful spots in Thailand. For the hardy, a rewarding experience is the trek to **Three Pagodas Pass**, through which Burmese armies mounted on elephants passed Hannibal-like on their way to engage royal Thai forces on the Chao Phya plains.

Fifty miles (80 km) north of Bangkok is the old royal city of **Ayutthaya**, Thailand's capital from 1350 to 1767. Even in a ruined state, it evokes the grandeur of the people who conquered the kingdom of Angkor Wat, controlled most of Laos and a major portion of the Malay peninsula. It was a larger and richer city than London or Paris during its time, but the golden age of Ayutthaya came to an end in 1767 when the Burmese besieged and utterly destroyed it.

Still, Ayutthaya stands as a fascinating link with Thailand's past. The ruined city is immense, best explored by bicycle or in the back of a *tuk-tuk* rented from outside the railway station. Sev-

The sun sets on Wat Mahathat.

FOOD, GLORIOUS FOOD!

Thai cuisine is one of the delights of its culture. The ubiquity of fresh seafood, meats, fruits and vegetables, and the numerous ways the Thais combine them make dining one of the highlights of a stay in Thailand. Dishes are generally spicy but some are only slightly spiced.

The base for Thai cuisine is rice, a long-grained variety that is among the tastiest in the

world. On top of this, the Thai ladles a variety of meat and vegetable dishes. Thais have also adopted a number of Portuguese, Chinese and Indonesian dishes which use a minimal amount of hot spices.

As with butter in French food, and water in Japanese dishes, the base ingredient in much of Thai food is coconut milk - a rich, creamy liquid which provides a gentle flavor. The flavor is further enhanced by the addition of garlic, lemon grass, cumin, cardamon, tamarind, ginger, coriander, and laced with ample amounts of chilis, the hottest being the tiniest called the *prink kee noo*, the "mouse drop-

ping" chilies. Additional flavor is usually achieved by splashing on a bit of *nam plaa,* a clear sauce made from the juices of salted, pressed baby shrimps.

Among the "must" dishes are soups like *Tom Yam Goong,* a spicy, sour shrimp-filled concoction. It is served in a metal tureen that is wrapped around a mini-furnace heated by charcoal so that it remains piping hot throughout the meal. *Pho Taek* ("The Fisherman's Net Bursts") is a similar liquid containing a variety of seafoods.

Gai Tom Ka, a chicken dish, is often served as a soup or ladled over rice, rendering the long grains even tastier. This non-spicy dish is a favorite among foreigners. There are dozens of curries (*gaeng* in Thai) but among the most popular are *Gaeng Karee,* a hot curry; *Panaeng Nua,* a dry curry with beef; *Gaeng Gai,* chicken curry; and *Gaeng Kieo Wan,* green beef curry.

Chinese in origin, but with a secure place in Thai cuisine, is *Plaa Jaramet Nung Kiem Bue,* steamed pomfret with Chinese plum and bits of ginger. *Gaeng Joot* is a non-spicy curry, a clear broth filled with glass noodles, minced pork and mushrooms. *Gaeng Musselman* is an unspiced curry. It consists of pieces of beef or chicken, combined with potatoes and onions in a brown gravy and resembles a Western stew.

Those with tender palates may also prefer something sweet and sour: *Gai Pat Bai Krapao,* roasted sweet chicken pieces wrapped in a leaf; *Nua Phat Namman Hoi,* beef marinated in oyster sauce; *Kow Muu Daeng,* slices of pork on plain rice and *Kow Phat,* fried rice.

Thais are great snackers and nibblers, and have created a wide variety of tidbits to be eaten any hour of the day. Fried bananas dipped in honey; *salim,* a collection of multi-colored vermicelli noodles in sweetened coconut milk; make-it-yourself dishes with corn, lotus seeds, water-chestnut, tapioca, lychees, almost all served with crushed ice, and dozens of other interesting concoctions offered at market stalls.

Thai food is a feast for the palate and for the eyes.

eral sites are not to be missed. **Wat Phra Ram** is one of the older temples, begun in 1369 by the son of Ayutthaya's founder. Elephant gates stand guard at intervals around the old walls, and the central terrace is dominated by a crumbling *prang* to which cling mythological animals and various Buddha figures. **Wat Raj Burana** was the secret burial place of a cache of intricate gold ornaments not found until restoration work during the late 1950s. Little remains of **Wat Mahathat** across the road, apart from the base of its huge *prang* and the multitude of large stone Buddha heads in the surrounding gardens.

The nearest hills to Bangkok are in the massive **Khao Yai National Park**, which sprawls across parts of four provinces about 130 miles (205 km) northeast of the capital. This cool retreat is stocked with bungalows, motels, restaurants and even an 18-hole golf course. But the big attraction here is the jungle. Various trails and roads lead deep into the rainforest where wild elephants, tigers, bears, boars and deer still roam.

Bang Pa-in, once the royal summer palace, is closer to Bangkok and usually visited in the same day as Ayutthaya. It features a charming collection of palaces and pavilions used by the kings during the hot season. The pretty palace on the lake is a mixture of Italian and Victorian styles. There is also an ornate Chinese-style palace and a Thai-style pavilion in the middle of the lake.

Down around on the southeast side of Bangkok is the **Crocodile Farm** at Samut Prakan, claimed to be the largest of its kind in the world, with 30,000 of the watery reptiles. A brochure describes the farm as "a happy marriage between wildlife conservation and commercial enterprise."

The **Ancient City** just down the road reflects a millionaire's passion to recreate all of Thailand's architectural masterpieces in miniature. On a 200-acre plot fashioned in the shape of Thailand, you will find all the major monuments plus model villages from each of the country's major regions, a gathering task that took a decade to complete.

Jaw appeal at the Crocodile Farm.

PATTAYA AND BEYOND

Two hours southeast of Bangkok, **Pattaya**, "Asia's Riviera," lies along a 2-mile beachfront crescent lined with first-class hotels. Here one can swim, ride water-scooters, parasail, waterski, sail, or windsurf. Though the waters around Pattaya are somewhat murky, there is good diving off the outer islands, including a few shipwrecks. At **Bang Saray**, 12 miles (20 km) south, one can go deep sea fishing for mackerel, marlin and other game fish.

Ashore, there are motorcycles and jeeps for rent to explore the adjacent farm country. The local chapter of the cross-country running fraternity, the Hash House Harriers, runs through the countryside every Monday evening with ample beer afterwards. Air-conditioned sports emporiums offer snooker, bowling, and shooting ranges as well as outdoor archery and mini-golf ranges. Nearby is the world-class **Siam Country Club** golf course and the **Reo Ranch** with pure-bred Appaloosa-horses and acres of countryside to ride on.

At an adjacent beach, **Chomtien**, several complexes of thatched bungalows offer rustic yet tranquil living. Also located here is the **Pattaya Park** with water-slides and other water recreation facilities for children. A new race track has been installed for weekend stock car races.

For culture, the **Elephant Kraal** in Pattaya offers daily shows during which elephants demonstrate their skills. **Nong Nooch**, 9 miles (15 km) south of Pattaya, has afternoon shows of Thai boxing, sword fighting, dancing, cockfighting, and elephants. It also has a unique cactus garden and orchid nursery.

Converted fishing trawlers travel to the outer island of **Koh Larn** whose prosaic name of "Bald Island" has somehow been transformed through tourist brochure hyperbole into "Coral Island" though the coral has long since disappeared. Its waters are very clear and its beaches wide with white sand.

The same shopping items offered in Bangkok are found in Pattaya but generally at lower prices. Several shops have resident artists who paint oil portraits from live sittings or photographs.

Pattaya is known for its seafood. Succulent fish, shellfish, fresh vegetables and fruits are blended into mouth-watering dishes. Thai, Asian, and Continental cuisines are found in abundance. Wash it down with excellent Singha or Kloster beers or the local brew, Mehkong, a cane whisky with a powerful, yet smooth-tasting punch.

South Pattaya comes into its element once the sun goes down. There are lounges with a-go-go girls but far more popular are the open-air bars where you can nurse a beer and watch the girls, in outlandish costumes, watching you.

Pattaya also has several discos that operate into the wee hours. Popular, especially among Asian travelers, are burlesque shows featuring male transvestites garbed in fabulous costumes mouthing the word to hit songs. Piano bars are also in abundance.

Pattaya has one of the finest golf courses in the country.

Situated 42 miles (67 km) beyond Pattaya is the commercial center of **Rayong**. The town is famed for its *nam plaa* or fish sauce, the *sine qua non* of Thai condiments. Sauce production is a local cottage industry, and many homes have backyard factories. A small silver fish that abounds in the gulf is allowed to decompose for about seven months to produce the ruddy liquid, filtered and bottled on the spot.

Most travelers skip through Rayong and head straight for the docks at **Ban Pae**, about a dozen miles (20 km) farther east. The waterfront is a patchwork quilt of brightly colored fishing boats, drying shrimp, seafood restaurants and tourist touts who inevitably ask if you want a boat to **Ko Samet**, a tropical paradise off the coast. You can see Samet from the waterfront, but it takes about half an hour to reach it by boat.

Ko Samet is another one of those idyllic Thai locales that has been adopted by overland backpackers in their quest for the ultimate uncrowded beach. The island is endowed with thatched bunga-lows, cheap eats and great beaches. Best of all, Samet is protected within the confines of a national park, which means that unlike other popular Thai beaches, growth will be substantially limited. Most ferries land at **Na Dang** village on the north shore, but the most popular beaches – **Haat Sai Kaew**, **Ao Phai** and **Ao Wong Deuan** – are on the east coast. You can either walk, or hop in the back of a mini-pickup taxi.

The island also has a place in history: Samet is remembered by students of Thai literature as the place where Sunthorn Pu, an undaunted romantic poet who lived in the 19th century, retired to compose some of his works. A sort of Walden Pond of Thailand.

Even farther out on the cutting edge of Thai tourism is **Koh Chang**, the country's third largest island but one of its most secluded. Chang sits in the gulf near the Cambodian frontier, famous for both its wild boar and the **Maiyom Waterfall**. Off the northern tip, some of the largest sharks in the gulf cruise near a rock outcrop.

An exotic underwater world awaits the diver and snorkeler.

PENINSULAR THAILAND AND PHUKET

Thailand's deep south – a long, narrow peninsular embracing 14 provinces – is a richly beautiful area of wild jungle, rocky mountains and broad beaches of powdery white sand. On one side are the placid waters of the Gulf of Thailand, on the other coast is the Andaman Sea. Taken as a whole, this region offers a marvelous variety of distractions – from seafood and skindiving, to temples and untouched rainforest.

Countless large and small islands ("*koh*" in Thai) are scattered down this narrow strip of land that leads to Malaysia. Except for a few of the larger islands like Phuket and Koh Samui, which have evolved into major tourist centers, few of them ever see visitors. Travelers in no particular hurry would find this the sort of terrain which lends itself perfectly to languid island hopping.

Royal Beaches: The provincial capital of **Phetchaburi**, 103 miles (165 km) southwest of Bangkok, has several worthy sights. The skyline is dominated by **Khao Wang**, a wooded ridge crowned by a rambling 19th-century palace complex called the **Phra Nakhon Khiri** (Holy City Hill), built for King Mongkut. The hillside also offers a fine vista of Phetchaburi and the surrounding countryside. Just north of town is **Khao Luang Cave**, a huge cavern with numerous Buddha images that are illuminated by natural shafts of light.

About 22 miles (35 km) farther south is **Cha-Am**, with a casuarina-fringed beach that has long been popular with wealthy Thais. There is a large, modern resort here, and a selection of more modest beach bungalows. Horses can be hired for rides along the surf.

The neighboring town of **Hua Hin** is Thailand's oldest major beach resort. Hua Hin gained royal repute after two summer palaces were built on the beach here in the 1920s. King Prachadipok was vacationing at **Klai Klangwan** ("Far From Worries") palace during the bloodless military coup of 1932, which ended 700 years of absolute monarchy in Thailand.

Remnants of the 1920s linger. The tiny **railway station** is a gem, with its own royal waiting room beneath ornate Thai-style roof. Across the tracks is the **Railway Golf Course**, the first links in Thailand and still one of the best. Fronting the beach is the magnificent **Railway Hotel**. Recently renovated, it retains an air of gentility, with ceiling fans, teakwood bars and a topiary filled with giant green creatures.

Koh Samui: Almost 450 miles (710 km) south of Bangkok is **Surat Thani**, a busy shipbuilding, fishing and mining center on the right bank of the Tapi River. The town itself has little worth seeing, but this is the jumping-off point for journeys to various idyllic islands in the Gulf of Thailand.

From Surat Thani, it's a one-hour journey by bus to either **Ban Don** or **Don Sak**, from where boats depart regularly to **Koh Samui**. This is one of the prettiest islands in the gulf, a place blessed with superb beaches, jungled hillsides and cool waterfalls whose beauty is rivaled by few other places in Thailand. For the moment, Samui is primarily the domain of overland backpackers. But with the recent inauguration of an airport (and flights from Bangkok), more upmarket resorts are in the cards.

Samui's lifestyle is relaxed, its people laidback. Until the advent of tourism, coconuts were the mainstay of the island's economy – a sophisticated economy which uses monkeys as labor-saving devices to pluck coconuts from trees. The smell of roasting coconut meat still pervades the island.

At last count, Samui boasted more than 200 bungalow complexes with rooms ranging in price from US$6 to US$30 per night. **Na Thon** is the island's largest town, but the main concentration of bungalows are at **Lamai Beach** on the southeast coast and at **Chaweng Beach** on the east coast. Simple food is cheap and delicious. And the variety of tropical fruit – coconuts, papayas, bananas, mangoes, pineapples and jackfruits – boggles the mind.

Phi Phi Island offers unspoilt beaches and crystal-clear waters.

An even more remote island is **Koh Phangan**, directly north of Samui and accessible by ferry from Na Thon Bay. **Rin Beach** is the island's main attraction, but there are at least a dozen bays ideal for swimming or snorkeling. Even farther out and less populated is the **Ang Thong** archipelago, recently gazetted into a national park comprising 20 small islands. Charter boats and tours can be arranged in Koh Samui.

Phuket: The island of **Phuket** calls itself the Pearl of the South, and for sheer natural beauty, few islands can matched it. Tall jungled hills, an incomparable coastline, picturesque coconut plantations and rice farms, white-sand beaches and azure waters – all the things that tourist brochures promise – are found in Phuket. Phuket made its first fortunes from tin and rubber, but the island's natural beauty was such a magnet for beach lovers that it rapidly developed into a major tourist resort.

The heaviest development has taken place at **Patong**. While planning has been somewhat haphazard, the beach offers a wide variety of watersports along its wide, white sands. Many of Phuket's major hotels are here, many of them built bungalow-style in deference to a building code stipulating that no hotel can rise higher than a palm tree.

To the north is **Surin Beach** with a bungalow complex set along a pretty hillside and a golf course where putters compete with grazing water buffaloes for space on the greens. South of Patong are **Kata** and **Kharon** beaches, popular with visitors who have lots of time on their hands. Very early on, Kata's charm was noticed by Club Med, which built its second Asian resort there.

Near Phuket's southern tip is the beautiful cove of **Nai Harn**, easily the prettiest spot on the island. However, its natural splendor has been somewhat compromised by a large hotel which does not succeed in blending into the hillside. **Rawai**, at the southern extremity of the island, is a fishing village populated by *chao lay* or sea gypsies, and bands of rovers who once plied the oceans but have now settled on several

A perfect hideaway island off Krabi.

260

of Thailand's southern islands. Around the corner from Rawai is the **Promthep Peninsula**, favored for its splendid views of the surrounding islands at sunset.

To the east of Phuket town is **Koh Siray**, another sea gypsy village, and the **Phuket Aquarium**. Near the intersection of the road to Kata and Kharon beaches is a temple called **Wat Chalong**. East of the intersection is **Ao Chalong**, a charming little fishing village with excellent restaurants. It is also the departure point for **Loan Island**, now being developed as a tourist resort.

Divers will find few reefs as inviting as those off the **Similan Islands**, a few hours by boat to the northwest of Phuket. Coral reefs of astounding beauty hold a rich variety of sea life and make the Similans one of Southeast Asia's premier scuba diving area.

Among the other wonders of Asia is the island group of **Phang-nga**, two hours north of Phuket. Board a long-tailed boat and take a dawn cruise through the bay, among limestone monoliths seemingly lifted from Chinese brush paintings. One of them, **Ko Ping Gun**, served as a setting for the early James Bond film, *The Man with the Golden Gun*. Another, **Koh Pannyi**, is a Muslim fishing village set on stilts.

A few hours to the south of Phuket is **Phi Phi Island** with coves of remarkable beauty. Barely developed, its beautiful beaches are set among limestone monoliths that mark the southern end of the Phang-nga group and give the island the look of Bora Bora.

Krabi: On the mainland opposite Phuket is a small beach town called **Krabi** which has only recently caught the eye of globe-trotting travelers. Krabi and its hinterland are marked by eerie limestone outcrops that seem to leap from the earth trailing a green canopy of vegetation behind them. These are the landbased cousins of the islands that dot the sea around Phi Phi. Old black junks with yin and yang talismans painted on their bows often berth at Krabi after voyages from Penang and farther south. From the docks you can catch boats to Phi Phi.

Exploring Tham Khaew, one of the many fascinating caves in Phang-nga Bay.

CHIANG MAI
AND THE NORTH

"The Dawn of Happiness," as **Sukhothai**'s name translates, marks the dawn of Thailand's existence as a nation. And for a city which started from a small federation of principalities of a people newly emerged, Sukhothai accomplished wonders in the 150 years of its short history.

The level of development is immediately evident in the ruins of its temples and palaces which are among the most impressive in Asia. Among the most important are **Wat Mahathat**, **Wat Phra Pai Luang**, and **Wat Si Chum** with its giant Buddha. The Museum contains numerous pieces of the gracefully flowing bronze Sukhothai Buddha images, considered the zenith of Thai sculptors' skill.

Chiang Mai, The "Rose of the Northern Hills," is Thailand's second largest town. The years since it was founded in 1296 have laid a patina of antiquity on its temples and buildings that has enhanced its beauty.

Set in a valley ringed by low hills, Chiang Mai is encircled by a stout wall and defensive moat which today serves as a fishing and swimming pond for children. Once a town of quaint wooden buildings, its charm has been diminished somewhat by the introduction of concrete shophouses of no particular distinction. Yet, riding a *samlor* (pedicab) along a backlane or on an evening drive along the banks of the **Ping River**, its abundant charm is immediately evident.

Wat Phra Singh, Chiang Mai's most important temple, was founded in 1345 and contains a Buddha image said to have been created in Sri Lanka and transported to Chiang Mai. Of special note at Wat Phra Singh is the *ho trai* or library, a beautiful wooden structure set atop a high stucco base on which float carved *theps* (angels).

Wat Chedi Luang's original *stupa* or spire must have been an imposing

The well-preserved Wat Chiang Man, the first temple to be built by Mengrai, founder of Chiang Mai.

structure before an earthquake destroyed it in 1545 reducing its height from 300 feet (90 meters) to 200 feet (60 meters). Its remains stand behind the present temple, which is richly decorated with mirror mosaics and gilded vines, and contains a large standing image of the Buddha.

Built in 1297, **Wat Chiang Man** is Chiang Mai's oldest temple. Behind it stands a *chedi* buttressed by rows of stucco elephants facing the four cardinal directions. Above them is a handsome spire sheathed in gilded bronze.

Located some distance from the center of town, **Chedi Si Liem** is a superb example of a style of architecture peculiar to the North. A steeply rising four-sided pyramid, it is divided into tiers with ranks of standing Buddha images set in niches surveying the large courtyard in which it stands.

Perhaps the most beautiful stucco carvings in the north are found at **Wat Chedi Chet Yot**. Wishing to honor the Buddha on the 2,000th year of his birth, King Trailoka in 1455 sent 30 architects and artisans to Bodhgaya, India where the Buddha is said to have reached enlightenment. They returned to build a rectangular block with a single spire (*yot*) surrounded by six smaller spires making a total of seven (*chet*). Its appeal lies in the 70 stucco figures who seem to float on the building's outer walls, their hands clasped in prayer.

Wat Ku Tao, a Burmese-style temple, is itself of little architectural note but its *chedi* is one of the most intriguing in Thailand. Five globes, like upturned monks' alms-bowls, are stacked one atop the other in decreasing order of size. Like Wat Arun and many other *chedi,* its stuccoed surface is decorated with seashells and fragments of porcelain plates shaped into flowers.

While Chiang Mai celebrates the same holidays as Bangkok, it has one of its own which occurs during the cool month of February. The Flower Festival features a floral parade and cultural shows utilizing the blooms that flower in the crisp hill air. Chiang Mai celebrates *Songkran* a week later than Bangkok

Freshly-painted umbrellas are spread out to dry in the village of Borsang.

and in a much more boisterous fashion. Expect to be drenched several times if you venture into the streets, all in the spirit of fun.

The most popular of Chiang Mai's many markets is the **Night Market** on Chiang Klan Road. In the cool of the evening, shops selling local products are swamped with Thais and visitors looking for bargains. Sidewalk cafes offer drinks and snacks and the opportunity to watch the passing crowds.

Chiang Mai's most famous landmark sits atop a hill called **Doi Suthep** on the outskirts of the town. Legend says that when the 14th-century monk Sumana was looking for a site for a new temple, he placed a holy relic on the back of an elephant, instructing his disciples to erect the temple at the spot where the elephant rested. The elephant must have had a sadistic bent because it led the disciples up the steepest hill in the district, trumpeting three times at the summit before lying down.

To appreciate the disciples' zeal in following the elephant, drive the 10 miles (16 km) up the winding road to the base of the final hill and then trek up the stairs with its serpent balustrade to the temple itself. Survey the panorama of Chiang Mai in the distance or rest in the shadow of the tall golden spire and its beautiful brass umbrellas.

Many of Chiang Mai's attractions are found outside the city. To the west across the Ping River, the 7.5-mile (12-km) road to **Borsang** is dotted with workshops creating the art objects for which the North is famed: namely silverwork, carved work, gold and lacquer *objets d'art*, ceramics, celadon pottery, and woven silk.

At Borsang, the "Umbrella Village," women fashion Chiang Mai's famous umbrellas. The umbrellas are marvels of engineering: tiny bamboo pieces are intricately bound with thread and covered in oiled paper or silk and painted with bright designs. The umbrellas come in a variety of sizes with the largest sufficient to cover a substantial party.

North of Chiang Mai is the **Mae Sa Valley**, a new resort area of bungalows

Spectacular rock formation at Mae Klang waterfall, Doi Inthanon National Park.

set in bucolic splendor along the banks of the burbling **Mae Sa River**. The area serves as a starting point for walks into the surrounding jungles.

In Mae Sa Valley, as in several other locales outside Chiang Mai, is a training school where elephants are taught the techniques of moving huge teak logs out of the forests. It is also possible to mount a *howdah* and ride for a short distance on elephant back, a bumpy experience not likely to convince the rider to trade in his car. Farther up the valley is picturesque **Mae Sa Waterfalls**, a series of cataracts that, depending on the season, crash or dribble over the rocks.

The northern hills are home to a half dozen hilltribes. Tour companies in Chiang Mai arrange treks lasting several days for visitors to observe the hilltribes close-up, which include overnight stays in Yao, Hmong, Karen, E-kaw, and other villages.

Northwest Frontier: Wedged in mountain scenery that is among the most breathtaking in Southeast Asia, **Mae Hong Son** fits into the map of Thailand like the overlooked last piece of a jigsaw puzzle. Secluded by jungle ridges and framed on the north and west by the Shan states of Burma, the province is just now awakening from years of neglect by the outside world.

Hilltribes like the Karen, Meo, Shan, Lisu and Lahu easily outnumber the ethnic Thais, adding intrigue to the ill-kept secret that Mae Hong Song lies at the crossroads of border smuggling routes. The provincial capital goes by the same name, but Mae Hong Son town bustles only early in the morning when the market is in full swing.

Mae Hong Son can be reached by a 40-minute flight from Chiang Mai, or via an 11-hour bus ride that winds through the Ob Luang Gorge.

Much farther down along this western border is **Mae Sot**, another interesting frontier town and one with a definite touch of Burma. Mae Sot thrives as a sort of backwoods trading post, a town that likes to think of itself as slightly above the law. In fact, it's not unusual to see ordinary citizens clutching automatic weapons as they walk down the main street in town. The place is a smuggler's delight, a confusion of short streets, sidewalk stalls, bicycles and pedestrians where just about anything can be bought or sold. From Mae Sot it's a 3-mile (5-km) journey to the banks of the **Moei River** which marks the border with Burma.

Golden Triangle: After visiting Chiang Mai, you can continue into the northern crown of Thailand, an area somewhat romantically tagged the "Golden Triangle." The name alone is enough to conjure visions of druglords and opium smugglers. But nowadays, northern Thailand earns more money off the tourist trade, leaving most of the illicit business to the inaccessible parts of neighboring Burma and Laos.

About 62 miles (100 km) north of Chiang Mai is a bustling town called **Chiang Rai**, often used as a base camp for explorations into deeper parts of the Golden Triangle. According to legend, King Mangrai founded the town in 1262 after his favorite elephant ran away and

Poppies, the object of much attention.

he tracked it to the banks of the Kok River. Despite this early start, Chiang Rai has only recently cast off its sleepy ways and entered the world of tourism.

Several local temples are of interest. **Wat Prasingh** has been restored too many times to allow for accurate dating, but documents suggest the 15th century or earlier. Right behind is **Wat Phra Keo**, believed to have been the original residence of the Emerald Buddha which is now in Bangkok. To the west rises **Ngam Muang Hill**. Inside the *wat* atop the hill, a reliquary is believed to contain the bones of King Mangrai, placed there by one of his sons.

Chiang Rai has recently become a center for arranging elephant treks into the surrounding jungle and hilltribe country, and longtailed jetboat journeys along the Kok to its confluence with the Mekong River.

From Chiang Rai, a highway leads north about 18 miles (29 km) to **Mae Chan**. Formerly a center for silverwork, this tiny district town now serves as a trading post for Akha and Yao people.

Many hilltribes reside in the mountains and valleys around Mae Chan. The apex of the Golden Triangle is another 21 miles (34 km) north at Mae Sai, directly across the frontier from Burma.

To get a glimpse of the mighty Mekong River, head east from Mae Sai to the lovely riverside town of **Chiang Saen**. Scholars believe that the town was founded at the end of the 13th century and strongly fortified about 100 years later. However, the ancient capital was destroyed in the 18th century by Rama I in order to prevent it from falling into the hands of invading Burmese. A few relics of the 13th-century city remain today.

Just west of town stands **Wat Pa Sak**, whose name derives from the use of 300 teak (*sak*) trunks for the original enclosure. Close to the western gate stands **Wat Chedi Luang**, a bell-shaped *chedi* with an octagonal base that rises nearly 200 feet (60 meters). In the same complex is a branch of the **National Museum**, with a good assortment of bronze Buddhas and other Chiang Saen art.

Lovely Lisu ladies.

The Northeast: As the deep south is colored by the culture of Malaysia, the northeast is tinted by the culture of its neighbors to the east. Its ruins show the imprint of the Khmer genius that created Angkor Wat, and its language, festivals and traditions have their genesis in Laotian culture.

Near Sakhon Nakhon is **Ban Chieng** which many archaeologists think may have been the birthplace of the Bronze Age. On display are skeletons which have been unearthed from huge burial mounds as well as bronze artifacts and pottery with distinctive and highly original patterns.

Of the many Khmer ruins, those at **Phimai** northeast of **Korat** are the best known. Recently restored, the 12th-century sandstone temple and its extensive courtyard incorporates the key architectural components and decorations found at Angkor Wat, which is one of the most brilliant creations of the ancient architects.

The most popular northeastern festival is the **Elephant Round-up** which takes place is **Surin** each November. Years ago, elephants were trapped in the jungles and trained to work in teak forests, transport goods, and fight in wars. At Surin, visitors will be able to see how wild elephants are captured, demonstrate their dexterity, including their soccer skills, and, as a grand finale, be treated to a mock war between two armies in which the elephants serve as the tank corps.

The Rocket Festival celebrated in **Yasothon** is a fertility rite and a great time of riotous celebration before the villagers get down to the hard work of planting rice. The rockets are home-made affairs of bamboo packed with gunpowder and gaily launched with much singing and laughter. They are fired into the sky for the purpose of persuading the Rain Goddess, *Mae Prasop*, to send sufficient supplies of rain earthward to water the crops. The rites, celebrated on a Sunday in May, are preceded by daylong bacchanalian festivities with a distinct air of *Mardi Gras* bawdiness.

The elephant roundup is a prime tourist attraction.

TRAVEL TIPS

GETTING THERE

BY AIR

Brunei International Airport in Bandar Seri Begawan offers connections to Hong Kong, Singapore, Bangkok, Kuala Lumpur, Jakarta, Manila, Taipei, Darwin, Kuching, Kota Kinabalu and Balikpapan. There is a B$12 airport tax (B$5 for flights to Singapore and Malaysia) payable on departure. The tax can be paid in Brunei or Singapore dollars. There is no reduction on the departure tax for children, but infants (under two years of age) are exempted. The Brunei Tourist Information Bureau has an office at the airport that is open during normal business hours.

BY SEA

Other than flying, the only link between Sabah and Brunei is by sea. There are daily ferries between B.S.B. and Labuan, a small island off the southwest coast of Sabah. As an alternative, you can catch a speedboat to Lawas, the northernmost port in Sarawak, and from there make your way by bus or taxi to Kota Kinabalu. High-speed ferries to Labuan and Limbang can be booked at the kiosk in front of the Customs House on Jalan McArthur in B.S.B.

BY LAND

There is only one land route into Brunei: from Miri in Sarawak, via Kuala Belait, to Bandar Seri Begawan. The journey entails at least two changes of bus: at the Baram River in northern Sarawak and in Kuala Belait after you cross the border into Brunei. You may also have to change bus in Seria. If you start early enough, the Miri-B.S.B. trip can be done in a single day. The B.S.B. bus station is on the ground floor of the multi-story car park on Jalan Cator near the Brunei Hotel.

TRAVEL ESSENTIALS

VISAS & PASSPORTS

Visitors entering Brunei must be in possession of a valid passport. Citizens of Belgium, Canada, Denmark, France, Germany, Indonesia, Japan, Luxembourg, Maldives, Netherlands, Philippines, South Korea, Sweden, Switzerland and Thailand do not require a visa for stays of up to 14 days. British, Singapore and Malaysia passport holders do not require visas for stays of up to 30 days. Holders of other passports must have a valid visa. Visas can be obtained at Brunei embassies overseas. If there is no embassy in your country, try the nearest British diplomatic mission.

MONEY MATTERS

The Brunei dollar is approximately equivalent to the Singapore dollar. At time of going to press, the exchange rates were roughly B$1.60 to the US$. Bank hours in Bandar Seri Begawan and other towns are 9 a.m. to 3 p.m., Monday to Friday, and from 9 a.m. to 11 a.m. on Saturday mornings. Brunei currency comes in denominations of 1, 5, 10, 50, 100, 500 and 1,000 dollar notes and 1, 5, 10, 20 and 50 cent coins. International credit cards such as Visa, Mastercard, American Express and Diners are accepted at major hotels, restaurants and shops.

HEALTH

It's fair to say that Brunei is one of the safest countries in Asia from a health and hygiene point of view. Malaria, cholera and smallpox have all been eliminated since independence. RIPAS Hospital in Bandar Seri Begawan is comparable to the best in Asia, and there is a nationwide network of smaller hospitals and clinics. Bottled water is advisable for visitors.

WHAT TO WEAR

Brunei is a typical equatorial country, with a hot and humid climate. Thus, light and casual cotton or silk clothes are most appropriate. Shoes should be removed whenever entering a mosque or private home. Being a devout Muslim country, it's also important to remember that women should cover their head, knees and arms when entering a mosque or other holy place, and generally refrain from wearing shorts, mini-skirts or sleeveless dresses. For men, bathing suits, shorts and tank top T-shirts are frowned upon when worn away from the beach or pool. Men may be requested to dine in suits and ties at some formal occasions.

CUSTOMS

Duty free allowances for Brunei are 200 cigarettes, 50 cigars or 250 grams of tobacco; one-sixth gallon (0.76 liters) of perfume or toilet water. Since January 1, 1991 it has been illegal for Brunei passport holders to import alcohol into the country. Foreigners are allowed to bring in two bottles of wine or spirits and 12 cans of beer for their own use. Importation of narcotics, weapons and pornography is strictly forbidden. As in Singapore and Malaysia, drug trafficking is punishable by death.

GETTING ACQUAINTED

TIME ZONES

Brunei Standard Time is the same as Singapore and Malaysia, eight hours ahead of Greenwich Mean Time.

CLIMATE

Although the climate in Brunei could be termed perpetually tropical – hot, humid and sunny – there are subtle variations in season that correspond to those in adjoining Sabah and Sarawak. The rainy season is generally November and December. The period from April to July is usually the driest, coolest part of the year. Temperatures can range as high as 90° F (32° C) in the daytime and down to 71° F (22° C) at night.

LANGUAGE

Bahasa Malay is the official language, but English is widely spoken or understood.

BUSINESS HOURS

The overlap of Muslim custom and modern business makes opening hours a bit complicated in Brunei. Government offices are open 7:45 a.m. to 12:15 p.m. and 1:30 p.m. to 4:30 p.m., Monday to Thursday, and Saturday. They are closed on Friday and Sunday. During the Muslim fasting month of *Ramadan*, government offices are open 8 a.m. to 2 p.m. Private offices, especially multinational corporations, generally follow 8 a.m. to 5 p.m. business hours from Monday to Friday. Shops are usually open daily from 8 a.m. to 6 p.m., with some open until 9 p.m.

CULTURE & CUSTOMS

Other then the aforementioned advice about clothing and shoes, it's important never to walk in front of someone at prayer nor touch a copy of the *Koran* in a mosque. It's considered rude in Brunei to pound your right fist into your left palm, and to point or beckon someone with your index finger.

If you need to point, use a clenched fist with your thumb sticking out. If you want someone to come toward you, wave your entire hand with the palm facing down. Members of the opposite sex do not shake hands in Brunei, while men prefer a light handshake rather than the vigorous shake common in much of the West.

It is considered extremely impolite to eat or drink in front of a Muslim between sunrise and sunset during the month of *Ramadan*. Better to take your meals within the confines of an international hotel or private home. Be sure to ask before taking photos of people, especially members of the royal family.

GETTING AROUND

FROM THE AIRPORT

Brunei International Airport is less than 8 miles (12 km) from the center of Bandar Seri Begawan. Normal travel time into the city is 15-20 minutes. Taxis cost B$20-30. Hotel transportation is normally available if you provide the hotel with your flight number and arrival time.

TAXIS

Taxis are a scarce commodity in Brunei, so book them well in advance. They are not metered, so it's advisable to negotiate a fare before setting out. Fares range from B$10 for a short trip in the city center to more than B$100 for a journey from Bandar Seri Begawan to Kuala Belait.

PUBLIC TRANSPORT

Owing to the country's affluence and the fact that most citizens have their own vehicles, very little public transportation is available in Brunei. You could wait hours for a city bus.

RENT-A-CAR

Given the dearth of taxis and public transport, perhaps the best way to see Brunei is to hire a car. Avis has desks at Brunei International Airport and the Sheraton Utama. The price for an economy-sized sedan is roughly B$100 per day. Cars with drivers are available for about B$360 a day (10 hours). The great thing about Brunei being a major oil producer is the fact that gas is dirt cheap – only 47 cents per liter.

WATER TRANSPORT

Small launches flit back and forth between the Bandar Seri Begawan waterfront on Kampong Ayer, the "water-village" in the middle of the Brunei River. The standard fare for a trip straight across the river is 50 cents. For charter journeys, the price is negotiable, but you shouldn't pay more than B$15-20 per hour.

WHERE TO STAY

Brunei is a tiny country, so don't expect a lot of choice when it comes to accommodation. There is just one hotel in the "international" category (Utama Sheraton), and a handful at lower levels.

HOTELS

Ang's Hotel, Jalan Tasek Lama, P.O. Box 49, B.S.B. 1900, Tel: 02-243553
Maximillian Grill serves Western food while Cempaka Cafe offers Western, Malay and Chinese cuisine. Other facilities: swimming pool, beauty salon, banquet rooms, IDD, in-house movies. Rates: B$118-138 single; B$128-148 double; B$350 suite.

Brunei Hotel, 95 Jalan Pemancha, P.O. Box 50, B.S.B 1900, Tel: 02-242372/9
80 rooms; coffee shop. Other facilities: conference rooms, IDD, color TV. Rates: B$150-190 single; B$175-210 double; from B$240 suite.

Hotel Sentosa, 93 Jalan McKerron, P.O. Box 252, Kuala Beliat, Tel: 03-234341
Rates: all rooms B$135.

Seaview Hotel, Lot 3678 Jalan Maulana, P.O. Box 127, Kuala Belait, Tel: 03-332651/5
Rates: B$130 single; B$155 double; B$280 suite.

Sheraton Utama Hotel, Jalan Bendahara, P.O. Box 2203, B.S.B.Brunei 1922, Tel: 02-244272
156 rooms; Melati coffee shop and Heritage restaurant serve local and international food; lounge and poolside terrace. Other facilities: pool, gym, business center, meeting and conference rooms; in-house movie channels, IDD. Rates: B$210-240 single; B$230-260 double; from B$480 suite.

FOOD DIGEST

DINING

Indigenous food in Brunei is similar to that found in neighboring Malaysia. Expect rich and spicy fare. Steamed white rice and fried noodles are common bases; coconut in one form or another is used in many dishes. Seafood, chicken and beef are popular. Fresh tropical fruits like mango, durian, rambutans and bananas can be found in abundance depending on the season. Bandar Seri Begawan also has a number of modest Chinese and Indian restaurants, and Western food is available in the big hotels as well.

SHOPPING

The Brunei Arts and Handicrafts Training Center is situated along the waterfront, about a two-minute drive east of downtown Bandar Seri Begawan. Specialties here are textiles, baskets, brocade, silver and brass. You can often see craftsmen making their works. Prices tend to be higher than elsewhere in Southeast Asia.

GETTING THERE

JAKARTA

Coming from outside the Indonesian archipelago you have two main options: through Jakarta's new international airport at Cengkareng 12.5 miles (20 km) west of Jakarta or through Ngurah Rai Airport near Denpasar on the neighboring island of Bali with connecting flights to Yogyakarta. Airport tax on international flight departures is Rp. 11,000. On the domestic flights the departure tax is Rp. 4,000 per person.

A new highway links Cengkareng with Jakarta and buses operate at regular intervals to Gambir Station in the city's center.

BY SEA

If you're one of the lucky ones with plenty of time (and money), an ocean cruise to Indonesia should not be missed. Luxury cruise liners offer fly/cruise arrangements which allow you to fly to Bali and other ports where you can play in the sun, then catch your ship on the way home or vice versa.

Several other big shipping companies run ships both big and small. However, most of them carry cargo with limited space for passengers. Check with the harbor master for prices. It's often cheaper to go to the captain himself and pay for your fare.

TRAVEL ESSENTIALS

VISAS & PASSPORTS

All travelers to Indonesia must be in possession of a passport valid for at least six months after arrival and with proof (tickets) of onward passages.

Visas have been waived for nationals of 30 countries for a visit not exceeding two months. These countries are: Australia, Austria, Belgium, Brunei,

Canada, Denmark, Finland, France, Germany, Greece, Iceland, Ireland, Italy, Japan, Lichtenstein, Luxembourg, Malaysia, Malta, Netherlands, New Zealand, Norway, Philippines, Singapore, South Korea, Spain, Sweden, Switzerland, Thailand, United Kingdom and United States of America.

Entry and exit for those who do not require visas must be through the air or seaports of Jakarta, Bali, Surabaya, Medan, Manado, Biak, Ambon, Batam, with the addition of Pekanbaru airport. For other ports of arrival and departure, visas are required. For citizens of countries other than the 30 listed above, tourist visas can be obtained from any Indonesian Embassy or consulate. Two photographs are required and a small fee is charged.

Visas are also free for registered delegates attending a conference which has received official approval.

Business visas for five weeks can be obtained on application and extensions are approved at the discretion of the immigration authorities.

Surat jalan is a letter from the police permitting the bearer to go to certain places. It is advisable to carry one when traveling in some of the outer islands but in Java, it is only required in such out-of-the-way places as the Ijen plateau. If in doubt check with a good travel agent. In Jakarta, a *surat jalan* may be obtained in an hour or two at Police Headquarters (Markas Besar Kepolisian Republik Indonesia) in Jalan Trunojoyo (Kebayoran Baru).

MONEY MATTERS

The exchange rate for a US$1 was about Rp. 1,915 at time of going to press. It is advisable not to exchange large sums of money if you plan to be in Indonesia for more than a month.

Foreign currency, in banknotes and traveler's checks, is best exchanged at major banks. Banks in many smaller towns are not necessarily conversant with all foreign banknotes, so it is advisable to change currencies in the cities. Your *rupiah* may be freely converted to foreign currencies when you are leaving the country.

Traveler's checks are a mixed blessing. Major hotels, banks and some shops will accept them, but even in the cities it can take a long time to collect your money (in small towns, it is impossible). Credit cards are usable if you stay in the big hotels. International airline offices, a few big city restaurants and art shops will accept them, but they are useless elsewhere.

HEALTH

If you intend staying in Indonesia for some time, particularly outside the big cities, gamma-globulin injections are recommended; they won't stop hepatitis, but many physicians believe that the risk of infection is greatly reduced. Diarrhea may be a problem: it can be prevented by a daily dose of doxycycline, an antibiotic used to prevent "traveler's diarrhea." Obtain this from your doctor at home. At the first signs of stomach discomfort, try a diet of hot tea and a little patience. Stomach reactions are often due to a change in food and environment. Tablets such as Lomotil and Imodium are invaluable cures. A supply of malaria-suppressant tablets is also highly recommended. Make sure the suppressants are effective against all the strains of malaria. It was recently discovered that a malaria strain was resistant to the usual malarial prophylactic (chloroquine). Consult your physician.

All water, including well water, municipal water and water used for making ice, <u>MUST</u> be made safe before consumption. Bringing water to a rolling boil for 10 minutes is an effective method. Iodine (Globoline) and chlorine (Halazone) may also be used to make water potable. All fruits should be carefully peeled before eating and no raw vegetables should be eaten.

Last but not least, protect yourself against the sun. Tanning oils and creams are expensive in Indonesia, so bring your own.

WHAT TO WEAR

Informal wear is suitable and comfortable. However, since this is a predominantly Muslim and conservative country, observances of local customs is important. Men may wear T-shirts or cotton shirts with short sleeves, and open sandals. Women should not wear dresses, skirts or shorts that are too short, and topless sunbathing is frowned upon. In cities, towns and villages, shorts are not a good idea — save them for the beach. In mosques, the legs should be covered to below the knee, and some mosques will provide scarves for the head and arms. When visiting government offices and passing through immigration points, long trousers and skirts are looked upon favorably.

CUSTOMS

Visitors may bring in 200 cigarettes, 50 cigars or 100 gms of tobacco; one liter of wine or spirits; a reasonable amount of perfumes; gifts worth up to US$250 per adult or US$1,000 per family.

GETTING ACQUAINTED

TIME ZONES

Indonesia is divided into three time zones. Java and Bali are on West Indonesia Standard Time, which is seven hours ahead of Greenwich Mean Time.

CLIMATE

Most of Indonesia has a typical tropical climate, which means that it is generally hot and humid throughout the year. However most islands also have their own micro-climates depending on their geographical position and maximum altitudes.

As a general guide average annual temperature at sea level is about 78°F (26°C). Rainy seasons vary from island to island. In Bali and Java you can expect wet weather between November and April. It can get quite chilly at night in highland areas and a light jacket or sweater is recommended.

LANGUAGE

Indonesia's motto, *Bhinneka Tunggal Ika* (unity in diversity) is seen in its most driving, potent form in the world of language. Although there are over 350 distinct languages and dialects spoken in the archipelago, the one national tongue, *Bahasa Indonesia*, will take you from the northernmost tip of Sumatra through Java and across the string of islands to Irian Jaya.

Bahasa Indonesia is both an old and new language. It is based on Malay, which has been the *lingua franca* throughout much of Southeast Asia for centuries, but it has changed rapidly in the past few decades to meet the needs of a modern nation.

Although formal Indonesian is a complex language demanding serious study, the construction of basic Indonesian sentences is relatively simple.

A compact and cheap book — *How to Master the Indonesian Language*, by Almatseier — is widely available in Indonesia and should prove invaluable in helping you say what you want to say. Indonesian is written in the Roman alphabet and, unlike some Asian languages, is not tonal.

Indonesians always use their language to show respect when addressing others, especially when a younger person speaks to his elders. The custom is to address an elder man as *bapak* or *pak* (father) and an elder woman as *ibu* (mother), and even in the case of slightly younger people who are obviously VIPs, this form is suitable and correct. *Bung* (in West Java) and *mas* (in Central and East Java) roughly translate as "brother" and are used with equals, people your own age whom you don't know all that well, and with hotel clerks, taxi drivers, tour guides and waiters (it's friendly, and a few notches above "buddy" or "mate").

BUSINESS HOURS

Government offices are open from 8 a.m. to 3 p.m., Monday to Thursday, 8 a.m. to 11:30 a.m. on Friday, and 8 a.m. to 2 p.m. on Saturday.

Commercial offices are generally open from 9 a.m. to 1 p.m. and from 2 p.m. to 5 p.m., Monday to Friday, although workers often leave early on Friday.

Shops tend to stay open from 9 a.m. to at least 6 p.m. everyday. Many department stores and larger shops are open until 9 p.m.

GETTING AROUND

DOMESTIC TRAVEL

Indonesia, for those that can afford it, is aviation country. The national flag carrier, Garuda, serves both international as well as domestic routes. The only carrier using jet airplanes on domestic routes, it has several flights from Jakarta to all main provincial cities. Several flights run daily from Jakarta to Bali, Medan, Ujung Pandang, Manado, Balikpapan and other destinations. Shuttle flights run to Surabaya, Semarang, Bandung and Bandar Lampung.

Merpati also offers regular services to 100 destinations within Indonesia. Of special interest are the "pioneer flights" to remote areas not served by other airlines. Merpati is particularly active in eastern Indonesia, serving the small islands and interiors of Sulawesi, Kalimantan and Irian Jaya. Besides Garuda and Merpati, there are several privately owned airlines with both scheduled and charter services.

Garuda operates an air-travel pass. Called the "**Visit Indonesia Air Pass,**" it allows for a number of flights for one payment:

Visit 1: flights between five cities of your choice as long as they are completed within no more than 10 nights. Price: US$300.

Visit 2: flights between 10 cities of your choice as long as they are completed within no more than 20 nights. Price: US$400.

Visit 3: flights between 33 cities of your choice as long as they are completed within no more than 60 nights.

The pass is operated only by Garuda and can be obtained in Japan, Australia, New Zealand, Europe and the United States. The pass is *not* for sale in Singapore. Airport tax must still be paid by the passenger.

Whether you have this air-pass or not, you are likely to use the domestic air network in Indonesia. **Garuda**, **Merpati** and **Bouraq** are the principal carriers, between them covering a veritable labyrinth of destinations. The travel information under the regional listings that follow includes a selection of just a few of the flights that might come in useful. Prices are rounded up to the nearest US dollar, *but should be treated as rough guidelines only* since the companies concerned change prices at short notice. Care has been taken to select routes that relate to the locations covered in this book. If you intend traveling by plane frequently, you should get a copy of the timetables and latest fares from the respective company. A seemingly endless variety of itineraries can be planned. The three domestic airline offices are located at:

Garuda Indonesian Airways, Wisma Dharmala Sakti, Jl. Jend. Sudirman 32, Tel: 588707

Merpati Nusantara Airlines, Jalan Angkasa 2, Jakarta, Tel: 411650

Bouraq Indonesia Airlines, Jalan Angkasa 1-3, Jakarta, Tel: 655170

THINGS TO DO

JAKARTA

There are many "musts" in Jakarta, but be forewarned about trying to do too much. Two major sights or areas of the city a day are enough. Take a siesta or a swim in between to recover from the heat. Get an early start in the cool morning hours, do your errands and sightseeing, then get in out of the noonday sun. Venture out again in the late afternoon and early evening, when the weather has cooled off and the crowds are thinner.

City Orientation: At Jakarta's center lies **Medan Merdeka** (Freedom Square), a vast parade ground crisscrossed by broad ceremonial boulevards, with the National Monument towering in its midst. Going north, the major artery is Jl. Gajah Mada/ Jl. Hayam Wuruk, two one-way roads with a canal separating them. This is the older, commercial area of town, horribly congested throughout much of the day and practically deserted at night. At the north end of this artery lies the old colonial city and the old harbor, now both major tourist sights. To the east along the coast are Ancol, a sprawling entertainment complex, and Tanjung Priok, the port.

The "main street" of Jakarta is now **Jl. Thamrin/ Jl. Jendral Sudirman**, which connects Medan Merdeka (the new satellite suburb). Many international hotels, office buildings, theaters, restaurants and nightclubs are on this street. To the east of Jl. Thamrin lie the older colonial residential areas of **Menteng**, **Cikini** and **Gondangdia**, with their luxurious mansions and tidy, tree-shaded streets. **Jl. Imam Bonjol/Jl. Diponegoro** is "Embassy Row," lined with many of the finest mansions in Jakarta and worth a quick drive or walk-through. Many shops, boutiques and restaurants are in this area, as is TIM, the arts center of Jakarta.

Public Transport: Taxis are by far the most practical way of getting around the city. Despite an increase, fares remain reasonable. It costs about Rp. 3,000-5,000 for most cross-town journeys. Cabs are available at any hotel and easily hailed on major thoroughfares. President and Bluebird are the largest and generally the most reliable companies. Radio cabs may be summoned by phone. Be sure the meter is on when you get in, and that it stays on for the entire journey. Some cabbies will try and take you for a ride. Try to rent a cab by the hour if you intend making a lot of stops. Tipping is not customary, but drivers rarely have change, so carry some with you and even then be prepared to round off to the nearest Rp. 500.

YOGYAKARTA

Most foreign visitors to Yogya arrive by air. **Garuda** has several daily flights from Jakarta's Cengkareng International Airport and it is often possible to bypass Jakarta completely by hopping on the first plane to Yogyakarta upon arrival from overseas.

The first-class **Bima Express** train that plies the Jakarta-Yogyakarta-Surabaya route nightly in either direction is Java's finest - comfortable air-conditioned sleeper cars with small two mattress bunk compartments, a sink and a table. The schedule is less than ideal, nonetheless. The Bima leaves Jakarta Kota Station at 4 p.m. and arrives in Yogya 10 hours later, which means that your sleep is interrupted and you travel by night. At US$11 one way, it's about a quarter of the price of an air-ticket. The **Fajar Utama** and **Senja Utama Yogya** trains

from Jakarta cost much less (US$5-7) but they are slower and not air-conditioned.

Inter-city buses always travel at night. The Jakarta-Yogyakarta run takes about nine hours and costs less than US$8. From Bandung, it's only six hours and costs about US$6. The more expensive Mercedes buses are air-conditioned.

From Semarang or Solo or other nearby cities, you're better off taking a mini-bus, with services all day from dawn to dusk. Cost is only US$1.20 from Solo, US$2.50 from Semarang.

WHERE TO STAY

JAKARTA

Luxury Class
(above US$100 per night)

Jakarta now has five five-star hotels. Three have extensive grounds and sports facilities: the **Grand Hyatt**, the **Borobudur Intercontinental** and the **Jakarta Hilton**. In addition to Olympic-size swimming pools, tennis courts, squash courts, health clubs, jogging tracks and spacious gardens, they also boast discos and a full complement of European and Asian restaurants.

Borobudur Intercontinental (840 rooms), Jl. Lapangan Banteng Selatan, P.O. Box 329, Jakarta, Tel: 3805555

Grand Hyatt Jakarta, Jl. M.H. Thamrin, P.O. Box 4546/JKT 10045, Jakarta 10230, Tel: 335551

Jakarta Hilton International (396 rooms), Jl. Jend. Gatot Subroto, P.O. Box 3315, Jakarta, Tel: 5703600

Le Meridien Jakarta, Jl. Jend. Sudirman, Kav 18-28, Jakarta 10220, Tel: 588250/1

Mandarin Oriental (455 rooms), Jl. M.H. Thamrin, P.O. Box 3392, Jakarta, Tel: 321307

First Class
(US$60 to US$100 per night)

Horison Hotel (350 rooms), Jl. Pantai Indah, Taman Impian Jaya Ancol, P.O. Box 3340, Jakarta, Tel: 680008

Hotel Indonesia (666 rooms), Jl. M.H. Thamrin, Jakarta 10010, Tel: 320008

Hotel Wiaata International, Jl. M.H. Thamrin, P.O. Box 2457, Jakarta, Tel:320308

The Aryaduta (340 rooms), Jl. Prapatan 44-48, Jakarta 10110, Tel: 376008

Patra Jasa Hotel, Jl. Jendral A. Yani No. 2, Bypass Jakarta 10510, Tel: 410608

President Hotel Nikko (354 rooms), Jl. M.H. Thamrin 59, Tel: 320508

Sahid Jaya Hotel (514 rooms), 86, Jl. Jendral Sudirman 86, P.O. Box 41, Jakarta, Tel: 5704444

Sari Pacific Hotel (521 rooms), Jl. M.H. Thamrin 6, P. O. Box 3138, Jakarta, Tel: 323707

JAVA

Anyer Beach Hotel, Jl. Raya Karnng Bolong, Anyer Serang 42166, West Java, Tel: 510503

Grand Hotel Preanger (63 rooms), 81, Jl. Asia Afika, P.O. Box 124, Bandung, Tel: 022-430682

Hyatt Regency Surabaya, Jl. Jenderal Basuki Rakhmat, 124-128 Surabaya, East Java, Tel: 511234

Istana Hotel (34 rooms), 21-24, Jl. Lembong, Bandung, Tel: 022-433025

Kumala Panghegar (65 rooms), 140, Jl. Asia Afrika, Bandung 40261, Tel: 022-52141

Motel Gununosari Patra Jasa, Jl. Ounungaarl, Surabaya, East Java, Tel: 68681, 65435, 65436

Patra Jasa Motel, Jl. It. Juanda 132, Bandung, West Java, Tel: 81664, 82590

Patra Jasa Motel, Jl. Tuparev No. 11, Cirebon, West Java, Tel: 29402, 27696

Panghegar Hotel (123 rooms), 2, Jl. Merdeka, Bandung, Tel: 022-430788

Patra Jasa, Jl. Sisingamangaraja, Semarang 50232, Central Java, Tel: 3144418

Samudra Beach Hotel, Pelabuhan Ratu, Sukabumi 41265, Tel: 23 or Jakarta 340601

Savoy Homann Hotel (100 rooms), 112, Jl. Asia Afrika, Bandung, Tel: 022-432244

Sheraton Inn Bandung (112 rooms), 390, Jl. Ir. H. Juanda, Bandung 40135, Tel: 022-81335

YOGYAKARTA

First Class
(US$35 and above per night)

Ambarrukmo Palace Hotel (240 rooms), Jl. Adisucipto, P.O. Box 10, Yogyakarta, Tel: 88488

Hotel Garuda, Jl. Malioboro 72, Yogyakarta, Tel: 486353

Puri Artha (60 rooms), Jl. Cendrawasih 9, Yogyakarta; Tel: 5934-5, Telex: 25147

Sriwedari (70 rooms), Jl. Adisucipto, P.O. Box 93, Yogyakarta, Tel: 88288

Sahid Garden (64 rooms), Jl. Babarsari, Yogyakarta, Tel: 3697

FOOD DIGEST

JAKARTA

Dining in Jakarta can be a delightful experience though, on the whole, restaurant meals are expensive here by Indonesian standards (about twice the price of a meal in the provinces), and the food is highly uneven in quality. Locals seek out obscure roadside stalls (*warung*) for a special *soto* or *sate* but too many visitors are hit with a stomach bug and this can ruin a week or more of your stay. It is possible to eat a good meal in a clean restaurant for US$2 and truly excellent Indonesian or Chinese food can be had for US$5 a head. With the exception of Western-style food and service, a meal at the best restaurants will rarely cost more than US$10 per person, all-inclusive. Seafood of any sort is excellent.

INDONESIAN FOOD

Ayam Bulungan (Javanese Fried Chicken), Jl. Bulungan I, No. 64, Kebayoran Baru, Tel: 772005

Hotel Marunda Restaurant, Wisata International, Tel: 320408, 320308

Natrabu Restaurant (Padang), Jl. H. Agus Salim 29A, Tel: 335668

Roda (Padang), Jl. Matraman Raya 65-67, Tel: 882879

Sari Bundo (Padang), Jl. Ir. H. Juanda 27, Tel: 358343

Sari Kuring (Sundanese Seafood), Jl. Batu Ceper No. 55A, Tel: 362203

Sari Nusantara, Jl. Silang Monas Timur, Tel: 352972

Senayan Satay House, Kebon Sirih 31A, 6, Jl. Pakubuwono VI, Tel: 7390521

CHINESE FOOD

The premier banquet houses for **Chinese Food** are the **Blue Ocean**, the **Cahaya Kota** and the **Istana Naga**.

For Szechuan food, try the pricey but delicious **Spice Garden** in the Mandarin Hotel or the **Summer Palace**. Hakka food is the specialty of the **Moon Palace**.

While visiting the Chinatown/Kota area, or in fact for a light lunch anywhere, it is *de rigueur* to sample a bowl of Chinese noodles with chopped pickled vegetables and beefballs (*mee bakso*). The largest noodle house in Chinatown is **Bakmi Gajah Mada**.

Bakmi Gajah Mada, 25, Blok M, Jl. Gajah Mada 92, Tel: 624689

Blue Ocean, 5, Jl. Hayam Wuruk, Tel: 366650

Cahaya Kota, Jl. Wahid Hasyim 9, Tel: 333077

Istana Naga, Jl. Jen. Gatot Subroto (Kav. 12, Case Building), Tel: 511809

Moon Palace, Jl. Melawai VII 15A, Tel: 711765

Spice Garden Restaurant (Szechuan), Mandarin Oriental Hotel, Jl. M.H. Thamrin, Tel: 332969

Summer Palace, Tedja Buana Building, Jl. Menteng Raya, Tel: 332989

EUROPEAN FOOD

If you insist on eating **European Food** in Jakarta, then experience the colonial atmosphere (and cuisine) of Dutch Batavia. This is best done at the magnificent **Oasis Restaurant**, a turn-of-the-century mansion turned eatery. Specialities of the house include a flaming sword shishkebab and the traditional Dutch colonial *rijsttafel* ("rice table") consisting of 20 Indonesian dishes served by 16 attractive young ladies. *Rijsttafel* is also the speciality of the **Club Noordwijk**, which has a *tempo deoloe*

"olden times") atmosphere in a somewhat less regal setting. Both establishments provide nightly musical entertainment. A less expensive place for *Indische* colonial food and atmosphere is the **Art and Curio Restaurant** located near TIM, the performing arts center of Jakarta.

Art and Curio Restaurant (Dutch Colonial), Jl. Kebon Binatang III/8A, Cikini, Tel: 322879

Brasserie Le Parisien (French), Aryaduta Hyatt Hotel, Jl. Prapatan 44, Tel: 376008 ext. 141

Club Noordwijk (Colonial/Dutch), Jl. Veteran, Tel: 353909

The Club Room (French), Mandarin Oriental Hotel, Tel: 321307

George & Dragon Pub & Restaurant (English), 32, Jl. Telukbetung, Tel: 325625

Jaya Pub (sandwiches & soups), Jaya building, Jl. M.H. Thamrin 12, Tel: 325633

Jayakarta Grill, Sari Pacific Hotel, Jl. M.H. Thamrin 6, Tel: 359141 ext. 1481

Le Bistro (French), Jl. K.H. Wahid Hasyim 75, Tel: 364277

Oasis Restaurant (Continental), Jl. Raden Saleh 47, Tel: 326397, 327818

YOGYAKARTA

The pilgrimage point for fried chicken lovers from all over Java (and all over the world now) is **Nyonya Suharti**'s (also known as *Ayam Goreng "Mbok Berek,"* after the women who invented this famous fried chicken recipe), located 4 miles (7 km) to the east of Yogya on the road to the airport (a short distance beyond the Ambarrukmo on the same side). The recipe is one of the best-kept culinary secrets in Indonesia - the chicken is first boiled and coated in spices and coconut, then fried crisp and served with a sweet chili sauce and rice. Excellent when accompanied by pungent *petai* beans and raw cabbage. Indonesians patronize the place in droves, and you can see Jakartans in the airport lounge clutching their take-away boxes of Nyonya Suharti's chicken for friends and family back home.

Nasi Padang fanatics also rave about the fare at **Sinar Budi Restaurant**, at Jl. Mangkubumi 41, about 500 meters north of the railway tracks on the left (opposite the cinema). Mutton *brani opor*, beef *rendang* and *gulai ayam* (chicken curry) await you at a moment's notice. Be sure to ask for their spicy potato chips (*kentang goreng*) - Sinar Budi's answer to the barbecue flavored variety in the West.

The Yogya speciality is *gudeg* - a combination

plate consisting of rice with boiled young jackfruit (*nangka muda*), a piece of chicken, egg, coconut cream gravy and spicy sauce with boiled buffalo hide (*sambal kulit*). The famous spot in Yogya for *gudeg* is **Juminten** at Jl. Asem Gede 22, Kranggan 69, just north of Jl. Diponegoro. The other *gudeg* restaurant of note is **Bu Citro**'s, located just opposite the entrance to the airport out on Jl. Adisucipto (a good place to eat while waiting for a flight). Most restaurants in Yogya also serve the dish, and there is excellent *gudeg* just north of Taman Sari on the eastern side of Jl. Ngasem.

Western food is now readily available in Yogya, and not just in the large hotels. The **Legian Garden Restaurant** serves excellent steaks, chops, sautéed fish, avocado seafood cocktails, yoghurt and corn and crab soup. Everything is very reasonable, the beer is cold and the vegetables are not overcooked. Enter via a well-marked doorway around the corner from Jl. Malioboro - Jl. Perwakilan 9 (Tel: 87985). The Legian Garden now has a branch, called **The Rose**, on the southern side of Jl. Solo - the same menu and prices but more atmosphere. For more money, the **Gita Buana** offers air-conditioning and low lighting at two locations: Jl. Diponegoro 52 A and out at Jl. Adisucipto 169 by the Ambarrukmo hotel. **The French Grill** in the Arjuna Plaza hotel (Jl. Mangkubumi 48) is also good, and they have puppet and dance performances every other night. **The Pesta Perak** (Jl. Tentera Rakyat Mataram 8) offers an Indonesian buffet in a pleasant garden setting.

There are several fine Chinese restaurants in town. The old standby and favorite of the local Chinese community is the **Tiong San**, at Jl. Gandekan 29, a block west of Malioboro. But the best seafood and, probably also the best Chinese food, is to be had at **Sintawang**, north of Jl. Diponegoro at Jl. Mageland 9, on the west side of the street.

CULTURE PLUS

YOGYAKARTA

Tourist performances are not necessarily any less authentic or in any way inferior (as some people insist), even though they are frequently shortened or excerpted versions of the originals, adapted for the benefit of foreign audiences.

What they do lack, of course, is a Javanese audience, and as the audience is as much a part of

most performances as the players (especially in Java), you should try if at all possible to catch a village or *kampung* shadow play or dance-drama. Being here at the right time to see one is just a matter of luck. Check with the **Tourist Information Office** (Jl. Malioboro 16) and travel agencies for up-to-date information.

GAMELAN

A *gamelan* orchestra is struck to accompany all of the dances and puppet shows listed below, and you can hardly avoid hearing recorded *gamelan* music everywhere you go in Yogya.

• Visit the **Kraton Gamelan Rehearsals** on Monday and Wednesday mornings from 10:30 a.m. to noon.

• Concerts are also staged at the **Pakualaman Palace** on Jl. Sultan Agung every fifth Sunday Minggu Pahing beginning at 10. No admission charge.

• And if somehow you seem to be missing all the other performances, then you can always go over to the lobby of the Ambarrukmo Palace Hotel, where a small *gamelan* ensemble plays daily from 10:30 a.m. to 12:30 p.m., and then again from 3:30 p.m. No admission charge.

WAYANG KULIT

This is truly the most influential Javanese art form, the one that traditionally has provided the Javanese with a framework through which to see the world and themselves. Not surprisingly, many foreigners have become fascinated by the shadow play (even if very, very few of them are able to understand the dialogue), and there is quite a voluminous literature in Dutch and English on the subject. Traditional performances are always at night, beginning at 9 p.m. and running until dawn.

• **The Agastya Art Institute** (Jl. Gedong Kiwo MD III/237), a private *dalang* (puppeteer) school, stages "rehearsal" excerpt performances for the benefit of tourists every day except Saturday, 3 p.m. to 5 p.m. US$3 admission.

• Another tourist excerpt performance is at **Ambar Budaya** in the Yogyakarta Craft Center opposite the Ambarrukmo Palace Hotel every Monday, Wednesday and Saturday from 9:30 p.m. to 10:30 p.m. US$3 admission.

• On the second Saturday of each month, Radio Republik Indonesia broadcasts a live all-night performance from the pavilion to the south of the Kraton, **Sasono Hinggil Dwi Abad**. Begins at 9 p.m. No admission charge.

• You can also try the **Habiranda Dalang School** at Pracimasono on the northeastern side of the *alun-alun* town square, where there are often informal training sessions or rehearsals in the evenings, 7 p.m. to 10 p.m., except Thursday and Sunday. No admission charge.

• *Wayang kulit* in an air-conditioned restaurant with dinner is the latest thing at the French Grill in the **Arjuna Plaza Hotel** (Jl. Mangkubumi 48) Tuesday nights at 7 p.m.

JAVANESE DANCE ·

• There is a rehearsal of the **Kraton Dancers** every Sunday from 10:30 a.m. to 12 a.m. US$0.50 admission.

• The Mardawa Budaya School, one of the best in Yogya, now stages a wide selection of dance excerpts in an aristocratic *pendapa*, **Dalem Pujokusuman**, Jl. Brig. Jend. Katamso 45, every Monday, Wednesday and Friday evening from 8 p.m. to 10 p.m. US$3 admission.

• Of course, if you happen (or plan) to be here between May and October around the full moon, don't miss the **Ramayana Ballet** at Prambanan. This is a so-called *sendratari* spectacular with a cast of thousands but without any dialogue. Get a round-trip "package" ticket out to Prambanan and back, including the US$4 admission from any travel agent or from the Tourist Information Center on Jl. Malioboro (about US$11).

• And if you prefer comfortable, hotel surroundings with dinner and refreshments, try the nightly "cultural show" at the **Ambarrukmo Palace Hotel**.

The regular performances listed above are all excellent. You should also visit some of the schools during the day to observe how Javanese dance is taught and studied. Most of these shools are situated in quite interesting surroundings – what are or used to be beautiful and elegant homes of members of the royal family.

•**Krido bekso Wirama**, Dalem Tejokusuman, Jl. K.H. Wahid Hasyim. The first school to teach Javanese dance outside the Kraton.

• **Siswo Among Bekso**, Dalem Poerwodiningratan, Jl. Kadipaten Kidul 46. They have frequent student performances.

• **Mardawa Budaya**, Jl. Brig. Jen. Katamso 45. Regular tourist performances (see above).

• **Pamulangan Beksa Ngayoyakarta**.

• **Bagong Kussudiarjo**, Jl. Singosaren 9, off Jl. Wates. The best-known Javanese "modern" dancer and choreographer. He was one of the artists who helped to invent and develop the *sendratari* art-dance-drama in the 1950s. Still an energetic writer, teacher and choreographer.

• **Indonesian Dance Academy (ASTI)**. This is one of five government tertiary-level dance schools in the nation and they get all the most promising young dancers from the Yogya area. Visit the school out on Jl. Colombo. This is where the most innovative Javanese dancing is found.

SHOPPING

WHAT TO BUY

Jakarta is not known as a shopper's paradise - imported goods are heavily taxed and domestic manufactures can only rarely compete in quality, though they are cheap. The good buys are hence limited mainly to two categories: handicrafts and antiques, with certain exceptions - notably pirated cassette tapes and locally produced designer clothes.

BATIK

Batik Keris, with showrooms in Sarinah, has the largest selection of *batik* in Jakarta, particularly yard goods and inexpensive *kain*. Another big Solo-based *batik* maker, **Danar Hadi**, specializes in finer *tulis* work fabric and ready-made shirts and dresses. Connoisseurs will want to stop in at the shop of designer **Iwan Tirta**. For *batik* paintings, Yogya-based **Amri** is the best known artist. Smaller, quality boutiques selling a range of clothes and fabrics include **Srikandi** and other shops on Jl. Palatehan I (Blok M, Kebayoran) and in the **Hilton Bazaar**.

Amri Gallery, Jl. Utan Kayu 66E

Batik Keris, Jl. Jend. Sudirman 9, Ratu Plaza

Danar Hadi, Jl. Raden Saleh 1A, Tel: 3423900

HANDICRAFT

The first stop for handicrafts of every description is the **Handicraft Center** in the Sarinah Jaya Department Store in Kebayoran. Here you can get everything from baskets to cane chairs to leather sandals. Then for paintings, carvings, *wayang* puppet and other "art" items, spend an afternoon or evening at the **Art Market** (*Pasar Seni*) in Ancol, where you can observe craftsmen at work and are welcomed to chat with them.

The **Indonesian Bazaar** at the Hilton Hotel has a number of up-market boutiques selling quality *batik*, jewelry and *wayang* puppets. Many of the antique and art shops at Jl. Kebon Sirih Timur Dalam, Jl. Majapahit and Jl. Palatehan (Kebayoran) also sell handicrafts. A few shops, such as the **Irian Art and Gift Shop** specialize in tribal handicrafts and primitive art.

ANTIQUES & CURIOS

These are available throughout the city, but especially on **Jl. Kebon Sirih Timur Dalam**, where there are several tiny shops with names like **Bali**, **Bima**, **Djody** and **Nasrun** - all stocked with old furniture, weavings, masks, puppets and porcelains. Nearby **Johan Art** has one of the largest collections of old Chinese porcelains; they will refund your money if good are found to be unsatisfatory after purchase, a rarity in Jakarta. Farther down Jl. Wahid Hasyim is a shop specializing in pewter ware: **The Banka Tin Shop**. Several other shops are on Jl. Haji Agus Salim (Jl. Sabang). All the above are within walking distance of Sarinah or the Sari Pacific Hotel.

There are also concentrations of antique and art shops in other areas of the city:

• The **antique market** on Jl. Surabaya, near Embassy Row (Jl. Diponegoro) consists of about 20 stalls set in a row. Porcelains, puppets, tiles, brass and silver bric-a-brac, much of it new but made to look old, spill forth onto the sidewalk. Nearby, two homes house a cache of antique Dutch furniture: Alex Papadimitriou's, and the Srirupa Shop.

• A new row of chic boutiques, galleries and studios catering to the foreign community and wealthy Jakartans is located in Kebayoran on **Jl. Papatehan I**. The new Sarinah Jaya Department Store is next door, and Aldiron Plaza/Blok M is within walking distance.

Bangka Tin Shop, Jl. Wahid Hasyim 178

Djelita Art Shop, Jl. Palatehan I/37

Djody Art & Curio, Jl. Kebon Sirih Timur Dalam 22

Irian Art and Gift Shop, Jl. Pasar Baru 16A, Tel: 343422

Johan Art Curios, Jl. H. Agus Salim 59A

Majapahit Arts & Curios, Jl. Melawai III/4, Block M

FURTHER READING

From the *Insight Guides* stable comes a range of travel guides, specially designed to help make your visit an unforgettable one.

More than 13,600 islands comprise the most extraordinary collection of places and people on earth.

Once the hub of the lucrative spice trade, this city still retains the romance of the past.

The best introduction to charming neighborhood streets and relaxed village lifestyles.

GETTING THERE

BY AIR

Bali's Ngurah Rai International Airport, which straddles the narrow Tuban Isthmus south of the island, is served by many daily flights from Jakarta, Yogyakarta, Surabaya and various other cities in Indonesia. Several weekly international flights arrive directly from Sydney, Melbourne, Perth and Darwin in Australia (Quantas and Garuda). Only Garuda and Singapore Airlines fly here from Europe and Singapore. Other international airlines fly only as far as Jakarta and you must then transfer to Garuda to reach Bali.

Flights to Bali from Jakarta's Cengkareng International Airport are frequent throughout the day, and you can generally catch a connection if you arrive before 6 p.m.

GETTING AROUND

Balinese roads are a parade ground, used for escorting village deities to the sea, for funeral cremation processions, for filing to the local temple in Sunday best, or for performances of a trans-island *barong* dance. They are also now increasingly crowded. The volume of traffic has increased dramatically over the past two decades.

In the end, the best way to see Bali is on foot. Away from the heavily-traveled main roads, the island takes on an entirely different complexion.

PUBLIC TRANSPORT

The local system of pick-ups and mini-buses (collectively known as *bemos*) and intra-island buses is efficient and inexpensive. You can get from one end of the island to the other for less than Rp. 4,000. Almost every *bemo* in Bali may be chartered by the trip or by the day, with the driver, by telling him where you want to go and then agreeing upon a

price. Most drivers are willing to go anywhere on the island for Rp. 40,000 a day (which is what they normally make hauling passengers).

TOURS

Expert daily bus tours, with well-informed multilingual guides are run by many travel agencies. They range in price from Rp. 14,000 for a half-day jaunt to Ubud or Sangeh/Mengwi, up to Rp. 40,000 for a full-day cross-island trip up to Kintamani or Besakih, including a *barong* dance in Batubulan, lunch and several stops at shops and temples.

You can also design your own private guided tour, in an air-conditioned car with a chauffeur/guide, which allows you to establish the itinerary and the amount of time spent at each sto–Rp. 60,000 to Rp. 120,000. The most experienced agents for the demanding traveler are **Bil** and **Pacto**.

TAXIS

There is a taxi service from the airport, with fares ranging from Rp. 6,000 (to nearby Kuta Beach) on up to Rp. 20,000 (to Ubud). Traveling to Sanur, Denpasar and Nusa Dua costs about Rp. 12,000.

Taxis and minibuses are for hire at every hotel, just with a driver, or with an English-speaking driver/guide. Rates are Rp. 60,000 to Rp. 80,000 per day. Often there is little difference (other than the price) between simply renting a car for a day (many drivers speak good English) and going on a professionally guided tour.

PRIVATE TRANSPORT

Car Rentals: The best way to get around the island independently is to rent a self-drive car, available in Kuta, Sanur or Denpasar. You must have a valid International Driving Permit. The most commonly rented vehicles are old beat-up **VW Safari** convertibles (Rp. 60,000 per day/Rp. 400,000 per week), although newer (sometimes air-conditioned) Suzuki Jimny's are also available for a bit more money (Rp. 70,000 to Rp. 80,000). You buy the gas. Buy the extra insurance also. Book a car through your hotel or from **Avis**, Bali Hyatt, Sanur, Tel: 88271 ext. 85023 or **Bali Car Rental**, Jln. By-pass Ngurah Rai, Sanur, Tel: 88550, 88359. Test-drive it before paying.

Motorcycle Rentals: Convenient and inexpensive. Be aware that the roads are crowded and traffic is dangerous – your chances of an accident are uncomfortably high. Each year several tourists are killed in motorbike accidents, and many more injured. If you do rent a bike, ride slowly and defensively.

The cost of hiring a motorbike is usually a matter of bargaining, and varies greatly. The usual price of a 100cc or 125cc machine is Rp. 6,000 to Rp. 12,000 per day, or Rp. 40,000 to Rp. 60,000 per week (paid in advance).

WHERE TO STAY

SANUR

Sanur is for gracious living, peace and quiet – more international but far less cosmopolitan than frenetic Kuta. Foreigners have been staying in Sanur since the 1920s, and they know how to take care of you here. Seek out the lovely Sanur temples, particularly when they are having their anniversary ceremonies (*odalan*), every seven months.

There are many excellent first-class hotels in Sanur, that you cannot go wrong. The main choice is between the convenience and luxury of a big four-star hotel or the quiet and personality of a private bungalow by the sea (at two-thirds to half the price). Reservations are advisable during the peak season: July to September and December to January. Prices quoted below do not include the obligatory 21% tax and service surcharge.

First Class
(above US$35 per night)

Alit's Beach Bungalow, Jl. Raya Sanur, P.O. Box 102, Denpasar, Tel: 88567

Bali Beach Hotel, Jln. Hang Tuah, Sanur 80001, Tel: 88511

Bali Hyatt Hotel, Sanur 80001, Bali, Tel: 88271-7

Bali Sanur Puri Dalem Bungalows, Jl. Raya Sanur, P.O. Box 306, Denpasar, Tel: 88421-2

Hotel Bali Beach Intercontinental, Sanur, P.O. Box 275, Denpasar, Tel: 88511/7

La Taverna Bungalows, Jl. Tanjungsari, Sanur, P.O. Box 40, Denpasar, Tel: 88497

Santrian Beach Hotel, Jl. Tanjungsari, Sanur, P.O. Box 55, Denpasar, Tel: 88181/3

Sanur Beach Hotel, Jln. Semawang, Sanur, P.O. Box 279, Denpasar, Tel: 88009/88011

Segara Village Hotel, Jl. Segara, Sanur, P.O. Box 91, Denpasar, Tel: 88407/8, 88021/2

Sindhu Beach Hotel, Jl. Sindhu, Sanur, P.O. Box 181, Denpasar, Tel: 88351-2

Tanjung Sari Hotel, Jl Tanjungsari, Sanur, P.O. Box 25, Denpasar, Tel: 88441

Intermediate Range
(US$15 to US$35 a night)

Bali Sanur Irama Bungalows, Jl. Tanjungsari, Sanur, Denpasar, Tel: 88423/4

Bintang Bali, Sanur 80001, Tel: 53292

Diwangkara Beach Hotel, Jl. Raya, Sanur, P.O. Box 120, Denpasar, Tel: 88577, 88412

Hotel Ramayan, Jl. Tanjungsari, Sanur, Denpasar, Tel: 664359

Laghawa Beach Inn, Jl. Tanjungsari, Sanur, Denpasar, Tel: 88494, 88214

Mars Hotel, Jl. Raya Sanur, Sanur, P.O. Box 95, Denpasar, Tel: 88211

Narmada Bali Inn, Jl. Sindhu, Sanur, P.O. Box 119, Denpasar, Tel: 88054

KUTA

Kuta is like a malignant seaside Carnaby Street of the '60s. Chaotic, noisy, lots of hype, but a great playground. Originally what drew visitors to Kuta was the wide beach and the surf, and it still has the best seafront on the island, now cluttered with hundreds of hotels, restaurants, bars, boutiques, travel agencies, antique shops, car and bike rentals, banks, cassette shops and wall-to-wall tourists.

Though there are now many first-class hotels, the 3-mile (5-km) strip still caters best for the economy traveler who likes to be in the thick of things. The Legian end of the beach is the probably the best place to stay for any period of time – much quieter and more relaxed.

Kuta Beach has so many bungalows, beach hotels and homestays (*losm*en) that no list is ever complete, nor is it really needed. Drop in, shop around and explore. However, note that reservations are necessary for the larger hotels during July to September and December to January.

First Class
(above US$35 a night)

Bali Anggrek Inn, Jl. Pantai Kuta, P.O. Box 435, Kuta, Tel: 51255

Bali Garden Hotel, Jl. Kartika, Kuta, Tel: 52725

Bali Oberoi, Kayu Aya, Legian, P.O. Box 351, Denpasar, Tel: 51061

Bali Padma, Jl. Padma 1, Legian Beach, P.O. Box 1107, Bali, Tel: 51723

Dynasty Shangri-La, Jl. Kartika Plaza, Kuta, P.O. Box 2047, Denpasar, Tel: 52403

Kartika Plaza, Kuta Beach, P.O. Box 84, Denpasar, Tel: 51067

Kul Kul Beach Resort, Jl. Pantai, Legian Beach, P.O. Box 97, Kuta, Bali, Tel: 52520

Kuta Beach Club, Jl. Bakungsari, P.O. Box 226, Kuta, Tel: 51261

Legian Beach Hotel, Jl. Melasti, Legian, P.O. Box 308, Denpasar, Tel: 51365

Pertamina Cottages, Kuta Beach, P.O. Box 121, Denpasar, Tel: 51161

Poppies Cottages, P.O. Box 378, Denpasar 80001, Tel: 51059

Ramada Bintang Bali Resort, Kuta Beach, Tel: 53292/3

Natour's Kuta Beach Hotel, Jl. Pantai Kuta, P.O. Box 393, Denpasar, Tel: 51461

Intermediate Range
(US$15 to US$35 a night)

Bali Mandira Cottages, Jl. Padma, Kuta, Tel: 51381

Sahid Bali Seaside Cottages, Kuta Beach, Tel: 53855

NUSA DUA

Bali Hilton International, Nusa Dua, Tel: 71102

Bali Resort Palace, Jl. Pratama, Tanjung Benoa, Nusa Dua, Bali 80361, Tel: 72026

Bali Tropic Palace, 34A Jl. Pratama, Nusa Dua, Tel: 72130

Club Bualu, P.O. Box 6, Nusa Dua, Tel: 71310, 71320

Club Med Bali, P.T. Bali Holiday Villages, Lot No. 6, Nusa Dua, Tel: 71520

Grand Hyatt Bali, P.O. Box 53, Nusa Dua, Tel: 71188

Hotel Nusa Dua, P.O. Box 1028, Denpasar, Tel: 71210

Hotel Putri Bali, P.O. Box 1, Nusa Dua, Tel: 71139

Melia Bali Sol, P.O. Box 1048, Nusa Dua, Tel: 71510

Mirage Bali, Jl. Pratama, 12 Tanjung Benoa, P.O. Box 43, Nusa Dua, Tel: 72147

Nusah Indah Hotel, P.O. Box 279, Denpasar, Tel: 88011

Sheraton Lagoon Nusa Dua Beach, P.O. Box 2044, Kuta 80361, Tel: 71327

UBUD

Amandari, Kedewatan, Ubud, Tel: 95333, Fax: 95335

Hotel Campuan, Ubud, P.O. Box 15, Denpasar 80001, Bali, Tel: 95137, Fax: 35428

Kupu Kupu Barong, P.O. Box 7, Ubud, Gianyar, Bali, Tel: 35663, Fax: 23172

Puri Saraswati, Main Road, Central Ubud, Ubud 80571, Bali, Tel: 95164

Ulun Ubud Cottages, Sanggingan, Ubud, P.O. Box 333, Denpasar 80001, Fax: 35190 SUNDT 1A, Cable: SUNDT DPR

FOOD DIGEST

WHERE TO EAT

The **Tanjung Sari Hotel Restaurant** has a formidable reputation for Indonesian *rijsttafel* and a sublime atmosphere. A bamboo *tingklink* orchestra provides the ideal accompaniment to dinner in a cosy, antique-filled dining area by the beach. The restaurant's new menu has a more creative nouveau-Bali slant, and the famous Bar, designed by Australian artist Donald Friend, is an elevated position overlooking the sea.

At **Kuri Putih**, in the Bali Sanur Irama Bungalows, chef Nyoman Sana of Ubud has at last brought his kitchen to Sanur. Try the barbecued specials from the grill and help yourself to side dishes from a tempting buffet salad bar.

Telega Naga, opposite the Bali Hyatt, is a spectacularly stylish Szechuanese restaurant in a lake, designed by Hyatt architect Kerry Hill. The food is good and the prices are non-hotel. Try the "Chicken with Dried Chili Peppers," the king prawn and the duck dishes.

The best Italian food in Bali is available at **Trattoria Da Marco**, where Reno and Diddit da Marco have guarded their reputation and clientele foe 15 years now. Try the grilled fish, *spaghetti carbonara*, bean salad and their steaks, truly the best in Bali.

La Taverna is part of the Hongkong-based chain of Italian restaurants in Asia. The Sanur branch is a charming bar and open dining area on the beach, with a menu that features imported cheeses, French pepper steak, seafood and pizza from a real pizza oven.

For more local flavours, try the inexpensive **Beach Market** (on Jl. Segara right at the beach), a little outdoor restaurant run by Sanur's mayor. Great for lunch (*sate, nasi goreng* and fresh fried fish) or dinner (grilled lobster), with delicious Balinese desserts, all at unbeatable prices.

New restaurants seem to open daily in Kuta, from small fruit salad and yoghurt stands by the beach to large Chinese, French or seafood establishments. The quality of the food goes up and down as cooks come and go, so we list here only a few old standbys where you can hardly ever go wrong. Ask around though for tips on the latest "in" restaurant.

Made's Warung on Jl. Pantai hasn't missed a beat in its metamorphosis from one or two foodstalls on the main street of a sleepy fishing village to a hip Cafe Voltaire in the St Tropez of the East. It has great food (spare ribs, Thai salad, escargots, turtle steaks, home-made ice-cream, chocolate mousse, capuccino, fresh-squeezed orange and carrot juices, breakfast specials).

Poppies, down a narrow lane, is another Kuta fixture. Avocado seafood salads, pate, tacos, grilled lobster, steaks, shishkebab and tall mixed drinks pack this garden idyll to capacity during the peak tourist seasons. Get there early to get a table.

Bali Indah and **Lenny's** are both first-rate for Chinese cuisine and seafood. Try the crab-in-blackbean-sauce at Bali Indah. And for fresh lobster or fried tuna fish steaks, go over to the **Yasa Samudra** Hotel (at the end of Jl. Pantai Kuta) and dine under the stars by the sea.

In Legian, the **Blue Ocean Hotel**'s beachside cafe is a popular gathering point for breakfast and lunch. And farther down, in Seminyak, **La Marmite** (also known as **Chez Gado-Gado**) serves Balinese "nouveau cuisine" in a secluded open-air location by the beach. The after-dinner disco on Saturday nights is the happening thing. The **Kura Kura** restaurant in the Bali Oberoi hotel, several miles beyond Legian is perfect for that special occasion. A quiet poolside overlooking the ocean. Go there for the sunset, dinner and drinks. Very romantic. Try the pepper duck, or grilled lobster.

CULTURE PLUS

DANCES

The best way to see Balinese dances, *wayang kulit* puppet shows and *gamelan* orchestras is to attend a village temple festival. There is one going on somewhere on the island almost every day. Ask your hotel, or consult the **Bali Post Calendar**, available from most shops. In the fine print beneath are listed the names of villages having ceremonies and the type of celebration (it is not 100 percent accurate, however).

Public performances are also given at various central locations all over the island. These are mainly for the benefit of tourists only. Some of the best dancers and musicians in Bali participate in tourist performances, and for them it's a good source of income. The Bali Hyatt has a plush disco, the **Matahari** with deejays and music provided by Juliana's of London.

Also in Sanur, the **Karya Restaurant**, the **Purnama Terrace** (in the Bali Hyatt) and the **Kul Kul Restaurant** (book for the Frog Dance night) are the island's best venues for dinner and a show under the stars.

The **Nusa Dua Hotel** at night is a spectacle in its own right – go there for its Ramayana Night and dine in opera box-like seats surrounding an open-air stage.

NIGHTLIFE

For hot, pulsating nightlife with loud, gyrating crowds and ear-shattering music, make your way over to the Kuta Beach side. This formerly somnambulant beach village is now on the go day and night.

A number of watering holes along Jalan Legian and Jalan Buni Sari stay open as longas there are people. Casablanca and The Pub, to mention just two, serve chilled Bintang beer in chilled mugs.

SHOPPING

WHAT TO BUY

Bali is a great place to shop. Hundreds of boutiques and roadside stalls have set up all over the island, and thousands of artisans, craftsmen, seamstresses, woodcarvers, painters, etc. are busy supplying the tourist demand.

WOODCARVINGS

You are sure to find good woodcarvings in the shops along the main roads in **Mas** (particularly well-known is Ida Bagus Tilem's Gallery and Museum). Also try the villages of **Pujung** (past Tegalalang north of Ubud), **Batuan** and **Jati**.

All types of indigenous wood, ranging from the butter-colored jackwood to the inexpensive bespeckled coconut, are sculpted here in bold designs which set the standards for carvers elsewhere on the island. Woods imported from other islands – buff hibiscus, rich brown Javanese teak and black Sulawesian ebony are also hewn into delicate forms by Balinese craftsmen.

PAINTINGS

The artist's center is **Ubud**, including the surrounding villages of **Pengoseken**, **Penestanan**, **Sanggingan**, **Peliatan**, **Mas** and **Batuan**.

The famous **Neka Gallery & Museum** and the **Puri Lukisan Museum**, both in Ubud, will give you an idea of the range of styles and the artistry achieved by the best painters. Thereafter visit some of the other galleries in the area: **Gallery Munut**, **Gallery Agung** and the gallery of the **Pengoseken Community of Artists**. Examples from every school of painting active in Bali can be found here as well as canvasses of young artists portraying festivals and dancers.

GOLD & SILVER

The centers for metal working are **Celuk** and **Kamasan**, where all such ornaments are on sale at reasonable prices. **Kuta** is another center for export gold and silver wares. For traditional Balinese jewelry, visit the shops on Jl. Sulawesi and Jl. Kartini in **Denpasar**.

HANDICRAFTS

Bamboo implements, *wayang kulit* figures and ornaments made of coconut shell and teakwood are sold at most souvenir shops. Bonecarvings can be had for good prices at **Tampaksiring**, while plaited hats and baskets are the specialty of the women of **Bedulu** and **Bona**.

Sukawati market and the row of stands opposite **Goa Gajah** are the best places to buy baskets. **Klungkung** market also has some finely worked traditional wares.

The **Handicraft Center** (Sanggraha Karya Hasta) in Tohpati, Denpasar, has a collection of handicrafts from Bali and the other islands of Indonesia, such as baskets and weavings. Open 8 a.m. to 5 p.m. daily, closed Mondays.

The morning market at **Pasar Badung** in Denpasar is also an eye-opener. Coral-lined alleys will lead you to a ceremonial knick-knacks section selling baskets of every shape and size.

ANTIQUES

Try the shopping arcades of major hotels for truly outstanding pieces (at outstanding prices). In **Kuta**, Angang's and the East West Artshop have the best collection of antiques and primitive artifacts.

In **Denpasar**, there are several antique shops

along Jl. Gajah Mada up near the town square end. Also on Jl. Arjuna, Jl. Dresna, Jl. Veteran and Jl. Gianyar. In Sanur, the shops are along Jl. Sanur.

The many antique shops adjacent to the Kerta Gosa in **Klungklung** house collections of rare Chinese porcelains, old Kamasan wayang style paintings, antique jewelry and Balinese weavings. Prices are reasonable.

Singaraja has some of the best antique shops in Bali, too. They're all on the main roads of this northern city.

FURTHER READING

From the *Insight Guides* stable comes a range of travel guides specially designed to help make your visit an unforgettable one.

APA's pioneering guidebook will help bring the magic of Bali to any journey.

This handy guide offers personalized and well-outlined routes in the land of mist and mystique.

This introduction to the Balinese countryside takes the visitor away from the usual tourist haunts.

GETTING THERE

Depending on where you are coming from, it may be difficult to get a direct flight to some of the less-developed destinations in the Indonesian archipelago. However, connecting flights from Jakarta or Bali are readily available.

WHERE TO STAY

LOMBOK

Lombok Intan Laguna, Senggigi, Mataram, Tel: 23680

Seleparang Hotel, Jl. Pejanggik 40, Cakranegara, Tel: 22670

Senggigi Beach Hotel, Senggigi Beach, Mataram, Tel: 23430

Sheraton Senggigi Beach Resort, Senggigi Beach, Mataram

Suranadi Hotel, Jl. Raya Suranadi, Mataram, Tel: 23686

NUSA TENGARA

SUMBAWA

Losmen Lila Graha, Jl. Belakang Bioskop, Bima, Tel: 740

Losmen Saudara, Jl. Hasanudin, Sumbawa Besar, Tel: 21528

Suci Hotel, Jl. Hasanudin No. 57, Sumbawa Besar, Tel: 21589

Tambora Hotel, Jl. Kabayon, Sumbawa Besar, Tel: 21555

KOMODO

There are several large and comfortable bungalows at the **PPA Camp** in Loho Liang. Both dorm-style rooms and twin rooms are available. Each cabin has two toilet/bathrooms and an overnight stay costs about US$4. Cheap meals of rice and fish are available. Total capacity is 80 beds.

SUMBA

Elim Hotel, Jl. Achmad Yani No. 35, Waingapu, Tel: 32/162

Losmen Lima Saudara, Jl. Wanggametti No. 2, Waingapu, Tel: 83

Losmen Pelita, Jl. Udayana, Waikabubak

Rakuta Hotel, Jl. Veteran, Waikabubak

Sandalwood Hotel, Jl. Matawai, Waingapu, Tel: 117

Surabaya Hotel, Jl. Eltari No. 2, Waingapu, Tel: 117

FLORES

Losmen Karya, Ruteng

Losmen Mutiara, Jl. Pelabuhan No. 31, Labuhanbajo

Losmen Komodo Jaya, Labuhanbajo

Wisma Agung, Jl. Wae Cos No. 10, Ruteng

Wisma Sindha, Jl. Yos Sudarso, Ruteng

SUMATRA

MEDAN

Angkasa Hotel, Jl. Sutomo No. 1, Medan, Tel: 322555

Danau Toba International, Jl. Imam Bonjol No. 17, P.O. Box 490, Medan, Tel: 327000

Dirga Surya Hotel, Jl. Imam Bonjol No. 6, Medan, Tel: 321555

Garuda Hotel, Jl. Sisingamangaraja No. 27, Medan, Tel: 22775/324453

Garuda Plaza International, Jl. Sisingamangaraja No. 18, Medan, Tel: 326255

Hotel Patrajasa Parapat, Kp. Sluhan-Parapat, Medan, Tel: 41796, Fax: 41536

Pardede International, Jl. Ir. H. Juanda No. 14, Medan, Tel: 323866

Polonia Hotel, Jl. Jendrai Sudirman No. 14, Medan, Tel: 325300/325700

Sumatera Hotel, Jl. Sisingamangaraja No. 21, Medan, Tel: 24973/324807

Way Yat Hotel, Jl. Asia No. 44, Medan, Tel: 27457/27575

BRASTAGI

Rose Garden Hotel, Jl. Peceren, Brastagi

Rudang Hotel, Jl. Sempurna, Brastagi

PRAPAT/LAKE TOBA

Astari Hotel, Jl. Pulau Samosir, Prapat, Tel: 41219/41725

Danau Toba International, Jl. Pulau Samosir, Prapat, Tel: 41583/41719

Natour Hotel Prapat, Jl. Marihat No. 1, Prapat, Tel: 41021/41081

Patra Jasa Prapat, Jl. Siuhan, Prapat, Tel: 41796

Silintong, Jl. Tuktuk Siadang, Pulau Samosir, Tel: 41345

Toba Beach, Jl. Pangembatan, Tomok, Pulau Samosir

BUKITTINGGI

Benteng Hotel, Jl. Benteng No. 1, Bukittinggi, Tel: 22115

Denai Hotel, Jl. Rivai No. 5, Bukittinggi, Tel: 21460/21511

Dymen's International, Jl. Nawawi Nos. 1,3,5, Bukittinggi, Tel: 21015/22781

Limas Hotel, Jl. Kesehatan No. 34, Bukittinggi, Tel: 22641/22763

Minang Hotel, Jl. Panorama No. 20, Bukittinggi, Tel: 21120

PADANG

Bouganville Hotel, Jl. Baginda Aziz Khan No. 2, Padang, Tel: 22149

Mariani International, Jl. Bundo Kandung No. 35, Padang, Tel: 25410/25466

Muara Hotel, Jl. Gereja No. 34, P.O. Box 10, Padang, Tel: 25600/21850

Padang Hotel, Jl. Baginda Aziz Khan No. 28, Padang, Tel: 22563

Pangeran Hotel, Jl. Dobi No. 3-5, Padang, Tel: 262333/31

RIAU ARCHIPELAGO

Batam Island Country Club, Tanjung Pinggir, Sekupang, Batam, Tel: 22825 or Singapore 225-6819

Batam Jaya Hotel, Jl. Raja Ali Haji, P.O. Box 35, Batam, Tel: 58707/58348

Batam View Hotel, Jl. Hang Lekir,, Nongsa, Batam, Tel: (Singapore) 235-4366

Hill Top Hotel, Jl. Jlir, Sutami No. 8, Sekupang, Batam, Tel: 22482

Mutiara Panghegar, Jl. Yos Sudarso 12A, Pekanbaru, Tel: 07-612-3667

Riau Holiday Inn, Jl. Pinang II No. 53, Tanjung Pinang, Bintan, Tel: 22573/22644 or (Singapore) 737-5735

Sampurna Jaya Hotel, Jl. Yusuf Kahar No. 15, Tanjung Pinang, Bintan, Tel: 21555/21269 or (Singapore) 532-4711

Turi Beach Resort, Nongsa, P.O. Box 55/BAM, Batam, Tel: 21543 or (Singapore) 235-5544

KALIMANTAN

BANJARMASIN

Maramim Hotel, Jl. Lambung Mangkurat No. 32, Banjarmasin, Tel: 4958/4835

New River City Hotel, Jl. R.E. Martadinata No. 3, Banjarmasin, Tel: 2983

Perdana Hotel, Jl. Brig. Jen. Katamso No. 5, Banjarmasin, Tel: 3276

Hotel Sabrina, Jl. Bank Rakyat No. 21, Banjarmasin, Tel: 4442/4721

BALIKPAPAN

Benakutai Hotel, Jl. P. Antasari, Balikpapan, Tel: 21804/21813

Budiman Hotel, Jl. P. Antasari, Balikpapan

Grand Park Hotel, Jl. P. Antasari, Balikpapan, Tel: 22942

Kaltim Hotel, Jl. Kampung Baru Tengah, Balikpapan

Mirama Hotel, Jl. May. Jen. Sutoyo, Balikpapan, Tel: 22960/61

Puri Kencana Hotel, Jl. Gajah Mada No. 14, Balikpapan

Tirta Plaza, Jl. D.I. Panjaitan No. 51-52, Balikpapan, Tel: 22324/22364

SULAWESI

UJUNG PANDANG

Makassar Golden Hotel, Jl. Pasar Ikan 52, Ujung Pandang, Tel: 22208

Marannu City Hotel, Jl. Sultan Hasanuddin 3, Ujung Pandang, Tel: 5087

Toraja Cottage, Paku Bola Salu, Rantepao, Tel: 84146

Victoria Panghegar Hotel, Jl. Jen. Sudirman 24, Ujung Pandang, Tel: 21428

MANADO

Kawanua City Hotel, Jl. Sam Ratulangi 1, Manado, Tel: 52222

MALUKU

Amboina Hotel, Jl. Kapitan Ulupaha No. 5, Ambon City, Ambon, Tel: 41725

Mahu Village Resort, Mahu Village, Saparua Island, Tel: 3529

Manise Hotel, J.W.R. Spratman, Ambon City, Ambon, Tel: 42905

Mutiara Hotel, Jl. Raya Pattimura, Ambon City, Ambon, Tel: 3075

IRIAN JAYA

Hotel Dafonsoro, Jl. Percetakan, Negara Jayapura, Tel: 21870

Hotel Triton, Jl. Achmad Yani No. 52, P.O. Box 33, Jayapura, Tel: 21218

Losmen Sederhana, Jl. Halmahera, Dekat Sarinah, Jayapura, Tel: 21291

FOOD DIGEST

LOMBOK

Balinese-style roast suckling pig (*babi guling*) prepared by the Lombok Balinese beats anything on the mother island. You can arrange a feast through your hotel or driver, and be sure to ask if it can be served in one of the spacious courtyards of a Lombok Balinese home. You can also arrange for *tuak* (palm toddy) to go with the pig, and a folk dance performance.

The old Chinese restaurants of Jalan Pabean in Ampenan (the **Tjirebon** and the adjacent **Pabean**) are both centrally located and good, favorite hang-outs for budget travelers. The Tjirebon has cold beer and steak with chips (don't eat the salad).

Many of the Arab restaurants of Mataram serve both Yemeni and Lombok dishes. The **Taliwang** on Jalan Pejanggik features *ayam pelicing* – the searing hot curried chicken that is Lombok's specialty. The nearby **Garden House Restaurant** serves both Chinese and Indonesia food.

In Cakranegara, the restaurants tend to cluster along Jalan Selaparang. The **Asia** and the **Harum** serve Chinese food. The **Minang** has *nasi Padang*, while the **Istimewa** and the **Hari Ini** both serve *ayam pelicing*. For Western dishes, try the **Selaparang Hotel**.

Both the **Surandai Hotel** (in Surandai) and the **Wisma Soejono** (in Tete Batu) enjoy good reputations for tasty, fresh fish taken from their ice-cold ponds.

NUSA TENGARA

SUMBAWA

Try the **Aneka Rasa** in Sumbawa Besar for Chinese or local food as well as cold beer. In Bima, your best bet is the **Rumah Makan Anda** near the cinema, which serves both Chinese and Indonesia food including delicious crayfish.

KOMODO

There are no restaurants. Bring your own food and cook it at the **PPA Camp** in Loho Liang.

SUMBA

Waingapu has several good restaurants including the **Rajawali**, the **Feni** (on Jl. Tribrata) and the **Jakarta** (on Jl. Achmad Yani).

FLORES

Flores is not a gourmet paradise. Skip the *warung* and eat at your *losmen* or hotel. Among the better bets are the **Losmen Komodo Jaya** and the **Losmen Mutiara** in Labuhanbajo, or the **Agung** in Ruteng which serves up Chinese food.

SUMATRA

MEDAN

Medan is a good place for eating. The **Tip Top Restaurant** at No. 92 Jalan Jend. A. Yani is known for its excellent Padang good, curried mutton brains and extravagant choice of ice-cream. The **Garuda Restaurant** on Jalan Pemuda also has Padang food along with a thirst-quenching choice of fruit juices.

At night, one of the best places to visit is **Selat Panjang**, an alley behind Jalan Pandu with stalls serving Chinese food, satay and fruit juices. Another open-air eatery is the swimming pool on Jalan Sisingamangaraja – famous for its *satay*.

Medan is also highly regarded for its durians. The best months are August and September, when the street stalls offer the fruit in abundance at just about unbeatable prices.

Among other recommended restaurants you can find in Medan are:

Bali Plaza (Chinese), Jl. Kumango No. 1A, Tel: 514852

Cafe De Marati (European), Jl. Gatot Subroto, Tel: 321751

De'Bour (Asian and European), Hotel Dharma Deli, Jl. Balai Kota No. 2, Tel: 327011

De'Plaza (Asian and European), Garuda Plaza International Hotel, Jl. Sisingamangaraja No. 18, Tel: 326255

Toshiko Yokohama (Japanese), Hotel Danau Toba International, Jl. Imam Bonjol No. 17, Tel: 327000

PRAPAT/LAKE TOBA

Most of the restaurants in Prapat are on Jalan Pulau Samosir and Jalan Sisingamangaraja. Among them are the **Asia Restaurant** for Chinese and Indonesia dishes, and the **Wisma Danau Toba** for both Asian and European cuisine.

BUKITTINGGI

Dymen's Hotel (Asian and European), Jl. Nawawi No. 1, 3, 5, Tel: 22781

Ria Sari (Minang-style cuisine), Ngarai Sianok Shopping Center, Jl. Jend. Sudirman No. 1, Tel: 21503

Simpang Raya (Minang), Muka Jam Gadang, Tel: 22585.

PADANG

Chan's (Chinese), Jl. Pondok No. 94, Tel: 22131

Hang Tuah (Asian and European), Hotel Hang Tuah, Jl. Pemuda No. 1, Tel: 26556/7/8

Machudum's Bar & Restaurant (Asian and European), Hotel Machudum, Jl. Hiligo No. 45, Tel: 22333/23997

Mariani Hotel Restaurant (Asian and European), Hotel Mariani, Jl. Bundo Kandung No. 35, Tel: 35421

Phoenix (Chinese), Jl. Niaga No. 138, Tel: 21304

RIAU ARCHIPELAGO

Set at the mouth of the Straits of Malacca, the seafood is excellent in the Riau islands, especially on Batam. Among the specialties are chili crab, garlic prawns, *gulai ikan* (fish curry), fried squid and grilled lobster. There are many tasty seafood stalls along the shore at **Pantai Batu Besar** and along **Nongsa Beach**, plus a night hawker center at **Lubuk Baja** in Nagoya village.

There is also a night market with food stalls in Tanjung Pinang, the main town on neighboring Bintan Island.

Batam Island Country Club (Chinese and Indonesian), Tanjung Pinggir, Sekupang, Batam, Tel: 22825

Batam View Hotel (Asian and European), Jl. Hang Lekir, Nongsa, Batam, Tel: 22281

Pagi Sore (Padang-style cuisine), Lubuk Baja, Nagoya, Batam

Panjang Restaurant (seafood), Tanjung Pinang, Bintan

Rejeki Restaurant (seafood), Pantai Batu Besar, Batam

Riau Holiday Inn (Asian, European and seafood), Jl. Plantar II No. 53, Tanjung Pinang, Bintan, Tel: 22573

Tunas Baru Seafood Restaurant, Jl. Imam Bonjol, Block E, No. 42, Nagoya, Batam, Tel: 58498

KALIMANTAN

BANJARMASIN

Prambanan (Javanese), Perdana Hotel, Jl. Brig. Jen. Katamso No. 5, Tel: 3276.

Maramim Hotel Restaurant (Asian and European), Jl. Lambung Mangkurat No. 32, Tel: 4958/4835

BALIKPAPAN

Mirama (Asian and European), Hotel Mirama, Jl. May. Jen. Sutoyo, Tel: 561/562

Rainbow Coffee Shop & Restaurant (European and Chinese), Blue Sky Hotel, Jl. Letjen Soeprapto No. 1, Tel: 22267

SULAWESI

UJUNG PANDANG

The seafaring Makassarese are famous seafood cooks who employ simple yet delicious recipes. Their most famous dish is *ikan Bakar* – red snapper or sea bass grilled over an open flame, served with rice and spicy *sambal*. Though it's best eaten while sitting on the wooden benches of a waterfront *warung* in the company of Bugis sailors in town for the night, you may also sample it in the more gentile settings of the **Asia Baru Restaurant** at Jalan Salahutu No. 2.

Other restaurants serving a mix of Chinese, Indonesian and Western food include **Hilman** at Jalan Jampea No. 2, the upmarket **Bamboo Den** on Jalan G. Latimojong, and the waterfront **Sea View** on Jalan Panghibur.

If seafood isn't your thing, another local specialty is *soto makassar*, a thick, nutritious soup made from various parts of the water buffalo. Try it in the afternoon at **Soto Daeng** near the Istana cinema, or at roadside *warung* all over town.

Other recommended restaurants in Ujung Pandang:

Happy (Asian and European), Jl. Sulawesi, Tel: 22947

Wisma Ria (Asian and European), Jl. Pasar Ikan

MANADO

Cakalong (Asian and European), Kawanua City Hotel, Jl. Sam Ratulangi No. 1, Tel: 3771

Dua Raya (Chinese), Jl. P. Tenoban No. 46, Tel: 2236

MALUKU

The Moluccan lifestyle is reflected in a rather basic cuisine. Sago is the staple food in the south, supplemented by sweet potatoes and cassava. Fish is the main source of protein, with meat and fowl reserved for special occasions. The *kanari* nut, similar to an almond, goes into a sauce for *gado-gado*-style salads. In the north, saffron rice eaten with curry or satay is very popular.

Families of mixed Arab and Chinese heritage have a more varied cuisine and eat more meat. Eurasian Moluccans favor a Dutch-style cuisine with such dishes as red-bean soup with pork trotters, and fish in white sauce. Dining out is not a widespread habit, though coffee houses serve lunch. A number of food stalls and small restaurants are beginning to appear to cater to the many immigrant workers who live in the islands.

Amboina Bakery, Jl. A.Y. Patty, Ambon City, Ambon

Halim Restaurant, Jl. Sultan Hairun, Ambon City, Ambon, Tel: 97126

Tirta Kencana Coffee House, Amahusu village, Ambon

IRIAN JAYA

Jayapura, the capital of Irian Jaya province, has a large Bugis population, so *ikan Bakar* is the meal of choice. The alley behind the Impor-Expor Bank near the *bemo* terminal is lined with *warung* serving *ikan akar* and satay.

Two recommended restaurants are the **Cahaya** on Jalan Achmad Yani Jayapura, and **Hawaii** on Dekat Sarinah. Both serve European and Asian food.

SHOPPING

WHAT TO BUY

LOMBOK

Traditional textiles are the best buy on Lombok. Visit the villages where the threads are woven by hand: **Sukarare** for *tenun Lombok*; **Pujung** for *kain lambung*; **Purbasari** for *kain Purbasari*; and **Balimurti** for the sacred *beberut* cloths. **Labuhan Lombok** on the east coast produces fine blankets.

The best weaving factories for contemporary textiles are in **Cakranegara**. Many of Bali's resident Italian couturiers purchase cloth from a shop called **C.V. Rinjani** next door to the Hotel Selaparang. The stockroom often has leftovers from bolts of top designer fabrics. The silk *sarungs* and matching *selendang* scarves are highly regarded among the rag trade cognoscenti of Bali and Jakarta.

Selamat Ryadi weaving factory in the Arab quarter at No. 10 Jalan Ukir Kawi (one block north and one block west of the Pura Mayura Water Palace) is another excellent source of yard goods. The nearby **Balimurti** factory produces weaving in the traditional *Purbasari* style.

Lombok's bamboo baskets are extremely decorative and sturdy. Many are produced in the eastern villages of **Kotaraja** and **Loyok**. Ceramic pots and earthenware are also beautifully crafted and elegantly shaped here. The bustling **Sweta Market** (just east of Cakranegara) and the **Cakranegara Market** to the west of the Pura Meru temple offer numerous bamboo, ceramic as well as wooden crafts.

Sudirman's antique shop is situated a few hundred meters down a side lane off Jalan Pabean in Ampenan (enter from opposite the *bemo* station, but be sure to ask directions). *Kris* blades, old weaving, religious effigies and other antiques (both old and new) are for sale here.

SUMBA

People flock here from all over the world to buy traditional Sumbanese *ikat* cloth. But you should shop carefully, as many inferior work is for sale. Look for smoothly curved lines as a sign of good work. The intricacy of the patterns is also important. Check to see if the colors are clean or if the dyes have run into each other (if there are white patches in the design, they should be sharp and clean).

Bargain with great determination – final prices could well be one-third the original asking price. Most *ikat* come in pairs – one as a bodywrap and one as a shawl. Prices can range from US$10 for mass-produced throw-away *ikat* to more than US$500 for a family heirloom (although these are increasingly hard to find).

The villages of **Prailiu** and **Mangili** outside Waingapu are the main centers of the Sumba weaving industry. **Melolo** on the southeast coast is also a good source of old Sumbanese handwoven fabrics.

Another unusual item for sale in Sumba are tiny metal disks shaped like a woman's vagina. These were traditionally used as part of a bride's dowry, but Western women now purchase them to use as earrings.

MEDAN

Medan's markets offer handicrafts from all over Sumatra and Java. A number of antique shops offer a good choice of merchandize. Among the shops worth visiting are: **Borobudur** (textiles, masks and statues), **Arafah** (paintings and carvings), **Aslo** (paintings), **Rufino** (paintings and statues) and **Selatan** (paintings), all on Jalan Jend. Achmad Yani.

For *batik* you should try **Pasar Ikan Lama** on Jalan Perniagaan between Jalan Yani and the railway tracks. Most of the souvenir shops along Jalan Yani also sell *batik* as do some shops on Jalan Arifin. Some shops such as **Batik Keris** and **Danar Hadi** on Jalan Arifin sell *batik* either by the meter or ready made.

LAKE TOBA

Nearly 20 years of tourism has unfortunately almost exhausted the supply of genuine antiques in the Toba and Karo districts. Reproductions of Batak tribal calendars and buffalo-horn medicine pouches are all too common now. A real antique is just as likely to turn up in Medan (try **Toko Bali** at No. 68 Jalan Jend. Jani or **Indonesia Art Shop** on the same street).

Some Toba entrepreneurs offer to take visitors on "antique safaris" around the countryside, but prices are invariably high. However, there is still good Chinese porcelain available along with Dutch silver coins.

The greatest, although most macabre, find is a Tungkat carved magic wand. Real wands contain phial of slaughtered baby's blood. Because they are considered so powerful, the asking price for authentic wands is upwards of US$1,000. Genuine Batak spirit figures can still be found, though the mini Batak houses are mostly of contemporary origin. Batak weaving and *kain ulos* are good buys, but you must be prepared to bargain hard.

WEST SUMATRA

West Sumatra is renowned for its beautiful handloomed *songket* cloth and fine embroidery, and for its silverwork and woodcarving. Though weaving is practiced in a number of communities, the best known source is **Silungkang**, a small town on the Agam Plateau where the brightly colored silk *songket sarungs*, scarves and headwear – all richly interwoven with gold – are made.

Another popular center is **Pandai Sikat** near Padangpanjung, on the main road between Padang and Bukittinggi. Loomed by women working in small cottage industry shops, it takes from a few weeks to a few months to finish a set consisting of a *sarung* and matching scarf. Pandai Sikat is also known for its embroidery and woodcarving.

Silversmiths working in **Kota Gadang**, near Bukittinggi, produce fine spider-web filigree work. In **Sungaipuar**, a small village 20 minutes from Bukittinggi, blacksmiths still pound out anything from spoons to agricultural implements.

KALIMANTAN

The center of attention for anyone interested in Borneo arts and crafts is Dayak culture. The work of the indigenous tribes of the island display an extraordinary sense of design. The characteristic geometric patterns used in portraying scenes of jungle life bear unmistakable Chinese and Hindu-Javanese influences.

Ikat (tie-dying) is the most common weaving technique. Bark fibers, plant dyes and earth dyes were used originally, though greater use is being made of commercial yarn and dyes these days. Dayak cloth is as good, if not better, than the famous *ikat* of Sumba.

More than any other ethnic group in Indonesia, the Dayaks are famed for their beadwork. Thousands of tiny glass beads are used to decorate purses, tobacco pouches, scabbards, baby-carriers, basket lids, hems, caps and headbands. The Penan are famous for their yellow-and-black beadwork.

Another popular craft is basketry. A wide variety of baskets in traditional two-tone patterns can be purchased.

Sex roles differentiate most Dayak crafts. Men are more at home carving wood and working metal, while the women tend more towards plaiting, weaving, beadwork and tattooing.

SULAWESI

Toraja woodcarvings and weaving are the most popular handicraft items sold in Sulawesi. Ujung Pandang has a number of good antique shops. Try **Art Shop** on Jalan Somba Opu for statues, carvings, *batik*, *sarungs*, baskets and leather. **Asdar Art Shop** farther up the same street has paintings, carvings, silk *sarungs* and basketwork. Nearby on Somba Opu are two other good art and craft shops: **Mutiara Art Shop** (statues, carvings, *sarungs*, sea shells and animal hides) and **Paleori Art Shop** (paintings, bamboo and Toraja weaving).

IRIAN JAYA

Many people automatically associate New Guinea arts and crafts with the famous Asmat tribe of Irian Jaya. Simple colors – earth-red, black and white – are the Asmat trademark. The demand for Asmat carvings has increased greatly in recent years. The United Nations has restored the prestige of the master-carvers by giving them a recognized place as teachers in the education system which is part of a special project funded by the UN.

One of the best places to buy Asmat carvings is the **Asmat Handicraft Project** at Dinas Perindustriaan, Kotakpos 294 in Jayapura. There is also an official warehouse on Jalan Batu Karang outside Jayapura, off the main road to Hamadi. The **Cama** shop in Jayapura sells carvings, as does the souvenir counter at Sentani Airport.

FURTHER READING

From the *Insight Guides* stable comes a range of travel guides, specially designed to help make your visit an unforgettable one.

More than 13,600 islands comprise the most extraordinary collection of places and peoples on earth.

Much more than a field guide, this book answers the call of all wildlife lovers.

GETTING THERE

BY AIR

Few first sights in Malaysia can compete with the elegant M$52 million Subang International Airport that greets air passengers at Kuala Lumpur. Its bold design came as such a novelty to the sleepy landscape of Subang, 14 miles (22 km) from the city center, that several myopic citizens ran into trouble. "The first victim," reported a newspaper several days after the official opening in 1965, "was an airport porter who walked right into a glass pane at the north arrival hall. He injured his nose but did not break the pane which is quite strong and thick."

Kuala Lumpur's airport serves about 20 international airlines linking key cities of the world to Malaysia and providing the country with more than 90 percent of her visitors. Nearest international connections are with Singapore, a pleasant 35-minute flight away, and with Bangkok, an hour and 20 minutes away. Malaysia's capital is also accessible by air from Sabah and Sarawak or Penang Island to the north.

An airport tax of M$15 for international flights and M$5 for flights to Singapore and Brunei is payable on departure from all Malaysian airports.

BY SEA

Sailors first glimpse Malaysia from bustling Port Klang (previously called Port Swettenham), 26 miles (42 km) west of Kuala Lumpur, or from the historic port of Penang, an ancient sanctuary for those once escaping the wrath of mainland lords. A number of cargo-cum-passenger ships and cruise liners call regularly at both ports.

BY RAIL

THE ORIENT EXPRESS

The operators of the fabled London-to-Venice Orient Express are launching a new luxury train in Southeast Asia. From November 1992, the Eastern and Oriental Express will make one round trip a week between Singapore, Kuala Lumpur and Bangkok. The journey will take 41 hours and cover a distance of 1,943 km. The E&O will pass northbound through Kuala Lumpur every Thursday. There will also be a stop at Butterworth for Penang. The standard of comfort, service and cuisine on board the train will be of the highest quality. Prices will start at US190 for the trip between Kuala Lumpur and Singapore and reservations can be made from spring 1992, via travel agents, or by contacting the E&O London office in Tel: (071) 928-6000. Fax: (071) 620-1210.

BY LAND

Train tracks have a legacy in Malaysian lore. An inscription along the railway 3 miles (5 km) from Telok Anson reads: "There is buried here a wild elephant who in defense of his herd charged and derailed a train on the 17th day of September 1894." Though elephants have ceased being so chivalrous, smooth tracks still cut through the jungles roamed by wildlife, making train travel a chance to peek into the forested hinterland without having to slow down.

The more casual traveler can pick up a "shared" taxi at Johor Bahru, just across the causeway from Singapore, and settle down to a 6-hour drive to Kuala Lumpur, without spending more than M$20. The secret of the bargain is that four or five passengers share one taxi. Bus fares are more reasonable on the air-conditioned express to Kuala Lumpur departing Singapore daily from the Lavender Street bus terminus at 9 a.m. and 9 p.m. for the 8-hour ride. They also do a service up the East Coast.

TRAVEL ESSENTIALS

VISAS & PASSPORTS

Valid passports and a health certificate of vaccination against yellow fever are required, if traveling from an infected area. Citizens of countries enjoying diplomatic relations with Malaysia do not need a visa for stays not exceeding three months. However, this does not apply to citizens of communist countries, Israel, or South Africa, who must have visas to enter Malaysia.

MONEY MATTERS

The Malaysian *ringgit* (dollar) is a sound currency which has been in circulation since 1957, and at time of press, it is valued at around M$2.73 to the US$. Singapore and Brunei dollars are of somewhat greater value, and no longer circulate freely in Malaysia. The importation of traveler's checks and letters of credit is unlimited. Visitors are allowed to bring in or take out with them any amount of Malaysian currency. It is much easier to take out cash if it has been declared upon arrival.

Banks offer better rates, and so do money changers with offices in downtown shop houses. If you are not in a rush, avoid changing money in the arcades of luxury hotels, since many of these shops levy a service charge by offering lower exchange rates: usually 2 to 4 percent. Deal directly with a bank or a licensed money changer and have plenty of local currency on hand when traveling to small towns and in rural areas.

In the more flashy, chic quarters of the larger towns – in department stores, shops, first-class restaurants and hotels – traveler's checks change hands easily. Bring your passport along when cashing traveler's checks: a formality which must be observed before heading off the beaten track where such checks are unacceptable. Established credit cards – Visa, Diner's Club, American Express, Carte Blanche – are honored in the major cities. Several hotel chains maintain their own credit card system. But when traveling through Malaysia, nothing could be better than the coin of the realm.

HEALTH

Travelers have few worries in a country where the health standards are ranked among the highest in Asia.

Water is generally safe for drinking, but it is safest to drink boiled water, tea, coffee, or bottled beverages. Coffee shops in small towns sell fresh fruits and bottled drinks. Fresh hot food, cooked on the spot, has made *nasi goreng* (fried rice) and *mee goreng* (fried noodles) the local equivalents of hot dogs and meat pie.

WHAT TO WEAR

Light, cool, comfortable clothes, for both men and women, fare well in Malaysia where informal styles prevail throughout the year. *Batik* cotton fashions, on sale everywhere, are an easy "in" to local color. Well-worn airy shoes or sandals are a favor to the feet. For some formal occasions, men may be requested to dine in suits and ties; but sport shirts are otherwise the ubiquitous Malaysian style for anything from cocktails to floor shows. Ladies are at liberty to take any hint from Vogue's summer pages, though when visiting mosques and outlying Malay villages, women should dress modestly. Shorts, tiny T-shirts and miniskirts have yet to win acceptance in Asian towns and villages.

CUSTOMS

Import duties seldom affect the average traveler, who may bring in 225 grams of tobacco or cigars, or 200 cigarettes and one liter bottle of liquor duty free. Used portable articles are normally exempted from import tax. Narcotics, pornography, daggers, and walkie-talkies are strictly prohibited. Prominent "Death to drug traffickers" signs are everywhere.

GETTING ACQUAINTED

GOVERNMENT & ECONOMY

Malaysia is the official name of the former British colony of Malaya.

Independent since 1957, the Malaysian government is regulated by the Parliament comprising the Yang di-Pertuan Agong (King or Supreme Sovereign) and two Houses: the House of Representatives and the Senate. The executive functions of the government are carried out by the Cabinet, led by Datuk Seri Mahathir Mohamad who became Prime Minister in 1981. His party was voted back into power in 1990.

The population of approximately 17 million comprises Malays (59 percent), Chinese (32 percent), Indians and Dayaks spread over 13 states. The capital city of Kuala Lumpur has more than one million people.

Until recently tin and rubber were the major export items, supplying 35 percent and 40 percent of the world's total output, respectively. But manufacturing surpassed basic commodities as the most important export segment in the late 1980s. Oil and natural gas products are rapidly growing in importance. Malaysia's major trading partners are Japan and the United States.

TIME ZONES

Malaysian Standard Time is eight hours ahead of Greenwich Mean Time, which means that clocks are set the same as Singapore but one hour ahead of Thailand.

CLIMATE

A tropical sun and clouds laden with the makings of a sudden downpour compete for the skies of Malaysia, with the odds on the sun. Malaysia's seasons follow the monsoon winds, which splash rains inland from September to December on the West Coast of Peninsular Malaysia, only to be overtaken by sunshine within the hour. Rains arrive later on the East Coast of Peninsular Malaysia and in Sabah and Sarawak, where umbrellas sell well from October to February. Malaysia's weather, however, is generally warm, humid, and sunny all the year round. The highlands, both during the day and at night, and the lowlands in the evening are comfortably cooler, which may explain why Malaysia's night-life is liveliest outdoors.

BUSINESS HOURS

In an Islamic nation with a British colonial history, weekly holidays vary. In the former Federated States which were united under the British – Selangor, Malacca, Penang, Perak, Pahang and Negri Sembilan – there is a half-day holiday on Saturday and a full-day holiday on Sunday. The former Unfederated States, which remained semi-autonomous under British rule – Johor, Kedah, Perlis, Trengganu, and Kelantan – retain the traditional half-day holiday on Thursday and full-day holiday on Friday. Saturday and Sunday are treated as weekdays.

In all government institutions, the workday begins at 8:15 a.m. and ends at 4:15 p.m., with time off on Fridays from noon to 2:30 p.m. for communal *Jumaat* prayers at the mosques. Most private business stick to the 9-to-5 routine. Shops start to close at 6 p.m. Large department stores keep their cash registers ringing past 9 p.m.

LANGUAGE

In Kuala Lumpur, chances are that the taxi driver knows a smattering of four languages. Among Malaysia's urban population, people shift tongues with neighborhoods. Malay is the national language, used officially in all government departments. English is widely spoken by people from all walks of life, along with the clicking sounds of Tamil, brought from South India, and a half dozen Chinese dialects – Cantonese and Hokkien predominating in the towns.

A traveler can step into the most unlikely small town coffee shop and encounter a shopkeeper with a Senior Cambridge Certificate. Almost every village, however small, harbors a linguist. One way to find out who he or she is is to enter the nearest snack bar, order a soft drink and wait for the word to get around that a *turis* or *tamu* (guest) is in town. Eventually, the local translator will appear.

GETTING AROUND

BY AIR

Since Malaysian Airline System (MAS) first took to the skies in 1972 as the national flag carrier, it has come a long way in providing services not only to international cities but also between cities within Malaysia. Its fleet flies from Kuala Lumpur to Alor Star, Penang, Kota Bharu, Kuala Trengganu, Kuantan, Ipoh, Malacca, Johor Bahru, Kota Kinabalu, Kuching and vice-versa.

In Sabah and Sarawak, internal air transport is just as efficient and regular too. Daily scheduled return flights connect towns like Kota Kinabalu with Labuan, Lahad Datu, Sandakan, Tawau, Bintulu, Kuching, Miri, Semporna, Tomanggong, Pamol, Kudat, Keningau, Ranau, Long Semadoh, Lawas, Limbang, Bario, Long Seridan, Marudi, Mukah Sibu, Kapit, Belaga, Simanggang, Bakalalan, Long Sukang and Long Lellang.

Special economy tourist flights are also available from Kuala Lumpur to Penang, Kota Kinabalu, Kuching, Johor Bahru and Kota Bharu; and from these towns back to Kuala Lumpur.

A visitor must bear in mind, however, that the visit passes issued for entry into the Malay Peninsula do not automatically entitle the holder entry into Sabah and/or Sarawak. A different pass must be obtained before setting out.

RAIL TRANSPORT

The main railway line runs right from Singapore in the south to Thailand in the north, passing through the entire Malay Peninsula with stations at major principal cities and towns such as Johor Bahru, Kuala Lumpur, Gemas, Segamat, Ipoh and Butterworth. Another line branches off from this main one at Gemas to run northeast to Tumpat on the east coast.

On these two lines, more than a dozen trains run throughout the day and into the night. Passengers can choose from air-conditioned first-class coaches in the day trains and first-class cabins with single or double berths in the night trains.

For the casual traveler, sleeping berths are available in the second-class and sleeperettes in the third-class coaches.

The Malayan Railway – or *Keretapi Tanah Melayu*, as it is called – is known for its punctuality. Many tourists have touted it as one of the few in Asia which keeps to published times of arrivals.

Fares are extremely reasonable. For example, the fare from Kuala Lumpur to Singapore ranges from M$25 for second class with no air-conditioning to M$55 for first class with air-conditioning.

For foreign tourists, KTM offers a railpass for unlimited travel in any class and to any destination. The cost is M$85 for 10 days and M$175 for 30 days.

WATER TRANSPORT

Water transport is no longer so important as a means of getting around Malaysia, except in Sarawak where roads are still few and far between.

Several ferry services still exist, however. The most important services are between Penang and Butterworth; Langkawi and either Kuala Perlis and Penang; Mersing and Tioman Island.

PUBLIC TRANSPORT

BUSES

Most of the principal cities have their own regular scheduled bus services. Inter-state long-distance travel by bus is common, as it is reliable and relatively cheap.

The MARA Express has regular services connecting Kuala Lumpur and Singapore in about 7 hours for M$17 (air-conditioned).

TAXIS

Taxis remain one of the more popular and cheap means of transport, especially on a shared basis. You can hail them by the roadside, hire them from authorized taxi stands, or book them by telephone calls. In the latter case, the mileage is calculated from the stand or garage from which the vehicle is hired.

TRISHAWS

This is the most novel mode of transport recommended for short trips. Except in Penang, where passengers are seated on a sun-hooded carriage in front of the cyclist or pedaler, a trishaw is a bicycle with a side carriage for the passengers.

PRIVATE TRANSPORT

You'd rather drive yourself around? You may, if you possess a valid international driving license (a foreign licence has to be appropriately endorsed by the Ministry of Road Transport). You must be at least 23 years old but not more than 60.

Most of the international rent-a-car agencies have offices here. Rental cost is calculated on a per-day or per-week basis; it ranges from M$125 to M$300 per day and from around M$700 to M$1500 per week.

Collection and delivery service is usually free if within city limits. Some firms levy a repositioning charge if you wish to "rent it here, leave it there." Motorcycles can also be rented from some of these agencies.

CAR RENTAL AGENCIES

Avis Rent-A-Car, 40, Jln. Sultan Ismail, Kuala Lumpur, Tel: 03-241-0561/3500

Budget Rent-A-Car, 20A, Jln. Telawi, Bangsar Baru, K.L., Tel: 03-255-1044

Hertz Rent-A-Car, 4th Floor, Ming Building, K.L., Tel: 03-232-9125

MOTORING ADVISORIES

Malaysia's road system is extensive and has some of the finest metal-surfaced rubberized highways in Southeast Asia, covering a total distance of 18,560 miles (29, 934 km). The main trunk road in West Malaysia runs northwards from Singapore to the Thai border.

The East-West Highway is a recently completed project which connects Butterworth in Penang to Kota Bharu in Kelantan.During the monsoon season from December to January, heavy rains may make road travel between Kuala Trengganu and Kota Bharu in the northeast difficult.

WHERE TO STAY

One may sleep in Malaysia in numerous styles: enamored by the old-fashioned elegance of a colonial lodge; tucked in a sleeping bag in an alpine mountain hut; soothed by Chinese singsong in a tiny hotel in midtown; or serenaded by the crickets outside the family guestroom of a Dayak longhouse in Sarawak.

Most Malaysian small towns do not offer the cosmopolitan facilities of a worldwide hotel chain, but they do provide the personal touch, simplicity, and cleanliness of a wayside inn. A typical urban street is dotted with small budget hotels renting simply furnished rooms for around M$10 to M$20.

KUALA LUMPUR

Carcosa Seri Negara, Taman Tasik Perdana, Tel: 03-230-6766

Dashrun Hotel, 285, Jln. Tuanku Abdul Rahman, Tel: 03-292-9314, 292-9271

Equatorial Hotel, Jln. Sultan Ismail, Tel: 03-261-7777

Federal Hotel, 35, Jln. Bukit Bintang, Tel: 03-248-9166

Fortuna Hotel, 87, Jln. Berangan, Tel: 03-241-9111

Furama Hotel, Kompleks Selangor, Jln. Sultan Ismail, Tel: 03-230-1777

Grand Central Hotel, Jln. Raja Laut, Tel: 03-441-3011

Hilton Kuala Lumpur, Jln. Sultan Ismail, Tel: 03-242-2122/2222

Holiday Inn City Centre, Jln. Raja Laut, Tel: 03-293-9233

Holiday Inn On The Park K.L., P O Box 10983, Jalan Pinang 50732, Tel: 03-248-1066

Hotel Grand Pacific, Jln. Tun Ismail/Jln. Ipoh, Tel: 03-442-2177

Hotel Malaya, Jln. Hang Lekir, Tel: 03-232-7722

Kuala Lumpur International, Jln. Raja Muda, Tel: 03-292-9133

Kuala Lumpur Mandarin, 2-8, Jln. Sultan, Tel: 03-230-3000

Malaysia Hotel, Jln. Bukit Bintang, Tel: 03-242-8033

Merlin Hotel, Jln. Sultan Ismail, Tel: 03-248-0033

Ming Court Hotel, Jln. Ampang, Tel: 03-261-8888

Miramar Hotel, Jln. Birch (Maharajalela), Tel: 03-2489122

Pan Pacific Kuala Lumpur, Jln. Putra, Tel: 03-442-5555

Park Avenue, 16, Jln. Imbi, Tel: 03-213-8383

Parkroyal Hotel, Jln. Sultan Ismail, Tel: 03-242-5588

Plaza Hotel, Jln. Raja Laut, Tel: 03-298-2255

Regent of Kuala Lumpur, Jln. Sultan Ismail, Tel: 03-242-5588

Shangri-La Hotel, 11, Jln. Sultan Ismail, Tel: 03-232-2388

Shiraz Hotel, 1 & 3 Jln. Medan Tuanku, Tel: 03-292-0159

South East Asia Hotel, Jln. Haji Hussein, Tel: 03-292-6077

Sungei Wang Hotel, 74-76, Jln. Bukit Bintang, Tel: 03-248-5255

The Lodge, Jln. Sultan Ismail, Tel: 03-242-0122

Wisma Belia, 40, Jln. Lornie, Tel: 03-232-6803

YMCA, Jln. Kandang Kerbau, Brickfields, Tel: 03-274-1439

YWCA, Jln. Tun Sambathan, Tel: 03-274-1439

JOHOR

Desaru View Hotel, Tanjung Penawar, Kota Tinggi, Tel: 07-838221

Holiday Inn Johor Bahru, Jln. Dat Sulaiman, Tel: 07-322800

Merlin Inn, Lot 5435, Jln. Bukit Meldrum, Tel: 07-228851

Mersing Merlin Inn, 1st mile Endau Road, Mersing, Tel: 07-791311

Tioman Island Resort, Pulau Tioman, P.O. Box 4 86807, Mersing Johor, Tel: 07-445445

KEDAH

Langkawi Island Resort, Pantai Dato' Syed Omar, Kuah, Tel: 04-788209

Mutiara Beach Resort, Tanjong Rhu, Langkawi, Tel: 04-788488

Pelangi Beach Resort, Pantai Cenang, Langkawi, Tel: 04-789799

KELANTAN

Hotel Perdana, Jln. Mahmud, Kota Bahru, Tel: 09-785000

Pantai Cinta Berahi Resort, Pantai Cinta Berahi, Tel: 09-781307

Temenggong Hotel, Jln. Tok Hakim, Kota Bahru, Tel: 09-783130

MALACCA

Hotel Admiral, Jln. Mata Kuching, Tel: 06-226822

Malacca Straits Inn, Jln. Bandar Hilir, Tel: 06-221101

Malacca Village Resort, Ayer Keroh, Tel: 06-323600

Merlin Inn Malacca, Bangunan Woo Hoe Kan, Jln. Munshi Abdullah, Tel: 06-240777

Ramada Renaissance Hotel, Jln. Bendahara, Tel: 06-248888

Regal Hotel, 66, Jln. Munshi Abdullah, Tel: 06-222433

Shah's Beach Hotel, 6th Mile, Tanjung Kling, Tel: 06-226202/222

PAHANG

Club Mediterranean, Cherating, Tel: 09-591181

Coral Beach Resort, 152, Sungai Karang, Kuantan, Tel: 09-587544

Foster's Lakehouse, Ringlet, Cameron Highlands, Tel: 05-996152

Fraser's Hill Bungalows, Fraser's Hill, Tel: 093-382201

Genting Hotel, Genting Highlands Resort, Tel: 03-211-1118

Highlands Hotel, Genting Highlands Resort, Tel: 03-211-2812

Hyatt Kuantan, Teluk Cempedak, Kuantan, Tel: 09-525211

Merlin Hotel Fraser's Hill, Jln. Lady Guillemard, Tel: 09-382300

Merlin Inn Resort, Tanah Rata, Cameron Highlands, Tel: 05-941205/211

Merlin Inn Resort, Teluk Cempedak, Kuantan, Tel: 09-522388

Pelangi Hotel, Genting Highlands Resort, Tel: 03-211-3813

Ramada Beach Resort, Balok Beach, Kuantan, Tel: 09-587-544

Samudra Hotel, Jln. Besar, Kuantan, Tel: 09-522688

Strawberry Park, Tanah Rata, Cameron Highlands, Tel: 05-941166

Ye Olde Smokehouse Hotel, Brinchang, Tanah Rata, Cameron Highlands, Tel: 05-941214

PENANG

Casuarina Beach Hotel, Batu Ferringhi, Tel: 04-811711

Continental Hotel, 5, Jln. Penang, Tel: 04-26381

E & O Hotel, 10, Farquhar Street, Tel: 04-375322

Garden Inn, 41, Jln. Anson, Tel: 04-363655

Golden City Hotel, 12, Lorong Kinta, Tel: 04-27281

Golden Sands Beach Resort, Batu Ferringhi, Tel: 04-811911

Holiday Inn Hotel, Batu Ferringhi, Tel: 04-811601

Merlin Inn, 126, Jln. Burmah/Anson, Tel: 04-376166

Ming Court Hotel, 202A, MacAlister Road, Tel: 04-368588

Mutiara Beach Hotel, Jln. Teluk Bahang, Tel: 04-812828

Penang Mutiara, No. 1 Jln Teluk Bahang, Tel: 04-812828

Rasa Sayang Hotel, Batu Ferringhi Beach, Tel: 04-811811

Shangri-La Inn, Jln, Magazine, Tel: 04-622622

YMCA, 211, Jln. MacAlister, Tel: 04-362211

SELANGOR

Holiday Inn Shah Alam, Plaza Perangsang, Persiaran Perbandaran, 40000 Shah Alam, Tel: 03-5503696

Hyatt Saujana Hotel, Subang International Highway, P.O.Box 111, 46710 Petaling Jaya, Tel: 03-7461188

Merlin Subang Hotel, Jln. SS12/7, Subang Jaya, Tel: 03-733-5211

Petaling Jaya Hilton Hotel, 2, Jln. Barat, P.J., Tel: 03-755-9122

Subang Airport Hotel, Subang Airport, Subang, Tel: 03-746-2122

TRENGGANU

Hotel Warisan, 65, Jln. Sultan Ismail, Tel: 09-622688

Pantai Primula Hotel, Jln. Persinggahan, Tel: 09-622100

Tanjung Jara Beach Hotel, 8 miles Dungun, Tel: 09-841801

FOOD DIGEST

WHAT TO EAT

That Malaysia is a gourmet's delight is a threadbare statement. Variety begins not only with the different types of foods available but also with the flexibility in dining environments. Flexibility stretches from eating in a plush restaurant with a formal setting and attentive waiters, to the open-air roadside stalls.

During your stay, you should try to eat at these stalls, which are *the* place to try local specialties in home-cooked styles. The most hygienic of travelers is assured that it is perfectly safe to eat here, even though he may imagine his bowl of noodles being peppered by dust as cars whiz past.

The different peoples that comprise Malaysia's multi-racial population provide the country with enough tastes to please every palate. Of the different types of foods available, the most popular and unique are Malay, Chinese and Indian.

MALAY FOOD

Malay food is generally rich and spicy. Although each state has its distinctive style of preparation and taste, ingredients are common to all.

White steamed rice (*nasi*) is the staple grain. Ample use is made of seafood, chicken and meat. Coconut forms a basis for many dishes. The juice is refined drink and the meat is usually grated and squeezed to obtain coconut milk (*santan*). This gives a dish its taste and texture.

Perhaps the best known of Malay dishes is *satay*,

slivers of barbecued beef or chicken dipped in hot peanut sauce. It is best eaten along with sliced cucumbers, onions and *ketupat* (steamed rice wrapped in coconut leaves).

Nasi padang is the best option for a filling meal of rice with a variety of curry dishes. Dishes are usually arranged on display at the stalls - there will be fish, beef and vegetable curries, among others - and customers select their meal from these.

The fingers of the diner's right hand are used to knead rice and spices before tucking them into his mouth. Nowadays a fork and spoon are common, though it is generally agreed that manual eating brings out the food's fullest flavor.

Other typical dishes worth trying include *tahu goreng*, fried cubes of soya bean curd and fresh sprouts with a spicy peanut dressing; *gado gado*, a salad of delicately steamed raw vegetables; *laksa*, another type of spicy soup made of fine noodles and fish stock; *mee rebus*, boiled noodles; and *mee siam*, Thai-style noodles.

Of note is the local dessert, *gula melaka*, made by topping sago with coconut milk and a syrup made of palm sugar - a guaranteed mouth-watering dish for the sweet tooth.

CHINESE FOOD

Chinese foods are found in abundance in Malaysia. You will do well to taste Teochew porridge, Hainanese chicken rice (rice cooked in chicken stock and served with delicately steamed chicken pieces), Hakka *yong tau foo* (beancurd stuffed with meat), Hokkien fried *mee* (noodles fried with pieces of meat, prawn and cuttlefish) and Chinese *laksa* (which differs from the Malay version)

INDIAN FOOD

Indian cooking is characterized by its complex and generous use of spices. With the exception of restaurants in big hotels which might modify their Indian dishes to cater to unaccustomed palates, Indian food here is just like what you would find in India. The crowning dish, most would agree, is the *nasi briyani*, a mixture of saffron and rosewater with rice steamed in milk and meat stock. An artificial yellow coloring gives this dish its other name, "yellow rice." For a greater variety of dishes at one sitting, one should try rice with various vegetables and meats.

Alternatively, these dishes can be eaten with *chapati*, an unleavened pancake, or *paratha*, a white flour dough. The Indian *rojak* - a selection of different foods like potatoes, eggs, cuttlefish, prawns and fish cake - is best eaten by dipping into a hot sweet-sour gravy.

At an outdoor eating place, one can usually eat both Chinese and Malay foods at the same meal, as stalls selling different types of food are usually neighbors. But remember not to mix the cutlery from

WEST MALAYSIA

a Muslim stall with that of a Chinese. For example, do not use the fork from the *mee rebus* stall to eat your Chinese *laksa*. Muslims consider pork an unclean food, and will never use it in their cooking. Chinese, on the other hand, use it in most of their dishes.

FRUITS

Malaysia is a veritable Garden of Eden of fruits all the year round, but besides the all-time tropical favorites such as golden pineapples, sweet papaya, juicy water-melon and all sorts and sizes of bananas, there's a host of others you may not have seen before. Many are seasonal - all are delicious.

Durian is king of fruits to the Malaysian. Once you survive the powerful smell, the taste is indescribably delicious. No two durians taste alike but some claim it is best likened to fruity-creamy-caramel.

Rambutans have marvelous hairy red-tinged-with-gold skins. The flesh is rather like lychees, juicy and sugar-sweet.

Mango comes long or rounded, green or yellow, and the golden flesh inside is soft, sweet and luscious.

Mangosteen is purple on the outside, white, sweet and juicy inside. The mangosteen ripens at the same time as the durian and they go well together. The Chinese believe that the "heatiness" of the durian is balanced by the "coolness" of the mangosteen.

Nangka or **Jackfruit** is the huge green fruit which you can often see on trees in the villages covered with sacks or paper bags to protect them from birds. The pulp is juicy and chewy at the same time. It can be eaten both raw and cooked and even the seeds are edible.

Starfruit, yellow and shiny, is a good thirst quencher. Cut it horizontally into star-shaped wedges and dip it in salt.

Pomelo looks and tastes like a sweet, overgrown, slightly dry grapefruit.

Buah Duku: To open a *duku*, just squeeze gently. The flesh is sweet and with a sour tinge. You'll probably eat dozens of *dukus* at one time, but watch out for the hard greenish center which can be bitter.

Buah Susu, literally translated "milk fruit," is better known as passionfruit. There are many different varieties, all equally delicious. Crisp-skinned and orange from Indonesia, purple from Australia and California, the local ones have soft, velvety yellow skins. The gray seeds inside are sweet and juicy.

SHOPPING

SHOPPING AREAS

Where to buy? At modern multi-story shopping complexes, night markets (*pasar malam*), bazaars, fairs, sidewalk stalls, night-time lantern markets, special Saturday night markets, cottage industries where visitors buy handicrafts direct from the craftsmen, duty-free shops . . . the list goes on and on. There is certainly no shortage of places to shop.

But it is usually unwise to shop at a place you have been taken by a taxi driver or an unlicensed tourist guide: part of the price you pay for an article could well be the commission for your "guide." It might be safer merely to wander around and choose a shop with window-shopping appeal.

WHAT TO BUY

BATIK

Although *batik* printing did not originate here - it was first introduced from Indonesia some centuries ago – it has always been popular in Malaysia, especially in the state of Kelantan. Nowadays, a great part of the industry has moved into sophisticated art salons and boutiques in Kuala Lumpur.

Batik printing is an art of fabric printing using wax-resistant dyes. A pattern is drawn on virgin fabric (once invariably cotton but now any material). Molten wax is applied to certain areas of the motif to protect them from contact with the dye. After the first dyeing, the wax is boiled away. The process is repeated according to the number of colors desired. The result is dazzling prints with pure rich color and attractive designs.

Prices range widely depending on the type of material used, the exclusiveness of the design, and the number of colors used.

KAIN SONGKET

This is another kind of cloth which is distinctively Malay. It is a very luxurious materials - handwoven silk with gold or silver threads.

Often made into shawls or evening dresses, it can cost as much as M$500 a piece if rated first-class in terms of design, workmanship and material.

SILVERWORK

This is another cottage industry of Malaysia. Silver is daintily and delicately crafted into items like brooches, pendants, belts, jewelry boxes, bowls and rings by skilled artists.

In some places, visitors can watch these artists at their work. Kampong Sireh, a suburb of Kota Bharu, is one such place where it is possible to buy wares at factory prices and to have pieces made to order.

There is a large handicraft center in Kuala Lumpur (near the Tourist Information Office in Jalan Tun Perak) where a good range of jewelry and other items can be purchased.

PEWTERWARE

Products made from this 97 percent Straits-refined tin are widely regarded as good buys.

Vases, beer mugs, water jugs, trays and coffee/tea sets are some of the items into which the metal can be fashioned. It was in the factory at 231 Jalan Tunku Abdul Rahman, Kuala Lumpur, that Selangor Pewter made its debut as the world's finest.

KITES & TOPS

Kite-flying and top-spinning have been popular pastimes in Malaysia for as long as one can remember. Hence, Malaysia has some of the most skilled makers of kites and tops.

Even if you don't care tuppence for any of these two sports, you may purchase them for decorative and ornamental purposes from handicraft centers both on the east coast and in Kuala Lumpur. A large kite, for example, might be a good substitute for that conventional poster in your living room.

FURTHER READING

From the *Insight Guides* stable comes a range of travel guides, specially designed to help make your visit an unforgettable one.

More than 280 superb photographs and an entertaining text capture the heart and soul of Malaysia.

The perfect guide for a short-term stay in Malaysia's most dynamic city.

Personal itineraries and recommendations help to make your stay in the old colonial settlement a memorable one.

This book assumes the role of a friend who will guide you through the streets and beaches of this fascinating island.

GETTING THERE

The state capitals of Sabah and Sarawak (Kota Kinabalu and Kuching) are connected by air with a number of regional capitals, including Singapore, Manila and Hong Kong. The national carrier, Malaysia Airlines, operates daily flights form Kuala Lumpur. There are also daily flights to destinations in the interior.

WHERE TO STAY

SABAH

KOTA KINABALU

Asia Hotel, 68-69, Jl. Bandaran Berjaya, Tel: 088-53533/53638

Central Hotel, 5-7, Jl. Tugu Kampung Ayer, Tel: 088-53522/51544

Hotel Shangri-La, 75, Bandaran Berjaya, P.O. Box 11718, Tel: 088-212800, Fax: 212078

Hyatt Kinabalu International, Jl. Datuk Salleh Sulong, 88994 Kota Kinabalu, Tel: 088-221234, Fax: 225972/242488

Jesselton Hotel, 69, Jl. Gaya, Tel: 088-225985

Sabah Inn Hotel, 25, Jl. Pantai, Tel: 088-53322/53177

Tanjung Aru Beach Hotel, Locked Bag 174, 7 km from Airport, Tel: 088-58711, Fax: 217155/216585

KUDAT

Kinabalu Hotel, No. 1, Block C, Sedco Shophouse, P.O. Box 82, Tel: 088-62693/62494

RANAU

Perkasa Mt Kinabalu Hotel, W.D.T. 11, 89309 Ranau, Kundasang, Tel: 088-889511

SANDAKAN

Hong Kong Hotel, 18, Jl. Tiga, Tel: 089-212292

Mayfair Hotel, 24, Jl. Prayer 1/F, Tel: 089-45191/2

New Sabah Hotel, 18, Jl. Singapura, Tel: 089-218711/949

Paris Hotel, 45, Jl. Tiga, Tel: 089-218488/493

Sabah Hotel, Km. 1, Jl. Utara, Tel: 089-213299

TAWAU

Ermas Hotel, Jl. Utara, Tel: 089-773300

Malaysia Hotel, 37, Jl. Dunlop, Tel: 089-772800

Oriental Hotel, 10, Jl. Dunlop, Tel: 089-771500

SARAWAK

KUCHING

Aurora Hotel, McDougall Road, Tel: 082-240281/6

Borneo Hotel, 30, Jl. Tabuan, Tel: 082-244121

Holiday Inn Damai Beach Resort, Jl. Tanjung Batu, Tel: 082-411777

Holiday Inn Kuching, Jl. Tunku Abdul Rahman, Tel: 082-423111

Kuching Hilton, Jl. Tunku Abdul Rahman, Tel: 082-248200/1

Palm Hotel, 29, Jl. Palm, Tel: 082-240231

BELAGA

Belaga Hotel, Belaga Bazaar, Tel: 084-461244

Huan Kilah Lodging House, Belaga Bazaar, Tel: 084-461259

BINTULU

Kemena Lodging House, 78, Keppel Road, Tel: 086-31533/33377

Li Hua Hotel, 2.5 Mile, Miri-Bintulu Road, Tel: 086-35000

LAWAS

Country Park Hotel, Lot 235 & 236, Jl. Trusan, Tel: 085-85522

Lawas Federal Hotel, 8, Jl. Masjid Baru, Tel: 0845-85115

LIMBANG

National Inn, 62A-69A, Jl. Buang Siol, Tel: 085-22922/8

MARUDI (BARAM)

Hotel Zola, Lot 14-15, Queens Square, Tel: 085-55991/55025

MIRI

Gloria Hotel, 27, Brooke Road, Tel: 085-416699

Park Hotel, Kingsway, P.O. Box 241, Tel: 085-414555

SIBU

Premier Hotel, Jl. Kampong Nyabor, Tel: 084-23222

Sarawak Hotel, 34, Cross Road, Tel: 084-333455

PARKS & RESERVES

SABAH NATIONAL PARKS

Head Office: Sabah Parks Board, Jl. Tun Fuad Stephens, P.O. Box 10626, 85806 Kota Kinabalu, Tel: 088-211585/211881

Mt Kinabalu National Park:
Beds in dormitories available at M$3 to $15 per night. Also available are twin-bed cabins and basement rooms at M$50 to $80 per night; duplex chalets and single-story cabins at M$150 to $200 per night; double-story cabins at M$180 to $250 per night.

On Mount Kinabalu:
Beds in three basic huts available at M$1 to $4 per night. Beds in more luxurious **Laban Rata Rest House** are M$25 per night.

Poring Hot Springs:
Beds in dormitories available at M$2 to $8 per night; rooms in two cabins are M$60 to $100 per night.

Tunku Abdul Rahman National Park:
The **resthouse** on Pulau Mamutik sleeps 12 and can be rented for M$160 per night through the Parks Board office in Kota Kinabalu. Camping is permitted on all islands with prior permission.

Turtle Islands National Park:
The **Pulau Selingan Rest House** offers a four-bed chalet for M$120 per night, or cabins from M$20. Enquire at the District Office in Sandakan.

SARAWAK NATIONAL PARKS

Head office: Sarawak Parks Board, Jl. Gartak, off Jl. Mosque, Kuching, Tel: 085-246-6477/248988

Bako National Park:
Accommodation available in rest houses (from M$44), hostel cabins (from M$1 per person) and permanent tents (from M$1 per person).

Niah National Park:
The **Niah Visitor's Hostel** charges from M$2.50 per person for beds in dormitory rooms.

Gunung Mulu National Park:
Hostels inside the park charge M$5 per night for beds in dormitory rooms.

FOOD DIGEST

SABAH

KOTA KINABALU

Arirang Restaurant (Korean), Block 6, No. 69, Bandaran Berjaya, Tel: 088-221528

Azuma (Japanese), A237, 3rd Floor, Wisma Merdeka, Tel: 088-225533/212511

Gardenia Steak & Lobster Bar (Western), 55, Jl. Gaya, Tel: 088-54296/52307

Rama Restoran (Malay), Block 6, No. 67, Bandaran Berjaya, Tel: 088-217193

SANDAKAN

Garden Terrace Restaurant (Chinese, Malay and Western), Sabah Hotel, Km 1, Jl. Utara, Tel: 089-213999

Kuala Lumpur Restoran (Malay), 1st Floor, Leboh Tiga near corner of Jl. Lima

SARAWAK

KUCHING

Aurora Restaurant (Malay), Aurora Hotel, Jl. McDougall, Tel: 082-240281/6

Jubilee Restaurant (Indian), 49, Leboh India

Malaya Restaurant (Indian-Muslim), 53, Leboh India

Meisan Szechuan Restaurant (Chinese), Holiday Inn Kuching, Jl. Tunku Abdul Rahman, Tel: 082-423111

Serapi Restaurant (Western and seafood), Holiday Inn Kuching, Jl. Tunku Abdul Rahman, Tel: 082-423111

BINTULU

Anika Restaurant (Chinese), 27, Hock Peng Complex, Tel: 086-31391

Bismi Restaurant (Indian), 27, Jl. Sommerville

Kinto Restaurant (Chinese), 28, Law Gek Soon Road, Tel: 086-31016

Mandarin Palace (Chinese, Malay and Western), Holiday Beach Hotel, Jl. Tanjung Datu

MIRI

Akhabar Restaurant (Indian), Kampong Dagang

Kah Hing Restaurant (Chinese), 29, Brooke Road, Tel: 085-31322

Kok Chee Restaurant (Chinese, Malay and Western), Park Hotel, Kingsway, Tel: 085-414555

SIBU

Hock Chii Lew Restaurant (Chinese), 28, Blacksmith Road, Tel: 084-21254

Metropole Restaurant (Indian Muslim), 20, Pulo Road, Tel: 084-24189

New Capital Restaurant (Muslim), Tanah Mas Building Complex

SHOPPING

SABAH

Sabah is famous for its *tamus* or open-air markets, which take place each week in towns and villages throughout the state. *Tamus* were encouraged by the British colonial government because they brought people from remote tribes and regions together. It's still that way today. Farmers come down from the hills to sell their produce. Bajau cowboys come to the *tamu* to buy and sell horses, and there are also water buffalo for sale. A colorful array of fruits and vegetables are sold alongside betelnut, baskets and household goods. In between you can browse through a great assortment of tribal souvenirs – handmade baskets, hats, beadwork and metal jewelry. It's best to go early in the morning when most of the heated bargaining takes place. The largest and most famous *tamu* takes place in Kota Belud every Sunday. Other weekly markets are Beaufort (Saturday), Ranau (1st of every month), and Tenom (Sunday).

Antiques and more valuable tribal crafts are becoming harder to find. The Kadazàn people make intricate weavings, multi-colored hats and cloth dolls, while the once nomadic Murut tribe is famous for its wooden blowpipes. Pottery is a specialty of the Chinese and Malay people living along the coast. Two of the best places to look for native arts and crafts are the shop at the **Sabah Museum** and the **Sabah Handicraft Development Corp** (above the tourist office) in downtown Kota Kinabalu. Two private shops selling tribal items are **Borneo Handicrafts** (Ground Floor, Lot 51, Jalan Gaya) and **Sabah Handicraft Centre** (Ground Floor, Lot 49, Bandaran Berjaya).

SARAWAK

Sarawak's many ethnic groups produce a vast array of art and craft items. The designs are distinctive: intricate motifs that often depict animals and spirits, featuring diamond-shaped and spiral lines.

The Dayak tribes in particular are known for their handicrafts: large metal earrings originally used to stretch the lobes of Kenyah, Kayan and Penan women, handwoven baskets, hats and mats, beaded pouches, rattan bags and bamboo containers. Featured in the Dayak woodcarving repertoire are spirit figures, masks, miniature coffins, walking sticks, war shields and huge burial poles, best described as the Bornean equivalent of the North

American totem pole. Among the musical instruments produced by the jungle tribes are bamboo flutes, fiddles, harps and gongs and an indigenous four-stringed instrument called the *sape*.

Weaving is yet another specialty. The Iban tribe makes blankets, jackets and skirts from natural fiber they harvest from the jungle. Down on the coast, Malay people weave fabulous *kain songet* and *kain berturus* sarongs, shawls and headgear – distinctive for their gold and silver threads. The ethnic Chinese concentrate on ceramics, producing decorative vases, flower pots and other pottery pieces that combine traditional Chinese and Dayak designs.

Craft shops concentrate in Kuching. One of the best is the **Sarawak Art Shop** in the New Wing of the Sarawak Museum, which sells wood carvings, baskets and bags, various tribal hats, *batik* paintings, beaded jewelry and Iban blankets. Other places to browse are the **Borneo Handicraft Shop** at 6 Jalan Tun Abg Hj Openg, **the Sarawak Batik Art Shop** at 1 Lebuh Temple, **Sarawak House Art Shop** at 39 Wayang Street, and **Thian Seng Goldsmith** at 48 Main Bazaar, which offers antiques and local handicrafts in addition to gold. Best bet for pottery is the Old Airport Road (Jalan Penrissen) with such shops as **Hua Lian Pottery** and **Joo Yee Ceramic Factory**.

FURTHER READING

From the *Insight Guides* stable comes a range of travel guides, specially designed to help make your visit an unforgettable one.

Much more than a field guide, this book answers the call of all wildlife lovers.

GETTING THERE

BY AIR

The majority of visitors arrive and depart from Manila by air. Some 200 international flights arrive in Manila weekly. Ninoy Aquino International Airport and the domestic terminal are centrally located. Mactan International Airport off Cebu in the south and Laoag International Airport in Ilocos Norte in the north also have international flights.

BY SEA

Freighters and cruise ships take advantage of the excellent harbor of Manila Bay, although most travelers prefer to arrive by air. The government is adamant about protecting tourists from endangering themselves by traveling on small craft between East Malaysia (Borneo) and the country's southernmost islands. Muslim rebels and continuing piracy make this exotic route inadvisable.

TRAVEL ESSENTIALS

VISAS & PASSPORTS

All visitors to the Philippines must have valid passports. Citizens of countries with which the Philippines has diplomatic relations and who are staying in the country for not more than 21 days, do not need a visa provided they have tickets for their onward or return journeys. Visas may be obtained from Philippine diplomatic and consular offices abroad.

MONEY MATTERS

The monetary unit of the Philippines is the *peso* (P). There are 100 *centavos* to a peso. At time of press, the exchange rate fluctuates around 27 pesos to a

U.S. dollar. The U.S. dollar, pound sterling, Swiss franc, Deutsche mark, Canadian dollar, Italian lira, Australian dollar and the Japanese yen are all easily converted. Outside Manila, the U.S. dollar is widely accepted after the peso. Traveler's checks can be easily cashed, and major credit cards are accepted.

HEALTH

Yellow fever vaccination is required upon arrival from infected areas, except for children under one year of age, who are, however, subject to isolation when necessary.

WHAT TO WEAR

Light and loose clothes are most practical. Pack a sweater though if you intend to go to the mountains. At formal gatherings Filipino men mostly wear the *barong tagalog* (Tagalog shirt). This is a long shirt with side slits, worn untucked. Traditionally it is made in white or pastels out of a very fine silk called *jusi*. The shirt is so transparent that a white T-shirt is always worn underneath. As for Filipino women, they often wear the *terno* for formal occasions. This is a long gown with huge "butterfly" sleeves and elaborate embroidery on the skirt and bodice. When visiting churches and mosques, remember that short shorts and any excessive or provocative dress is inappropriate.

CUSTOMS

Tourists may bring in the following items free of duty: (1) Personal effects: A reasonable amount of clothing for personal use; a small quantity of perfume; (2) Tobacco and alcoholic beverages: 200 sticks of cigarettes or 250 grams of tobacco; two bottles of alcoholic beverages of not more than one liter each. Departures involve an airport tax of P220 (US$8) for international flights and P15 for domestic (US$0.50).

GETTING ACQUAINTED

TIME ZONES

The Philippines is 8 hours ahead of Greenwich Mean Time. All year round sunrise is about 6 a.m. and sunset about 6 p.m., give or take 30 minutes.

CLIMATE

The best months to travel to the Philippines are from December to May during the dry season. From June to November, temperature hovers around 80°F (21°C). January is the coldest month with 78°F (25.5°C); the hottest is May with 83°F (28°C). Humidity is high, ranging from 71 percent in March to 85 percent in September.

BUSINESS HOURS

Shops open from 9 a.m to about 7 p.m., Monday to Saturday. In Manila, many shops catering to tourists stay open on Sundays. The Philippine attitude of *bahala'na* (whatever happens) prevails outside Manila so shops don't usually stick to rigid schedules. Government and business hours are from 8 a.m. to 5 p.m, Monday to Friday, with a lunch break from noon to 1 p.m. Banks are open from 9 a.m. to 4 p.m., Monday to Friday.

LANGUAGE

Most Filipinos are bilingual, with English still the basic language in business, government, schools and everyday communications. *Pilipino*, based on the Tagalog dialect, is the national language. There are 111 dialects and 87 languages spoken in the archipelago. Aside from English, Spanish is spoken fluently by a number of Filipinos.

Mabuhay, the first Pilipino word most tourists encounter, means "welcome" as well as "long live." *Po* and *ho* are traditional expressions of respect still in everyday use, especially when addressing elders. *Salamat*, meaning "thank you," is one of the most useful words you will ever need to learn. Try it and watch the smiles break out on the faces of your new Filipino friends.

GETTING AROUND

DOMESTIC AIR TRAVEL

Transportation around the archipelago emanates from the country's hub, Manila. Flying is quick and cheap and Philippine Airlines, Aerolift and Pacific Airways Corporation, the country's domestic carriers cover the country with their routes. For those with time to spare, transportation possibilities include bus, train, car and boat travel.

Philippine Airlines is the major domestic (and international) carrier operating to over 40 domestic points. Up-and-coming airlines competing with the flag carrier include Aerolift, (Daet, Cebu, Boracay, Bohol, Dipolog, Lubang and Busuanga) and Pacific Airways Corporation (Lubang, Boracay and Busuanga). Listed below are the telephone numbers of the three airlines.

Aerolift, Tel: 817-2361/818-8711
Pacific Airways Corporation, Tel: 832-2731
Philippine Airlines, Tel: 832-0991/3166

WATER TRANSPORT

Manila and Cebu are the two centers of shipping. Be advised that inter-island boat travel will only suit those prepared to "rough it." The effort is rewarding however, as some of the ports served by the steamers have hardly changed in decades – and the bonus is that seemingly half the local populace greets arriving boats down at the wharf. Tickets on major lines (e.g. Manila-Cebu) can be booked through travel agencies. Again, the low fares are a pleasant surprise.

PUBLIC TRANSPORT

WITHIN MANILA

In Metro Manila, the bus and jeepney rates are P1.50 for the first 4 kilometers plus 25 centavos for every kilometer thereafter.

Tricycles (motorcycle with a side-car attached) are sometimes available for short trips on the side streets.

There are also air-conditioned Love Buses with terminals in Escolta in Binondo, Manila, The Center Makati and Ali Mall in Cubao, Quezon City. Rates are P10.

Taxi fare is P7.50 at flagdown for the first 500 meters and P1 for every 250 meters thereafter for non-air-conditioned taxis; and P12.50 for air-conditioned ones. Taxis can be found almost everywhere, especially near hotels, shopping centers and cinemas. Always have small change available and pay in pesos.

Metrorail, which is a 10-mile (15-km) overhead railway system, charges a flat rate of P3.50 at any point along Taft and Rizal Avenue, from Baclaran to Monumento in Caloocan City.

The Pasig River ferry operates from Lawton near the Central Post Office to Guadalupe near Makati. The fare is P9.50 one way.

TRAINS

Train travel is only for the very brave with lots of time to spare. Only one line operates out of Manila. The train from Manila's Tutuban Station in Tondo runs south to Legaspi City from where you can visit Mayon Volcano in the Bicol region.

BUSES

The central Luzon region near Manila and areas surrounding provincial capitals have a reasonable road system. Dozens of bus companies operate services to the main tourist centers of Luzon and fares are low by Western standards, e.g. The 5-hour journey from Manila to Baguio costs less than P100.

PRIVATE TRANSPORT

You can rent station wagons, bantams, coasters, buses, jeepneys and air-conditioned limousines. Cars may be rented with or without a driver. Charges vary according to type of vehicle.

Hourly rates are available, charges are at one-sixth the daily rate. In excess of 6 hours, daily rates apply. A valid foreign or international driver's license is acceptable.

CAR RENTAL AGENCIES

Avis Rent-A-Car, G & S Transport Corp., 311 P. Casal Street, San Miguel, Manila, Tel: 742-0887/2871

Hertz Rent-A-Car, China Banking Corp. Building, Paseo de Roxas corner Villar Street, Makati, Metro Manila, Tel: 832-5325/831-8541

J Rent-A-Car, 1573 Yakal Street, Sta. Cruz, Manila, Tel: 26-4732

WHERE TO STAY

The Philippines offers a wide range of accommodation to suit every budget from beach resorts and pension houses to apartments and luxury hotels.

Manila boasts 10 deluxe hotels. The city has been well organized for tourism and conventions. The Department of Tourism and the Philippine Convention and Visitor's Bureau have an excellent network of promotion offices all over the world to provide information and in some cases even make hotel reservations. For detailed information and rates, contact the Tourist Information Center, Department of Tourism, 2nd floor, T.M. Kalaw Street, Rizal Park, Manila, tel: 599-031.

MANILA

DELUXE

Century Park Sheraton, Vito Cruz Cnr Adiatico St. Malate, Metro Manila, Tel: 522-1011, Fax: 521-3413/5275

Hotel Intercontinental, 1 Ayala Avenue, Makati Commercial Center, Makati, Metro Manila, Tel: 815-9711

Hotel Nikko Manila Garden, Makati Commercial Center, Makati, Metro Manila, Tel: 810-4101

Hyatt Regency Manila, 2702 Roxas Boulevard, Pasay, Metro Manila, Tel: 831-2611, Fax: 833-5916

The Mandarin Oriental Manila, Paseo de Roxas Triangle, Makati, Metro Manila, Tel: 816-3601

Manila Hotel, Rizal Park, Manila, Tel: 47-00-11

The Manila Midtown Hotel, P. Gil corner Adriatico streets, Ermita, Manila, Tel: 59-39-11

Manila Peninsula, Ayala Avenue corner Makati Avenue, Makati, Metro Manila, Tel: 819-3456

The Westin Philippine Plaza, Cultural Center Complex, Roxas Boulevard, Manila, Tel: 832-0701

Silahis International, 1990 Roxas Boulevard, Ermita, Manila, Tel: 57-38-11

FIRST CLASS

Admiral Hotel, 2138 Roxas Boulevard, Ermita, Manila, Tel: 57-20-81

Ambassador Hotel, 2021 A. Mabini Street, Malate, Manila, Tel: 50-66-11

Holiday Inn Manila, 3001 Roxas Boulevard, Ermita, Manila, Tel: 59-79-61

Manila Pavilion Hotel, Maria Orosa Street, corner U.N. Avenue, Ermita, Manila, Tel: 57-37-11

Philippine Village Hotel, MIA Road, Pasay City, Metro Manila, Tel: 833-8081

BAGUIO CITY

Baguio Park Hotel, Harrison Road, Tel: 442-5656

Hotel Monticello, Maryheights, Kennon Road, Tel: 442-6566

Hotel Nevada, Loakan Road, Tel: 442-2400

BACOLOD CITY

Bascon Hotel, Gonzaga Street, Tel: 231-41

Sea Breeze Hotel, St Juan Street, Tel: 245-71

Sugarland Hotel, Singcang, Tel: 224-62

BATANGAS

Punta Baluarte InterContinental, Calatagan, Tel: 818-3185/3628

BORACAY

Club Panoly, Manila office, Tel: 818-9985/815-9601

Costa Hill Resort, Manila office, Tlx: 63936

Friday's Beach Club, Manila Office, Tel: 521-5040

Lorenzo Beach Club, Quezon City office, Tel: 990-719

Palm Beach Club, Manila office, Tel: 832-0304

Paradise Garden, Manila office, Tel: 522-2685

CAVITE

Puerto Azul Beach Hotel, Ternate, Tel: 57-47-31 to 40

CEBU

Argao Beach Club, Dalaguete, Tel: 702-00

Badian Island Beach Club, Badian Island, Tel: 613-06

Cebu Beach Club, Buyong, Mactan Island, Tel: 702-00

Cebu Plaza Hotel, Lahug, Tel: 924-31

Coral Reef Hotel, Barrio Agus, Mactan Island, Tel: 792-03

Costabella Tropical Beach Hotel, Buyong, Mactan Island, Tel: 854-75

Magellan International, Gorordo Avenue, Lahug, Tel: 746-13

Maribago BlueWater Beach Resort, Buyong, Mactan Island, Tel: 838-63

Montebello Villa International, Banilad, Cebu City, Tel: 850-21

Tambuli Beach Resort, Buyong, Mactan Island, Tel: 702-00

ILOILO

Amigo Terrace Hotel, Iznart-Delgado streets, Iloilo City, Tel: 748-10

Del Rio Hotel, M.H. Del Pilar Street, Molo, Iloilo City, Tel: 755-85

Isla Naburot, Iloilo, Tel: 761-12

Sarabia Manor Hotel, Gen. Luna Street, Iloilo City, Tel: 727-31

Sicogon Resort, Carles, Iloilo, Tel: 792-91

FOOD DIGEST

WHAT TO EAT

Nowhere else is the Philippines' long history of outside influences more evident than in its food...the experience of a lifetime. Philippine cuisine, an intriguing blend of Spanish, Malay and Chinese influences, is noted for the use of fruits, local spices and seafoods. Food to the Filipino is an integral part of local art and culture, and the result is a tribute to the Pinoy's ingenuity in concocting culinary treats from eastern and western ingredients.

Filipinos eat rice three times a day, morning, noon and night. It is a "must" to sample a Filipino breakfast of fried rice, *longaniza* (native sausage) and fish, which is normally salted and dried accompanied by tomatoes and *patis* (fish sauce) on the side.

When ordering it's best to watch the Filipinos. Even before the food arrives, sauce dishes are brought in and people automatically reach for the vinegar bottle with hot chili, or the soy sauce which they mix with *kalamansi* (small lemons). Grilled items are good with crushed garlic, vinegar and chili. It's a good idea to start a meal with *sinigang*, a clear broth slightly soured with small nature fruit and prepared with *bangus* (milkfish) or shrimp.

Some typical Philippine dishes worth trying are *tinola* which is made with chicken, and *pancit molo* which is a dumpling made of pork, chicken and mushrooms cooked in chicken or meat broth. *Adobo* is pork in small pieces, cooked for a long time in vinegar with other ingredients such as chicken, garlic and spices and then served with rice.

A typical feast dish, *lechon* is suckling pig stuffed with tamarind leaves and roasted on lighted coals until the skin is crackling and the meat tender. It is generally served with liver sauce. *Sinanglay*, another festive dish, is fish or piquant crabs with hot pepper wrapped in leaves of Chinese cabbage, and then cooked in coconut milk.

Other Filipino favorites include *lumpia* – a salad of heart-of-palm and small pieces of pork and shrimp wrapped in a crepe and served with garlic and soya sauce and *kare-kare* which is oxtail, knuckles and tripe stewed with vegetables in peanut sauce and served with *bagoong*, an anchovy based sauce.

Puddings are generally made with coconut rice or coconut milk. Among the most famous is *bibingka*, which consists of ground rice, sugar and coconut milk, baked in a clay oven and topped with fresh and salted duck eggs. *Guinatan* is a coco-pudding which is served with lashings of coconut cream. Ice creams are made in several fruit flavors such as *nangka* (jackfruit), *ube* and mango as well as the more usual vanilla, chocolate and strawberry.

THINGS TO DO

First and foremost the Philippines is renowned for its beaches. Choose from Boracay, Cebu, Puerto Galera, Camiguin, Bauang La Union, Sicogon, Batangas, Laoag and hundreds more. If you tire of sun and sand try heading for the hills of Baguio and the fabled rice terraces of Banawe, visiting Bontoc and Sagada en route.

Visitors looking for something different might consider climbing Davao's Mt Apo, diving in Palawan, golfing in Batangas, walking on Camiguin, visiting the tribal people in Zamboanga and Sulu or fiesta hopping around the islands.

Having "done" Manila, anyone with time to spare would do well to check out the following day trips, if daytrips are your thing: Corregidor, Tagaytay and Taal Volcano, Villa Escudero, Sarao Jeepney Factory, Las Piñas Bamboo Organ, Hidden Valley Springs, Pagsanjan Falls and Batangas Philippine Experience.

For official tour guides registered with the Department of Tourism, telephone Manila: 599-031.

Baron Travel Corporation, Pacific Bank Building, Ayala Avenue, Makati, Metro Manila, Tel: 817-6696

Far Travel Inc., Asian Plaza I Building, Makati, Metro Manila, Tel: 815-1425

Sarkies Tours Phils., Inc., J.P. Laurel Building, M.H. del Pilar Street, Ermita, Manila, Tel: 59-76-58

Southeast (Phil) Travel Center, 451 Pedro Gil, Ermita, Manila, Tel: 50-66-01

Sundowner Travel Center, 1430 A. Mabini, Ermita, Manila, Tel: 521-2602

SHOPPING

WHAT TO BUY

The Philippines is an old Asian shopping emporium, dating back to the days when its coastal towns sold pearls, beeswax and tortoise shell to trading vessels all the way from Arabia. Today, the emphasis is on handicraft, woodcarving and the gifts of the sea. Almost all major cities are worth a shopping trip but a limited schedule that takes you to Manila, Cebu, Baguio and Zamboanga yields sufficient reward.

BASKETRY

Philippine baskets are now found in many fashion capitals of the world, thanks to enterprising Pinoys who have at last seen their export potential after years of having taken them for granted. With all of their varying regional designs and recent streamlining, Philippine baskets are both the scholar's and the plain old shopper's delight. Made out of a range of natural fibers from the bamboo, the rattan vine, the nipa bush and various palms, these baskets come in a whole range of sizes and purposes, both functional and decorative.

Baskets are found all over the tourist shops and also in bazaar-like display under the Quiapo Bridge, in the heart of Metro Manila. The Baguio market up in the mountain province is also worth a visit because it is where the antique designs of the mountain province converge with baskets from all over the Philippines, from Bicol through the Visayas and Mindanao.

Note also that there is a special line of baskets that have lately caused collection fever among the more knowledgeable Philippine-watchers. These are the smoked fish traps and locust baskets, as well as the lunch containers bought off the huts of Northern

Luzon where they are considered family heirlooms. So popular are these antique baskets that a line of endeavor has sprung up in the north – "cooking" new baskets woven in the old design to look as though they have stood beside a smokey Igorot hearth for decades.

MATS

First cousin to the baskets, Philippine mats are fascinating bits of local color recruited to line the walls of hotels. They range from the natural-colored *pandan* mats of most of Luzon to the playfully designed ones of Leyte and Samar in the Visayas and the dramatic geometries of Basilan and Sulu in Mindanao. What you find in Manila can be severely limited, with the exception of the Quiapo Bridge market, but finding yourself in Cebu, Davao or Zamboanga is the perfect opportunity to stock up on these inexpensive bits of folk art.

HANDICRAFTS

Abaca hats, placemats, coasters, bamboo trays, shell wind-chimes, ceramic pots and gewgaws are all over the tourist shops around the airport, Makati Commercial Center and the Ermita tourist belt. The macrame fever is also in full blush in these places, in shirts, blouses, bags and dresses, planters and wall hangings.

EMBROIDERY

Very few guests, in the country for the first time, resist the attractions of Philippine embroidery. The *barong tagalog* has now gain international fame and has many versions, from the thousand-peso Pierre Cardin type to the humbler *polo barongs* (short-sleeved) much beloved by casual tourists. Depending on your tastes, you can choose the translucent pineapple fiber, *jusi*, for your material with the finest hand-embroidery, or the less expensive *ramie* with machine-embroidery (though you sometimes can hardly tell the difference). Go to the better-known houses.

There is no lack of embroidered clothes for women either – the *barong* dress shaped like the *barong tagalog* but longer, the embroidered kaftans and jelabas with matching scarves, bags and handkerchiefs.

JEWELRY

The most typically Philippine lines are shell and silver jewelry. Mother-of-pearl is perhaps the most popular, although coral and tortoise shell are also coming into their own. The best silver jewelry is to be found in Baguio where the guild-like training from St Louis University has today engendered much fine craftmanship.

You can also find many examples of wood and vine jewelry in the specialty shops of Ermita and Makati, as well as beadwork from the tribes, notably the necklaces, earrings and ornamental hair pieces of the T'boli, the Mangyan and the Igorot tribes.

ANTIQUES

The first smiths of the Philippines are recorded in Mindanao. To this day, they continue to manufacture gongs, jewel boxes, betelnut boxes, brass beds and cannon replicas. They're all over the tourist belt but if someone tries to sell you an "antique," check it out first with a knowledgeable shopping guide. There are also ceremonial canopies embroidered and sequined to celebrate royal Muslim weddings and feasts in these shops. They make lovely buys.

WOODCARVING

Giant hardwood carvings of the Igorot tribesman and his woman were among the first items of Filipiniana brought home by the Americans. What they did not see were other more fascinating things like the rice granary god carvings and the animal totems from Palawan that can now be found in the Ermita tourist belt.

SPORTS

GOLF

For most visitors to the Philippines, golf is a big attraction because the country has some of the finest courses in the world – including several championship courses. Teeing off amid lush tropical vegetation and water-laced inland resorts gives any golfer maximum enjoyment of the game. Also, because of the climate, golf is an ideal all-year-round sport.

To date there are more than 50 golf courses in the archipelago. Most are in Luzon, although there are some fine courses in the large cities of the Visayas and Mindanao. From its humble beginnings of a few thousand golfers in the 1920s, Philippine golf has become an increasingly popular sport with the advent of international golf tournaments and the development of well-appointed country clubs.

Green fees vary from links to links and are often slightly higher on weekends. Green fees vary from P100-500 plus rentals. Caddies, carts, golf clubs and shoes are available for hire on an hourly basis.

SKIN-DIVING

The archipelago is a skin-diver's paradise. Generally, the islands offer steep drop-offs, huge coral heads, large and small inlets, warm waters and fairly easy to obtain diving gear. Underwater photographers will have a heyday among the multicolored feather star, colorful coral gardens, clouds of tropical aquarium fish and schools of pelagic jacks.

Submarine cliff aficionados can experience the pulse-pounding thrill of swimming with schools of 30-pound garoupas, napoleon wrass and snappers, or witness the sinuous grace of a shark and the capacity of a 5-foot barracuda.

The best diving season in the Philippines is March, April, May and early June. During this period, seas all around are calm, rainfall is rare and waters are crystal clear.

Areas worth trying in Luzon include Balayan and Batangas Bays close by Punta Baluarte resort, Caban and Layag Layag, both on a small island and Devil point on Maricaban Island.

Cebu, too, offers both excellent diving close to shore and further offshore is the Hilurangan Channel between Cebu Island and Bohol to the south. There are many diver's guides on the subject and the Department of Tourism can also provide you with detailed information.

HORSE-RACING

Horse-racing is held generally on Tuesdays, Wednesdays, Saturdays and Sundays at San Lazaro Hippodrome and Santa Ana Race Track. Betting on horses is a big-time operation. Major races include the Gran Copa, National Grand Derby, the Founder's Cup and the Presidential Cup.

FURTHER READING

From the *Insight Guides* stable comes a range of travel guides, specially designed to help make your visit an unforgettable one.

This award-winning guide captures the charms of the Philippine archipelago.

Much more than a field guide, this book answers the call of all wildlife lovers.

GETTING THERE

BY AIR

The smooth descent over Singapore's harbor and city – a shoreline in business by day, an illuminated city planner's outline by night – is well worth a window seat on the nearest side.

Even before landing, you will see the airport's magnificent 257-foot (78-meter) tall control tower. Singapore's **Changi International Airport** projects an aura of grandeur. In addition to the national carrier, Singapore Airlines, it is the touchdown for 52 international airlines with more than 1,500 flights a week.

Since it opened in 1981, Asia's largest and most modern airport has provided for more than 20 aircraft movements every hour, facilities to handle more than 500,000 tons of cargo and more than 14 million passengers every year.

A second terminal opened in 1990 has doubled Changi's capacity, enabling it to cope with up to 24 million passengers. The two terminals are linked by the "sky train," an automated miniature rapid transit train system with a track length of 600 meters. This is the first of its kind outside the USA and Europe.

An airport tax of S$12 for international flights and S$5 for flights to Malaysia is payable on departure.

BY SEA

Sailors enter Singapore as did the ancients – through waterways which weave among tiny offshore islands once called the Dragon Teeth Straits.

From the early Chinese junks that braved the seas to trade dried fruits, sugar candy, tea or paper umbrellas, to steady tankers listing under the weight of the island's refined oil, the port of Singapore has been the hub of navigation on the eastern seas.

Three hundred shipping lines flying the flags of some 80 countries and serving 300 other ports call regularly. A ship arrives at and leaves the port every 10 minutes. Along with major ports like Rotterdam and Hong Kong, Singapore is rated one of the world's busiest.

Passenger lines serve Singapore annually from Australia, Europe, North America, India and Hong Kong. Entry formalities comply with standard immigration laws and, for quick orientations, the

Tourist Promotion Board is on hand to greet arrivals with a mobile information service on the sights of the town.

BY LAND

Singapore, surrounded by waters on all sides, is connected by road and rail with the Malay Peninsula by the Causeway.

The railway takes travelers to Singapore from Bangkok en route Haadyai, Butterworth and Kuala Lumpur. Express trains depart from Bangkok daily. The fare from Bangkok to Singapore is S$237 for air-conditioned first class down to S$106 for second class with no air-conditioning.

Three air-conditioned express trains run daily from Singapore to Kuala Lumpur and Butterworth in Malaysia. The morning train departs at 7:45 a.m., the afternoon service at 2:45 p.m., and the evening mail train at 10 p.m. You must change at Butterworth to continue on to Bangkok. For detailed fares and schedules, call the railway station on Keppel Road (tel: 222-5165). Reservations are accepted with advance payment, though arriving early for your train is advisable.

BY RAIL

THE ORIENT EXPRESS

The operators of the famed London-to-Venice Orient Express, are launching a new luxury train in Southeast Asia. From November 1992, the Eastern and Oriental Express will make one round trip a week between Singapore, Kuala Lumpur and Bangkok. The journey will take 41 hours and cover a distance of 1,943 km. The E&O will leave Singapore every Sunday, arrive back in Singapore every Friday, and depart that evening for an overnight excursion to Malacca. Passengers can look forward to a fabulous rail experience and enjoy unsurpassed comfort, service and cuisine.

Prices for the one way trip between Singapore and Bangkok will range from US$900 to US$2,940 depending on the class of accommodation. Reservations can be made from spring 1992, via travel agents, or by contacting the E&O office on Tel: (071) 928-6000. Fax: (071) 620-1210.

TRAVEL ESSENTIALS

VISAS & PASSPORTS

Visitors entering Singapore must possess valid national passports or internationally recognized travel documents. Visas are not necessary for a stay up to 14 days, provided the visitor has confirmed onward passage and adequate finances. Collective passports or travel documents are permitted for group travel in tours of five to 20 people. However, these regulations do not apply to nationals from communist countries or India who need visas to enter Singapore. Tourist visas are usually issued and extended up to a maximum of three months at the Immigration Office, Pidemco Centre (for enquiries, phone: 532-2877).

A certificate of vaccination against yellow fever is necessary only for those who have passed through or originated in infected countries, which includes most of Africa and South America.

MONEY MATTERS

Singapore issued its own currency in 1957, choosing native orchids to adorn its dollar. In 1976, a second generation of currency was issued, depicting birds of the region perched above the island's buildings and industries. A third series depicting a variety of sailing vessels is now in circulation. The Singapore dollar was valued at about 1.76 to the U.S dollar or 3.18 to the British pound sterling at the time of going to press. Brunei dollars are roughly equivalent to the Singapore dollar.

There are currently two sets of coins in circulation. The newer 10, 20 and 50 cents are smaller in size than the old ones. Malaysian dollars are about 40 percent lower in value and no longer circulate freely.

There is no limit on the amount of Singapore and foreign notes, traveler's checks and letters of credit brought into or out of the country.

Make no haste to change big money at luxurious hotels. Singapore's ubiquitous money-changers are government licensed and reliable. Often they give better rates than those of leading hotels which deduct a service charge of 5 to 10 cents Singapore currency on each U.S. dollar. Currency exchange rates at banks fluctuate each day, but only very slightly. Traveler's checks generally get a better rate of exchange than cash. It's best to deal directly with any bank or licensed money-changer. Banking hours are 10 a.m. – 3 p.m. Monday to Friday, and 9:30 a.m. – 11:30 a.m Saturday.

If you wish to deal with banks for your traveler's checks and other foreign currency transactions, it is advisable to do so on weekdays. Although most banks welcome such transactions, some do not handle them on Saturdays while others conduct them in small amounts only, based on Friday's rate.

Credit cards commonly accepted are Visa, American Express, Diner's Club, Carte Blanche, Asia Card, Master Charge Card and those of international hotel chains and airlines.

HEALTH

Inevitably the third word belonging to Singapore after "clean" and "green" is "healthy." Travelers have no worries in a place where one can drink water straight from the tap and consume food by the streetside. They can even participate in the hygiene campaigns like "Keep Singapore Pollution Free." The Republic lives up to this comforting reputation with efficient, contemporary medical facilities in numerous hospitals and clinics throughout the island. The closest anyone can come to a physical ailment originating in Singapore is over-eating and there is a quick cure for this: shopping on foot for a few hours.

WHAT TO WEAR

The daytime trend is pure casual comfort. Light summer fashions, easy to move in, are the right choice for a full day out in town. Wear a white shirt and tie for office calls. Evening dress is a more subtle combination of fads and formality. Only few plush nightclubs and very exclusive restaurants favor the traditional jacket and tie. Most hotels, restaurants, coffee houses and discos accept more casual wear of shirt-and-tie (or even shirts without ties) for men and pleasant dress suits for the ladies. However, jeans and T-shirts are a taboo at most discos. To avoid embarrassment, visitors are advised to call in advance to check an establishment's dress policy.

CUSTOMS

Singapore essentially remains a free port. Personal effects (including cameras and radios), 1 liter spirits, 1 liter malt liquor or 1 liter wine, non duty-free cigarettes are allowed. Narcotics are strictly forbidden as are firearms and weapons, which are subject to licensing.

GETTING ACQUAINTED

GEOGRAPHY & CLIMATE

Singapore, at the tip of the Malay Peninsula is about 80 miles (128 km) north of the equator and has an area of 250 square miles (626 square km). The Republic city-state consists of Singapore island and 57 other islets of which fewer than half are inhabited. The Government, not to be deterred by the limited land space, is constantly clearing swamps and jungles and reclaiming land from the surrounding waters.

About two-thirds of the island is less then 50 feet (15 meters) high and the highest point (Bukit Timah or "Tin Hill") stands at 585 feet (177 meters).

TIME ZONES

Singapore Standard Time is eight hours ahead of Greenwich Mean Time.

CLIMATE

Conversations jump from rain to shine. Shine wins out on most occasions since the climate is equally warm and sunny the year round. Temperatures teeter between 87°F (30.6°C) at noon and 75°F (23.8°C) at night, the daytime heat cooled by sea winds and ample air-conditioning.

Asia's subtle seasons follow the monsoons and, from November to January, high winds turn a bucket over Singapore. For 10 minutes, the city comes to a standstill under hawker stalls, arcades and umbrellas. Then as suddenly as they come, the rains vanish, leaving the pavements wet-washed, the lawns refreshed, and the umbrellas behind for sunshades.

BUSINESS HOURS

Government offices and commercial firms generally open between 7:30 a.m. and 9:30 a.m. on Monday to Friday. They usually close between 4 and 6 p.m., with an hour for lunch. Many offices are also open on Saturdays from 8:30 a.m. to 1 p.m.

Shops are open from 9 a.m. to 6 p.m. Monday to Saturday. However, shops catering to tourists tend to open at 10 a.m. and close at 9:30 p.m.

LANGUAGE

English is spoken and understood by nearly everyone in Singapore. Almost all signs are also in English. So the English-speaking visitor should feel quite at home. Mandarin and Malay are also widely spoken. Tamil is the mother tongue of the local Indian population, and a number of Chinese dialects such as Cantonese and Hokkien are also found in Singapore.

CUSTOMS

The customs, religions and languages of nearly every nation in the world have converged in Singapore during some time in its history. Adjectives beginning with "multi" are common sounds on the Singapore scene, and a cosmopolitan tolerance is part of the city's character.

With everyday etiquette relaxed and straightforward, visitors behaving courteously stand little chance of giving offense.

TEMPLES & MOSQUES

Removing one's shoes before entering a mosque or an Indian temple has been an unspoken tradition for centuries. Within, devotees do not smoke, though neither of these customs generally applies to Chinese temples where more informal styles prevail. Visitors are most welcome to look around at their leisure and are invited to stay during religious rituals. While people pray, it is understood that those not participating in the service will quietly stand aside.

A polite gesture would be to ask permission before taking photographs; the request is seldom, if ever, refused. Moderate clothing rather than brief skirts or shorts, is appropriate for a visit.

Most temples and mosques have a donation box for funds to help maintain the building. Contributing a few coins before leaving is customary.

TIPPING

Smiles follow tips everywhere. Singapore is no exception especially in the fashionable accessories of an affluent society like nightclubs, friendly bars and expensive restaurants. Here the magic number is 10 percent. Leading hotels are kind enough to do the tipping for you by adding a 10 percent service charge to every bill; a second time round is not necessary though neither is it refused. Bellboys and porters receive from S$1 upwards depending upon the complexity of the errand. Yet, beyond the international thoroughfares, tipping is exceptional. In small local restaurants, food stalls and taxis, the bill includes the service, and with thank you (*terima kaseh* in Malay), a smile will do.

LITTERING

Singapore has something else to boast about. It is clean and green. Much pain has been taken by the Government not only to keep it that way but also to inculcate civic-conscious habits in its citizens. Litter bins dotting the island at short distance intervals make it inexcusable to drop a litter (be it a bus ticket, a cigarette butt, or a sweet wrapper) anywhere else and if you do, it's a fine, of up to S$1,000.

SMOKING

Smoking is banned in cinemas, theaters, libraries, lifts (elevators), buses, taxis, government offices and air-conditioned restaurants. The offense carries a fine of up to S$500. Signboards that serve as reminders are on display in such places.

TOILETS

Failure to flush urinals and water closets after use in public toilets (hotels, shopping centers, cinemas etc.) can result in a S$500 fine.

GETTING AROUND

FROM THE AIRPORT

The airport is linked to the city center by the East Coast Parkway (20 minutes traveling time) and to the rest of Singapore by the Pan-Island Expressway.

There are three types of transport from the airport – private car, taxi or public bus. A surcharge, S$3 more than the fare shown on the taxi meter, is charged if you board the taxi at the airport. A 50 percent surcharge of the metered fare must be paid by the passenger if the taxi ride begins between 12 a.m. and 6 a.m. Taxi fare from the airport to hotels in the Orchard Road area should run about S$15 plus extras.

A number of public shuttle bus services run between the airport and nearby bus interchanges. For service numbers and routes, check the CAAS information counters in either terminal or the basement of Changi Terminal One. Bus No. 390, from the airport to Orchard Road, costs S$1.20 (air-conditioned) or 90 cents (non-AC).

BUSES

Nearly 250 bus services ply the paved roads of Singapore today, connecting every corner of the island. Bus rides in Singapore, though more crowded and slower than taxis are less expensive, and more exciting; absorbing the local travelers, minitowns and marketplaces with all the immediacy it takes to turn an experience into a memory.

Singapore has four kinds of buses: single-levels and double-deckers, air-conditioned and non-air-conditioned. They run from 6:15 a.m. to 11:30 p.m. on average, with an extension of about half an hour for both starting and ending times on weekends and public holidays. Fares are cheap: 50 to 90 cents for non-air-conditioned; 60 cents to S$1.20 for air-conditioned and structured according to fare stages. Have some change ready and ask the bus driver after boarding. Most buses are one-man operated (OMO) with no conductor.

For good value, purchase the Singapore Explorer tickets: S$5 for one day or S$12 for three days of unlimited bus rides. Available from travel agents and major hotels.

An especially helpful source, available at most bookstores and news-stands at 70 cents, is the **Bus Guide**. This booklet gives complete details of all bus routes including a section on bus services to major places of interest in Singapore for the benefit of tourists. Or call Singapore Bus Service, Tel: 287-2727 during office hours.

MASS RAPID TRANSIT

The Singapore government spent an estimated S$5 billion, for the Mass Rapid Transit (MRT) railway system project. It is Singapore's biggest single investment. The MRT system includes 42 stations spread over four lines and can carry about 600,000 passengers daily.

Fare collection is automatic: magnetically coded cards costs between 60 cents to $1.50. Stored value cards are valued at $12.

Depending on the station, the first train rolls out between 6 a.m. and 6:40 a.m. Monday to Saturday, and between 6:45 a.m. to 7:25 a.m. on Sunday and public holidays. The last trains are between 11 p.m. and midnight, and 15 minutes earlier on Sundays and public holidays.

TAXIS

Taxis are fast, easy and comfortable in Singapore. They come in various colors – black and yellow, blue, green and white, red and white – all with "SH" on their license plates. Each taxi is allowed a maximum of four passengers. All taxis in Singapore run on meters. If a driver insists his meter is broken, catch another cab. The flag fare is S$2.20.

There are a number of extra charges which you should be aware of:

* A surcharge of 50 percent on the metered fare is assessed between midnight to 6 a.m.

* A surcharge of S$3 for the purchase of a daily area license fee if you are the first passenger using the taxi to enter the Central Business District (CBD) during two peak periods: 7:30 a.m. to 10:15 a.m. Monday to Saturday and 4:30 p.m. to 6:30 p.m. during weekdays.

* A S$3 surcharge for taxi trips originating at Changi airport.

* A S$1 surcharge on trips out of the CBD restricted zone from 4 p.m. to 7 p.m. on weekdays.

* A S$2 surcharge if a taxi is booked through a telephone call to a taxi stand, or S$3 for a taxi booking made at least half an hour in advance.

Taxis on radio call are available at tel: 481-1211, 452-5555, 533-9009 and 250-0700 day and night. Tipping is optional and is discouraged by the government.

TRISHAWS

A direct descendent of the historical rickshaw – covered carriage pulled by man on foot – is the trishaw, a bicycle with a sidecar. This is a somewhat vanishing mode of transport among locals due to its slow speed, its lack of sophistication and the unending hassle over the fare with the rider who is often a stubborn grumpy man in his 60s.

However, it is fast becoming a hot favorite among visitors. Its selling point lies in the fact that it goes at a speed slow enough for its passenger to absorb what goes on around but fast enough to cover most of the picturesque sights of downtown within an hour. Full information of itinerarized trishaw tours at stand and prices is available at your hotel's tour desk.

A word of caution: for a ride by a free-lance rider, be sure you agree upon a fare before getting on. Licensed riders are distinguished from these by colored control badges.

RENT-A-CAR

In the free spirit of independent travel on and off the main roads of Singapore, rent-a-car services provide the wheels if you provide the valid driver's license. Self-drive cars cost from S$100 to S$350 a day plus mileage, depending on the size and comfort of your limousine. Contact any of the many companies renting cars through your hotel or the Yellow Pages – they will be the first to remind riders to bring along their passports. Two popular car rental companies are **Avis Rent-A-Car**, Tel: 737-1668 and **Hertz Rent-A-Car**, Tel: 734-4646.

WHERE TO STAY

As the island country with its abundant attractions continues to draw crowds, the accommodation sector is experiencing a boom which seems to live on and on and on...

In one month at least one hotel somewhere on the island is being renovated, while another is undergoing expansion and still another is computerizing its operations. Such keen competition among the hoteliers spells two words: variety and quality. Variety ranges from the deluxe that makes living like a king a slice-life (spending like one too, of course) to low-budget guesthouses for those whose only concern is for a roof above.

HOTELS

Most of the hotels listed below offer additional facilities such as conference room, banquet room, pool, health center, ballroom, discotheques, doctor, hairdresser, with TV and IDD in the guest rooms.

Allson, 101 Victoria Street., Singapore 0718, Tel: 336-0811
500 rooms; restaurants serving local, European. Japanese, Chinese and Thai food; bar; ballroom. Rates: S$140-180 single; S$160-200 twin; S$240-1000 suite.

Amara, 165 Tanjong Pagar Road, Singapore 0207, Tel: 224-4488
349 rooms; 8 restaurants serving local, European and Chinese food; bar; club and ballroom. Rates: S$190-280 single; S$200-290 twin.

ANA, Nassim Hill, Singapore 1025, Tel: 732-1222
462 rooms, restaurants serving local, European and Japanese food; bar and club. Rates: S$180-200 single; S$200-240 twin; S$260-1000 suite.

Apollo, 405 Havelock Road, Singapore 0316, Tel: 733-2081
332 rooms; restaurants serving local, Japanese and Chinese food; bar; club. Rates: S$120-140 single; S$160-180 twin; S$280 suite.

Asia, 37 Scotts Road, Singapore 0922, Tel: 737-8388
146 rooms; restaurants serving local and European food; bar. Rates: S$120-140 single; S$140-155 twin.

Boulevard, 200 Orchard Boulevard, Singapore 1024, Tel: 737-2911
529 rooms; restaurants serving local, European, Japanese and Indian food; bar. Rates: S$155-230 single; 185-260 twin; S$300-650 suite.

Cockpit, 6 Oxley Rise, Singapore 0923, Tel: 737-9111
182 rooms; Chinese restaurants; bar. Rates: S$130 single; S$150 twin; S$250 suite.

Concord, 317 Outram Road, Singapore 0316, Tel: 733-0188
509 rooms; 2 restaurants serving European and Japanese food; bar; Chinese nite-club. Rates: S$170-200 single/twin.

Crown Prince, 270 Orchard Road, Singapore 0923, Tel: 732-1111
303 rooms; restaurants serving local, European, Japanese and Chinese food. Rates: S$180-220 single; S$210-250 twin; S$530-1200 suite.

Dai Ichi (Harbour View), 81 Anson Road, Singapore 0207, Tel: 224-1133
420 rooms; restaurants serving Western, Japanese and Chinese food. Rates: S$120 single; S$150 twin; S$270-350 suite.

Dynasty, 320 Orchard Road, Singapore 0923, Tel: 734-9900
400 rooms; restaurants serving local, European and Chinese food, bar; ballroom. Rates: S$190-300 single; S$220-300 twin; S$500-2200 suite.

Excelsior, 5 Coleman Street, Singapore 0617, Tel: 338-7733
300 rooms; restaurants serving local, European, Japanese and Chinese food; bar. Rates: S$140 single; S$155 twin; S$300-1,080 suite.

Equatorial, 429 Bukit Timah Road, Singapore 1025, Tel: 732-0431
224 rooms; restaurants serving local, Chinese, Japanese and Swiss foods; genuine tea-house; business center. Rates: S$140-160 single; S$160-280 twin.

Furama, 10 Eu Tong Sen Street, Singapore 0105, Tel: 533-3888
354 rooms; restaurants serving local, European, Japanese and Chinese food; bar. Rates: S$150-170 single; S$170-190 twin; S$350 suite.

Goodwood Park, 22 Scotts Road, S'pore 0922, Tel: 737-7411
225 rooms half of which are suites; restaurants serving local Chinese, Japanese and continental food. Rates: S$355 single; S$400 twin; S$1,100 suite.

Hilton, 581 Orchard Road, Singapore 092, Tel: 737-2233
435 rooms; restaurants serving local, European and Chinese food; bar; ballroom. Rates: S$160-210 single; S$185-240 twin; S$320-1250 suite.

Holiday Inn Park View, 11 Cavenagh Road, Singapore 0922, Tel: 733-8333
350 rooms; restaurants serving European, Chinese and Indian food; bar; ballroom. Rates: S$190-200 single; S$220-290 twin; S$300-800 suite.

Hyatt Regency, 10 Scotts Road, Singapore 0922, Tel: 733-1188
791 rooms plus 352-room extension; restaurants serving local and European food; bar. Rates: S$190-290 single; S$220-320 twin; S$600-2,500 suite.

Imperial, 1 Jalan Rumbia, Singapore 0923, Tel: 737-1666
600 rooms; restaurants serving local, European, Chinese and Indian food; bar; ballroom. Rates: S$165-195 single; S$185-215 twin; S$330 suite.

Mandarin, 333 Orchard Road, Singapore 0923, Tel: 737-4411
1,200 rooms; restaurants serving local, European; Chinese and Japanese food; bar; club; ballroom. Rates: S$180-195 single/twin; S$250-900 suite.

Marina Mandarin, 6 Raffles Boulevard, Singapore 0103, Tel: 338-3388
557 rooms; 4 restaurants serving local, European and Chinese food. Rates: S$300-360 single; S$340-410 twin.

Meridien, 100 Orchard Road, Singapore 0923, Tel: 733-8855
419 rooms; restaurants serving local, European and Chinese food; bar; ballroom. Rates: S$190-245 single; S$210-280 twin; S$300-1200 suite.

Meridien Changi, 1 Netheravon Road, off Upper Changi Road, Singapore 1750, Tel: 545-7700
280 rooms; restaurants serving local, European and Chinese food; bar; ballroom. Rates: S$165-220 single; S$185-255 twin; S$300-1200 suite.

Novotel Orchid, 214 Dunearn Road, Singapore 1129, Tel: 250-3322
473 rooms; restaurants serving local and European food; bar. Rates: S$190-210 single, S$210-230 twin.

Omni Marco Polo, 247 Tanglin Road, S'pore 1024, Tel: 474-7141
603 rooms; restaurants serving local, European food; bar; club. Rates: S$300-400 single/twin.

Orchard, 442 Orchard Road, Singapore 0923, Tel: 734-7766.

350 rooms; restaurants serving European food; bar; ballroom. Rates: S$190-260 single; S$220-290 twin; S$450 suite.

Orchard Parade, 1 Tanglin Road, Singapore 1024, Tel: 737-1133
300 rooms; restaurants serving local, European and Chinese food; bar. Rates: S$200 single; S$225 twin; S$300 suite.

Oriental, 6 Raffles Boulevard, Singapore 092, Tel: 338-0066
515 rooms (no smoking floors): restaurants serving Chinese, European and Continental food; disco. Rates: S$295-350 single; S$330-390 twin.

Pan Pacific, 7 Raffles Boulevard, Singapore 0103 Tel: 336-8111
800 rooms. 9 restaurants serving local, European, Japanese, Chinese and Polynesian food; bar; ballroom. Rates: S$290-390 single; S$330-430 twin.

Peninsula, 3 Coleman Street, Singapore 0617, Tel: 337-2200
315 rooms; restaurants serving local and European food; bar; club. Rates: S$125-140 single; S$140-155 twin; S$280 suite.

Phoenix, Orchard Road/Somerset Road, Singapore 0923, Tel: 737-8666
300 rooms; restaurants serving local, European and Chinese food; bar. Rates: S$132-154 single; S$154-176 twin; S$210-250 suite.

Plaza, 7500A, Beach Road, Singapore 0719, Tel: 298-0011
355 rooms; restaurants serving local and European food; bar; club. Rates: S$130-160 single; S$150-180 twin.

Raffles, 1-3 Beach Road, Singapore 071, Tel: 337-8041
This historical landmark reopened on 16 September 1991 after two years and a S$100-million renovation. Raffles now has all the latest state-of-the-art facilities carefully hidden behind an early 20th-century facade. The new Raffles consists of suites only – 104 of them. Also back are the famous Long Bar, and Palm Court. Rates: S$600-6,000.

Regent, 1 Cuscaden Road, Singapore 1024, Tel: 733-8888
442 rooms; restaurants serving local, European and Chinese food; bar; ballroom. Rates: S$210 single; S$250 twin; S$500 suite.

Riverview, 382 Havelock Road, Singapore 0316, Tel: 732-9922
483 rooms; restaurants serving local, European, Japanese and Chinese food; bar; club. Rates: S$160-170 single; S$180-190 twin; S$400 suite.

Royal Holiday Inn Crowne Plaza, 25 Scotts Road, Singapore 0922, Tel: 737-7966
600 rooms; restaurants serving local, European and Chinese food; bar; ballroom. Rates: S$175 single; S$205 twin; S$380 suite.

Shangri La, 22 Orange Grove Road, Singapore 1025, Tel: 737-3644
810 rooms; restaurants serving local. European, Japanese and Chinese food; bar; ballroom. Rates: S$180-355 single; S$215-370 twin; S$470-2175 suite.

Sheraton Towers, 39 Scotts Road, Singapore 0922, Tel: 732-6888
412 rooms; 3 restaurants serving European and Chinese food; bar; club; ballroom. Rates: S$180-250 single/twin; S$350-1000 suite.

Westin Plaza, 2, Stamford Road, Singapore 0617, Tel: 338-8585
796 rooms; 11 restaurants serving local, European; Japanese and Chinese food; bar; ballroom.

Westin Stamford, 2 Stamford Road, Singapore 0617, Tel: 338-8585
1,253 rooms; 11 restaurants serving local, European, Japanese and Chinese food; bar; ballroom.

York, 21 Mt. Elizabeth, Singapore 0922, Tel: 737-0511
400 rooms, restaurants serving local, European and Chinese food; bar; ballroom. Rates: S$200-580 single; S$225-580 twin.

FOOD DIGEST

WHAT TO EAT

CHINESE

Cairncourt Restaurant, (Peking Szechuan), Cairnhill Hotel, 19 Cairnhill Circle, Tel: 734-6622

Changi Floral Mile Seafood, (Hong Kong), Blk 56, #01-1314, New Upper Changi Road, Tel: 443-8222

Cherry Garden, (Szechuan), The Oriental Hotel, 6 Raffles Boulevard, #01-200 Marina Square, Tel: 338-0066

Chui Garden Noodle House, (Cantonese), 345 Orchard Road, #01-02 Shaw House, Tel: 732-7578

Choon Seng Restaurant, (Seafood), 892 Ponggol Road, Tel: 288-3472

Goldleaf Restaurant, (Szechuan, Taiwanese), 160 Orchard Road, #04-11 Orchard Point, Tel: 737-7830

Happy Valley Noodle House, (Cantonese), 304 Orchard Road, #01-42 Lucky Plaza, Tel: 732-9918

House of Blossoms, (Teochew, Cantonese), Marina Mandarin, 6 Raffles Boulevard, #01-100 Marina Square, Tel: 338-3388

House of Four Seasons, (*Dian Xin*/Cantonese), 1 Empress Place, #01-03, Empress Place Building, Tel: 339-6833

Imperial Herbal Restaurant, (Herbal), Metropole Hotel, 41 Seah Street, Tel: 336-3611

Inn of Happiness, (Cantonese), Hilton International, 581 Orchard Road, Tel: 737-2233

Lei Garden Restaurant, (Cantonese), Boulevard Hotel, 200 Orchard Boulevard, Tel: 737-2911

Li Bai Restaurant, (Cantonese), Sheraton Towers, 39 Scotts Road, Tel: 737-6888

Liu Hsiang Lou, (Teochew, Cantonese, Szechuan and, Shanghainese), Allson Hotel, 101 Victoria Street, Tel: 336-0811

Long Beach Restaurant, (Seafood), 610 Bedok Road, Tel: 445-8833

Long Jiang, (Szechuan), Crown Prince Hotel, 270 Orchard Road, Tel: 732-1111

Loong Yuen, (Cantonese), Holiday Inn Park View 11 Cavenagh Road, Tel: 733-8333

Meisan Szechuan Restaurant, (Szechuan), Royal Holiday Inn, 25 Scotts Road, Tel: 737-7966

Min Jiang Seafood Restaurant, (Szechuan), Goodwood Park Hotel, 22 Scotts Road, Tel: 737-7411

Ming Palace Restaurant, (Cantonese),Orchard Parade Hotel, 1 Tanglin Road, Tel: 737-1133

Orchard King Prawn Restaurant, (Seafood), 96 Somerset Road, #01-05/06, UOL Bldg., Tel: 734-4079

Por Kee Restaurant, (Cantonese *dim sum* & roast meats), 76 Smith Street, Tel: 223-0814

Prima Tower, (Cantonese), 201, Keppel Road, Tel: 221-5600

Swatow Teochew Restaurant, (Teochew) Singapore Conference Hall, Shenton Way, Tel: 223-5471 100 Beach Road, #02-12/14, Tel: 292-9085

Tien Court, (Szechuan, steamboat), King's Hotel, 403 Havelock Road, Tel: 733-0011

Tung Lok Shark's Fin Restaurant, (Cantonese), 177 River Valley Road, #04-07/09 Liang Court, Tel: 336-6022

Xiang Man Lou, (Hong Kong *dim sum*), 79 Bain Street, Bras Basah Complex, Tel: 338-7885

Xin Zhang Jiang Restaurant, (Cantonese), Hotel Miramar, 401 Havelock Road, Tel: 733-0222

WESTERN FOOD

Barnacle Bill's (Continental), 10A Duxton Hill, Tel: 227-9630

Baron's Table, (Continental), Royal Holiday Inn, 25 Scotts Road, Tel: 737-7966

Blooms, (Continental), Orchard Hotel, 442 Orchard Road, Tel: 734-7766

Bologna, (Italian), Marina Mandarin, 6 Raffles Boulevard, Tel: 338-3388

Cafe Boulevard, (Continental), Orchard Parade Hotel, 1 Tanglin Road, Tel: 737-1133

Cafe Vienna, (Austrian, local and International), Royal Holiday Inn, 25 Scotts Road, Tel: 737-7966

Chico's 'N Charlie's, (Mexican/American), 541 Orchard Road, #05-01 Liat Towers, Tel: 734-0175

Coffee Garden, (International), Shangri-La Hotel, 22 Orange Grove Road, Tel: 737-3644

Compass Rose, (French and Continental), Westin Stamford Hotel, 2 Stamford Road, Tel: 338-8585

Da Paolo, (Italian), 66 Tanjong Pagar Road, Tel: 224-7081

Domus, (Italian), Sheraton Towers, 39 Scotts Road, Tel: 732-0022

Emmerson's Tiffin Rooms, (Continental and Asian), 51 Neil Road, Tel: 227-7518

Fourchettes, (Continental charcoal grill), The Oriental Hotel, #01-200 Marina Square, Tel: 338-0066

Gordon Grill, (Western and Scottish), Goodwood Park Hotel, 22 Scotts Road, Tel: 737-7411

Harbour Grill, (Continental), Hilton International, 581 Orchard Road, Tel: 737-2233

Hard Rock Cafe, (American), #04-01, HPL House, 50 Cuscaden Road, Tel: 235-5232

Jack's Place Steakhouse (Steaks)
Hotel Miramar, 401 Havelock Road, Tel: 703-0222
#02-117 Killiney Road, Tel: 737-7028, 734-2921
268 Orchard Road, #B01-00 Yen San Building, Tel: 235-7361

La Brasserie, (French), Omni Marco Polo Hotel, 247 Tanglin Road, Tel: 474-7141

La Boulangerie, (French), 500 Orchard Road, Far East Shopping Centre, Tel: 734-1576

La Brasserie Georges, (French), Hotel Meridien, 100 Orchard Road, Tel: 733-8855

Le Chalet Restaurant, (Swiss), Ladyhill Hotel, 1 Ladyhill Road, Tel: 737-2111

La Grande Bouffe, (French), 53/55 Sunset Way, Tel: 467-6847, 467-6078

Maxim's de Paris, (French), The Regent Singapore, 1 Cuscaden Road, Tel: 733-8888

Prego, (Italian), Westin Stamford Hotel, 2 Stamford Road, Tel: 338-8585 ext. 16310

Restaurant LaTour, (Continental), Shangri-La Hotel, 22 Orange Grove Road Tel: 737-3644

Shashlik Restaurant, (Russian), 545 Orchard Road, #06-19 Far East Shopping Centre, Tel: 732-6401

Steeple's Deli, (American deli), 19 Tanglin Road, #02-25 Tanglin Shopping Centre, Tel: 737-0701

The Hubertus Grill, (Continental), ANA Hotel, 16 Nassim Hill, Tel: 732-1222, ext. 1582

Trader Vic's, (International), Hotel New Otani, 177A River Valley Road, Tel: 338-3333

OTHER ASIAN FOOD

Alkaff Mansion, (Indonesian and Continental), 10 Telok Blangah Green, Tel: 278-9207

Annalkashmi, (Indian vegetarian), Excelsior Hotel, #02-10, 5 Coleman Street, Tel: 339-9993

Aziza's, (Malay), 36 Emerald Hill Road, Tel: 235-113

Bintang Timur Restaurant, (Indonesian), 14 Scotts Road, #02-08/13 Far East Plaza, Tel: 235-4539

Bombay Woodland, (South Indian vegetarian), 583 Orchard Road, #B1-06 Forum Galleria, Tel: 235-2712

Cafe Vanda, (Singapore & International), Paramount Hotel, 30 Marine Parade Road, Tel: 344-5577

Changi Cafe, (Singapore & International), Hotel Meridien Changi, 1 Netheravon Road, Tel: 542-7700

Empire Curry Inn, (South Indian), 3B-5 Lowland Road, Tel: 280-8655

Guan Hoe Soon, (Nonya), 214 Joo Chiat Road, Tel: 344-2761

Her Sea Palace Restaurant, (Thai), 583 Orchard Road, #01-16, Forum Galleria, Tel: 732-5688

Hotel Phoenix Coffee House, (Hawker food), Somerset Road, Tel: 737-8666

Keyaki Restaurant, (Japanese), Pan Pacific Hotel, 6 Raffles Boulevard, #01-300 Marina Square, Tel: 336-8111

Komala Vilas, (Indian vegetarian), 76/78 Serangoon Road, Tel: 293-6980

Korean Restaurant, (Korean), Specialists' Centre, #05-35, Orchard Road, Tel: 235-0018

Kurumaya, (Japanese), Dai-Ichi Hotel, 81 Anson Road, Tel: 224-1133

Luna Cafe, (Nonya & Singapore), Apollo Hotel, 405 Havelock Road, Tel: 733-2081

Maharani Restaurant, (North Indian), Far East Plaza, Scotts Road, Tel: 235-8840

Mayarani, (North Indian), Boulevard Hotel, Cuscaden Road, Tel: 732-2911

Nid's Place, (Thai), 164 Upper East Coast Road, Tel: 445-3371

Nonya and Baba Restaurant, (Nonya), 262-264 River Valley Road, Tel: 734-1382

Orchard Maharaja Restaurant, (North Indian), 25 Cuppage Road, Tel: 732-6331

Palm Beach Seafood, (Singapore seafood), National Stadium, West Entrance, Stadium Drive, Tel: 344-1474

Rajah Inn Restaurant, (Indonesian), 5001 Beach Road, #01-96 Golden Mile Complex, Tel: 298-5016

Rang Mahal Restaurant, (North Indian), Imperial Hotel, 1 Jalan Rumbia, Tel: 737-1666

Rasa Ria Cafe Restaurant, (Indonesian, Malay), 101 Thomson Road, #01-52 United Square, Tel: 253-8349

Restaurant Suntory, (Japanese), 402 Orchard Road, #06-01/02 Delfi Orchard, Tel: 732-5111

Saigon Restaurant, (Vietnamese), 4th Floor, Cairnhill Place, Tel: 235-0626

Senbazuru Japanese Restaurant, (Japanese), Hotel New Otani, 177A River Valley Road, Tel: 388-3333

Sushi Koharu, (Japanese), 14 Scotts Road, #02-23 Far East Plaza, Tel: 235-7172.

The Tandoor, (Kashmiri-Moghul Indian), Holiday Inn Park View, 11 Cavenagh Road, Tel: 733-8333

Tradewinds, (Malay), Hilton International, 581 Orchard Road, Tel: 737-2233

Unkai Japanese Restaurant, (Japanese), Furama Singapore Hotel, 10 Eu Tong Sen Road, Tel: 533-3888

Yunnan Inn, (Seafood), 21 Yuan Ching Road, Jurong Town, Tel: 265-4221

CULTURE PLUS

MUSEUMS

The National Museum, founded as early as 1823, had skeletons of a Sumatran rhinoceros, a horse and a tiger in its possession by 1877. Relics of Old Singapura's enigmatical past, like the cryptic "Singapore Stone" said to have been heaved into the river by a Malay strongman to prove his prowess to the king, survive in indecipherable fragments. The famous jewels of Majapahit – armlets of pale gold, six rings set with 11 inferior diamonds, and an odd jeweled clasp – are Singapore's opulent if slender link with the 14th century; not to mention a medieval Persian spittoon spotted on top of a junk heap by a Chinese collector in 1942.

The museum has its wealth stored in *kris* daggers, spears, idols, masks, belts of beads and betelnut boxes collected some years ago from the region's rarer civilizations. A walk through its galleries adds a hidden dimension of Asian history to the city's commercial skylines.

The National University of Singapore's Art Collection, housed in a separate wing, specializes in the pottery and porcelain of China illustrating 4,000 years of its manufacture. Collections also include a selection of ancient Indian sculpture and ancient Asiatic fabrics.

The National Museum is open from 9 a.m. to 4:30 p.m. (closed on Monday), including Sundays and public holidays. The National Art Gallery is in the same building. The gallery was opened in 1976 and displays the National Permanent Collection of Art as well as various local and international art exhibitions. Open from 9 a.m. to 5:30 p.m.

A group of volunteer guides called the "Friends of the Museum," conduct free tours around the National Museum everyday at 11 a.m., except Saturdays, Sundays and public holidays. Tel: 337-6077.

THEATERS

If you have seen a postcard depicting the statue of Sir Stamford Raffles standing in Empress Place, you'll probably have noticed a white building in its background. That white building is the **Victoria Theatre**, the oldest theater in Singapore, and it was originally conceived far back in 1854 as the Settlement's Town Hall, a place of meeting and social reunion, theatrical performances, balls and concerts. Tel: 337-7490 for bookings and information on current performance.

The modern **Kallang Theatre** (tel: 345-8488) and the **National Indoor Stadium** in Kallang are used for live performances including visiting Broadway and London stage productions and concerts. More avant-garde performances can be seen at **The Black Box** (tel: 338-4077) and the **Drama Centre** in Fort Canning Park (tel: 336-0005). One of Singapore's newest venues for stage plays and other live entertainment is the **Substation** on Armenian Street (tel: 337-7800) which also features theater workshops and art exhibits, as well as a flea market in Sundays.

SHOPPING

Those seeking out shopping venues in Singapore will find that the problem isn't where to go but rather which to go. Turn the corner of any street and chances are that you'll find a departmental store or at least a shopping center, a plaza, an emporium, some tiny shops along the footway of a row of shophouses, or a vendor with his merchandise sprawled out on a mat.

Singapore owes its deserving title of "Shoppers' Paradise" to two main facts. One, there is no import duty or sales tax on most items which makes it cheaper to buy them here than back home; and two, there is a wide variety of products here brought by exporters from all over who find Singapore a ready market due to its free trade policy. One scene, typical of Singapore, continues to mesmerize visitors: a brightly lit space that may or may not be enclosed occupied by vendors who take pride in their items which not only fill the shelves to the edges but spill out onto portable shelves or display stands placed just outside the shops.

The Yellow Pages is an extremely good aid for singling out specific shops to obtain your purchases. But for those who have to stretch precious time, it is advisable to shop at areas where you can find all your wants. Highly recommended areas are **Orchard/Tanglin**, **Chinatown/People's Park complexes**, **Holland Village** and **Arab Street/Beach Road**.

Wherever you shop, obey the two golden rules: bargain (except in departmental stores and other fixed prices shops); and do not buy at the first shop but compare prices.

FURTHER READING

From the *Insight Guides* stable comes a range of travel guides specially designed to help make your visit an unforgettable one.

Cityguide: Singapore serves a tropical dish of greenery and cultural diversity.

This book will bring you to the obvious and not-so-obvious corners of the surprising island state.

GETTING THERE

BY AIR

More than 50 international airlines call at Bangkok's Don Muang International Airport whose customs clearance and passport checks are relatively fast. Remember that Bangkok airport tax for outgoing passengers on international routes is 200 baht per person. The departure tax for domestic flights is 20 baht per person.

Although nearly all air passengers arrive and depart from Bangkok, there are international airports in Chiang Mai, Pattaya, Phuket and Hat Yai.

BY SEA

From Europe, companies such as Ben Line Steamers, Polish Ocean Lines and Nedloyd ship out to Bangkok. From the United States, Pacific Far East Line, American President Lines and State Lines go to Bangkok. There are also many ships sailing regularly from Japan, Hong Kong and Singapore. Inquire with local travel agents for schedules and fares.

BY RAIL

Except when it rains so hard that railroad tracks are submerged, Thai trains are reliable. You can get first-class, air-conditioned sleepers going anywhere within the country for less than 500 baht (US$22). There is daily railroad service between Singapore, Malaysia and Thailand. Fares between Singapore and Bangkok range from US$56 for a lower berth and a second-class cabin with no air-conditioning to US$237 for an upper berth in a first-class air-conditioned cabin.

ORIENT EXPRESS

Venice Simplon-Orient Express, operator of the fabled train in Europe, is launching a new luxury train in Southeast Asia. From November 1992, the Eastern and Oriental Express will make one round trip a week between Singapore, Kuala Lumpur and Bangkok. The journey will take 41 hours and cover a distance of 1,943 km. The E&O will pass northbound through Kuala Lumpur every Sunday, and southbound through Kuala Lumpur every Thursday. There will also be a stop at Butterworth for Penang. The standard of comfort, service and cuisine on board the train will be of the highest quality. Prices will start at US$190 for the trip between Kuala Lumpur and Singapore and reservations can be made from spring 1992, via travel agents, or by contacting the E&O London office on Tel: (071) 928 6000, Fax: (071) 620 1210.

BY ROAD

Roads in Thailand are excellent. Roads are being improved and extended into the more remote provinces, but apart from the southern road links with Malaysia, Thailand is virtually road-locked. At present there is no road access to and from Burma, a missing link in the Asian Highway that stretches from Turkey to Singapore.

There are three main roads crossing the Thai-Malaysian border in the south. Inexpensive taxis and minibuses ply the routes between major towns. Malaysia closes its border at 6 p.m. daily, so plan your itinerary in accordance.

In case you are driving or renting a car, please note that Malaysia prohibits any vehicle from Thailand that does not have an insurance policy. Most cars in Thailand do not.

TRAVEL ESSENTIALS

VISAS & PASSPORTS

All foreign nationals can stay in Thailand for up to 15 days without a visa. You can extend your stay for another seven days for 500 baht.

For a longer stay a visa must be obtained from Thai embassies or consulates abroad. Tourist visas cost US$12; applications must be accompanied by three passport-sized photos. Visas are granted for a period of 60 days, with a possible extension of another 30 days upon request for 500 baht. There is also the option of getting a 30-days transit visa at the cost of US$8. This can be extended for an additional 30 days for 500 baht. Anyone who wishes to leave Thailand and return before expiry of this tourist visa must first obtain a re-entry visa. This cost 500 baht and you should obtain it before departure.

Visas can be extended Monday to Friday from 8:30 a.m. to 3:30 p.m. at the Immigration Division, Soi Suan Plu, South Sathorn Road (Tel:286-9222); or between 8:30 a.m. and 2:30 p.m. on Saturday, Sunday and government holidays at the Tourism

Authority of Thailand, Rajdamnoen Avenue. There are also immigration officers in Chiang Mai, Pattaya, Phuket and Hat Yai.

A visa is valid for one entry within 60 days from the date of issue. Should the holder of the visa be unable to enter Thailand within this period, Thai embassies or consulates will generally extend the visa for a period not exceeding the period of validity of the applicant's passport, nor exceeding six months.

MONEY MATTERS

The unit of currency in Thailand is the *baht* (pronounced "baad"). One US dollar is equivalent to 25.4 baht (at time of press). One baht is divided into one hundred *satang*. Coins are valued at 25 satang (smaller gold coin), 50 satang (bigger gold coin), one baht (smaller nickel coin) and five baht (bigger nickel coin). The 25-satang coin is commonly called a *salehng*. Paper notes are valued at 10 (brown), 20 (green), 50 (blue), 100 (red) and 500 (purple).

Thai banks tend to be rather slow, so most tourists changed money at their hotel or money-changing kiosks. These kiosks are open 8 a.m. to 8 p.m. and trade at bank rates.

If you have traveler's checks in US dollars, they can be cashed at banks in all provincial capitals; so there is no need to carry unmanageable amounts of baht notes with you outside of Bangkok. Traveler's checks in other currencies, however, are best cashed in Bangkok. As a rule, hotel exchange rates are poorer than those offered by banks and authorized money changers.

Keep in mind that most hotels do not accept personal checks. Some hotels, restaurants and shops place a 3-5 percent surcharge on credit card purchases.

HEALTH

Incoming visitors need an International Certificate of Health, showing a smallpox vaccination within the last three years, if arriving from an infected area. Yellow fever inoculations are required by persons coming from or going to contaminated areas; children less than a year old are exempted.

If you are heading into jungle areas, you should be vaccinated against Japanese encephalitis. Precautions against malaria should also be taken.

In a country where people are as personally neat and cleanliness-conscious as the Thais, there are relatively few health hazards stemming directly from poor sanitation.

Tap water in Bangkok is considered relatively safe, but to be doubly sure, drink purified bottled water.

Travelers who have never reckoned with the tropical sun should keep in mind that noon is not the wisest time to sunbathe; you will earn a burn in just 15 minutes. If you are out touring, exposed to the elements, wear a straw hat or carry a paper parasol.

WHAT TO WEAR

Light and loose clothes are best suited to Thailand's climate. For the hot season, pack clothes that provide adequate protection from the direct sun – cotton is best, and umbrellas and sunglasses are highly recommended. For the rainy season, it is wise to carry clothes that dry quickly after a sudden downpour. For the four months from November to February, warmer clothes (at least sweater and warm socks for the chilly nights) are necessary in the North and other hilly regions, as there is no central heating or even household fireplaces.

Bangkok is highly westernized in its business and social dress, with provincial centers following suit. Certain restaurants require jackets and ties for dinner. At traditional ceremonies and formal gatherings, however, Thai women often prefer to don their ethnic silk costumes.

CUSTOMS

As with most countries, Thailand prohibits visitors bringing in illicit narcotic drugs and explicit pornography. Firearms require a permit from the Police Department. Goods that may be imported duty-free include 200 cigarettes, 50 cigars or 250 gm of tobacco; one liter of wine or spirits; a camera with five rolls of film; and a reasonable amount of personal effects.

Visitors are permitted to bring in any amount of foreign currency for personal use but must fill in a currency declaration form for larger sums. No one can bring in or take out of Thailand more than 500 baht. Holders of family passports are permitted to export 1,000 baht.

GETTING ACQUAINTED

GOVERNMENT & ECONOMY

Thailand is a constitutional monarchy. The head of state since 1946 has been King Bhumipol Adulyadej.

Almost 55 million persons make their homes in Thailand: nearly eight million of them live in Bangkok. Thailand has one of Asia's fastest growing economies, especially the manufacturing sector which has grown rapidly in recent years due to billions of dollars of foreign investment.

Rice is the major export crop. Nearly three million tons is exported annually, ranking second in the world. Thailand is the world's largest exporter of tapioca, second largest of rubber, and the fifth largest producer of tin. Teak, sugar cane, maize, tobacco and cotton are other important export crops. And fisheries rank high in the economy. The gross national product (1988) was US$57.2 billion. The per capita income (1988) was US$1,039.

TIME ZONES

Thailand is seven hours ahead of Greenwich Mean Time.

CLIMATE

Although Thailand is situated well within the tropics, there is a wide climatic range depending on the time of year and the part of the country. The Central Plains (including Bangkok), the hilly North, and the arid, flat Northeast share the same seasonal patterns. The so-called hot season spans March, April and May, although many foreign residents argue that it is hot throughout the year when it is not raining. Daytime temperatures in the hot season are in the 86°F(30°C) range and can reach 104°F (40°C), especially in the Northeast.

In June, the southwest Monsoon ushers in the rainy season with slightly lower temperatures but higher humidity. In Thailand, the monsoon season amounts to five months of unpredictable weather. Some days bring erratic rainstorms while others are clear and sunny. November ushers in the cool season, particularly in the North where night temperatures can drop to 8°C (46°F). Bring a sweater or jacket if traveling there between November and February.

The long isthmus in South Thailand, which straddles the Gulf of Thailand and the Indian Ocean, has a climate similar to that of Malaysia – subtle seasonal variations with the weather generally warm, humid, and sunny year-round. Rain is possible almost any time.

BUSINESS HOURS

Government offices are open from 8:30 a.m. to 4:30 p.m., Monday to Friday. Banks are open from 8:30 a.m. to 3:30 p.m., Monday to Friday. Shops are generally open from 9 a.m. to 6 p.m. every day.

LANGUAGE

English is widely spoken in major tourist destinations like Bangkok, Chiang Mai and Phuket. Otherwise, if you are traveling in rural areas, it helps to have a working knowledge of Thai.

CULTURE & CUSTOMS

Some customs are important to keep in mind during a visit to Thailand. The Thais are far too genial and easygoing to expect a *farang* ("foreigner") to observe all their ways, but here, as anywhere, it helps to have a few general ideas about the *dos* and *don'ts* of polite society.

Perhaps the one area (besides showing proper respect for the monarchy) where they can be sticky is regarding behavior in a temple. Visitors are required to remove their shoes before entering the building containing the principal Buddha image, in front of which there will be people sitting about on the floor paying homage to the Buddha. Women are not allowed in the monks' quarters, nor should they hand anything directly to a monk. (Should the occasion arise when a woman *has* to give something to a monk and no man is around to perform the service, she places the object on a table or on the ground and then the monk is free to pick it up for himself).

GREETINGS

When Thais meet one another, they do not usually shake hands. The customary greeting is the *wai*, with the hands raised as if in prayer. Traditionally the higher the hands are held, the more respectful is the *wai*. By observing two people, you can therefore tell their respective ranks. But rank is a complicated matter in Thailand, involving, as it does, such things as age, occupation, and social position. For an outsider, it is enough to make the gesture.

As the feet are the lowest part of the body, it is considered rude in Thailand to point your feet at anybody, especially if the gesture is deliberate. Most Thais strive mightily to avoid doing so even accidentally, and as a result you seldom see people with their legs crossed, or if they are, they tend to keep the toes pointed carefully toward the floor.

DRESS

Thais are extremely neat in their appearance and even in a slum, it is rare to see anyone who is really dirty or unkempt; mechanics, covered with grease and grime at the end of the day, emerge from their evening bath as spotless as if they had never come within reach of an engine. (All Thais bathe at least once a day and usually twice.) To say that someone is *mai rieb-roi* ("not neat") is almost as serious as saying that he is *mai -suparb* ("not polite"), and very often it is the same thing; disorderliness can be regarded as rude in certain circumstances.

Although among some younger, westernized Thais – those you see roaming about Bangkok shopping centers – it is considered smart (*sa-mart*) to dress in the loose, semi-hippie garb of Western teenagers, to the great majority of the population it is simply *mai rieb-roi*. Similarly, to conservative Thais, there are polite and impolite colors – a brightly colored dress is acceptable on a young girl but not on an older woman, who ought to wear somber shades or pastels. (There are even colors for certain days; Sunday, for example, is the only day when almost anyone can wear red without being considered *mai-suparb* in the extreme).

As a general rule, of course, foreign visitors are not included in all these strictures, and as long as you look reasonably presentable (even in a *mai-suparb* color) you are not likely to get a second look on the street.

PUBLIC BEHAVIOR

It is common to see two Thai men holding hands as they walk along the street – a sign, incidentally, of simple friendship; nothing else – but very rare to see a man and woman doing it, for public displays of affection between the sexes is an old and strong taboo. During the Vietnam war, when Bangkok was a major rest and recreation center for thousands of American servicemen, one of the most frequent criticisms leveled at them was their public behavior with bar girls, innocent though most of it was by American standards. The experience has left many well-bred Thai girls wary about even being seen with a *farang* for fear she will be held in contempt by others.

GETTING AROUND

FROM THE AIRPORT

From Don Muang Airport to Bangkok 14 miles (22 km) south, air-conditioned sedans offer 24-hour service, while buses leave every half-hour. Tickets cost 300 baht and 100 baht respectively.

Public taxis are not metered. Be sure you first agree on a fare, normally between 180 and 200 baht. Bus fares are 3.50 baht for a regular bus and 15 baht for an air-conditioned bus. Pick-up points for public taxis and buses are just outside the airport gate.

Across the highway, is the Don Muang Railway Station. A train ride to Bangkok costs 4 baht. However, this is recommended only for visitors with light luggage.

DOMESTIC AIR TRAVEL

Thai Airways (do not confuse it with Thai International) and Bangkok Airways link major cities throughout the country. In the north, there are daily flights to Chiang Mai, with stops at Phitsanulok, Phrae, Nan, Lampang, Chiang Rai and Mae Hong Son. In the northeast, there are daily flights to Ubon

Rajthani, with stops in Udon, Nakhon Phanom, Khon Kaen and Loei. The south-bound schedule includes the island resort of Phuket, as well as Hat Yai, Trang and Pattani.

WATER TRANSPORT

Thailand has an estimated three million kilometers of navigable waterways. Most visitors limit their water travel to trips around Bangkok, or possibly the daily launch to Ayutthaya on the *Oriental Queen*. Cost of that excursion is 650 baht including lunch. Hotels in Bangkok and all provincial capitals can arrange localized excursions.

The Thai Navigation Company has three passenger-cargo ships that travel south from Bangkok, down the Gulf of Siam and South China Sea, to Koh Samui, Songkla, Pattani and Narathivat. Departures are Wednesday and Saturday. Full nine-day cruise rates average about 1,000 baht.

RAIL TRANSPORT

Thai trains are comfortable and reliable, though they are crowded all year round. The State Railway of Thailand runs international express, express, rapid, ordinary and diesel railcar services in three passenger classes over an extensive and well-maintained network. Costs are very reasonable.

Two railpasses are now available. The Red Pass is valid for 20 days. It costs 3,000 baht for adults and 1500 baht for children, including all supplementary charges such as sleepers and air-conditioning. The Blue Pass is also valid for 20 days at a cost of 1500 baht for adults and 750 baht for children, but this does not cover extras.

For information and reservations call the Bangkok Railway Terminus at 233-7010, or Hua Lampong Station at 223-3762.

PUBLIC TRANSPORT

Air-conditioned coaches and ordinary buses run from Bangkok to every town in Thailand. 2,744 buses are operated by the State Transport Company over 134 routes to all 72 provinces; and another 2,246 buses operate on 147 routes within or between the provinces. In Bangkok, there are three major bus terminals:

Northern & Northeastern routes: Taladmochit, on Paholyothin Road, Tel: 282-6660.

Eastern route: Ekamai on Kukhumvit Road, Tel: 392-2520. This is the route that goes to Pattaya and points beyond.

Southern route: Sam Yaek Fai Chai on Charansanitwongse Road in Thonburi, Tel: 411-1337.

Numerous private buses and coaches also ply routes between major cities. Check with local agencies for schedules and fares.

PRIVATE TRANSPORT

It is possible to rent cars with major agencies in Bangkok. Indeed, there are 27,400 miles (43,840 km) of national and provincial highways in Thailand, and another 7,500 miles (12,000 km) under construction. But most signs are in the Thai language only, driving can be hazardous for the uninitiated, and other forms of transportation are universally recommended to visitors. Chauffeur-driven rentals are usually best, but this will cost 1500 to 2400 baht per day.

TRANSPORTATION IN BANGKOK

Buses: The Bangkok Metropolitan Transit Authority (BMTA) runs blue-and-white city buses. Route numbers in front and on the back, can be checked against maps sold in most bookstores. Buses are usually very crowded during the rush hours in the morning and afternoon, but are relatively vacant at other times during the day. Bus fares start at 2 baht for the first 10 kilometers, with an additional one baht for the next 10 kilometers.

Air-conditioned buses, also run by the BMTA, link major places in Bangkok. They are quite comfortable and not so crowded. Fares start at 5 baht for the first 8 kilometers and 2 baht for each additional kilometer.

Taxis: All taxis are air-conditioned. Bargaining is essential, as taxis do not have meters. Many drivers do not speak English, so have your hotel desk write your destination in Thai and suggest the approximate fare. Short trips usually cost a minimum of 60 baht; a trip from the Grand Palace to the major hotel districts should be around 100 baht.

Pedicabs: Commonly known as *sam-lor* or *tuk-tuk*, they consist of a motor-scooter around which a two-seat carriage has been built. They are worth trying for short trips. Prices start at 30 baht; again, bargaining is essential.

Boats: Numerous ferries and express boats ply the Chao Phya river and major *klongs*. In addition, several day and night cruises can be booked through major hotels. Going rate for renting private jetboats along the river bank is 300 to 500 baht per hour, regardless of the number of passengers.

WHERE TO STAY

HOTELS

There is no telling just how many hotels there are in Thailand. They exist all over the country and their standards range from deluxe international inns to small, simple establishments catering to on-the-move hitchhikers.

Fluctuations in exchange rates and rampant inflation make it virtually impossible to pinpoint hotel rates. As a general rule, rates are highest in luxury hotels found in resort cities and provinces like Bangkok, Chiang Mai and Pattaya. It is always advisable to call ahead or check with a travel agent about the latest prices. Most lodgings add an 11 percent hotel tax and a 10 percent service charge.

You may rest assured that finding a hotel that suits your needs and budget is never a task. The following list will give an idea of what is available in Bangkok.

BANGKOK

Airport Hotel, 333, Chert Wudthakas Road, Don Muang, Tel: 566-1020

Ambassador, Soi 11 Sukhumvit Road, Tel: 254-0444

Bangkok Center, 382 Rama IV Road, Tel: 235-1780

Bangkok Palace, City Square, Petchburi Road, Tel: 251-8874

Dorchester, 21 Soi Kotoey, Pratipat, Tel: 279-2641

Dusit Thani, 946 Rama IV Road, Saladang Circle, Tel: 233-1130

Grand Hyatt Erawan, 494 Rajdamri Road, Tel: 733-1188

Fortuna, 19 Sukhumvit Road (Soi 5), Tel: 251-5121

Grace, 12 Sukhumvit Road (Soi 3), Nana North, Tel: 252-9170

Hilton International Bangkok, Nai Lert Park, North Wireless Road, Tel: 253-0123/0671

Indra Regent, Rajprarob Road, Tel: 251-1111

Le Meridien President, 135/26 Gaysorn Road, Tel: 253-6550/0444

Mandarin, 662 Rama IV Road, Tel: 233-4980

Manhattan, Soi 15, Sukhumbit Road, Tel: 252-7141

Miramar, 777 Mahachai Road (Samyod Road), Tel: 222-1711

Montien, 54 Suriwongse Road, Tel: 234-8060/7060

Narai, 222 Silom Road, Tel: 233-3350

Oriental, 48 Oriental Avenue, New Road, Tel: 234-8620

Peninsula, 295/3 Suriwongse Road, Tel: 234-3910

Ramada, 1169 New Road, Tel:234-8971

Regent Bangkok, 155 Rajdamri Road, Tel: 251-6127

Royal Orchid Sheraton, 2 Captain Bush Lane, Siphya Road, Tel: 234-5599, Fax: 236-6646

Shangri-La, 89 Soi Wat Suan Pla, New Road, Tel: 236-7777, Fax: 236-8579

Siam Inter-Continental, Rama I Road, Tel: 253-0355

PHUKET

Club Med Phuket, Karon Sub-District, Muang District, Phuket, Tel: 381455-60, Fax: 381462

FOOD DIGEST

WHAT TO EAT

The problem of eating in Bangkok, as one gourmet has observed, is not so much where as what. The city probably has a more diversified selection of restaurants than any other capital in Asia, with the possible exception of Tokyo, with a range running from cheeseburgers to *sukiyaki* and almost everything in between. Within a relatively small area you can eat Mexican, French, German, Italian, Scandinavian, Hungarian, Japanese, Vietnamese, Korean, English, American, Laotian, Filipino, Indian, Indonesian, Swiss, Burmese and Austrian – and not, in most cases, vague approximations but the real thing prepared by cooks from the country in question. Half a dozen provinces of China are represented, from bland Cantonese to spicy Szechuan, offering not only such splendors as Peking Duck but esoteric oddities like duck tongues and chicken breast stuffed with bird's nest.

You can dine on Central, Northern, Southern, and Northeastern Thai food, either in fairly basic surrounding or in lavish, air-conditioned comfort while watching a show of folk and classical dancing. Your hotel bookshop will probably have a number of restaurant guides to help you make a choice; one that is recommended is *Eating Out In Bangkok* by Harry Rolnick, a highly personal but dependable compilation by a long-time resident of Bangkok.

Except for weekends, reservations are usually unnecessary, even at the fanciest restaurants; only one hotel restaurant requires a jacket and tie.

ROADSIDE KITCHENS

Inveterate snackers, Thais like to eat when the mood strikes them, at almost any hour of the day or night. Their philosophy regarding food is quite simply, "Eat when you are hungry." Wherever you go in Thailand you will see them around a noodle vendor's bicycle or at one of the temporary sidewalk stalls that spring up as if by magic wherever people are likely to be working or passing by – eating a bowl of rice noodles garnished with a bit of fried meat and coriander, a delicate little pancake folded around a sugary sweet, or a deep-fried banana fritter.

These portable kitchens, using only the basics in equipment – usually only a brazier of charcoal and a few pots and pans – turn out culinary delights remarkably complex by any standards.

NIGHTLIFE

The nighttime world of Thailand needs no introduction. Nightlife is as important to Bangkok visitors as sandy beaches are to Hawaii or cherry blossoms to Japan.

Thai nightlife is centered around nightclubs, bars, massage parlors and–more recently – discotheques, all of which exist in almost all corners of the country.

Musical entertainment, provided by pop groups

or solo vocalists, is available at the larger hotels. It is difficult to know just what is featured since hotels rotate their acts. Call to check first.

For a cheaper way to enjoy an evening drink and perhaps a meal with musical accompaniment, there are many open-air restaurants around Bangkok – especially along Lard Prao Road – where live bands play music of Thai modern genre and (occasionally) Western.

If your idea of a well-spent evening is jiving to the latest sounds, drinking and chatting with beautiful hostesses, visit any of the bars and nightclubs on Patpong Road or Soi Cowboy (off Soi 21, Sukhumvit Road). These bars are famous for their open and friendly bargirls. Most of them also stage floor shows, with the first show starting about 10 p.m.

Fancy trying Bangkok's famed massage parlors? Try those along Patong II Road (the small road parallel to the main Patpong Road) or on Petchburi Road. A massage will cost from 120 baht per hour upwards although much depends on the class of establishment…and how elaborate a massage you require.

SHOPPING

WHAT TO BUY

Shopping is a pleasure, not only because of the variety of things to buy but also because of the ubiquity of Bangkok's air-conditioned shopping centers where it is possible to get a good deal of your buying done without being laid out by the heat. The following are some of the things Thailand is noted for, both the quality and the price in most cases being superior to anywhere else.

THAI FABRICS

Thai silk is too well known to need any introduction – in quantity, in assorted weights, in meters, or made up into clothes and other items.

It may, however, be useful to note that the quality of silk is not always uniform, and in some shops that offer suspiciously good bargains, the cloth may have been cleverly interwoven with rayon or some other synthetic; stick to better-known shops unless you are good at telling. Handwoven Thai cotton is less famous and unjustly so, for it is a soft but durable material that is wonderful for dresses, upholstery, and other uses. In many shops, you can get the cotton

in the same colors and prints as the silk at around 40 to 50 baht a meter.

JEWELRY

Gold in Thailand is considerably cheaper than in Europe or the United States, and the craft of making modern jewelry – as distinct from the traditional Thai designs – has progressed to the point where many tourists now rank Bangkok ahead of Hong Kong. Best buy among native stones is the sapphire, blue or black, star or plain; also you can sometimes find good rubies from Cambodia and Burma. Most stones are less expensive than in the West. For something different, look at the Thai princess ring, which has nine tiers set with nine different precious and semi-precious stones.

HANDICRAFTS

If you are going to Chiang Mai, where most of the Thai handicrafts come from, wait and buy them there. Otherwise, look for the hill tribe embroidery, laquerware, painted umbrellas, woodcarvings, basketwork, and delightful fish mobiles made of woven bamboo which Thai mothers hang over cribs as pacifiers. The government-sponsored Narayana Phand, on Larn Luang Road in Bangkok, is a good place to buy these.

CELADON

This was originally made in Thailand during the Sukhothai period, died out, and was revived about 20 years ago. Vases and lamp bases are good buys; complete dinner sets are also available as well as a variety of souvenir pieces.

DOLLS

For collectors, there is a wide selection in classical dance costumes or depicting the various hill tribes of the North.

BRONZEWARE

Long one of the most popular buys with tourists, bronzeware now comes in plain, modern designs as well as the traditional Thai ones. You can get everything in it from complete cutlery sets to salad bowls; look also for bronze temple bells to hang on a terrace or patio. At several shops you can get bronzeware that has been siliconized so that it will not tarnish.

SPIRIT HOUSES

There are some charming ones in the shape of little Thai-style houses which are not too bulky to send or carry.

ANTIQUES

Best buys are Chinese porcelains and furniture, carvings from Thai temples. Sawankhalok (a porcelain made near Sukhothai in the 14th century), old Thai paintings, silver betelnut boxes, Burmese tapestries and wooden figures. Fakes abound, especially with Buddha images, so know what you are doing or go to the best shops. For most Buddhist art of Thailand, a permit is required from the Fine Arts Department before the pieces can be taken out of the country. The good shops will take care of this complicated job for you.

SHOPPING AREAS

The **Central Department Store**, with its five branches in Silom, Chidlom, Wangburapa, Ladya and Ladpraw, is the best place for a visitor who does not have enough time to travel around the country to shop for gifts from various provinces. Goods from all over the globe are also on sale here. (Prices are fixed; credit cards and personal checks are accepted.)

Thai Daimaru has two branches; one in Rajdamri Arcade on Rajdamri Road and the other at Phra Kanong on Sukhumvit Road. It sells mostly imported goods from Japan. (Prices are fixed; credit cards and checks are accepted.)

The Mall Shopping Center on Rajdamri Road offers for sale goods from all around the world at fixed prices. **Robinson Department Store** has three branches; Rajdamri, Victory Monument and Stam Square. You will find a good range of ready-made clothes here at fixed prices.

Those who like bargaining will find small or big shops on almost every street of Bangkok offering everything from rubber bands to jewelry. A few big shops accept credit cards and checks, but most prefer cash.

FURTHER READING

From the *Insight Guides* stable comes a range of travel guides, specially designed to help make your visit an unforgettable one.

An informed and superbly-photographed guide to the land of gentle smiles.

One of the Orient's most exciting, exotic cities comes to life in *Cityguide: Bangkok*.

Itineraries designed for an idyllic stay in this island paradise.	Personalized recommendations for the active and inquisitive visitor.	Antiquities and forest splendor await you in this ancient capital.

ART/PHOTO CREDITS

INDEX

H

I

J

N

Q

R

T

X-Z